BACK INTO FOCUS

The Real Story of Robert Capa's D-Day

CHARLES R. HERRICK

CASEMATE

Pennsylvania & Yorkshire

Published in the United States of America and Great Britain in 2024 by
CASEMATE PUBLISHERS
1950 Lawrence Road, Havertown, PA 19083, USA
and
47 Church Street, Barnsley, S70 2AS, UK

Hardcover Edition: ISBN 978-1-63624-473-0
Digital Edition: ISBN 978-1-63624-474-7

A CIP record for this book is available from the British Library

Printed and bound in the United Kingdom by CPI Group (UK) Ltd, Croydon, CR0 4YY
Typeset in India by DiTech Publishing Services

For a complete list of Casemate titles, please contact:

CASEMATE PUBLISHERS (US)
Telephone (610) 853-9131
Fax (610) 853-9146
Email: casemate@casematepublishers.com
www.casematepublishers.com

CASEMATE PUBLISHERS (UK)
Telephone (0)1226 734350
Email: casemate@casemateuk.com
www.casemateuk.com

Cover image: (front) A cropped portion of Capa's first set of five photos showing troops debarking.
(Robert Capa © ICP/Magnum Photos)
(back) U.S. Army troops wade ashore on Omaha Beach during the D-Day landings, 6 June 1944.
(Chief Photographer's Mate Robert F. Sargent, U.S. Coast Guard/Wikimedia Commons)

Contents

Acknowledgements

This book evolved from a comment I posted on the *Alternate History: Robert Capa on D-Day* project some nine years ago. Along the way, many people have lent a hand, directly or indirectly, to help this book reach its current form. Chief among them is Allan (A. D.) Coleman, critic, historian, educator and curator of photography. He leads the *Alternate History* project, which first questioned the Darkroom Accident myth. He permitted me to challenge other aspects of Capa's D-Day saga, and proved an invaluable advisor, font of information and skilled editor. A big nod to Pulitzer Prize winner J. Ross Baughman, another member of Allan's team, who started this all by originally posting the first serious challenge to the Darkroom Accident myth. Rob McElroy, professional photographer, daguerreotypist and photo historian from Buffalo, NY, is another key team member who not only provided the first evidence that the Lab Accident myth was wrong but showed commendable patience with my ignorance in all things photographic. I also owe a debt of gratitude to Tristan da Cunha, Photographe Retoucheur and another *Alternate History* team member; not only did he put the final nail in the coffin for the Darkroom Accident myth, but freely provided photographic expertise I sorely needed. Pieter Jutte, amateur historian and Normandy guide, was an excellent source for obscure but vital observations and details most professional historians overlook. The esteemed Patrick Peccatte and the "passionate amateurs" of the PhotosNormandie project are another amazing source for information and insights. Along the way I received help from many organizations and people, such as Toni Kiser of the National WWII Museum; the staff of the Eisenhower Presidential Library; NARA; Colonel Robert R. McCormick Research Center, First Division Museum at Cantigny; the USS Landing Craft Infantry National Association and many others. And thanks to Tom Hogan and the many like him who contacted me along the way to contribute countless nuggets that helped to flesh out the fine details. Thank you, all. For any I have overlooked, please be assured it is only due to senior memory loss, and not to a lack of gratitude.

Separate thanks go to Peter Marshall, photographer extraordinaire, whose exceedingly positive review of my first post provided much needed reassurance when so many in the arts and media were crying, "Burn the heretic!"

And finally, my grateful appreciation to my wife for not only putting up with, but materially helping the grumpy old codger in the basement.

A Note to the Reader

For a smoother reading experience, footnotes have been included only where additional explanations are called for in the text. Citations and sources are included as endnotes.

Introduction

"If you didn't get the picture at the exact instant, you kept the meaning in mind, and you faked the picture, or reframed it. . . .. I was enough of a journalist to realize that you invent a good picture. I was the pioneer of the made-up picture. The faked, invented picture."

DAVID SCHERMAN—CAPA'S FELLOW *LIFE* PHOTOGRAPHER DURING
THE NORMANDY INVASION

"There is something wrong with the values of a journalistic world that accepts as an important image a photograph that so clearly depends on the caption for its authentication."

PHILLIP KNIGHTLY—OBSERVATION WHILE QUESTIONING
THE AUTHENTICITY OF CAPA'S ICONIC FALLING SOLDIER PHOTO

Any effort to trace the activities of Robert Capa is at least partially an exercise in futility. So much of his legend is, well, a legend, that pinning down verifiable facts is difficult. The persona of Robert Capa was itself fabricated, an invention of Endre Friedmann and his girlfriend who hoped the idea of a mysterious, rich American at the head of their photo agency would bring credibility and boost sales. Having invented this character, young Endre soon stepped forward and assumed the identity of his fictional boss: Robert Capa. Capa burst onto the international stage with sensational images taken as he covered the Republican side of the Spanish Civil War. Though he billed himself as a photojournalist, he was at least as much partisan propagandist, and there is ample evidence that some of his photos of that conflict, to include some of his most famous, were staged events that he passed off as genuine combat actions. Whether one merely considers this aggressive self-promotion and creative marketing, or one recoils at the ethical implications, it set the tone for his subsequent career. With Capa one is never quite sure where the facts ended and the façade began; where the truth withered away, and the legend flourished.

The Past as Prologue

The most famous photo of Capa's early career purported to capture the moment a Spanish Republican soldier was shot as he advanced under fire—the "Falling Soldier" photo—and was published in the 23 September 1936 issue of the French *Vu* magazine. Capa was just 22 at the time and on his first assignment as a war photographer. Superficially, it was a powerful image, seemingly confronting the reader with death the moment it occurred. Or at least it might have been, except for the fact that when *Vu* published that photo, it also published another Capa photo showing a second soldier apparently being shot at precisely the same spot, with identical framing and almost identical pose as the original "casualty." The two photos appeared to have been taken just moments apart. Despite this obvious evidence of staging, *Vu*'s caption faithfully presented them as actual combat scenes, using language that was flowery, almost romantic. Still, with the two pictures published side-by-side, alert readers could draw their own conclusions regarding authenticity.

The "Falling Soldier" next appeared the following summer in *Life* magazine. This time it was published without the second photo, so American readers were not privy to evidence that the photo was perhaps not what it seemed. The photo, and the purported context, were widely and uncritically accepted at face value, and became embedded in popular culture. To some familiar with combat, however, the image always rang false; photographers are almost never ahead of troops advancing under fire. In fact, such positioning of a photographer relative to his subject in combat is virtually always an indication of a staged shot. Nevertheless, the image quickly became celebrated both as powerful symbol of the cause of the Republican forces and as a great achievement in the photographic arts. The 3 December 1938 edition of *Picture Post* went so far as to proclaim him the "Greatest War Photographer in the World."

Capa gave interviews discussing the circumstances of the "Falling Soldier" in 1937 (shortly after the *Life* spread) and in 1947. In both interviews he gave detailed—if not entirely consistent—descriptions of the combat action leading to the picture, going so far as to claim he remained pinned down under fire until dark, when he was finally able to crawl to safety. In neither interview did he mention the photo of the second soldier's "death." More significantly, in his second interview he claimed that he merely aimed his camera blindly, holding it above his head over the edge of the trench, and snapped the photo without seeing the action. It was pure luck that supposedly accounted for the famous picture. On its face this is ludicrous. It is even more so when we consider the second photo with identical framing showing the "death" of the second soldier. Identical framing showing two different men getting shot, in nearly identical poses, at the precisely same spot, just minutes apart? With a camera blindly aimed and shutter blindly activated? It simply is not credible.

As a result of these questions, an element of controversy has hovered over the "Falling Soldier," with a number of authorities questioning its authenticity. Capa partisans, however, remained loyal. To maintain the authenticity of the "Falling Soldier" photo, a theory was advanced that acknowledged, yes, Capa was staging some shots, but while staging those shots, a real sniper "just happened" to really shoot one of the actors (in the exact same spot and in the same pose as the second unwounded actor's feigned death), and it was this coincidental, actual shooting that

Capa captured in the "Falling Soldier" photo. Various "experts" were put forward to bolster the authenticity of the "Falling Soldier," going so far as to even point to the pose of the soldier's hand as proof that he was truly shot.[1] Seldom has the photographic community been so eager to see a man killed.

This die-hard loyalty to an untenable position was made even more unreasonable by the revelation that on another occasion, Capa and his girlfriend worked with the Chapaiev Battalion's communist political commissar to film a mock attack arranged by the latter.[2] It, too, was passed off as actual combat, but his apologists excused it as probably being a recreation of an actual attack." The simple fact is that Capa was a propagandist working to advance the cause of the Republican forces. Staging scenes was part and parcel of his craft, as was misrepresenting them as genuine events.

Other Capa loyalists, unable to maintain the fiction that the photo was not staged, resorted to rationalization. While acknowledging the possibility or even likelihood of fakery, they claimed that the photo nevertheless was "very good as a symbol of a moment in our history and of our conscience" or "its symbol and message are authentic." In other words, these apologists hold that a lie that has emotional impact—especially one which supports their political bias—is not only morally acceptable but can be proclaimed a great artistic achievement. Richard Whelan, Capa's adoring biographer and eventual guardian of the Capa archives, dismissed questions about the fakery as "both morbid and trivializing," insisting instead that the significance of the picture was symbolic, "not in its literal accuracy as a report on the death of a particular man."[3] But if that is valid, what does it do to Capa's claim to being the "Greatest War Photographer in the World" if he merely captured staged scenes in a safe area? And does that not reduce his work to mere crass propaganda? The ethical implications are stark.

The debate over authenticity of the "Falling Soldier" was decided in 2009 when José Manuel Susperregui, Professor, University of the Basque Country, proved that this set of photos was actually taken near Espejo, which is some 30 miles from the Cerro Muriano location Whelan concluded was the site of the action.[4] This difference indisputably revealed Capa's "Falling Soldier" and the other shots in that set as staged fakes. On the date Capa took his photos in late August 1936, Espejo was at least 15 miles behind the lines. Fighting was indeed taking place in the vicinity of Cerro Muriano at that time, which is why the photos were falsely attributed to that location, but there was no combat at Espejo on that date. Combat eventually did reach Espejo later (on 22 and 26 September 1936), but this was three weeks after Capa took his photos, and, coincidentally, was almost simultaneous with their publication in *Vu*.

This should give the historian pause. Capa's first spectacular photo, taken on his very first combat assignment at the tender age of 22, has proven to be a fake. Not only was his photo a fake, but the derived persona of frontline cameraman bravely snapping shots while pinned down has been proven to be built on a false foundation as well. But it would take 73 years to reveal the fraud.

If Capa learned anything from his Spanish Civil War experience, it was that his fictional accounts would be accepted at face value by publications and public alike. Concluding his analysis of Capa's "Falling Soldier" photo, Susperregui stated:

> Finally, the results of this study call for a revision of historical research on Robert Capa that is based on Falling Soldier. His archives, including 70,000 negatives mostly related to the five wars he covered, deserve to be treated with as much rigor as possible in order to deepen and improve knowledge of his work.

And that is precisely the intent of this book. To apply that same rigor to Capa's D-Day photos and the descriptions of the events surrounding them which he himself provided.

D-Day: The Sixth of June

As a result of the foregoing, the wise analyst must rigorously examine Capa's combat photos before accepting their authenticity or accuracy. The tactic of misrepresenting the context of his photos had proven a success at his very first outing, and there is no reason to believe he suddenly mended his ways thereafter. It should be remembered that it was just seven years and 10 months between Capa's faked "Falling Soldier" and his D-Day photos.

This current exploration does not question whether Capa's D-Day photos were staged in a safe area, as was the case with the "Falling Soldier." Clearly his Omaha Beach photos were taken on that dreaded beach and were taken on 6 June 1944. Rather, the focus is to examine various aspects of their purported context to determine whether they have been presented to the public accurately. In addition to examining precise location, exact time and combat conditions at the moment his photos were snapped, this work will also examine his actions and movements from the time he was alerted in London on 29 May 1944 until he returned to Portland Harbor on 7 June.

But separating the Capa "legend" from the facts is always a difficult task, and that is never truer than when it comes to his D-Day photos. The difficulty stems in no small part from his own quasi-autobiography—*Slightly out of Focus* (1947)—which he initially penned with hopes of a screenplay. To put it mildly, many of the events he related smack of hype, exaggeration or outright fabrication.

As just one example of the latter we turn to that memoir's account of his role in the invasion of Sicily (July 1943).[5] Capa claimed he rode with the first night's paratrooper drop (the night of 9/10 July) as a non-jumping photographer, then parachuted behind enemy lines in Sicily with the reinforcing echelon of paratroopers on the third night of the invasion (11/12 July). He then claimed he spent four days isolated behind enemy lines, "blowing up little bridges" before linking up with an American unit. The reality was far different. Even Richard Whelan, Capa's staunch defender, had to admit that the Sicily passages were "the most heavily fictionalized section of *Slightly out of Focus*."[6]

The actual events were far less glamorous. When he arrived in Tunisia, Capa had wrangled accreditation with a US Army Air Forces troop carrier unit that was slated to drop the paratroopers;[7] he was not accredited to the paratroopers. He did not fly at all on the initial invasion drop, despite his claim to have ridden along as a non-jumping photographer that night. It was only on the subsequent drop of reinforcements two days later that he conducted his picture-taking jaunt; and instead of jumping, returned to Tunisia on the aircraft. He did not jump at any time during the Sicilian campaign. As he described the excursion in a letter to a friend, "I jumped at the chance—and fortunately not out of the plane."[8]

The truly amazing part of this tall tale is that by the time *Slightly out of Focus* was published, the world had known for three years how he arrived in Sicily, but critics chose to accept the fabricated version anyhow. Capa landed in Sicily accompanying the Air Force troop carrier unit's ground echelon, which arrived by means of a Landing Ship, Tank (LST) at the port of Licata at least 10 days after the invasion began. In fact, this actual seaborne trip to Sicily was documented in the *Sicily Campaign* story, which was published by *Illustrated* magazine in its 13 May 1944 issue as a prelude to the Normandy invasion.

And this is far from the sole instance in which Capa's fanciful narrative ignores even the evidence of his own photos. At the surrender of Palermo, he claimed to have served as the official interpreter between the American and Italian generals. Yet his photos (*The Surrender of Palermo*, in *Life*'s 23 August 1943 issue) show he was far too busy moving about and snapping pictures, while also showing an Italian who was interpreting for the generals.[9]

That kind of wild invention might be the norm for Hollywood screenplays that are "inspired by true events," but it hardly makes a sound foundation for historical inquiry. Capa himself made no pretense that his quasi-autobiography was constrained by the truth. The dustjacket of the original edition of *Slightly out of Focus* included this caution to the reader:

> Writing the truth being obviously so difficult, I have in the interests of it allowed myself to go sometimes slightly beyond and slightly this side of it. All events and persons in the book are accidental and have something to do with the truth.

That was a good hint that not everything in the book should be considered factual. Subsequent editions did not include a dustjacket, however, and many readers never saw that warning.[10] As a result, far too many readers, critics and even some historians have chosen to accept Capa's tales as gospel. Perhaps it is a testament to our cultural need to believe tall tales that accounts for his fabrications surviving and even flourishing despite his own pictorial evidence that proves them false.

Hyped or not, his accounts of events have often seemed to be the only evidence as to what may, or may not, have happened. As a further complication, many of the Capa anecdotes have come to us through third persons whom Capa regaled with his exploits in social settings. The variance in details suggests such accounts may have been "exaggerated" by alcohol when told by Capa, or confused in the retelling by his audience. In one derivative account, he accompanied Patton's end-run amphibious landings on the north coast of Sicily (he did not). In another hand-me-down account,[11] on 6 June 1944 his ship sank, and he swam for 45 minutes before being fished out of the water (also false). In a sketch outline for a screenplay by Robert Wise, Capa not only landed with the first wave of troops on Omaha Beach, but charged ahead of them on the beach, placing himself in the crossfire between German defenders and attacking American invaders just to get good shots of the advancing troops.[12] In this manner, Capa was fancifully placed so far up the beach that he was literally the lead man of the invasion (also, clearly, false).[13] War stories, like fish tales, do not improve with time, retelling or alcohol.

Capa's D-Day fame can largely be attributed to the fact that he apparently was the only press photographer to actually land on Omaha Beach during the first few hours of the invasion (at least one military photographer landed on Omaha Beach almost an hour before Capa). As a result, five of his photos are among the few pictures

Figure 1. The International Center of Photography digitally recreated this contact sheet from the surviving images of Capa's negatives at the request of A. D. Coleman. (Robert Capa © ICP/Magnum Photos)

of the early landings from the perspective of the GI *on the beach*. Regardless of the artistic and technical merits of his photography—or lack thereof—if a newspaper or author needed a picture of early conditions on the invasion beach, there were few choices, and Robert Capa's images had been heavily promoted by *Life* magazine. His photos became iconic not so much through merit as by default. There simply was no other widely known source.

And yet, his few pictures perfectly illustrate the frustration with the Capa legacy. We cannot even agree how many photos he took. In Capa's own memoir he said he exposed two rolls of 35mm film on the beach (72–76 images), but two pages later said he took 106 pictures when discussing that film. In a D+3 interview with *Life's* Charles Wertenbaker, the number was 79 "of the fighting on the beach"; yet in the same interview, Capa said he spent an hour and a half before he used up all his film, which would seem to imply more pictures than that. Richard Whelan (Capa's authorized biographer) put it at 72 "during the landing," which is close enough to Capa's two rolls. Complicating this accounting, Capa took 60 pictures in 120 format with his Rolleiflex camera after he boarded a landing craft to leave the beach; these are sometimes conflated with the beach film to totally confuse matters.

The Darkroom Accident Fable

At the risk of jumping ahead of the story, it is necessary to provide some context now on a topic that will be covered in more detail in a later chapter. When Capa's D-Day film was sent off to *Life's* New York offices, on D+2, there were just 10 images from his time on the beach. That was a pitifully small number, all things considered, and explanations were sought. *Life's* home office was initially under the impression that seawater had ruined most of the film, and implied that in the 19 June 1944 issue that carried Capa's D-Day photo spread. Apparently, this conclusion was based on a cryptic comment Capa penciled in on a page of caption notes that said, "Film like everything got wett [*sic*] by landing."

The explanation had changed after Capa returned to London during the last half of July. There he supposedly learned that an accident in the darkroom at *Life's* London office had ruined 90 percent of his film. Three years later he included this explanation in *Slightly out of Focus*, going on to add that an excited darkroom assistant had turned the heat too high in the drying cabinet, causing the emulsion to run on most of the film, thereby ruining all but eight of 106 images. The fact that his claim of 96 ruined images was directly contradicted two pages earlier by his claim that he exposed just two rolls (72–76 exposures) on the beach seems to have been lost on most readers. But with publication of that book, the Darkroom Accident fable became canon and the accepted explanation for the small number of photos.

After Capa's death in 1954, the Darkroom Accident fable became the sole property of John Morris, who, as *Life's* London photo editor on D-Day, was Capa's boss and the man who the darkroom worked for. There is no record of any statement by any of the other darkroom employees, and Morris's telling and retelling of the events were the only source for additional details. And he included many more details, weaving a dramatic story of a race against the clock to meet the next deadline. As the only surviving member of the events at *Life*'s London office, Morris gave a seemingly endless series of interviews in later years, to the point that his narrative has all but eclipsed Capa's.

Just how many "surviving" images from the beach were there (i.e., excluding the 120 format film exposed after he left the beach)? As noted above, Capa claimed "only eight were salvaged." Wertenbaker's account claimed only seven survived. The International Center for Photography has in its files a digitally recreated contact sheet which purports to contain all Capa's surviving negatives (Figure 1); it has nine exposures. In addition to these nine, there is the famous "Face in the Surf" picture which, although the original negative is missing (and not included in the digitally recreated contact sheet), was part of Capa's photo spread published by *Life* on 19 June 1944 and has been reproduced countless times since. In addition to these, John Morris, the standard bearer of the Darkroom Accident story, claimed there was an eleventh negative that was not worth printing, but that negative seems to have been lost—if it ever existed in the first place. Whelan, apparently believing Morris, also claimed 11. Despite no evidence of an eleventh image, the photos have somehow become popularly known as "the Magnificent Eleven."

And that's our challenge in a nutshell. They are the most famous photos of D-Day, yet we cannot even agree how many were snapped or how many of them survived the darkroom. If these details are so hopelessly muddled, one can easily imagine how difficult it is to verify less-central aspects of Capa's D-Day legend.

Then things took a dramatic turn. The combined efforts of A. D. Coleman, J. Ross Baughman, Rob McElroy and Tristan da Cunha definitively debunked this Darkroom Accident story; the scenario described by Capa and Morris simply could not have produced the kind of film damage that supposedly resulted in the loss of so many pictures.[14] Seventy years of intricately woven narrative had been dismantled. Which then raised the obvious questions: if the bulk of his film was not in fact ruined by inept developing, then what really happened to those missing images? Or were those few "surviving" photos all that Capa managed to take on D-Day?

All of which poses a problem for an attempt to trace Capa's actions that day. It is only prudent to approach Capa's own accounts with at least a moderate measure of skepticism. Yet the paucity of corroborating accounts can make it difficult to verify or contradict parts of his tales. Fortunately, there is enough data on D-Day in general (if not Capa in particular) that with a little digging, we can shed some light on the matter. Further, for reasons we'll explore later, Capa happened to land at a point on Omaha Beach that saw an unusual convergence of photographers. By carefully comparing their products with Capa's anecdotes, we can draw some useful conclusions.

Capa vs Capa

The two basic versions of Capa's D-Day experiences come from Capa himself. Unfortunately, they are so different in detail that they confuse more than they clarify. The first version comes from an interview he gave fellow *Time* and *Life* reporter Charles Wertenbaker on Omaha Beach on D+3 (9 June). It is a terse, barebones account.[*] The entire experience—from arriving off Omaha Beach on his attack transport to his return to England the next day—is covered in just three paragraphs.[15] The simple, direct narrative coupled with the proximity to the actual events makes for a deceptively convincing read. The dearth of details, however, makes it most unsatisfactory for a historian. Worse, many of the passages are plainly incorrect. This account has generally been lost to oblivion, overshadowed by his second, more widely circulated version.

As noted above, in 1947 he penned his memoirs—*Slightly out of Focus*—hoping to have them made into a movie. In this book, the details of his life were heavily embellished, and his story of D-Day was no exception. The two-page narrative had grown to seven pages.[16] Picturesque but unverifiable anecdotes involving new characters were added. (One of those characters penned a detailed account of his own adventures that day but made no mention of encountering the world-famous Capa.) Capa's description of the scene on the beach became far bloodier and more gruesome. The number of pictures he supposedly took grew from 79 (the tally cited in the Wertenbaker interview) to 106. Even his mutterings to himself while under fire had morphed into much more picturesque language.

In his original 1944 version, Capa made no mention of where he was slotted in the landing sequence, but he gave a boarding time for his landing craft (0600 hours) that would have placed him roughly in Wave 13 or 15. In the 1947 version he claimed to have landed with Co. E in the "first wave." In this later version, he quietly omitted what time he departed his transport, merely claiming they assembled on deck in the dark at 0400 hours and left the reader to assume he departed shortly thereafter.

Complicating matters greatly are the two books by Capa biographer Richard Whelan (*Robert Capa*, 1985, and *This Is War!: Robert Capa at Work*, 2007). Whelan was well aware of Capa's habit of sacrificing truth for the sake of a good story, and although he frequently pointed out Capa's digressions when he recognized them, he remained a loyal advocate for the core of the Capa mythology. His later book, *This Is War!,* served as a follow-up to the first and amplification of Capa's wartime work using extensive additional research. Unfortunately, that additional research often turned up more details which called Capa's accounts into question. As a result, Whelan was forced to invent increasingly unbelievable scenarios to make sense of

---

[*] Wertenbaker had just become the head of the *Time/Life*'s London office. He spent D-Day offshore aboard the US First Army's command ship the USS *Achernar* (*AKA-53*).

the contradictory data. This is especially true for D-Day, as Whelan had to invent a convoluted sequence of events involving Capa landing not once, but twice, on Omaha Beach that morning.

All of this poses a challenge for those hoping to piece together a truthful version of events. The scale of differences is so marked that choosing between versions is extremely difficult. One cannot even place blind faith in the original, terse version, as its description of when and where he took photos does not match the surviving photos themselves.

The best we can do is to use his versions only as uncertain guides, doubtful trail makers which we must then try to either confirm or disprove at every step. In some few instances, there are points of congruity between the versions, and we can grant those greater credibility. But not much.

Life and Editorial Spin

Not all the blame for the hype and exaggeration of Capa's D-Day legend can be attributed to Capa himself. As with all the major press outlets, management at *Life* worked hard to push the brand and to convince its readers they had the best reporters, the best photographers and, as a result, best coverage. As always, circulation was the goal.

The Army had specific plans for Capa, as documented in the detailed landing tables which were part of the operation's plan: he would be one of two press photographers riding in with an infantry unit, with one photographer arriving in Wave 13 and the other in Wave 15.[17] But that order was a closely guarded secret. When Capa was whisked away from his London flat and dropped into a pre-invasion marshalling camp, he had no idea which unit he would accompany, much less where in the landing sequence he would be fitted. None of his bosses in London were supposed to know either and, apparently, they did not. According to *Slightly out of Focus*, it was only after he had embarked on his assault transport and that ship was actually en route to Normandy that Capa supposedly chose to land in the first wave.[18] Even if this anecdote were true, it would have been a decision his superiors in London could not possibly have known, as he had been cut off from them for a week at that point. And the London office would be kept in the dark for days to come. When Capa sent his film back to London the day after the landings, he included no caption notes for his D-Day film rolls and only the scantiest message indicating which rolls of film contained "the action." Nothing else.

As a result, when *Life* editors in London or New York composed captions for his beach photos, they had little idea when or where he was *supposed* to have landed, and absolutely no idea when or where he *did* land. So, they guessed.

Those editorial guesses loyally hyped the company image. They placed their photographer in the first wave of the invasion. Good marketing; questionable ethics.

So, the origin of at least part of the Capa D-Day myth would seem to lie at the feet of others. Of course, *Life's* little white lie perfectly fit Capa's own carefully cultivated persona of the "Greatest War Photographer in the World." He subsequently not only embraced the marketing lie, but he also expanded on it in his later retellings of the event.

These are important points. Any effort to honestly determine the facts of Capa's D-Day adventure is invariably met with charges of revisionist history. Such charges fail for the obvious reason that *there is no history to revise.* Instead, we have corporate spin and a "memoir" that Capa himself admitted wasn't constrained by truth, rather was intended to lead to a Hollywood screenplay. There is no sin—but much virtue—in deconstructing illusions of this sort. In fact, these circumstances all but demand a dispassionate examination of the facts.

Legacy or Legend

Since his premature death in 1954, Capa has been elevated in popular esteem to almost saint-like status. Partially this is due to the understandable tendency to excessively emphasize the positive attributes of one who has died "before his time." In a similar vein, there is a natural reluctance not to speak ill of the dead, so there has been remarkably little interest in closely scrutinizing the fanciful aspects of *Slightly out of Focus.* In this factual void, succeeding generations have had little option but to accept those fables as true, no matter how dubious they seem. As John Hersey concluded in his review of *Slightly out of Focus,* "The text is just the inventor's invention about himself."[19] The man had indeed become the myth.

And it is an endearing myth. Capa was a charming man and a raconteur of the first order. Sociable, entertaining, even lovable. He was also an inveterate gambler, an excessive drinker, a womanizer, and, judging from his memoir, not a particularly truthful person. In short, he was a lovable rogue, the kind of person you know has serious flaws, but you choose to ignore them because you just can't help yourself from being swept up by the legend.

And that is a problem. When a man's legacy has become little more than a self-generated series of romanticized and fanciful anecdotes, how should history treat it? Is there an obligation to "protect" a legacy that includes so very much that is false? Or is there an obligation to winnow out the facts and judge that man by his actual accomplishments? And if we succeed in doing this, are we prepared to face the man that may be revealed?

Once the Capa legend is stripped away from the Capa legacy, we are mostly left with his photographic record. And here too we encounter a quandary. The hard truth which many wish to ignore is that Capa's photos are not especially technically good. Nor did he pretend they were. As he told Leon Danielle, "The main thing is to get the right mood and feeling. Technique is not important."[20]

But even this raises problems. What is the "right mood and feeling"? Who decides what is right? Why not choose the accurate or factual mood and feeling? Are faked but apparently powerful photos more to be prized because they convey someone's opinion of the "right mood and feeling"? Do photos that are presented in a false or misleading context—thereby setting a false mood and feeling—constitute great photography? Or is it merely the sly contextual packaging of the photos that elevates (but distorts) the value of the pictures? Capa has been lauded as the one honest photographer of his generation, but how can this be, knowing as we do of his history of faking pictures? How is honesty being defined? Capa primarily was a photographer for news magazines, and the readers of that medium expected to see pictures of actual events, to see a moment of truth frozen in time. But is that what they got?

And that's the rub, where the interests of historian and photojournalist conflict. The historian is not interested in protecting a legacy. He is interested first in factual details, from which conclusions may then be drawn. The photojournalist, especially one using the art to further political ideas, is more concerned with creating an emotional response, whether grounded in truth or not.

Bare Bones

In very rough outline, the Capa legend had him arriving in the invasion area on the attack transport USS *Samuel Chase*. He landed with troops of the 16th Regimental Combat Team (RCT) on Omaha Beach, most likely on the Easy Red sector. After spending an undetermined period on the beach taking an undetermined number of photos (both are confused by conflicting claims), he fled to a Landing Craft, Infantry (LCI), which had beached nearby. From there he was taken back to the same USS *Samuel Chase* and arrived back in the UK early on 7 June. He sent his film by courier to *Life*'s London offices and took a ship back to Omaha Beach. And, as noted above, according to legend all but a few of his pictures were ruined during the developing process.

Now, let's see if we can determine what really happened.

PART I

To the Normandy Coast

"Writing the truth being obviously so difficult, I have in the interests of it allowed myself to go sometimes slightly beyond and slightly this side of it. All events and persons in the book are accidental and have something to do with the truth."

ROBERT CAPA, FROM THE DUSTJACKET OF THE ORIGINAL EDITION OF
SLIGHTLY OUT OF FOCUS

"I like the truth sometimes, but I don't care enough for it to hanker after it."

MARK TWAIN

CHAPTER ONE

A Change of Scenery

"When you're in the fighting you don't go where there's fire, but you go where there's pictures."

ROBERT CAPA'S ADVICE TO SOLDIERS OF THE 165TH SIGNAL
PHOTO COMPANY BEFORE D-DAY

As 1944 began, Capa was stuck in Italy, and he was none too happy about it. He had both personal and professional reasons to leave Italy and return to London. On the personal side, he hadn't seen his girlfriend, Elaine Parker, since the previous June. She worked in the Office of War Information in London, and while technically still married and still sharing quarters with her husband, she seemed to have a free-ranging social life that included Capa on a semi-serious basis and other men on a casual basis. Capa could not write to Pinky (the nickname was due to her hair color) at her home address due to the husband, so his letters were sent to the *Time/Life* office in London, where Elizabeth Crockett (Crocky), who was one of the staff and a friend of Capa's, held the letters for Pinky to pick up. The last time he'd seen Pinky was during a brief stay in London, but that interlude lasted just a couple of weeks. Whether either Capa or Pinky were truly in love with the other is open to question, as both appeared to treat the relationship as something of a game. But Capa longed to see his Pinky again, if for no other reason to find out if she really was interested in being "his."

On the professional side of things, Italy was proving to be something of a dead end, bordering on a stalemate. Allied lines had been stopped dead north of Naples. Terrain, mud, cold and tenacious German defenses hampered Allied attacks and resulted in tactical defeats and high casualties. To break this stalemate, the Allies decided to make an amphibious "end run" farther up the Italian peninsula at Anzio to turn the German defenses.

There are two versions describing how Capa became involved with this landing, his own version naturally sounding much more heroic.[1] In his autobiography, he gave a rather embellished summary of his just-completed "five months at the front," which ended at his arrival back in Naples preparing to leave for the United Kingdom.

While Capa packed for departure to the UK, Bill Lang (the head of the Naples *Time/Life* bureau) pointed out the mass of amphibious shipping in the harbor. Something was up. Despite his fatigue and war weariness, Capa couldn't resist an opportunity to be part of an amphibious invasion. "Can I still get in on the show?" he claimed he asked Lang.

But even Whelan saw through this façade.[2] The fact is that upon arrival in Naples, he found that the Fifth Army Public Relations Office had already slotted him for the invasion. He was shanghaied, not a volunteer. Much to his dismay and against his wishes, Capa would be covering the same Ranger units he had briefly visited a few months earlier. He frankly dreaded the prospect. William Stoneman (Chicago *Daily News*) was also tagged with the job, and stated both he and Capa were "scared to death" at the news. He also stated that Capa's first reaction was to procure a case of Spanish brandy to fortify his courage on the trip.

The amphibious assault took place on 22 January 1944. The first waves landed unopposed at 0200 hours; Capa claimed he boarded his landing craft at midnight, implying he landed in the early waves. The truth was once again a bit different. Capa didn't step ashore until after daybreak. The excuse was that he couldn't take pictures in the dark. While true, the corollary was that by the time he did land (a time much in doubt), the action had moved far inland, and he was in no position to capture it in the daylight. Although *Life* used his photos from the operation, they were the still picture equivalent of B-roll images. Generic shots of rear area activity. Things ashore would soon change. The Germans reacted swiftly, and cautious efforts to expand the beachhead over the next week met increasing resistance, with indications of a powerful German counterattack soon. A major attack to break out of the beachhead made some gains, but was defeated, and resulted in the loss of two Ranger battalions on top of other casualties. Capa's narrative of his time in Anzio is so sketchy and sparse that he didn't even take notice of the disaster suffered by his purported friends in the Rangers.

With stalemate at every turn in Italy in general, and Anzio in particular, combat in the "soft underbelly of Europe" held little interest for Capa.

On the other hand, Great Britain was quite another story. It was apparent to everyone that the long anticipated cross-Channel assault had to happen soon. Both Eisenhower and Montgomery left the Mediterranean Theater for London that very January, so it was obvious that the vast quantities of men and materiel which had been amassed in the United Kingdom were going to be put to lethal use soon. Allies and Axis alike knew invasion was coming and the suspense was such that people on both sides just wanted to get it over with. The only questions were when and where.

This prospect offered Capa much better opportunities to ply his trade and beckoned him strongly. The prospect of a cross-Channel attack posed the additional lure of a faster return to his beloved France, most especially Paris. And then there was the not inconsiderable fact that while biding his time in London, Capa would enjoy a far more luxurious lifestyle than Anzio could offer, especially with Pinky close at hand.

And so Capa looked to end his isolation on the increasingly besieged Anzio beachhead.

Homecoming

As if on cue, deliverance appeared. Capa claimed he received a message from a friend in the Army Air Corps IX Troop Carrier Command (transport airplanes) informing him that the unit was being transferred to London, and his friend had a plane waiting for Capa in Naples. With this invitation in hand, and with no apparent regard for the necessity of receiving either Fifth Army or *Time/Life* authorization, Capa claimed he managed to leave the beachhead "at the end of February" (1944) on a hospital ship headed for Naples.[3]

Almost everything in that was an exaggeration. In fact, Capa wasted little time extricating himself from Anzio. A 3 February 1944 cable from Capa shows he had already received travel orders to go to London and was preparing to leave "as soon as possible." Four days later, John Morris (the *Life* photo editor in London) cabled New York that "Capa advised he is expecting to arrive here by the 15th, but I hear he's at the Anzio beachhead and I don't see how he will make it."[4] He did leave the beachhead, and did so long before the end of February, as evidenced by the fact that on 10 February 1944 he flew from Naples to Algiers, meaning he left Anzio at least several days previously.[5] He hadn't even been in the beachhead two weeks. From Naples he still had to get to London. A 13 February 1944 letter from Allied Force Headquarters Public Relations Branch to the British Consul in Algiers, which sought the Consul's endorsement, stated Capa's trip to London was urgent, so we can assume he left Algiers en route to London shortly after that date.[6] And since the British Consul's endorsement was required, it would seem Capa hitched a ride on a British diplomatic courier aircraft. This also indicates that Capa's assertion that his friend had an aircraft waiting for him was merely a fabrication to exaggerate his importance.

About the only item Capa got right was that his friend's unit did transfer to the UK in February, though even then, he got the unit designation wrong. It was the 52nd Troop Carrier Wing, which was being assigned from the I Troop Carrier Command in Sicily, to the IX Troop Carrier Command in the UK. And it didn't go to London. Capa's autobiography didn't bother much with getting dates or details correct.

Despite this supposed urgency, we don't know exactly when he arrived in the UK. Capa made virtually no reference to specific dates during this period and effectively left more than a two-month void in his narrative. Recall that he claimed to have left Anzio "at the end of February." While leading into a description of his *second* night back in London, he set the scene by describing the city's atmosphere in *May* 1944.[7] Not March. *May*.

Whelan's biography is almost equally vague on the topic. He stated Capa arrived in London just in time for the Baby Blitz. The Baby Blitz reference—alluding to the abortive German renewed bombing offensive against England in early 1944—is misleading. This renewed bombing offensive began the night of 21/22 January 1944, but Capa stepped ashore at Anzio, Italy on the morning of 22 January, so Whelan must have been mistaken. John Morris merely recalled that Capa arrived in late February.[8] Kershaw's *Blood and Champagne* placed Capa arriving in London in early April 1944.[9] So much for both firsthand and secondary sources.

A letter from Pinky to Elizabeth Crockett (the staffer in the *Time/Life* London office) dated 6 March 1944 might be more helpful.[10] In it she gleefully announced that Capa was home with her in London. Whelan's notes also included a reference to "Crockey's Letter" ([sic]; possibly the same letter from Pinky) which recounted a party Capa attended at the home of Derek and Jean Tangye in Mortlake that was damaged by one of the Baby Blitz raids as the party was underway. While the German raids were anything but precision bombing at this point, there appears to have been only one raid during this period that would have interrupted the party. The Baby Blitz raids for the night of 20/21 February 1944 (a month into the Baby Blitz) were concentrated in the Fulham, Putney and Cheswick areas, which encompassed the Tangyes' residence (at the time, Thames Bank Cottage in Mortlake). Assuming that this letter is accurate and not just another tall tale—Capa made no reference to a narrow escape or attendance at a Tangye party—this placed him back in the UK at least by 20 February, which dovetails nicely with the request a week earlier to give him priority for transportation from Algiers to the UK.

The only other hint of a date that Whelan provides is that Capa supposedly attended a parachute school in late March conducted by the 82nd Airborne Division in the Leicester area.[11] Whelan placed Capa in jump school in March based on a photo which supposedly showed the photographer wearing parachutes and reading a newspaper while sitting in a plane. The headlines of that paper provided Whelan with an approximate date. Unfortunately, Whelan did not provide that photo, and an extensive search has failed to turn it up. More importantly he is clearly wrong, as will be made clear in later paragraphs. For our purposes, it is sufficient here merely to point out that SHAEF hadn't even begun to look for volunteer parachutists among the correspondents until sometime after 24 April, at least a month after Whelan had Capa in jump school.[12] Capa didn't attend a jump school until later that summer.

The Better Part of Valor

Whenever he did arrive in London, he landed in a city in the embrace of invasion fever, as he put it. Although details were closely guarded secrets, it was plain to everyone that plans and preparations were being frantically perfected. Among the myriad of details that planners addressed was the matter of representatives of the media: print columnists and reporters, broadcast journalists and photographers. All had to be accommodated—at least to some degree—with due consideration to the power and reputation of their employers, and the nations they represented. The matter of media quotas was thorny. In the words of COL Barney Oldfield, then a lieutenant in the SHAEF Public Relations Division:

> One of the troubles in the mounting up for Normandy was the great numbers of war correspondents who wanted, or professed to want, to be in the so-called "first-wave." In it was the lure of the front-page by-line and the established reputation for all time.[13]

"First wave" in this case referred to the mass of troops arriving in the first 24 hours—or even the first week—rather than those in the first landing craft to hit the beach. The initial group of American invasion units coming by sea was divided into three echelons. Force O, carrying the 1st Infantry Division, would land on Omaha Beach. Force U, carrying the 4th Infantry Division, would land on Utah Beach to the west. Following these would come Force B, carrying in the 29th Infantry Division. All told—and including hundreds of smaller attached units—that amounted to roughly 90,000 men and 12,000 vehicles due to land during the first 24 hours. In addition, airlift would carry most of two airborne divisions for parachute drops. In this context, the loose use of the term "First Wave" was far different from its normal military denotation.

While every newsman worth his salt wanted to be *on hand* for the assault, most were not eager to be *in the front ranks* of that assault. The war correspondents were, after all, civilians, not soldiers. So, while there was keen competition to get a spot in the invasion shipping, there was little competition to be with those who would storm the beach. The distinction between *war* correspondent and *combat* correspondent may be lost on the public, but reporters knew the distinction was a potentially fatal one.

So, when Lieutenant Colonel Jack Redding of the SHAEF Public Relations Division staff called in individual reporters to ask them if they had any preferences about which unit they wanted to accompany ashore, he was not overwhelmed with volunteers for the assault elements. John "Beaver" Thompson (*Chicago Tribune*) had become famous for jumping into combat with paratroopers in both the North Africa and Sicily invasions. At this point, however, his paper had had enough of his risk-taking and ordered him not to jump in the upcoming invasion of France. Thompson apparently was none too eager to press his luck with the seaborne forces, either. He told Redding that he wanted to be assigned to General Bradley's First Army headquarters (commanding the landings on the two American beaches), which would sit out the actual storming of the beaches on a command ship and not land until a few days after D-Day. As it would turn out, his colleagues Don Whitehead (AP) and

John O'Reilly (*New York Herald Tribune*)—both veteran war correspondents with frontline experience—told Redding the same thing. They preferred coming in with Bradley rather than with the assault waves. Partly this choice could be attributed to the better access to the general (and the information the general had access to) as well as the excellent communications systems on the command ship that would facilitate getting their reports out. But it was also plainly true that the bloody assault on the defenses of Hitler's Atlantic Wall, whose defenders had four years in which to fortify, was hardly something these reporters wanted to witness firsthand and at hand-grenade range.

For some reporters, even Bradley's command ship was too close to the action. Ernie Pyle was looking forward to taking his editor's not entirely humorous advice to come in late, with the tenth echelon or after. Pyle was thinking of not landing until a week or two after D-Day.[14]

As it would turn out, few of these reporters got their wish for a safe billet. John MacVane (NBC radio) claimed he did get his wish, but he portrayed himself as something of a fire-eater. Having been run out of France by the German invasion in 1940, he claimed that he wanted to be in the forefront of the Allied return. He'd been on the Dieppe Raid—though it was aborted before his craft landed—and his brief frontline coverage of fighting in North Africa hadn't been enough to sicken him of combat. He wanted to land early, and he asked to land with the 1st Infantry Division, a unit he knew and trusted from North Africa.[15]

We have no record of what Capa may have requested, but we know what he *did not want* and *what he actively avoided*.

The first hint we have of what Capa's role would be in the invasion was found in a 24 April SHAEF Public Relations Office memo identifying accredited correspondents and the component to which they were assigned.[16] It listed Capa as assigned to the US Army Air Forces (USAAF) still photo pool. That would have perfectly suited his desires. He would have remained in England amid its (relative) luxuries and near Pinky. And the USAAF wasn't known for taking many civilian still photographers on missions. They were normally relegated to taking pictures at air bases.[*]

But that ideal billet was perhaps just too good to last.

In late April or early May, Oldfield was assigned the task of recruiting correspondents to accompany the two airborne divisions, either parachuting in or landing by glider.[17] *Life* magazine nominated Capa and fellow *Life* photographer Bob Landry for this honor—but being nominated is not the same as volunteering. Recall that three years later Capa would include in *Slightly out of Focus* the fabricated account of jumping into Sicily with the 82nd Airborne Division back in 1943. Yet when

---

[*] Capa claimed to have flown on several bombing missions to Italy from North Africa, but even Whelan discounts this. For all this claimed activity, there is virtually no photographic evidence, and what there is, is ambiguous, not clearly showing it was from a combat mission.

Oldfield and *Life* tried to give him an opportunity to actually "walk the walk" in 1944, Capa made himself scarce.

By May 1944, Capa and Landry had missed several dates to attend the parachute training course set up at Chilton-Foliat by the 101st Airborne Division (which was tasked to qualify volunteer correspondents for D-Day), and as time was getting short, Oldfield set out to find them. He finally caught Capa in his flat where he was throwing an enthusiastic party. When enough liquor had flowed to spawn reckless bravado, Oldfield managed to have Capa, Landry and a Larry Lesueur (a "volunteer" from CBS) sign the necessary waivers, and all agreed to meet the next morning for the trip to the jump school.

The next morning, none of the three showed up. When Oldfield finally managed to contact Landry and Lesueur, both claimed they had badly sprained their ankles stepping off a curb getting into a taxi after the party and couldn't possibly attend the course. Capa, they said, was supposed to let Oldfield know what happened when he showed up at the rendezvous. Capa didn't even bother with an excuse. He simply did not show up and could not be reached. Perhaps Capa thought if he never showed up for jump school, he could return to his much safer original assignment to the USAAF still photo pool. If so, he figured wrong.

When Redding eventually gave up on the three, he instead assigned them slots to come in with naval shipping, embedded with various Army units. And thus, Capa ended up with the ground forces still photo pool, not the air forces still photo pool. And this bit of collective hooky-playing also explains why no press photographers landed with the airborne forces on D-Day.

As noted earlier, this anecdote also rules out Whelan's assertion that Capa attended jump school in late March 1944.[18] The SHAEF Public Relations staff was still unsuccessfully trying to get him to that school two months later. But having incorrectly jump-qualified Capa before D-Day, Whelan had painted himself in a corner. He needed an explanation why Capa did not jump on D-Day, and since Capa gave no hint on the matter, Whelan came up with what might sound like a plausible reason. Going back to the Italian Campaign, Capa had supposedly missed the Salerno landings—the much-awaited return to mainland Europe—because he was sequestered with the 82nd Airborne Division in preparation for an ill-conceived operation that would have them seize airfields near Rome. Although that operation was canceled at the last moment, it prevented the 82nd from initially participating in the Salerno invasion and served as Capa's excuse for missing those landings as well. Therefore, Whelan surmised, Capa probably begged off the Normandy airdrop for fear of a similar glitch leaving him in England with the grounded paratroopers while the seaborne invasion went ahead. As excuses went, it was poor. For one thing, Capa appears to have once again been embedded with the troop carrier wing for the Salerno operation, not the paratroopers. This is borne out by the fact that when the paratroopers did jump into Salerno to reinforce the beachhead, Capa did not go with them. For another thing, the Normandy invasion simply could not be mounted without the airborne component. But the average reader would not be expected to know those points, so Whelan's explanation sounded plausible.

Not all Capa's time in London was devoted to wine, women and merriment. The Public Relations Division had asked a few veteran photographers among the correspondents to share their expertise with the members of the 165th Signal Photo Company,[19] which would provide detachments to various First US Army units during the invasion and beyond. As with most of the units waiting in England for the invasion, the 165th was straight from the US, and had no combat experience. According to Oldfield, Capa took a cue from a Willie and Joe cartoon which showed a condom used to protect the muzzle of a rifle, and suggested the Army photographers use condoms to waterproof their film after a roll was exposed.[20] It seemed a good idea, and condoms were issued, in excess of the normal demands of recreation, to the men of the 165th.

According to Whelan, Capa provided another key bit of advice, though Whelan missed the full implications of it. "When you're in the fighting," Whelan quoted him, "you don't go where there's fire, you go where there are pictures."[21] This is one of a series of quotes, both by Capa and other war photographers, that begins to paint a disturbing vision of their journalistic ethics. Capa advised them to avoid fire, yet his photos often *supposedly* show men under fire? Then there's Scherman's quote on faking or reframing photos after the fact (see lead-in quote to the Introduction). And of course, there's Capa's own quote about jiggling the camera when taking a picture to introduce the impression of action. Such quotes, when coupled with Capa's faked photos during the Spanish Civil War, caution one not to take war photography at its face value. It's a bit of wisdom worth keeping in mind throughout the rest of this book.

The Correspondent Corps

Of the 540 correspondents that were accredited by SHAEF,[22] 467 had been assigned to cover one aspect or another of the invasion. Correspondents were assigned to all Allied forces and branches of the services that were engaged in the invasion: the air, naval and ground forces. By far the vast majority of these would remain in the UK for the invasion. Some would cross on naval shipping, and never step ashore—at least not in the first days. For D-Day and the following two weeks,[23] American forces were allowed 106 correspondents (not counting those assigned to naval forces). Fifty-seven would operate from London, 21 would cover USAAF operations and 28 would land with the American ground forces (First US Army) sometime in the first week. The most prized (or dreaded, depending on one's perspective) slots for correspondents were those assigned to the two beach assault divisions (1st Division at Omaha Beach and 4th Division at Utah Beach), and the two parachute divisions (82nd and 101st Airborne Divisions, landing behind Utah Beach). Within these four divisions, a mere 19 correspondents were embedded, and one of these was scheduled merely to ride in an aircraft to cover the airdrop and return to base with that aircraft. An additional nine correspondents were to cover the three major headquarters: V Corps, commanding Omaha Beach landings; VII Corps, commanding Utah Beach landings; and First US Army, in command of both corps. These nine correspondents would arrive offshore early on D-Day but stay aboard ship one or more days until their headquarters transferred to the beach.

Included in this group of 28 correspondents was a small still photo pool to cover the US First Army ground forces. In the 24 April 1944 memorandum, four photographers were identified for this pool. At that date, Capa was assigned to the US Army Air Forces still photo pool. As we saw above, he and his *Life* coworker Bob Landry were added to the First US Army ground still photo pool later, replacing two of the original photographers. Bert Brandt was the only original man of this pool to make the landings.

In the final weeks before the invasion, a small number of assault correspondents had second thoughts and pulled out. To my knowledge, the Army has never identified these men, nor does it appear a final comprehensive record of correspondent assignments for D-Day exists. One of the four still photo pool photographers apparently opted out. He has never been identified by either name or press organization, and his position in the 1st Division's landing tables was taken by broadcast journalist John MacVane.

In addition to the four pool photographer slots identified in the plans, a photographer from *Stars and Stripes* accompanied the Ranger assault at Pointe du Hoc, and three other press photographers were schedule to land later that day on Utah Beach. This latter group included Peter J. Carroll (AP) who Whelan mistakenly placed at Omaha Beach.* Carroll was featured in Jack Lieb's film documenting his crossing and landing with non-jumping elements of the 101st Airborne; they came in by sea and landed at Utah Beach just after noon on D-Day.[24]

There were, however, an additional 32 military photographers landing with these units—all from the Army's 165th Signal Photo Company—and unlike most of their civilian counterparts, they landed with motion as well as still cameras.

Except for those 19 press correspondents assigned to the assault units, most of the civilian correspondents covering D-Day never came close to setting foot on solid ground on 6 June. As noted above, nine would spend D-Day on ships with various headquarters, 21 were assigned to the USAAF and might (or might not) fly on D-Day and the remaining 57 who had not been slotted for D-Day would

---

* Whelan's error stems from a photo of *LCT-207* on Omaha Beach, which he included in W/TIW (p. 238). That photo is often credited to Carroll, even though he was not near Omaha Beach that day. The actual photographer remains unknown.

ship over sometime during the first week, much to their professed chagrin. Of the remaining 400-plus accredited correspondents, most stayed in London or hovered about the departure harbors. Some were assigned to other services, and while they did not step ashore, were present for D-Day. Walter Cronkite, for example was one of the few who flew with supporting bomber missions. Some, such as Joseph Liebling, were assigned to Navy or Coast Guard vessels which permitted them to make the harrowing ride to the beach and back in landing craft, but none of these set foot ashore for the first two days. Others remained on ships that anchored in the Transport Area some 10–13 miles off the invasion beaches. Despite this fact, many of these would later craft their tales such that it appeared they were in the "First Wave."

In the loosest, most generic sense, perhaps they were "First Wave," part of the first week's contingent of correspondents. But in the bloody business of combat, The First Wave has an altogether different, highly specific, literal meaning. The first wave is a place of honor, dread, and death; the first being far less tangible than the latter two. To be in the first wave and survive is a notable feat, simply because the chances of surviving are notably lower. Those reporters who later claimed credit for being in the first wave were trading on the blood-purchased credit of others, having risked little or nothing themselves. Sadly it was an all-too-common practice for correspondents to exaggerate how far forward they actually were.[*] The only reporters who truly landed with the first waves included those covering the airborne divisions; by 0400 hours, all four of them had boots on the ground in Normandy (the fifth, Wright Bryan (NBC/*Atlanta Journal*), was not scheduled to jump, only to cover the operation from the aircraft). At the beaches it was a similar story taking place a few hours later. Fewer than six correspondents assigned to Omaha and Utah beaches landed in the first three hours of the invasion, and none at Omaha Beach set foot on dry ground before 0820 hours (1 hour and 50 minutes after H-Hour)—no matter how loosely they crafted their stories later. Even then, they landed a full hour after the first cameraman from the Army's 165th Photo Company stepped ashore.

Capa would be the only one of the three civilian press photographers covering Omaha and Utah Beaches to step ashore before noon that day, and that was likely an accident.

---

[*] The practice even had a name, the Magic Carpet tactic, wherein a correspondent would gather details from witness who had been present at a location, and then the correspondent would write the story as if he'd been there himself. Based on Oldfield's account of the Normandy landings, Harry Gorrell (UP) used this tactic when he filed a story on the paratroopers' battle for the key city of Carentan.

CHAPTER TWO

Pressing Matters

"The camera is an excuse to be someplace you otherwise don't belong. It gives me both a point of connection and a point of separation."

SUSAN MEISELAS

The Still Photo Pool

The significance of Capa's final assignment to the US First Army still photo pool is often overlooked or minimized.

Under most circumstances, a correspondent was largely free to wander about in search of a story, often based on guidance from his bureau or suggested topics the public relations officers hoped to promote. This freedom was normally limited only by the geographic limits of the command's boundaries. But in certain types of operations, the number of correspondents that could participate was strictly limited by circumstances, and their freedom of movement limited even more so. Assault landings—air or amphibious—were the primary examples of this. Space aboard aircraft or assault shipping was at a premium, with every slot needed for key members of a small unit. And the very nature of those aircraft or landing craft limited a correspondent's ability to wander in search of a story. And yet assault landings were typically such important news events that every media outlet clamored for access.

The pool system was created specifically to deal with these situations. The military would make a limited number of slots available, hopefully ensuring a logical plan of coverage that would include print, broadcast and photographic coverage. The correspondents assigned would receive guidance on coverage topics from the military through a correspondent editor who supervised that pool. The material produced by the pool correspondents would be made available to all media outlets, ensuring maximum distribution of products. As a result, when Capa and Landry joined the ground still photo pool, they were in a real sense temporarily working for the Public Relations Division of the SHAEF staff, providing photos for all news outlets, and not just *Time* or *Life*.

Why, then, would *Life*, a weekly magazine, agree to take part in such an arrangement? It turns out this arrangement did offer *Life* some important advantages. Being part of the pool ensured *Life* would get photographers in at the earliest possible moment.[1] Initial plans restricted non-pooled photographers from deploying to France before D+14, which would be fatal to *Life's* publication timeline and reduce them to using the same limited pool of photos everyone else had access to, so getting a man on the pool was vital. While a small number of the best of the photos from the pool photographers would be selected for radio telephoto transmission and be snatched up for use by the daily press, a *Life* photographer assigned to the pool would still produce more than enough additional photos for exclusive use in detailed spreads in *Life's* weekly issue. So, a bureau with a photographer in the pool had a tremendous competitive advantage over other weekly outlets; not only was *Life* the only magazine in the ground still photo pool for American forces, but it had two of the three photographer slots.

The pool's primary initial task was to get photos of the initial landings back to London as quickly as humanly possible to feed the daily newspapers, and from the American perspective, that meant getting them stateside. The Public Relations Division published a memo covering "Photographic Policy," with the purpose of ensuring "complete photographic coverage of the operations of this command."[2] A "Public Relations Plan OVERLORD"[3] and a series of accompanying letters amplified this memo, such as one titled "Pictorial Coverage,"[4] which outlined procedures to "coordinate coverage between the newsreels and still photo war correspondents and the official military photographers to ensure cooperative, not competitive coverage." (Original emphasis.) These documents went so far as to provide seven pages of suggested photo topics, organized by air, sea and land forces, and were further broken down by phases, from marshalling to combat ashore.

A provision in the Pictorial Coverage memo would influence Capa's D-Day actions. "IT IS EXTREMELY IMPORTANT to get the first action on the beach and LEAVE FILM AT COLLECTING POINTS SO IT CAN BE RUSHED BACK. DO NOT CARRY THE LANDING FILM IN, as you advance with the troops." (Original emphasis.) While that advice was fine for most photographers who were not members of the pool (such as the many Army photographers embarked for the landings), it posed a challenge for the pool photographers. There would be no collecting points ashore in the immediate hours after the landing began, and backup plans involving couriers and fast dispatch boats didn't inspire much confidence.* The only certain method for the still pool photographers to get their hot products back to London quickly was to carry it back themselves.

This point was underscored by Charles Smith (International News Photos), who was the coordinator of the still photo pool. He told his pool photographers "that it

---

* On D-Day and the following days, these backup plans failed at every level.

would be okay if any of them saw a chance to rush back to London with their own negatives and thus beat the official Army courier system."[5] So much for ensuring "cooperative, not competitive coverage." Nevertheless, it was a realistic appraisal of the situation, and two of the three still photo pool photographers would heed Smith's advice. The third pool photographer apparently didn't land until D+2 due to mechanical trouble in his landing craft; by that time the need for a rapid return with film was past.

So, Capa was not there to hunt down a photo story for *Life* or follow the fighting inland. He was part of a small pool of correspondents whose activities were a coordinated part of the larger photo coverage of the operation, with priority to provide the daily papers with immediate photos from the initial landing waves.

And therein lies a key point, which will be developed more fully later. Capa's plan for the invasion could not have entailed stepping ashore, for that would almost certainly have precluded getting his photos back to London by the following day, because the fast attack transport ships, the first convoy headed back to the UK, were planning to start recovering their landing craft at 1030 hours in preparation to relocate to an outer anchorage. They were scheduled to sail back to the UK by noon.[6]

Further proof of Capa's D-Day role in assault landings can be found in another pre-invasion course he did not attend. During the first week of May, the correspondents who would be landing with the assault troops were taken to an amphibious and commando training camp in Scotland for a one-week course.[7] Neither Capa himself nor any biographer nor any historian has indicated Capa attended this course.

The Press vs the Press

In the current culture, where a press-vs-military conflict is virtually taken for granted, it is difficult to appreciate the nature of press relations at the time of the invasion.

In the space of five years, the Army had swollen from a force of 190,000 men in 1939 to more than eight million men in 1944. The difference between those two figures was exclusively made up of civilian volunteers and draftees. In 1939, the Army had a mere handful of public relations officers—the duty was normally assigned in addition to the officers' primary responsibilities. By the time of the Normandy landings, a robust public relations organization had evolved. Not surprisingly, it was staffed almost exclusively by personnel who had been either newsmen or public relations men in civilian life just months before. Indeed, it would be hard to point to many officers in the press relations sections between the ranks of lieutenant and lieutenant colonel who hadn't worked in the media before joining up.

As a result, the "military" press relations men were friends, colleagues, or at least professional associates of the correspondents. They were very much two faces of the same profession, and beneath any tension, there existed a bond which would be completely mystifying to the modern newsman.

Just as importantly, key senior officers at SHAEF and other headquarters were giants in the media themselves. The mere suggestion that Ted Turner serve in uniform as a senior officer on the Central Command staff during the Gulf War would be met with shock or laughter today, but David Sarnoff, pre-war head of RCA (which owned NBC), was a colonel (soon to be brigadier general) on Eisenhower's staff. William Paley (who had built CBS into a major network) was a colonel in Eisenhower's Psychological Warfare Branch (which at one point controlled the press relations office). As a result of men like Sarnoff and Paley filling senior positions, SHAEF press policies were to a large degree created, or at least shaped, by newsmen. The old truism again proved itself: where you stand on an issue largely depends on where you sit. It is easy to be a reporter demanding free access and unfettered communiques, but when serving in positions such as Sarnoff and Paley, you are forced to confront the moral and physical implications of those extremist positions. People's lives were at issue—if not the fate of nations—and some realistic middle ground had to be chosen. When the responsibilities for both sides of the issue were dropped into their laps, members of the press, whether in or out of uniform, instinctively sought that middle ground to one degree or another. It was a much different national culture.

And there was a "self-correcting" element, as well. To put it mildly, any "difficult" correspondent who bucked SHAEF's media policies—and in effect, bucked the media giants/SHAEF staff officers who had formulated those policies—was liable to find post-war employment opportunities scarce. The classic example of this was Edward Kennedy's (AP) intentional leak of the signing of the German surrender—before the German High Command could inform its units. Today Kennedy is portrayed as a victim of unreasonable military censorship, but at the time he was reviled by his peers in the correspondent corps and was openly attacked in print by his fellow press in the ETO. When learning the facts, the AP apologized to Eisenhower and later fired Kennedy.[8]

There was, of course, an inevitable degree of press chaffing under military rules, and from time to time—as we'll see later in this work—it erupted into near mutiny. But generally, the complaints were relatively minor, so much so that one latter-day commentator was reduced to mentioning the correspondents' unhappiness about having to wear uniforms in London (a requirement that was soon lifted) in the same breath as their unhappiness about censorship rules.[9] The military also became easy scapegoats for correspondents who needed an excuse for not being in on the invasion. Future Pulitzer Prize winner and correspondent Hal Boyle (AP) blamed his failure to be in on the invasion on the "fatheads" in the Army Public Relations office, who somehow committed the colossal blunder of leaving nine of the assault correspondents behind in the UK.[10] No surviving document indicates Boyle was ever one of the 28 assault correspondents, or that nine of them were mistakenly left in the UK. Nevertheless, he spent the next couple of days after the invasion in London putting forth another explanation for his safe billet: the Army, he claimed, was afraid of the bad publicity if a reporter of his fame were killed in action.[11]

There were also serious and legitimate sources of friction between the military and the press. No reporter of a free nation likes (or should like for that matter) being subjected to censorship, no matter how reasonable the intent or efficient the system. Further, since the press relied on the military for everything from life support to transmission of copy, many correspondents blamed the military for any failures in these arenas, whether real or imagined, excusable or inexcusable. The fact that these correspondents and their corporations could not possibly have provided that support for themselves in no way lessened the criticisms of some reporters.

Nevertheless, despite bumps in the road—and occasional large potholes—the military/press relationship was generally exceptionally good by current standards. There was no moral equivalency to the conflict, and despite the friction, all were clearly on the same team when it came to the need for victory. CBS news chief Paul White told his staff shortly before D-Day, "Remember, winning the war is a hell of a lot more important than reporting it."[12] Yes, things were that much different back then.

Eisenhower himself embraced the press to the extent that he considered them quasi-staff officers of his command. Accredited correspondents were not members of the military but were under the control of the commander of the force they accompanied. As the Regulations for War Correspondents Accompanying Allied Expeditionary Force in the Field (1944) stated, "War Correspondents, while holding licenses, have the status of officers and are subject to military or air force law, and are subject to direction by Naval authority …" In fact, if captured by the enemy, under the Geneva Convention they were afforded status equivalent to an Army captain. And, of course, they were required to wear appropriate military uniforms.

Truth or Consequences

When press relations had been introduced as a military staff function in WWI, it had resided under the intelligence staff sections, specifically under the psychological warfare department. This was recognition that while a free press is vital to a democracy, its products are accessible to the enemy as well. That information can either help or hurt the enemy just as it could help or hurt your own side. While psychological operations and press relations were broken out into a separate staff department in SHAEF's early days, and then further broken into two separate special staff sections by 13 April 1944, the concern over the threat posed by careless press reporting never lessened. As GEN Eisenhower himself put it to the SHAEF's accredited correspondents:

> With regard to publicity, the first essential in military operations is that no information of value should be given to the enemy. The first essential in newspaper work and broadcasting is wide-open publicity. It is your job and mine to try to reconcile these sometimes diverse considerations.[13]

In the case of Normandy, the press could deal a strategic blow from which the Allies might not easily recover. The German strategy for 1944 was to maintain a defensive posture against the Russians on the Eastern Front, while devoting maximum effort to defeating the looming Allied invasion of Western Europe.[14] If the invasion could be defeated, it was felt, the Allies could not launch another one for two years, by which time Britain would have exhausted its manpower reserves. The hope—the assumption—was that once the invasion was defeated, a negotiated peace with the western Allies might be possible, and the Reich could then focus all its might against the Russians. All this depended on the ability to smash the invasion, and that meant making the maximum number of German divisions available in the west in 1944.

To make German defensive efforts more difficult, the Allies developed a vast deception plan to aid the Normandy landings, one that encompassed demonstrations, feints, and misdirection from the Arctic Circle to the mid-East. Each deception plan was intended to draw off enemy divisions from the intended landing area and reduce the rate and weight of reinforcements. The intent of the most important of these deceptions—FORTITUDE SOUTH—was designed to convince the Germans that the landings in Normandy were not the main invasion, rather merely a preliminary, subsidiary operation that was to be followed by much larger landings in the Pas de Calais, commanded by Lieutenant General Patton.[15] The prospect of this second landing would pin down the 22 German infantry and armored divisions north of the River Seine, as well as armored divisions in the strategic reserve. With luck, this would keep them from responding to and crushing the Normandy landings before the Allies could land enough forces to secure the beachheads.

We now naturally view the 6 June 1944 landings as *the* invasion, but there was no indication that this was the case at the time. The Allies counted on keeping the FORTITUDE SOUTH deception working for weeks after D-Day. Maintaining the threat to Pas de Calais became a major subject of documents from Churchill, Eisenhower, the London War Cabinet and various SHAEF staff sections.[16] Every memo concerning press guidance and censorship rules forbade speculation whether Normandy was the main landing or whether there would be subsequent landings. There was to be no hint from the press or the various allied governments or militaries as to what might, or might not, be coming, unless it was a planned leak as part of the deception effort—and deliberate leaks were employed. Looming over it all would be Patton's vast phantom army pointing at the Pas de Calais.

But how could you sustain a deception so bold yet so fragile when every citizen was eagerly awaiting news of the impending invasion? How could you restrain a press corps that was just as eager to provide that news? The press was not aware of the deception plan; it was far too closely guarded for that. And yet to permit the press to fully report the scope of the landings was tantamount to destroying the carefully crafted deception plan, and informing the Germans that they were free to move those divisions from the Pas de Calais. Which would result in far more Allied lives lost, if not a disastrous defeat.

Part of the solution was to let the press trumpet the invasion, but limit the scope of press reports so that, to a German intelligence analyst, the open-source evidence would seem to point to Normandy being a large but limited affair—the diversionary operation the Allies had been grooming the Germans to expect. SHAEF forbade discussion of the allied order of battle in press reports, and released information on individual units only long after it was known the Germans had discovered those units for themselves. The Germans were to be misled by the (relatively) scanty factual media information and encouraged to 'see through' the actual operation and hold firm to their delusions regarding the Pas de Calais.

So, the media needed to be reined in to protect the deception effort, yet reined in in such a subtle manner that they were not aware of it. Quite simply, the press had to be unknowingly conscripted into the deception effort.

This deception effort was so sensitive that even key allies were left in the dark. De Gaulle was flown from hid headquarters in Africa to Britain only at the last minute to be informed of the Normandy landings. Even then he was kept partly in the dark; the details he was given pointed to Normandy being only preliminary landings. Allied discretion proved wise. By 4 June, the German intelligence services had full knowledge of the information de Gaulle had been given, thanks to a colonel on his staff who reported to the Nazis. Thankfully, the report had been "filed away and forgotten among the dross of 250 other, less accurate intelligence reports that the Germans received" just prior to the invasion.[17]

Sense and Censorship

All press reports were presumptively considered secret material until passed through a censor's review.[18] That would pose problems for correspondents in the first hours, and even days, after initial landings.

The mere act of stepping ashore in the initial stages of the invasion was as much a change in legal status as it was a physical movement. Simply put, once you stepped ashore, you stayed ashore. The only people to be taken off the beach were either survivors of sunken craft or casualties. Despite the "Greatest Generation" reputation, the military was overwhelmingly a conscript organization whose core was hastily mobilized, imperfectly trained and lacked solid discipline. Stragglers were a significant concern, especially those who naturally wanted to straggle off the beach and out of danger, so "straggler collection lines"—boundaries to the rear of which individuals were not allowed to pass without specific authority—were initially established at the waterline.[19] Both Army and Navy orders strictly limited who could be taken off the beach by watercraft. The primary vehicles for medical evacuation from the beach were supposed to be the Army's amphibious 2½ ton trucks (DUKWs), not Navy landing craft.[20] Policing the straggler problem would primarily be an Army concern, as the Navy wasn't intended to be significantly involved in carrying people off the beach. These commonsense straggler-control measures would pose a serious obstacle for correspondents ashore who wanted to carry their products back themselves.

Print and recording correspondents had to pass their products through censors in the beachhead (assuming the censors arrived early)[21] and then send their reports back via courier or by radio (assuming these were available early). This would be a bottleneck. The courier chain depended on the Army message center system, which could not operate effectively in the first few days after the landings. And the military radios could be expected to be too busy with operational traffic to spare much time for media traffic. In the first few days following the initial landings, this process would be slow and uncertain—but that was exactly the period in which the press demanded the most time-sensitive handling of copy.

For photographers, the problem was worse. While text or voice copy could be sent electronically, exposed film had to be hand-carried in classified pouches (it too was presumed to be secret material) back to the UK for developing and review by the censors.[22] So once a photographer stepped ashore—and was forced to remain there—his film was relegated to the military message center system for couriering all the way back to the UK, an even more time-consuming and uncertain process. It was so time-consuming that it would almost guarantee the photographer's pictures would miss the news cycle. And that would defeat the entire point of the still photo pool.

There were a few efforts to improve the odds. Beginning D-Day, a dispatch boat service was scheduled to run several times a day to pick up exposed film (and print copy) from the command ships and run it back to the UK.[23] It was a great idea, but still left a photographer on the beach with the problem of how to get his film quickly and reliably back to a command ship. Several photographers and reporters sought out a less conventional solution: they brought in carrier pigeons which would fly their products directly back to their bureaus in London for developing and censoring.

Despite the good intentions and detailed plans, experienced correspondents understood the friction of war and the immutable nature of Murphy's Laws. Pyle warned his editor that censorship would initially be tight, so his columns would probably arrive badly hacked up. He also warned that he probably couldn't get his copy out during the first few days.[24] This was the voice of an experienced correspondent.

As far as the still photo pool went, the smart play was to simply avoid the problem of getting film off the beach, and this could only be done by not stepping ashore. This would limit how much of the battle the pool could photograph, but it was better to get shots only of troops landing and get them back immediately, than it was to get more comprehensive coverage inland, but too late to meet the deadline. And this, as we'll see, is exactly what Bert Brandt (the other still photo pool man for Omaha Beach) did. He documented the ride in to the beach, the troops debarking, and then rode back to his transport without stepping out of his landing craft.

Helpers and Minders

All the preceding problems with media coverage of invasions had been encountered before in the course of amphibious landings in the Mediterranean. To overcome these problems and facilitate support of the press in general, SHAEF created a specialized unit: the 72nd Publicity Service Battalion.[25] While the battalion had psychological warfare and propaganda subunits, it also operated the Press Camp and was responsible for the care and feeding of the correspondents accredited to First US Army. Its duties included not just housing the reporters, but providing transportation, drivers and even facilitating transmission of copy to the rear. For this purpose, it would also oversee the operation of specialized military and civilian press transmitters.

None of this, of course, would be available in the first days of an invasion. To address this shortcoming, SHAEF allotted two small teams to support the press ashore on D-Day.[26] Each team consisted of two lieutenants, a driver, and a jeep with trailer, and carried a jeep-mounted low-power voice radio, a Morse code set and a wire recording machine (the precursor to the tape recorder). More powerful radios were not available on such short notice, but it was hoped the low-power sets could reach the UK. One team was tasked to support the press landing on Omaha Beach, the other Utah Beach.

On reaching the marshalling area in England, one of these teams immediately proved its value. It found that VII Corps planners had made no provisions for reporters to accompany any of the units going ashore, and none of the lower-level commanders was willing to disrupt the landing tables to accept last-minute additions of reporters. This press support team was able to get the corps commander's ear, and correspondents were slotted into the landings at the last moment. While good news for the reporters, it has posed a problem for historians. Due to this last-minute adjustment, we have no records that detail when and with whom some of the correspondents at Utah landed. As a result, we have almost no information on the actual landing and activities of the third D-Day still photo pool member, *Life*'s Bob Landry.

Unfortunately, almost none of the provisions intended to help the press file its reports worked out as planned on D-Day. As we'll see, the only reporters to succeed in quickly filing their copy were the ones who trusted in their own devices.

Starting Blocks

All the endless waiting, compulsive pre-invasion partying and obsessive planning finally came to an end in the last days of May 1944 when the "assault" correspondents were notified to report to the SHAEF Public Relations Office. The specific date is uncertain. Capa did not note the date. Kershaw put it on 28 May, while Whelan said 29 May and another source claimed 30 May. While Pyle and others were merely summoned by phone and traveled to the meeting place on their own, this apparently was not the case for Capa. A lieutenant from the Public Relations Office personally went to Capa's apartment to deliver the notification and help carry his baggage.[27] One can be excused for wondering whether this lone instance of personal notification, valet service and escort was intended to ensure Capa's reporting in as ordered, especially given his recent successful efforts to absent himself from parachute training. It is equally likely that Capa invented this personal escort to make himself seem more important.

John McVane (NBC Radio) provided a good description of mobilization of these correspondents and the secrecy that surrounded their work until they finally boarded their attack transports.[28] From the Public Relations Office, the assault correspondents were taken to the Press Training Center in Bristol where they were issued their invasion gear, including everything from clothing impregnated against gas attack, to battle harness, rations and a myriad of other items they would wear or carry in. Correspondents had been allotted 125 pounds for personal baggage,[29] and film shot by Jack Lieb (*News of the Day*) at the press camp showed they arrived with a bewildering array of suitcases, duffle bags, civilian sleeping bags and various boxes and cases. The handling of this baggage depended on the correspondent's mission. Correspondents scheduled to land with the assault regiments, such as John Thompson, could bring in only what was strapped to their bodies. Their excess baggage would be shipped over with the other cargo that made up the press camp, and the correspondents could reclaim it once the press camp had been established in Normandy. Those correspondents landing later in the flow manhandled much of their baggage ashore, as Lieb's movies showed. Although Bert Brandt was assigned to the D-Day still photo pool, he didn't actually land until several days after D-Day, and photos of him as he came ashore show the clumsy assortment of baggage he brought with him. At 125 pounds, the baggage allocation was generous enough to make life a bit easier. It allowed Ernie Pyle to include 11 bottles of booze. Given this, it is impossible to credit later claims that it was this weight limit that accounted for Capa running out of film on the beach on D-Day.

Although correspondents who were due to step ashore early on D-Day would initially take along only the gear that they carried in or on their assault vests, this could still be quite a load. McVane carried in a small typewriter but left the wire recording set behind on his attack transport; at 50 pounds he judged it too heavy to lug ashore.[30] Though not great compared to the loads carried by some of the assault infantry, loads such as these were quite heavy enough for civilian correspondents who had been enjoying the soft life of London for several months.

Capa's load was apparently one of the lightest. The photographic evidence we have of Capa on D-Day (as examined in detail later) seems to indicate he wore virtually none of the normal combat kit, and that he carried with him just a leather camera bag, large enough to carry only part of his camera gear, slung over a shoulder. Where

Capa left the rest of his camera gear, as well as the rest of his baggage, is a question we'll examine later in this analysis as it bears directly on his intentions that day.

At this point in the Bristol Press Training Center, most correspondents still had little idea of their place in the invasion. As a result of a personal invitation, Pyle knew he'd be with the First US Army headquarters, and the correspondents who had completed jump training knew they were headed to airborne divisions. Beyond that, information was sketchy.

It cleared up a day later when they boarded jeeps, this time to be dispersed to various unit marshalling areas. The first hint that Whitehead, Thompson, MacVane, O'Reilly, Brandt and Capa had as to their destination was when their jeeps rolled into the headquarters of the 1st Division, located in Blandford. It was something of a reunion as Capa, Whitehead, Thompson and MacVane had covered the 1st Division in its earlier fighting. LTC Redding (the officer in the Public Relations Office who made the assignments) clearly wanted to leverage their earlier working relationships to make up for the fact that the correspondents would only join their units a few days before the invasion. MacVane and Whitehead would cover the division headquarters. The remaining four would cover subordinate units of the division—Capa and Thompson for the 16th RCT, Brandt for the 116th RCT and O'Reilly for the division's artillery command.

O'Reilly was whisked off to link up with the division's artillery at another location. MacVane stated Capa and Brandt were then sent off to take photos of troops embarking at Weymouth, about 30 miles south of the division headquarters and, according to MacVane, to join their units. This raises an odd point. If Capa and Brandt were leaving to join their units, then why didn't Thompson go with them? He was assigned to the exact same unit as Capa. Yet MacVane was clear that Thompson remained at Blandford until 3 June.

Based on the embarkation schedule, Capa and Brandt's trip to Weymouth to photograph the embarkation must have been on 1 June. Images of the back of at least six of Capa's embarkation photos show they were cleared by censors on 6 June 1944, which proves that Capa was able to send an initial packet of these photos back to London. The captions on the back of these photos are nearly identical to the comments he scrawled on one of his pages of caption notes titled "Embarcation" [sic]. That page indicates the packet would have included two rolls of film from his Rolleiflex camera and one from one of his Contax cameras.

MacVane was also taken Weymouth to interview embarking troops and senior officers, though he seems to imply this was a separate trip, perhaps on a separate day. He sent his recordings to London for censoring. As with Capa's embarkation film, MacVane's recordings joined the pre-invasion media products that SHAEF was amassing for release once the official announcement of the invasion was made. After finishing his recordings, MacVane rejoined Whitehead and Thompson at Blandford until they embarked on 3 June.

After documenting the embarkation at Weymouth, Brandt apparently joined the 116th RCT, with whom he would cross the Channel, as MacVane didn't mention him again. Capa, too, dropped out of MacVane's narrative, never to reappear again. In fact, MacVane's attitude toward Capa seemed rather cool and limited to the least possible comment. Although Capa, MacVane, Whitehead and Thomson would all cross the Channel aboard the attack transport USS *Samuel Chase* (APA-26) and were apparently berthed together in the sick bay, MacVane omitted all mention of Capa during the passage and the landings. And in his wartime memoir, MacVane did not use a single Capa photo to illustrate his narrative, even though Capa captured many of the very scenes MacVane recounted. The embarkation photos he used were from another photographer covering the very same embarkation as did Capa.

On the other hand, Capa's disappearance from MacVane's account may be partly due to an early embarkation by the photographer, though even this isn't clear. The unit Capa was attached to boarded the *Chase* the afternoon of 1 June. Capa shot photos of the troops assembled on the quayside, loading onto landing craft, riding out into the harbor to the attack transport and embarking on the *Chase*. Two of his embarkation photos placed him at the top of the *Chase*'s accommodation ladder on the main deck as he took pictures of troops boarding.[31] From this we know he did set foot aboard the *Chase* that day, and it is possible he remained there. Kershaw, however, places his embarkation on 4 June, and Whelan is less precise, merely stating that Capa had several days of briefings at the 1st Division headquarters before boarding.

So, we simply don't know when he boarded. Capa was a man who enjoyed his pleasures, and it seems unlikely he chose to remain cooped up on a crowded ship for two days longer than necessary. Especially since the other three correspondents had a one-last-night-on-the-town party planned in the company of the division's public affairs officer. That wasn't something Capa would miss if he could help it. But our best evidence, MacVane's book, seems to indicate he did just that, by boarding on 1 June.

MacVane, Whitehead and Thompson remained at the division headquarters in Blandford until embarkation. About the only thing they knew for certain was who they would be covering. They had absolutely no idea where the landings would take place and weren't even entirely sure if it was the real invasion or just another rehearsal. It was the very fact that they hadn't been let in on any of the secrets of the invasion that made it possible for them to leave the estate for their party in the village.

On Sunday, 3 June 1944, the three correspondents left the 1st Division headquarters and were driven to Weymouth where they boarded their ships. Only then did they begin to learn the specifics of their missions, with the final formal briefing taking place at sea the night before the landings. That was when they learned Normandy would be the target, and the first they heard of Omaha Beach.

The pattern of these assignments will bear on our later discussions, so a summary of the correspondents on Omaha Beach is in order.[32] In most cases, correspondents would land in the entourage of a senior leader, a colonel or general officer. Whitehead and MacVane would land with Brigadier General Wyman, assistant division commander, in the division's advanced command post. Thompson would land with Colonel Taylor whose 16th RCT led the assault on eastern Omaha Beach. As noted above, these three, with Capa, were all aboard the same attack transport, the *Chase*. O'Reilly, aboard another transport, would land with Brigadier General Andrus, the First Division's artillery commander. Brandt's position has been variously noted as being with the 26th RCT or with the First Army Headquarters. In fact, he crossed (and returned) on the USS *Thomas Carroll* (APA-28), which had as its primary load a forward command element of the 29th Division, the rear command echelon of the 116th RCT (who led the assault on western Omaha Beach) and the 3rd Battalion of the 116th RCT.* As we'll see, this ship and its embarked troops had the same roles and similar landing times within the 116th RCT's plan as the *Chase* did within the 16th RCT's plan. Brandt's assignment, then, was parallel to Capa's, the only difference being they were in adjacent regiments.

A follow-on set of Omaha Beach reporters would arrive later on D-Day in the company of the two public relations lieutenants who were tasked with supporting and looking after the correspondents. These included Tommy Grandin (Blue Network) and Harold Austin (*Sydney Morning Herald*). They had no specific assignment within the division and were scheduled to land a few hours after H-Hour. In the event they were very much delayed.

As noted earlier, Charles Wertenbaker (recently appointed head of *Life*'s European Bureau) and Pyle were attached to Bradley's headquarters. They would remain off Omaha Beach for a few days until the headquarters and command post were established ashore.

So, where was Capa slotted? That, after all, is the question that lies at the heart of the Capa legend. It is a subject we'll consider in detail a bit further along.

---

* Although the 29th Division was slotted to land as part of Force O, elements of this division, to include its 116th RCT, were attached to the 1st Division and landed beginning at H-Hour on D-Day.

CHAPTER THREE

The Channel Crossing

"The best lies about me are the ones I told."

PATRICK ROTHFUSS

Which Ship?

One might think that a short sail across the English Channel would be a simple, straightforward event, but nothing involving Capa ever was.

Capa was *apparently* slotted to land with the 16th Regimental Combat Team (RCT), a combat formation built around the 16th Infantry Regiment. The regiment was a Regular unit consisting mostly of veterans of the fighting in North Africa and Sicily and had been tapped to be one of the two assault regiments for the landing on Omaha Beach. By the time numerous supporting units had been attached to the regiment, its strength had swollen to more than 4,500 men.

Most of the 16th RCT embarked on their transports at Weymouth Harbor, Dorset, England. The naval transportation included three large attack transports, several Landing Craft, Infantry (LCI), dozens of Landing Craft, Tank (LCT) and scores of smaller craft.[1] (See Appendix A for details of the assault craft discussed in this paper.) Capa claimed to have embarked on the USS *Samuel Chase*, one of the three attack transports. And so he did.

Unfortunately, there is a belief in some quarters that Capa embarked on the USS *Henrico*, the second of the 16th RCT's three attack transports. As we'll see later, the identity of Capa's ship will play a large factor in our investigation, so the point bears clarification now.

Some of Capa's pre-invasion photos show Landing Craft, Vehicular, Personnel (LCVPs) from the *Henrico* plying through the water (Figure 2 is one of those). The letters "PA-45" stencilled on the side at the bow indicate the craft belonged to APA-45, that being the hull number of the *Henrico*. From the perspective of these photos, it is clear Capa is an occupant of one of the craft. A caption that is often linked to this photo is vague enough to lead some to believe this is a photo of the actual run in to the beach on D-Day. If that were the case, then it would indicate Capa had crossed the Channel on the *Henrico*.

Figure 2. This Capa pre-invasion photo shows troops of the 16th RCT being ferried out to the USS *Samuel Chase* in landing craft provided by the USS *Henrico*. Taken between 1–3 June 1944 in Weymouth Bay, Capa was riding in a sister landing craft also heading to the USS *Chase*. (Robert Capa © ICP/Magnum Photos)

In fact, it is a photo of troops being ferried from the Weymouth quay out to where the attack transports were anchored in the roadstead, which was how the embarkation for those ships was conducted.

The fact that Capa took a ride in Weymouth Harbor aboard an LCVP from the *Henrico* does not indicate he boarded, crossed the Channel on that ship or landed on D-Day with its troops. The *Chase*'s after-action report included a section critiquing the embarkation process.[2] It noted that the embarkation orders called for 35 LCVPs to ferry the troops from the pier to the *Chase*. Because the *Chase* did not have 35 LCVPs, another ship had to be tasked to provide the extra craft. Obviously, this fell to the *Henrico*. Capa's own photos support this. One of his shots was taken from the stern of an LCVP, with PA-45 (the *Henrico*'s hull number) barely visible at the bottom of the frame, painted on the engine

Figure 3. Capa's photo showing his LCVP from the USS *Henrico* (APA-45) bringing troops to the USS *Chase* (APA-26). (Robert Capa © ICP/Magnum Photos)

Figure 4. One of two pictures Capa took of Sam Fuller. One documentary erroneously paired this photo with a caption note describing the ship underway and entering the English Channel. The ship is actually anchored at Weymouth. The squiggly lines are the censor's instructions to obscure harbor details. (Robert Capa © ICP/Magnum Photos)

hatch cover (Figure 3). That *Henrico* LCVP—with Capa aboard—is pictured in line behind another LCVP, waiting to offload its troops at the port side accommodation ladder of a ship whose hull number is clearly visible. The hull number is PA-26, the USS *Chase*.

Capa's presence in Weymouth Harbor aboard an LCVP from the *Henrico* does not indicate the *Henrico* figured in Capa's D-Day saga. *Henrico* landing craft were used to help ferry troops to the *Chase* during embarkation. It's as simple as that.

Unfortunately, the confusion over the *Henrico* was furthered by a combination of bad editing and a flawed memoir. Figure 4 is one of two Capa photos showing embarked troops sunning on the upper deck of a transport in Weymouth Harbor. A television documentary erroneously linked to this photo a set of caption notes which indicate the ship, and therefore Capa, was already underway for the French coast.*

---

* This photo was part of a roll (Contax 3) whose caption notes included topics of troops playing craps, examining invasion currency and sunning on the upper deck.

Figure 4 and its mate would fade to obscurity were it not for the man who was the subject of both shots. He was Corporal Sam Fuller, a writer before the war, who would go on to become a Hollywood director and producer. He notably wrote and directed the 1980 film *The Big Red One*, which followed the 1st Division through WWII and included a section on the Omaha Beach assault. Fuller and Capa had met previously, dating back to the Sicily operation. Five decades later Sam Fuller would claim that he crossed the Channel aboard the *Henrico* with the rest of the 2nd Battalion Landing Team (2nd BLT, a subunit of the 16th RCT), to which he said he was assigned.[3] The elements were thereby complete for misunderstanding. Between the incorrect pairing of that photo with the caption notes that stated the ship was already sailing, and Fuller saying he was on the *Henrico*, a legend was born that Capa, too, necessarily crossed the Channel on the *Henrico*.

Fuller is a troublesome character as far as this analysis is concerned due to the inaccuracies in his own autobiography. This requires an unavoidable digression. Fuller claimed that following Pearl Harbor, he volunteered for service, asking only that his induction be delayed a short time to permit him to finish a book. In fact, he was drafted (as opposed to volunteering) and didn't enter active service until 7 September 1942, nine months after Pearl Harbor.[4] Initially assigned to the 26th Infantry Regiment, his reputation as an author soon brought him to the attention of that regiment's new commander, COL Taylor. When COL Taylor was later transferred to command the 16th Infantry Regiment, he wanted to take Fuller with him for the purpose of chronicling the 16th's combat operations. In Fuller's telling of the story, however, he turned down such a soft billet, wanting instead to be in the thick of the fighting. The fact remains, however, he did transfer with COL Taylor and he was one of the authors of the 16th Infantry Regiment's WWII history.[5] While Fuller portrayed himself as an infantryman in the front ranks, CPT Karl Wolf, commanding the regiment's Company I, recorded that Fuller, as the regiment's public relations NCO, came down to observe one of their operations. There was no position formally authorized for a public relations NCO at regimental level, but Army policy directed units down to battalion level detail a member of their staff to perform those duties. And indeed, records show that Fuller was assigned to the regimental Service Company on D-Day—not to a rifle company (the Service Company included the regimental staff).[6] So, Fuller's autobiography, like many published almost six decades after the war, is rife with exaggerations or errors, and cannot be automatically accepted as fact any more than can Capa's.[7]

The important point for our immediate purpose is that on 6 June 1944, Fuller was in fact assigned to the regimental Service Company, not the 2nd BLT as he claimed. This fact is substantiated by the orders awarding him a belated Silver Star medal for his actions on D-Day; those orders stated he was a member of Service Company on that date.[8] And according to the regimental landing tables, the Service Company had *no one* embarked on the *Henrico*.[9] Fuller even provided evidence to undermine his own credibility; in his book he tells an anecdote of COL Taylor, the regimental commander, calling them together around a terrain model *after the ship sailed* for the invasion. The terrain model had first been set up in the marshalling camp for the regiment's mission briefings; it had then been packed up, moved and set up in the gym (an empty forward hold) aboard the *Chase*.[10] We have multiple, unquestioned sources verifying that Taylor embarked on the *Chase*, and that it was there on the *Chase* that Taylor held his gathering around the terrain model after the ship had sailed. If Fuller were present for COL Taylor's briefing during the crossing, then he had to have been on the *Chase*.

Clinching the issue falls to the memoirs of the regimental surgeon, of whom more will be heard later. On D-Day the surgeon came in on a Landing Craft, Mechanized (LCM) in Wave 13. While he was in the LCM, waiting for the rest of the troops to climb down the nets, he noted that "I tried looking at the densely packed men standing ahead of me and found myself fascinated by the olive drab color of Cpl. Sam Fuller's face. Poor Sam, looked as I felt."[11]

The surgeon crossed on the *Chase*. And the *Chase did* have members of the Service Company aboard. Fuller, therefore, was obviously on the *Chase*, too.

Perhaps Fuller placed himself on the *Henrico* in his memoirs to exaggerate his place in the invasion. Troops from the *Henrico* were in the earliest waves of the invasion, whereas the *Chase*'s troops did not come in until Wave 10 and later. So, claiming instead to be on the *Henrico* and landing with the 2nd BLT among the leading infantry waves would sound much more heroic back in Hollywood than admitting he was the much less warlike publicity flack for the regimental headquarters. Or perhaps 50-plus years had had dimmed his memory. Regardless, this apparent bit of exaggeration had the secondary effect of spawning the mistaken belief that Capa, too, crossed on the *Henrico*.

The plain fact is that Capa sailed on the *Chase*, just as he claimed. He took several photos of officers studying the regiment's terrain model in the *Chase*'s gym, one of which included COL Taylor. Other photos show Coast Guard coxswains being briefed on models of the approach lanes and photos of the coastline. Further, an artillery officer and a *New York Times* correspondent who were aboard the *Chase* recalled playing poker with Capa the night of the crossing.[12] And finally, Capa himself related an encounter he had with COL Taylor during the crossing.[13] There can be no doubt Capa arrived off the coast of Normandy aboard the *Chase*.

The invasion was originally scheduled for 5 June 1944, but was postponed for 24 hours due to bad weather. The slower elements of the invasion fleet had already set sail by the time the weather delay was decided late on 4 June and had to be recalled to the embarkation ports. To sustain the *Henrico* error, some sources claim that after the *Chase* returned to port from its aborted 4 June departure, Capa transferred to the *Henrico*. In this scenario, Capa would have been present for the briefings at the *Chase*'s terrain model during the false start and still have been present on the *Henrico* for the landings.

It is an argument based on error. The 16th RCT's attack transports, being substantially faster than the smaller landing craft, were slotted to sail much later in the departure schedule. As a result, the order for the weather delay came *before* the attack transports departed port. This is confirmed by the *Chase*'s war diaries; it remained at anchor for all of 4 June.[14] The one—and only—briefing conducted by COL Taylor at the terrain model took place the evening of 5 June after the *Chase*'s *sole sortie*. Again, Capa crossed on the *Chase*.

Whelan, however, clung stubbornly to the idea that Capa transferred to the *Henrico* at some unidentified point. Capa never mentioned doing so; and in fact, explicitly stated he crossed on the *Chase*. Whelan attempted to dismiss this fact by explaining that Capa would resort to "a bit of embroidery to make a good story even better." While true, in this case it was Whelan who resorted to a bit of embroidery, discarding one of the few facts Capa got right. Whelan cited Fuller's false claim about being on board the *Henrico* to bolster the idea that Capa transferred to that ship, but we've debunked that claim. There is no proof at all that Capa was aboard the *Henrico*, and as we'll see throughout this work, ample proof that he landed from the *Chase*. Whelan's invention of the transfer to the *Henrico* was an attempt to fabricate a scenario that would support the First Wave myth—a myth as false as the reputation it sought to support.

The Dilemma That Wasn't

In *Slightly out of Focus*, Capa told of a quandary he supposedly faced during the Channel crossing aboard the *Chase*: he needed to decide his place in the landing. He was torn between landing with Co. B, 1st Battalion Landing Team (BLT) of the 16th RCT, and landing with Co. E, 2nd BLT of the same regiment.[15] On the one hand, he mused, Co. B's objective looked more interesting—and safer (it would land at H+80, or 80 minutes after the 0630 H-Hour). On the other hand, Co. E's objective, though more dangerous (landing at H+01, or one minute after H-Hour), gave him an opportunity to work with a unit he had come to know in North Africa and Sicily, and with whom he had captured his best story. While pondering this choice, COL Taylor, the 16th RCT's commander, came by and supposedly offered Capa a third alternative: to land in a later wave with the regimental command group at H+95 / 0805 hours. It appeared to be a very safe alternative. After much soul searching, however, Capa declared he was a gambler, and decided to land in the "first wave" with Co. E. Company E was one of four specially organized and specially trained assault companies that the 16th RCT had slotted in Wave 3, coming in one minute after H-Hour. Though slotted in Wave 3, these companies would be the very first infantry to hit the beach in the regiment's sector (the first two waves consisted of tanks). For the unwary reader, Capa's voluntary decision to place himself in that dangerous First Wave was admirable, even heroic.

It was also pure bunkum. As we'll see in a later chapter, he had no choice in his landing slot, and did not land in the heroic circumstances he would later claim.

Sailing Orders

On 5 June, after months of planning, preparing, training and one false start, orders were issued for the invasion fleets to head to Normandy. According to its War Diary, the *Chase* began heaving on its anchor chain at 1721 hours and six minutes later was underway as part of the fast transport convoy.

Despite the near chaos caused by so many convoys steaming at various speeds in the same few clear lanes through the minefields, the *Chase's* deck log was deceptively routine, noting such minor items as the names of six sailors who had completed extra duty punishments. And in a sense, it *was* almost routine, notwithstanding the historic events that were about to unfold. There had been no submarine scares, no encounters with German E-boat raiders and no enemy air attacks. The fast transport convoy hadn't even run into a stray mine.

Capa had spent the passage in typical Capa fashion. After taking photos of COL Taylor and some of his officers studying the terrain model, he found a poker game to fill the hours. He also had his flask in which to seek comfort and courage, though he did not mention availing himself of it. Except for the anticipation and worry that occupied everyone's minds, it was as peaceful a transit as you could wish for. It was a peace, however, that saw many men unable to sleep.

Capa had taken pictures of the embarkation process (one roll of 35mm and two of 120 film) and once aboard the *Chase*, had taken photos of the *Chase's* coxswains being briefed (one roll of 120 film). These he had sent to London to be part of the prepared press release material that would be distributed once the invasion was officially announced. The 6 June 1944 censor's stamps on the back of these photos prove he did not take these rolls with him to Normandy. After dispatching that packet of film, there was more to document. He exposed three rolls of 35mm film, one roll focusing on each of these scenes: troops idling on the upper deck of the *Chase* while it was at anchor in Weymouth; photos as the *Chase* sailed out of Weymouth Bay; and photos of Army leaders being briefed around the terrain model. These he stowed with the rest of his baggage rather than risk losing them during the landing operation.[*]

At 0315 hours, the *Chase* let go the starboard anchor, one of 28 large ships positioned in the Transport Area, some 23,000 yards off Omaha Beach.[16] The timing was close. In just an hour, the *Henrico*, carrying the first waves of troops, would

---

[*] These rolls didn't reach the censors until 7 June based on the censor's stamp, indicating he didn't dispatch them until after his return to the UK that day.

begin lowering landing craft. The *Chase* would do the same, about an hour later. The die was cast, a metaphor that Capa, the gambler, would find appropriate, if he wasn't too distracted to think about it.

CHAPTER FOUR

D-Day: The Plan

"In preparing for battle I have always found that plans are useless, but planning is indispensable."

GENERAL DWIGHT D. EISENHOWER

"This operation is not being planned with any alternatives. This operation is planned as a victory, and that's the way it's going to be. We're going down there, and we're throwing everything we have into it, and we're going to make it a success."

GENERAL DWIGHT D EISENHOWER

Before further examining Robert Capa's D-Day saga, it is necessary to summarize the landing as it was *planned* to unfold. In a later chapter we'll examine how it transpired. The distinction between the two is important in understanding this bit of history, for the plan did not, as the military says, "survive contact with the enemy." Even today, much of the popular history of this battle presumes key elements went off without a hitch, when in fact they did not. Such bad assumptions sabotage well-intentioned analysis by later generations. In our case, we look no farther than Capa's landing for illustration. He claimed—and it has long been accepted as fact—that he landed in the first wave with Co. E, 16th RCT on beach sector Easy Red. After all, that *was* the plan for Co. E. But in fact, except for one landing craft—which Capa definitely was *not* on—Co. E's assault sections landed as much as 2,000 yards east of their intended target, and stepped ashore on Fox Green, instead. Therefore, if he landed with Co. E, he could not have landed on Easy Red. Conversely, if he landed on Easy Red, he could not have landed with Co. E. In an operation that saw so much go wrong, every "fact" must be validated before being used as a basis for analysis.

The Lay of the Land

Capa's tale is inextricably coupled with the saga of beach sector Easy Red. The reader may not understand the significance of this stretch of beach, but it may well have been the site of the decisive action on Omaha Beach. Dog Green's carnage may be better known, due in no small part to the movie *Saving Private Ryan*. And the eastern section of Dog White is known as the site of the 5th Ranger Battalion's penetration of the German defenses (where the famous motto "Rangers, lead the way!" originated). But Easy Red was perhaps the critical point. It was here that a combination of light German defenses and obscuring smoke first enabled a few units to cross the beach largely intact and scale the bluffs. It was here engineers were able to blow the equivalent of four complete gaps through the beach obstacles, two-thirds of the total gaps initially cleared on all of Omaha Beach. The combination of light enemy fire, a practical route to the top of the bluffs, and so many cleared lanes made it the most useful site for the rapid landing of follow-on forces. Initial units landing at Easy Red were instrumental in paving the way for opening the first, vital beach exit at the E-1 draw. Easy Red was the wedge that cracked the German defenses and served as the gateway to victory. As a testament to the importance of the area, the point above Easy Red where the German defenses were first penetrated was chosen as the site of that hallowed ground, the American Military Cemetery in Normandy.

As Easy Red is the scene of our investigation, let's look a bit closer. Easy Red was 1,850 yards long (just over a mile) and it, with the adjacent 1,135-yard-long Fox Green (to the east) were the target beach sectors for the 16th RCT. The critical terrain features on these beaches were the exits at the E-1 draw (slightly to the west of the center of Easy Red) and the E-3 draw (on the west half of Fox Green). Rapid opening of these exits was critical to getting heavy equipment and weapons off the beach and expanding the initial lodgment. Easy Red was the responsibility of the 2nd BLT, which would attack with rifle Co. E and Co. F in the assault waves, followed later by rifle Co. G and the battalion's heavy weapons of Co. H.

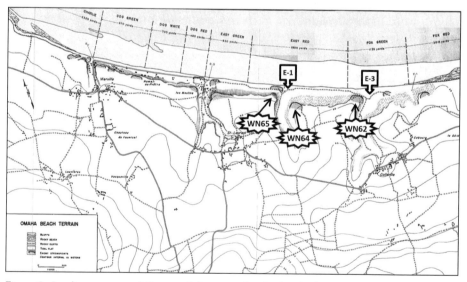

Figure 5. Landing sectors and German defenses on Omaha Beach. (US Army, *Omaha Beachhead, 6 June–13 June 1944*, with author's annotation)

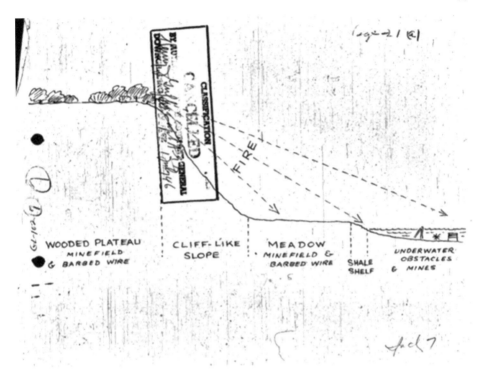

Figure 6. A sketch showing the terrain profile and principal features of the beaches in the 16th RCT sector. (From the 16th RCT's S-3 Combat Report, McCormick Research Center)

Three strongpoints were of interest to arrivals on Easy Red. On the western half of Easy Red lay the E-1 draw that led up to fields between villages of St. Laurent and Colleville-sur-Mer. Unlike the D-1, D-3 and E-3 draws, the E-1 draw did not have a village at the head of the draw, so road access up the draw was underdeveloped. This draw was near the boundary between the planned landing sectors of Co. E and Co. F of the 2nd BLT. The draw was guarded on the west by strongpoint WN65[*] and on the east by WN64. To the east of Easy Red, inside the boundary of the Fox Green beach sector, lay the E-3 draw whose exit led up to the village of Colleville-sur-Mer. Although it lay outside Easy Red's boundary, the western side of this draw was defended by WN62, which could bring fire from heavier-caliber weapons to bear on the eastern half of Easy Red. It was generally too distant for truly effective small-arms fire, but could still seriously harass landings on the nearer parts of Easy Red.

Approaching the beach, the first terrain feature encountered would be the tidal flats. Omaha Beach saw almost a 20-foot range from low to high tide. As a result, the tidal flats at Easy Red extended about 300–400 yards seaward at low tide but would be completely inundated at high tide. These flats were the location of the belts of beach obstacles which were intended to wreck landing craft. On Omaha Beach, the obstacles included

---

[*] In German, *Widerstandnestern*; literally 'resistance nests' in English. Commonly abbreviated to 'WN'.

450 log ramps and 2,000 poles/stakes (most topped by mines), 1,050 steel hedgehogs and 200 "Belgian gates" for a total of about 3,700 obstacles.[1] Except for these obstacles, the tidal flats provided neither cover nor concealment for assaulting troops.

With low tide on 6 June at about 0530 hours, and H-Hour at 0630 hours, the initial assault waves would have a distance equivalent to two to three football fields of open tidal flats to cross under enemy fire before reaching cover. This does not count the additional distance through the surf that the heavily burdened troops would have to wade from the ramps of their landing craft to the waterline, which could be as much as another 50 yards.

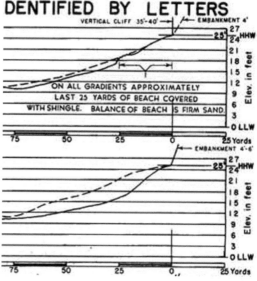

Figure 7. Four of eight beach profiles from Omaha Beach showing the shingle section and the embankment behind it. (From the Omaha Beach invasion map prepared by Commander, Task Force 122, 21 April 1944, PhotosNormadie)

Approaching the high tide mark, the last 25 yards or so steepened and was covered with small stones, called shingle or shale in contemporary documents (see Figure 7). Topping it was an even steeper embankment of sand dune. The portion of shingle that was normally covered by water at high tide was discolored, and usually showed up as a darker layer in photos. The sand layer (and parts of the shingle that were not discolored) appeared as a light layer above the discolored shingle. The height of the shingle and sand embankment varied along the beach. In the area where Capa landed (as we will determine later), the shingle was about 7 feet high, and the sand embankment was another 6–7 feet. Although this feature consisted of two distinct parts, most accounts simply referred to it as either the shingle or the embankment, while the Terrain Profile sketch included in the 16th RCT's S-3 Combat Report (Figure 6) refers to it as the Shale Shelf.

The shingle/sand embankment was a key feature. With a rise of 13–14 feet, it provided the first solid cover from direct fire as the troops waded ashore. That apparent safety could prove deceptive. By stopping to take cover at the embankment, troops prolonged their time in the prepared shoreline kill zone of the German defenses. The tendency to halt there was reinforced by a major barbed-wire obstacle the Germans constructed above the embankment. It was 10 yards thick and consisted of two parallel double-apron barbed-wire obstacles with concertina wire coils piled between them. Breaching this obstacle would take time, specialized equipment and organization—items that were all at a premium during the confused first minutes of an amphibious assault. All this was designed to keep troops stationary in a very

Shingle/Sand Layer

Discolored Shingle Layer

Figure 8. A view of the shingle/sand embankment on Easy Red. The lower, darker horizontal band is the result of ocean's discoloration of the shingle. The top, lighter band consists of shingle topped by a sand bank. (LT John W. Boucher, USNR)

confined area where they could be engaged by the primary defensive killing weapon: indirect fire. Worse, the stones themselves became secondary fragmentation when artillery or mortar rounds exploded, multiplying the casualty-producing effects.

The shingle/sand embankment also served as an obstacle to movement by tracked and wheeled vehicles. Between the slope and the loose surface covering, both types of vehicles could get bogged down. In addition, the stones tended to work in between the tanks' road wheels and tracks, causing the tracks to break or come off the road wheels, which was very difficult to repair under fire. As a result, the shingle/sand embankment would serve to trap vehicles on the beach flats until engineers could bulldoze a path through it.

The shingle/sand embankment no longer exists on Omaha Beach. It was removed by engineers following D-Day to facilitate unloading of ships and movement of supplies inland.[2] Visitors today will get no appreciation of the tactical significance of this embankment.

Just inland of the shingle/sand embankment was a small, unimproved beach road that ran the length of Easy Red. Beyond the road was an area commonly termed the beach flats (the "Meadow" in Figure 6), a relatively level area of sand and low dunes, 100–200 yards deep. It was heavily mined, had numerous belts of wire obstacles, and in some places was swampy. In some areas of Omaha, the flats also contained significant enemy defenses, such as trenches and antitank ditches, but these were mostly limited to the vicinity of the strongpoints that defended the beach exits. A notable feature of the Easy Red beach flats was the ruined house and outbuildings which lay immediately beyond the beach road in the eastern half of the sector. These were called the Roman Ruins in some reports. They are just visible in the right half of Figure 8, above the top dashed white line.

Beyond the beach flats were the bluffs (the "Cliff-Like Slope" in Figure 6), which were about 130 feet high along Easy Red, and whose slopes extended about 200 yards to the top. The slopes had patches of trees but were mostly open. They were not steep enough to prevent movement by infantry, but when combined with the liberal use of mines and wire obstacles, slowed progress significantly. The addition of effective enemy fire could halt movement altogether. At the top of the bluffs, enemy defenses were generally light, at least between the strongpoints.

Beyond the bluffs the land stretched out into small fields and farms bordered by thick hedges, with scattered small villages. The terrain was generally flat, except where cut by watercourses or where relatively small hills dominated the fields (the "Wooded Plateau" in Figure 6).

For the assault, two factors drove the selection of H-Hour: daylight and the tides.[3] The ground, sea and air forces each had optimal conditions for their part of the operation, and the selection of H-Hour had to make tradeoffs between these often-conflicting needs. Eventually planners chose H-Hour to be 0630 hours for Omaha (an hour after low tide). As with all compromises, there were advantages and disadvantages. On the positive side, at that point the initial landing craft would beach seaward of the obstacle belts on clear sand, and not have to gingerly pick their way through them. Also, with the beach obstacles exposed, it would be easier for engineers to destroy them. And landing on a rising tide meant that it would be easier for landing craft to retract off the beach after unloading. The obvious disadvantage, though, was that the initial waves would have a long distance to cover, under fire, across the exposed beach flats—a problem which hopefully would be mitigated by air and naval preparatory bombardments, both of which required visibility and argued for scheduling H-Hour after daylight.

Wave Action

The landing plan was a carefully orchestrated sequence of arriving units organized in waves, each with a specific task to accomplish to enable the following waves to accomplish their tasks in turn.[4] The timing of each wave was critical as that dictated how long a unit would have to accomplish its mission, and whether that task would be completed in time to facilitate the arrival of the next wave of troops.

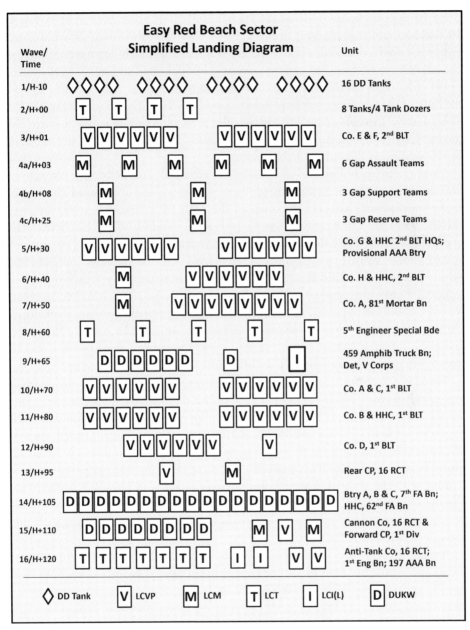

Figure 9. A simplified landing diagram showing the beaching sequence for the 16th RCT's Easy Red beach sector. A similar flow of units was scheduled for Fox Green. (Author)

The first elements ashore in the 16th RCT sector were supposed to be 32 Duplex-Drive (DD) tanks (Wave 1), which would be discharged from LCTs about 6,000 yards out to sea, and swim to the beach.[5] One company of DD tanks (16 tanks) would land on Easy Red, and the other company on Fox Green, both reaching shore 10 minutes before H-hour (H-10 minutes).[6] Ten minutes later, at H-Hour, 16 standard tanks would land from LCT's directly onto the beach (Wave 2) with eight tank dozers attached.[7] This company was slated to touch down straddling the boundary between Easy Red and Fox Green. Although the Landing Diagram annex to the order depicted these tanks evenly divided between Easy Red and Fox Green, the bulk of the company was targeted for Easy Red, as six tank dozers were needed to land there to support the six gap assault teams targeting that beach sector. In theory, Easy Red should have had 16 DD tanks, 12 standard tanks and six tank dozers landing at the outset of the invasion.

These tanks (excluding the tank dozers) were tasked with delivering "drenching fire" on enemy defenses, which hopefully would knock out or suppress enemy fire as the four infantry assault companies of the 16th RCT landed one minute later (H+01, Wave 3).[8] On Easy Red, Co. E, 16th RCT, would land on the western half of the sector, and Co. F would land on the eastern half. Simultaneously, Companies I and M (of the 3rd BLT) would land to assault Fox Green. Each assault company was subdivided into six assault boat sections, and each boat section was task-organized to initially work independently, proceeding to attack a specified objective. The boat sections would not regroup to operate as a company until after seizing their initial objectives. In theory, they would attack German defenses under cover of the tanks, and these infantry assaults would in turn cover the men of the Engineer Special Task Force as they landed and set about clearing the beach obstacles.

These engineers included 16 combined Army–Navy demolition units—termed gap assault teams (GATs)—and their supporting elements.[9] The gap assault teams would arrive in Wave 4a (H+03 minutes), followed by two supporting waves of engineers landing at H+08 and H+25. Across the length of Omaha Beach, each of the initial 16 gap assault teams was to blow a 50-yard-wide gap through the beach obstacles while they were still exposed by the rising tide. The eight gap assault teams landing with the 16th RCT were tasked to clear six gaps on Easy Red, and two on Fox Green. The eight tank dozers that landed three minutes earlier with Co. A's standard tanks at H-hour were tasked to support the gap assault teams, with one tank dozer allotted to each team.

At H+30, the second set of infantry waves would land, consisting of the support companies of the two lead BLTs. On Easy Red, this would include Co. G (Wave 5, H+30) and Co. H (Wave 6, H+40) as well as the 2nd BLT headquarters and a provisional antiaircraft battery hand-carrying .50 caliber machine guns. From this point on, waves would arrive every five to 10 minutes. The third set of infantry landings would start arriving at H+70 when the RCT's support battalion—the 1st BLT—began to arrive. Because much of the historical focus of the fighting at Omaha was on the infantry elements, the landing of this support BLT is sometimes referred to as the second or even third wave. It was the third *group* of infantry landings, but strictly speaking, formed the 10th, 11th and 12th waves. The following waves would continue to land, bringing in the rest of the 16th Infantry Regiment, as well as a vast array of vital attachments (artillery, more engineers, antiaircraft, mortar, medical, etc.), ending about 2 hours and 40 minutes after H-Hour. The next significant infantry landings were scheduled to begin at H+195 minutes (0945 hours), when the 1st Division's 18th RCT would begin to land on Easy Red.

At least that was the plan. Now, where did Robert Capa fit into this?

CHAPTER FIVE

Capa and the "First Wave with Company E" Myth

"The camera cannot lie, but it can be an accessory to untruth."

HAROLD EVANS

False Pretenses

When we left Capa, he was aboard the *Chase*, having just decided to land in the first wave with Co. E.[1] It was a bold decision. Co. E was one of the assault companies that was broken into independently operating boat sections. Though actually in the third wave, its troops would be the first infantry ashore. This would have been an incredibly unusual choice for the man. Capa had missed the Dieppe Raid, missed the North Africa landings, had come in 10 days after the Sicily invasion and had missed the Salerno landings. Although he later claimed he asked to get in on the show at Anzio,[2] the truth is the Army had assigned him to that landing without his knowledge and he was scared to death at the prospect.[3] Fortunately for him, he came ashore at least four hours after H-Hour at Anzio, and the landings were initially a cakewalk.* So the idea of Capa choosing to be at the very point of the spear as it struck Hitler's dreaded Atlantic Wall was an incredibly brave decision, and very much out of character for the man.

At least it would have seemed so if Capa actually made that decision.

The problem is that the major infantry elements of the 16th RCT shipped over on three transports: the USS *Chase*, the USS *Henrico,* and the British *Empire Anvil.*[4] The *Chase* had the 1st BLT embarked, which was the Regiment's *support* battalion, *not* one of its assault battalions. The regiment's assault battalions were embarked on the *Henrico* (the 2nd BLT) and the *Empire Anvil* (the 3rd BLT). And there's the rub.

If Capa were going to go in with Co. E, he would have to have shipped over on the *Henrico* because Co. E was part of the 2nd BLT (Companies E, F, G and H).

---

* "Cakewalk" insofar as the assault landing was concerned. The landing achieved tactical and strategic surprise and initially was barely contested. German opposition strengthened considerably in the following days.

Surprisingly few people have stopped to wonder how he could possibly have landed with Co. E when he was on the wrong ship. Whelan suggested Capa transferred from the *Chase* to the *Henrico* while still at anchor in Weymouth,[5] but we've proven that he crossed the Channel on the *Chase*. There's no indication he transferred to the *Henrico* early D-Day morning, or that his boat from the *Chase* stopped at the *Henrico* to pick up troops for the run in to the beach. Though generally unrecognized, the "First Wave with Co. E" myth required Capa's magical teleportation to another ship.

It is small wonder that in *Slightly out of Focus* Capa skipped over this point;* he simply boarded a landing craft from the *Chase* and the reader, having been led to *assume* the craft would magically be filled with men of Co. E (despite a small issue with time and space), then naturally proceeded with that assumption. Readers who paid attention, however, note that after making his Co. E declaration, Capa's narrative never once mentions them again. Never. After using them to construct a false façade of bravery, they were quickly discarded by the narrative.

The simple fact is that coming over on the *Chase*, Capa could not have landed in "the first wave" with troops from the *Henrico*, an entirely different ship. The infantry's assault boat sections were scheduled to land at H+01 / 0631 hours. These included 12 from the *Henrico* (six of which carried Co. E) and 12 from the *Empire Anvil*. The *Chase*, however, did not see its first craft land until H+70 / 0740 hours—more than an hour after H-Hour—and in Wave 10.

Despite this fact, Capa persisted in the fiction that he landed in the first wave. He even tried to maintain this fiction in the face of his own narratives, both of which directly undercut his claim. When originally describing his trip to the beach (to Wertenbaker on D+3), Capa said, "We waited for the first wave to go in and then I saw the first landing boats coming back and the black coxswain of one boat is holding his thumb in the air and it looked like a pushover."[6] Capa used much the same language in his 1947 *Slightly out of Focus*, stating, "The first empty barge, which had already unloaded its troops on the beach passed us on the way back ..."[†]

If he really had landed with Co. E in Wave 3, the only landing craft returning from the beach that he would have encountered were the much larger Landing Craft, Tanks (LCTs), which carried in the tanks of Waves 1 and 2. But these craft had a quartermaster who was tucked away in an armored wheelhouse, not a coxswain visible to passing craft. Nor could Capa's comments refer to the LCMs that brought in the gap assault teams (GATs) of Wave 4, some of which happened to land before the first wave of infantry. Capa's description of the encounter rules this out as LCMs had an armored box to protect the coxswain, so, again, the coxswain would not have been visible.

---

* As did Whelan in his earlier biography of Capa.
† Because he collapsed at least an hour's timeline into the following two sentences, he led the reader to assume he landed far earlier than facts would prove.

As a result, the "first landing boats" Capa witnessed returning from the beach can only refer to the smallest infantry landing craft: LCVPs. But the first wave of LCVPs carried in the initial assault companies scheduled to land at H+01 / 0631 hours in Wave 3, which included Co. E's. And Capa's narrative here makes it clear he didn't go in with them. In other words, he had to have landed sometime after Co. E. But how much later?

We have yet another data point that disproves the "First Wave with Co. E" fabrication. The six LCVPs loaded with the troops of Co. E were lowered to the sea at 0415 hours.[7] But ... in his Wertenbaker interview, Capa said, "just before 6 o'clock we were lowered in our LCVP and started for the beach."[*] Capa's own words place him about an hour and 45 minutes later in the landing sequence than Co. E's six assault sections. In *Slightly out of Focus,* as Capa embraced and amplified the "First Wave with Co. E" fabrication, he not surprisingly omitted the inconvenient fact of his actual embarkation time.

Let's look a bit further into this. According to Navy and Army plans, the LCVPs carrying Co. E were scheduled to be lowered into the sea more than two hours before their wave's beaching time and were scheduled to leave the Transport Area (where the transports anchored) 122 minutes prior to their beaching time.[8] Yet ... in *Slightly out of Focus* Capa stated he was lowered into the water barely more than 30 minutes before Co. E's landing time. Clearly something is wrong with Capa's claims. To put that in context, the distance between the shore and the Transport Area was 23,000 yards, or a little over 13 miles.[9] With a theoretical top speed of 14 miles an hour (12 knots) Capa's fully loaded LCVP could not physically have covered the 13 miles to the beach in the roughly 35 minutes between being lowered to the water just before 0600 hours and Co. E's landing time of H+01 / 0631 hours, even if we were to ignore the time required for assembly of waves, marshalling, departure line coordination, etc.. To make matters worse, the highest specified speed for LCVPs during the assault was just 6 knots.[10] So, we find that Capa's First Wave assertion would require us to accept a second physical impossibility.

We've only examined the second stage of his journey and already something is very wrong with the Capa legend. No matter what that legend says, he did not land in the first wave, and he did not land with Co. E.

Dispersion

We find further proof of this simply by returning to the actual landing of Co. E's boat sections.[11] As alluded to earlier, five of the company's six boat sections landed

---

[*] For the first waves, LVCPs were lowered by their davits to the level of the ship's rails, and troops would embark into the craft there—so-called "rail loading." When craft were already in the water, troops climbed down to them using cargo nets—a procedure known as "net loading."

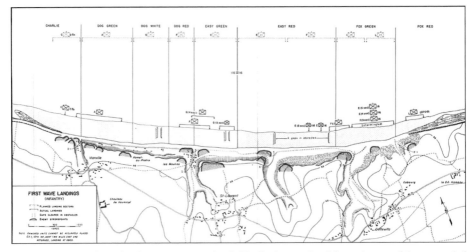

Figure 10. First infantry landings. Most units landed badly dispersed and far to the east of their intended sites. (US Army, *Omaha Beachhead, 6 June–13 June 1944*)

2,000 yards too far to the east, hitting Fox Green instead (Figure 10). The sixth boat section was "only" 1,000 yards off target, landing on the east half of Easy Red. In fact, it was virtually the sole boat section of the 16th RCT's assault teams to land on Easy Red. As for the remote possibility that Capa came in with this boat section, this was the section led by Lieutenant Spalding. This was probably the first section atop the bluffs that day and played a crucial role in opening the E-1 exit.[*] Spalding's landing experience in no way resembled Capa's stories or his photos.[†] Further, it is inconceivable that Capa came in with that storied boat section, and never mentioned it.[‡] Likewise, LT Spalding's detailed narrative of that day's events notably fails to mention the world-famous Capa being in his boat. It's abundantly clear Capa did not come in with the assault troops of Co. E on Easy Red. Most of Co E. didn't even land on Easy Red. Here Capa relied on the *planned* landing scheme to claim credit for a "first wave" landing on Easy Red, when the actual events show he could not have possibly done so—at least not with the assault waves.

---

[*] Both he and his assistant section leader, Technical Sergeant Streczyk, were awarded the Distinguished Service Cross for their actions that day.

[†] His Debarkation Set of photos—to be examined later—clearly shows the men of several waves ahead of him on the beach, which would not be the case if he were in the first wave.

[‡] Fuller, who also inaccurately claimed to have landed in the first wave, said he was on the beach when "TSGT Streczyck" [*sic*] of Spalding's platoon blew the first path through a wire barrier and opened up the E-1 exit. The wire was actually blown by SGT Olson, and it merely opened a footpath up the bluffs. That event occurred at least 90 minutes before Fuller landed with COL Taylor's party. The battle for the E-1 exit took place later and a few hundred yards away. Fuller seems to have inserted himself into several events that took place before he landed.

Putting the Lie to One's Own Lie

While these points are conclusive, the True Believers of the Capa legend may not be convinced. So let us turn to the evidence of Capa's own photos to discredit his "First Wave with Co. E" claim. The key point is the state of the tides, a consideration we will revisit several times in this analysis. The Navy published an invasion map of the Omaha Beach sector which addressed, among many other factors, the state of the tides during the invasion window.[12] The map went so far as to include beach profiles at a dozen or more locations on Omaha Beach. If we take the beach profile for Capa's landing site (which will be explained in a later section) and pair that with the state of the tide on the day of the invasion and when Co. E and the first infantry wave landed at H+01 (1 minute after H-Hour), we find the *waterline* was 225–250 yards from the shingle/sand embankment. Indeed, the water line was still more than 100 yards seaward of the *outer* obstacle belt.

The initial photos Capa took when he landed—taken while he was still on the ramp of his landing craft—show a much different scene. The tide had already progressed all the way through the obstacle belt and the waterline was far, far closer than the 250 yards it would have been at 0630 hours. Clearly, he landed long after H-Hour. Capa's claim to have come in on the first wave is indisputably false, revealed as such by his own photos.

His landing photos also provide the final nail in the "First Wave with Co. E" myth's coffin. Instead of landing with the First Wave, those photos show a large number of troops ahead of him, both in the water and clustered in the shelter of the shingle embankment.

While Capa's two versions of his exploits that day form the basis of his legend, the tellings and retellings by others have created different versions. Fuller later recounted details of Capa's landing, but not from firsthand observation. They met again years

Figure 11. A detail from Capa's Negative 32 showing the waterline within a short distance from the discolored bottom layer of the shingle. Clearly, he did not land at 0631 hours when the waterline was 250 yards from the shingle/embankment. (Robert Capa © ICP/Magnum Photos)

later in Hollywood, and, over drinks, swapped stories of the landing. Fuller's version of those stories was rife with factual errors and cast doubt on the more colorful aspects. Another example comes from Stephen Ambrose. In his book *D-Day, June 6, 1944: The Climactic Battle of WWII*, Ambrose unaccountably stated that Capa landed with Co. E in the "second wave", as opposed to the first wave.[13] And as we've already seen, Robert Wise's screenplay somehow placed Capa farther ahead on the beach than the first wave had reached, locating him between the leading American soldiers and German defenders as they slugged it out!

Despite the muddled sequence of events that Capa related, there is one important point in the foregoing that bears repeating. Because Capa was on the *Chase*, and because none of the *Chase*'s troops or craft landed until 0740 hours—as verified by the 16th RCT's combat reports—we have established a critical threshold.

We can say for a fact that Capa could not have reached any part of Omaha Beach before 0740 hours, at the very earliest.

CHAPTER SIX

A Second Look at the First Wave

"A picture is worth a thousand words. But dollars would be better."

ANON.

Additional Suspects

Just exactly who originated the "First Wave" myth? Suspicion would seem to immediately fall on Capa, but as the introduction indicated, that isn't necessarily the correct answer.

In conducting research, the most easily accessible sources tend to be books, followed by original government records. As a result, historical analysis mostly focuses on data obtained from those sources. Which is precisely the pattern this analysis has followed up to this point. We've focused on Capa's book, Wertenbaker's book, Whelan's book, Kershaw's book, Ambrose's book and many, many military records.

Let's break that pattern and see what we can learn from a periodical.

Capa's photos were featured in a seven-page spread in *Life*'s 19 June 1944 issue.[1] The spread opened with a half-page picture from Capa's negative 32, followed by a half page of text which broadly described the landing and set the context for the rest of the photos. The last paragraph, while introducing Capa's photos, had this to say:

> "The picture above and those on the next six pages were taken by LIFE photographer Robert Capa <u>who went in with the first wave of troops</u>." (Emphasis added.)

Nor was this an isolated comment. The magazine's caption for Capa's negative 29 had this to say:

> "The <u>first wave</u> of U.S. assault troops race through boiling surf to the beach." (Emphasis added.)

The caption accompanying Capa's negative 34 read in part:

> "<u>These men waited for second wave boats</u>, then followed the tanks up the beach." (Emphasis added.)

And the caption for negative 35 (looking *backwards* at troops behind Capa):

> "Men in the <u>second wave</u> also take cover until all their boats have come in." (Emphasis added.)

In case anyone might possibly miss the point, *Life really* wanted to make sure the reader believed Capa was in the first wave. By now it should be obvious that *Life* was heavily invested in the idea that their pictures came from the very point of the spearhead.

Now let's return to that issue's date—19 June (which actually hit the newsstands on 12 June)—and ask ourselves, how did the stateside editors at *Life* know that Capa had gone in on the first wave (or intended to)?

As discussed in an earlier chapter, the assault correspondents had no idea who they were assigned to until they reached the marshalling areas and had no idea of their exact slots in the landing tables until after boarding their transports. By the time they learned these facts, they were cut off from all communications with their bureaus—or anyone else on the outside. If we accept Capa's account in *Slightly out of Focus*, the case is even more certain; in this version, he hadn't decided which wave he would go in with until the evening before the invasion,[2] by which time the ship was at sea (on radio silence) and he could not relay that information to any of his bosses.

The next opportunity Capa had to contact his superiors was during his brief return to Weymouth the morning after D-Day. According to John Morris's account (his photo editor in London), Capa merely dropped a brief note into a pouch with his film. The content of that note has varied significantly as Morris told different versions,[3] but there are two points common to all versions: 1) it said something to the effect that the "action" was in the rolls of 35mm film, and 2) it contained nothing about his actual place in the assault. He provided no summary of his landing experiences, nor did he provide pages of caption notes to accompany the landing film (though the pouch did contain his pages of caption notes for the film he exposed during the Channel crossing). He then hopped on the next available boat back to France apparently without any other communication—at least neither Morris nor Capa said there had been. Morris did claim that at about 1800 hours (or 1830 hours, depending on the version Morris told) on 7 June, his office received a telephone call alerting him that the film was on the way to London, but Morris never claimed he talked to Capa at that time, that he took the call himself, that the call came from Capa himself, or that he received any more details during that call.[4]

In short, if Capa ever did intend to land with the first wave, he could not—and did not—communicate that decision with anyone in the *Life* hierarchy.

Is it possible that Morris was unofficially told of Capa's scheduled landing position by someone in the SHAEF Public Relations Division? Perhaps. Inside information does tend to be passed on. But this possibility quickly falls apart as far as the First

Wave myth goes. Even if the staff officer had perfect knowledge of the 1st Division's plans—which he certainly would not have access to—the most he would have known was that Capa was scheduled somewhere after Wave 10.* That could not have been the source of the First Wave myth.

So how is it that *Life*'s stateside staff published a seven-page spread claiming Capa came in with the first wave? Capa was not peddling the "First Wave" myth at that point. His D+3 (9 June) interview with Wertenbaker made no such claim. Quite the contrary, Capa frankly gave an embarkation time that would have put him ashore at best 95 minutes after H-Hour (and in the event, that wave actually landed almost two hours after H-Hour due to delays). This is a solid indication that he wouldn't have tried to mislead Morris two days earlier when he dropped his film in the pouch. Why set up the "First Wave" lie on D+1, then give an interview on D+3 destroying that fiction? It makes no sense.

So, if Capa did not originate the "First Wave" myth, then who did? Was it Capa's London editor Morris? Or someone stateside? It turns out we can narrow this down. Bernard Lebrun discovered an original radiotelephoto of Capa's negative 35 which was transmitted 8 June 1944.[5] Taped to the front of this photo is the original caption Acme Photo Agency (the company handling the pool photographs) provided with the photo. Remember, Acme's caption was created without input from Capa, who provided no caption notes for his beach photos.

The difference between Acme's original caption and the one *Life* ran in the following issue is instructive:

> Acme: W;894-6/8-(WP)-Working through beach obstacles men are seen struggling through water up to their necks on French coast. Machine gun fire took its toll here.
> Life: Troops crouch behind shallow-water obstacles (below) installed by Germans. Tanks out of camera field to the right move up to silence German fire. These men waited for second wave of boats, then followed the tanks up the beach. Two landing craft may be dimly seen at left. (Emphasis added.)

It is not surprising that *Life* had its own caption for this photo; most daily and periodical publications put their own twist on the bare-bones Acme captions.

What is notable, however, is *Life*'s inclusion of the "First Wave" theme. If these men are waiting for the second wave of boats, then these men—and the photographer—must have been in the first wave. Bernard Lebrun's photos were posted on Patrick Peccatte's website and Patrick included a survey of the captions used for this photo by several daily papers.[6] Though there were similarities, there were notable variations as well. The only publication, however, which made any mention of waves was, unsurprisingly, *Life*'s heavy-handed "First Wave" spread. The work of Lebrun and Peccatte makes it clear that the "First Wave" myth was confined to the realm of *Life*'s empire.

---

* The question of his exact landing wave will be addressed in detail in Chapter 10.

Spinning Disappointment

According to Morris, his team of *Life* photographers had landed six of the slots in the various still photo pools (air, naval and ground for British and American forces) but had produced virtually nothing for the effort on D-Day.[7] Frank Scherschel, riding with the US Army Air Forces got no photos due to overcast weather. Oddly enough, that was the same excuse Morris gave for David Scherman's failure to get useable pictures from the LST he was aboard off the coast of Normandy. No D-Day film was received from Robert Landry (scheduled to land at Utah beach) and its fate has been a mystery ever since. George Roger (who landed with the British) stepped ashore in "glorious anti-climax" and produced no usable images. Morris stated that Ralph Morse was assigned to ride on an LST outfitted to receive casualties, but he neglected to identify why Morse failed to produce any useable photos. By Morris's telling of events, all five of his *Life* staff photographers failed. There was only the lone contract photographer on whom to pin all hopes.

Of course, Morris's summary of their disappointing performance was disingenuously crafted to enhance his dramatic tale of waiting for Capa's pictures to return from D-Day. As we'll see, Scherman's film arrived in London in the same packet as Capa's, and five of his photos were in a six-photo, two-page spread in the very same 19 June 1944 issue as Capa's.[8] Scherschel reported that his aircraft dropped below the clouds to bomb, but there's no indication why his photos weren't used.

But Morris's theme is largely valid. The whole point of an amphibious landing is to put men ashore, and Morris's team had three photographers assigned to that task. And two (Roger and Landry) had for some season failed. Only Capa seems to have produced, and even then, only about 20 pictures (a number this analysis will revise in later chapters), of which only five were taken on the beach. The other 15 or so were shot while aboard various Navy landing craft and ships. And oddly—very oddly, in fact—his take for the day did not include a single photo of the trip from the attack transport or the run in to the beach.

The situation was even worse, for it seemed Coast Guard cameramen dogged Capa's steps and duplicated almost all his shots—or perhaps vice versa. A Coast Guard cameraman was aboard the *Chase* and captured pre-invasion shots like Capa's. Another Coast Guard cameraman rode a landing craft into Easy Read beach and captured a series of debarkation photos remarkably like Capa's—except the Coast Guardsman came in much earlier than Capa. When Capa boarded the LCI that took him from the beach, he discovered it had a Coast Guard motion picture cameraman aboard, and his film would turn out to be more dramatic than Capa's. Even back upon the *Chase*, a pesky Coast Guard cameraman took shots almost identical to Capa's, and it is uncertain which one snapped his photos first.

The sad fact was that *Life* had only five Capa D-Day photos that were truly unique: the five shots taken *while he was in the surf*. And even then, one could hardly miss the fact that every one of these five shots was pointing offshore. Not a single shot he took on the beach captured any fighting ashore, or even the advance of the troops around him as they moved to the embankment! Capa's production was disastrously poor, and it needed every bit of spin possible to make the best of what little there was.

One can only imagine the pressure *Life* must have felt to hype those few pictures. So, it comes as no surprise that the *Life* captions—along with the First Wave Myth—originated not in London, but in New York. According to Richard Whelan, the captions were written by Dennis Flanagan, an assistant associate editor in *Life*'s New York offices.[9] Flanagan recalled that "he relied on *The New York Times* for background information, and for specifics he interpreted what he saw in the photographs." He might even have had access to Wertenbaker's interview with Capa (the gist of it was included in the 19 June issue). It's extremely unlikely that Flanagan had any experience with amphibious warfare, and therefore had virtually no basis for his interpretations. Instead, it is probable that his interpretations were influenced by *Life*'s marketing culture. If they didn't get the *first* pictures back from the beach—which they didn't—then they had to have a sales hook to convince the public and/or corporate management that they had the *best* pictures. In the cutthroat business of weekly magazines, you had to have an edge. Even if you had to invent it.

You can imagine how Capa might then have become trapped between his own reputation and this fabrication and felt the need to sustain the corporate fable. And I sincerely doubt Capa found the effort distasteful. This is, after all, the same Capa who began his combat photography career by fabricating the context of his "Falling Soldier" photo. The "First Wave" myth fit perfectly with the mythos he had created through the years, and it only served to make him seem more intrepid. A disappointingly small haul of photos that, to be honest, were objectively less than spectacular, became elevated by the application of false context such that they cemented Capa's reputation. By the time he wrote *Slightly out of Focus* three years later, he clearly had embraced the "First Wave" myth as his own and invented a rich layer of additional details.

One final point. Note the way *Life* used the term "wave." As mentioned earlier, wave can have several interpretations, ranging from the military's term for a group of boats landing at the same time, to the generalized term referring to the vast number of men arriving in the first 24 hours. It's clear from *Life*'s captions that they were using the military's terminology, as they specifically referred to the landing craft that were close offshore as the next wave. As a result, we can give no credence to those who would excuse the "First Wave" fabrication based on it being a simple confusion over terminology.

CHAPTER SEVEN

D-Day: The Reality

"In every battle there comes a time when both sides consider themselves beaten; then he who continues the attack wins."

GENERAL ULYSSES S. GRANT

It is now necessary to see how the 16th RCT's landings proceeded in the first couple hours of the invasion. The events on Omaha Beach that day have been the subject of literally hundreds of books, and it is not the intent here to duplicate that extensive body of work. Nevertheless, at least a partial summary is necessary to understand the context of Capa's experiences.

Supporting Fires

Basically, the early hours of the invasion can be summed up as near disaster mitigated by a few strokes of good luck, doggedly determined soldiers and some solid leadership at just the right places.

The brief naval preparatory fires had little effect on the immediate beach defenses, though they did manage to keep German coastal artillery fire from threatening the naval vessels offshore.[1] They also ignited grass fires at several points on the beach, which had the dual effects of obscuring terrain features—which the landing craft needed for navigation to the correct beaches—while also obscuring troop landings from German observation and fire on some sections of the beach. Next, bombing by the Air Force struck too far inland and failed to impact the beach defenses, or blast craters on the beach that could be used for cover by landing troops. The planned saturation of the beach defenses by rocket-equipped LCTs was also ineffective. Finally, rough seas and an unexpectedly strong current plagued the landing craft and swept most of them far to the east of their planned landing sites. It was not a good start, and it quickly got worse.

Armor Landings

The story of the tank landings is hopelessly muddled, with no two sources agreeing. It began with Wave 1's 32 DD tanks which were allotted to the 16th RCT's sector.

They were due to land at H-10 minutes, but more than 80 percent were lost at sea because of the two tank company commanders deciding to launch their DD tanks in dangerously high seas. According to the 741st Tank Battalion's unit journal and after-action report, only two DD tanks managed to swim all the way to the beach; 27 of the remainder were swamped by rough seas.[2] The last three were landed directly on the beach by their LCT. All the five that made it ashore were from Co. B and they landed on their designated beach sector, Easy Red, though swept by the currents to the east end of that beach sector. Upon landing one was quickly disabled. The 16th RCT—which claimed six DD tanks made it to the beach—stated all six were landed directly on the beach by their LCTs, but "several were knocked out by enemy AT [antitank] and artillery fire after firing a few rounds," but this version is certainly not correct.

Each of the eight LCTs in Wave 2 (0831 hours / H+01 minutes) carried two standard tanks of Co. A, 741st Tank Battalion and one tank dozer. They came in with guns blazing. Elevated timber platforms had been built in these LCTs so that the front two tanks in each craft could fire over the ramp during the approach to the beach,[3] and extra ammunition was loaded aboard the LCTs so that this preparatory firing would not deplete the tanks' basic loads.[4] One tank, for example, fired approximately 50 rounds of 75mm during its run in to the beach.[5] These 16 standard tanks were supposed to be landed directly on the beach from their LCTs, astride the boundary between Easy Red and Fox Green. As six of the eight tank dozers were tasked to support the six gap assault teams for Easy Red, it follows that the 12 standard tanks also loaded on those LCTs were scheduled to land on Easy Red as well. Of the 16 tanks from Co. A, two tanks (and the accompanying tank dozer) were lost 20 miles offshore when their LCT sank after hitting a mine; the landing of two others (and their tank dozer) was delayed until after 0800 hours due to ramp problems; "some" of the remaining 12 unloaded in water too deep and were soon drowned out; and three were knocked out immediately after landing. The 741st reported the tanks that survived the first few minutes after landing—apparently no more than six—landed astride the boundary between Easy Red and Fox Green.*

As a result, fewer than a third of the planned DD and standard tanks were in action, most of which seem to have landed on the eastern part of Easy Red. These cumulative losses among the armor greatly reduced the suppressive fire the tank units were supposed to provide for the arriving infantry assault boat teams.

Records about the tank dozers are rather confused. The 741st Tank Battalion's reports recorded the landing of its own tank dozer platoon of four vehicles, although

---

* The confusion that day is illustrated by the fact that though the standard tanks of Co. A were reported by battalion to have landed "astride the boundaries of Easy Red and Fox Green," the statements of many of the surviving tank commanders indicate they thought they had mis-landed 1,000 yards west, near the E-1 draw; this may be explained by a battalion landing overlay that had the labels for the E-1 and E-3 draws switched.

other orders and the landing tables state there should have been six vehicles. Further, the 741st Tank Battalion's records made no reference at all to the actions or fate of the two attached tank dozers from the 610th Engineer Light Equipment Company. Being aboard the same LCTs as the tanks of Co. A, the tank dozers suffered parallel mishaps. Of eight planned tank dozers, one had a maintenance problem that delayed its Channel crossing until D+3 and one was lost with the two tanks 20 miles offshore when its LCT sank; the loss of these two tank dozers probably accounts for the discrepancy of two vehicles between the planned landing strength of six and the four vehicles of the tank dozer platoon that were reported to have actually landed. Of the remaining six, another tank dozer's landing was delayed until 0800 due to the faulty ramp. Another tank dozer was hit 100 yards offshore while still aboard its LCT and being inoperable, apparently was pulled off the LCT by another tank. A final tank dozer was quickly knocked out after landing. Of the three remaining tank dozers, one was a "toothless" tank that lacked its dozer blade. The specific landing sites for these tank dozers were not recorded in official reports, though we will be able to identify two of them later in our analysis.

Infantry Assault Companies

The assault boat teams of infantry (Wave 3) also had their problems. Companies E and F were scheduled to land on Easy Red. Upon landing, the troops typically were dropped in waist-deep water, or worse, and had to wade through 25–50 yards of surf with their heavy loads. They then had 250–300 yards or more of open tidal flats to cross under fire before reaching the shingle/sand embankment. But most did not land where scheduled. Company F's six craft were swept east several hundred yards by the current. They came in badly scattered, with one landing just on the Easy Red side of the boundary with Fox Green, and the remaining five scattered the length of Fox Green. Two landed directly under the guns of the WN62 strongpoint. As discussed earlier, Company E's boats fared worse. Five were swept 2,000 yards east, landing on the far side of Fox Green; scattered, suffering heavy losses and almost complete disorganization, they had no impact on the initial assault on Easy Red.

Only one boat section of Co. E (LT Spalding's) landed on Easy Red, and even this section landed 1,000 yards too far east, touching down on the eastern half of what should have been Co. F's target. It would prove to be a very fortunate mistake. Two additional boat sections landed on the east half of Easy Red, but both were lost elements of Co. E, 116th Regimental Combat Team,* which should have landed far to the west.

---

* The similarity between the numeric designations of the two assaulting regimental combat teams (the 16th and 116th) has been a point of confusion for some historians.

Of the 12 infantry boat sections, 16 DD tanks, 12 standard tanks and six tank dozers from the 16th RCT that should have landed on 1,850-yard Easy Red beach sector, only two boat sections (one of which was on the very boundary with Fox Green), five (or six) DD tanks and several standard tanks are believed to have actually landed there, and all were grouped on the eastern 500 yards of that sector. Mixed among this paltry force were added the two lost boat sections from the 116th RCT. While these were under relatively light enemy fire, they were out of touch with one another and did not operate in a coordinated fashion, at least not initially. The entire western half of Easy Red saw not a single infantry boat section land on it until about an hour after H-Hour, when a heavy weapons company from the neighboring assault regiment was mis-landed there.

On the 16th RCT's other beach, the story was equally bad. Companies I and L were supposed to have landed on Fox Green, but Co. I's landing craft got lost and didn't try to land until about 0800. Of its six landing craft, two swamped, three struck mines or were hit by artillery, and one was temporarily hung up on an obstacle. The company commander organized what men he could and proceeded to his objective. Company L's landing was 30 minutes late and it too landed out of sector, beaching on Fox Red, where no assault troops were supposed to land.[6] None of the assault infantry scheduled for Fox Green reached that beach within the first hour of the assault.

Gap Assault Teams

In theory, the gap assault teams of Wave 4a (scheduled for H+03 minutes) should have landed three minutes after the standard tanks and two minutes after the lead infantry. Because of the scattered and disorganized landings of the infantry assault boat sections, however, in many places the engineers of Wave 4a arrived ahead of the infantry, simultaneous with them, or in the worst cases, where no infantry of Wave 3 landed at all. As a result, most engineers could not benefit from the infantry's assault on the beach defenses.

But worse was to come. The success of the gap assault teams was closely dependent on the successful landing of the dozer tanks that came in on Wave 2. Each tank dozer had its supporting gap assault team number painted in large characters on its rear ventilation stack to aid the team in landing at the right spot when they arrived four minutes after the dozers. The tank dozer would then help clear the obstacles under the direction of the gap assault team commander.

But the mishaps that plagued the landing of Co. A's tanks hurt the gap assault teams, too. Six teams were scheduled for Easy Red and two for Fox Green; Team 9 was to be the farthest west, with the succeeding teams coming landing to the east in sequence.[7] Although the gap assault teams were supposed to clear lanes separated by 200–300 yards, most of Co. A's tanks, and their accompanying tank dozers, landed fairly concentrated near the boundary between Easy Red and Fox Green.

Even if the gap assault teams had landed at their planned locations, this meant most would neither have been covered by Co. A's tanks nor have had tank dozers on hand to support.

As with the infantry assault sections, most of the gap assault teams were also swept eastward.[8] Instead of six teams landing on Easy Red, only two did, and they ended up on the eastern half of that sector. Teams 11 through 16 landed on areas covered by effective enemy fire, lost heavily in men and equipment, and were hampered by infantry seeking cover among the obstacles they were trying to destroy; between them they managed to cut just one partial gap. Judging from the consistent eastward drift of the misdirected landings and the volume of fire they received, most or all of these landed on Fox Green under the guns of WN62 or WN61. Losses among these gap assault teams were so severe that most were rendered ineffective.

Due to the mishaps noted above, the gap assault teams received minimal support from the tank dozers. Pictorial evidence identifies only two of these tank dozers—#9 and #10—in action on D-Day, and both were on Easy Red. None of the tank dozers seem to have been in position to support the six gap assault teams that landed on Fox Green. Finally, the support wave of engineers (Wave 4b, H+08, including the reserve demolition teams) beached 20–60 minutes late, arriving out of sector on or near Fox Red and after the tide had covered much of the obstacle belts.

A Glimmer of Hope at the Roman Ruins

Amidst the mishaps, failures and chaos, there were bright spots. The lone boat section of Co. E (of the 16th RCT) that actually landed on Easy Red, beached in front of the ruined house (the "Roman Ruins") where German fire was initially light and ineffective. Behind the ruins, a small ravine in the bluffs offered a relatively covered route to the top. LT Spalding, the boat section's leader, got his men off the tidal flats, over the shingle and blew a gap through the wire on the beach flats. After being held up by a mined, swampy area and an enemy machine gun firing from the direction of the E-3 strongpoint (WN62), he got his men to the base of the bluffs and sent out a reconnaissance patrol. Spalding's section made it to the base of the bluffs losing just three men in the process.

In addition, most tanks that did make it to shore made significant, though generally unrecognized contributions. The standard tanks towed in trailers with extra ammunition, so they had plenty to fire. A disabled tank in front of the E-3 Exit fired 150 rounds of 75mm ammunition from its main gun at the strongpoints in front of it until the incoming tide flooded the turret and they had to "abandon ship."[9] One pair of tanks[10] fired 450 rounds of 75mm main gun ammunition plus "uncounted rounds of 30 caliber" machine-gun ammunition.* And in a crucial feat,

---

* The basic load for an M4 tank included almost 7,000 rounds of .30-caliber machine-gun ammunition.

the deadly 88mm antitank gun sited in WN61 (one of only two present on all of Omaha Beach) was knocked out by about 0710 hours by one of the surviving DD tanks.[11] Most tank commanders spoke of cooperation with the infantry commanders, who pointed out targets for them. Despite the chaos, a degree of ad hoc coordination and cooperation was effected.

Meanwhile, the relatively low volume of enemy fire on the eastern half of Easy Red permitted unexpected success for two gap assault teams. Both teams reached the shore relatively unscathed and were ready to go to work—an important indication of the *relative* lack of serious enemy fire in their landing areas. They are the only two teams in the 16th RCT sector known to have successfully beached at the same site as their supporting tank dozers. Instead of the planned landing site at the far western end of Easy Red, Team 9 landed a bit east of the middle of Easy Red where none of the Wave 3 infantry boat teams had arrived; nevertheless, it managed to clear its assigned 50-yard gap. It was aided by tank dozer #9, which is visible in an early D-Day photo taken in the center of this gap. (This photo will be examined later.)

Gap Assault Team 10 landed in the vicinity of the Roman Ruins on Easy Red, and in fact arrived early, just ahead of LT Spalding's boat section.[12] Team 10 landed right behind its tank dozer. "Clearing the infantry aside within twenty minutes of hitting the beach," it then managed not only to blow its assigned 50-yard gap, but also clear an additional double gap of 100 yards.[13] It received *no* enemy fire until *after* it set off its first demolitions shot, 20 minutes after landing.

Although fewer than the planned six lanes for Easy Red, these lanes were the only gaps cleared on the entire eastern half of Omaha Beach (where eight were planned)—and three were in the "sweet spot" on Easy Red in the vicinity of the Roman Ruins. Only the 100-yard double gap of Team 10 was initially deemed usable, however (presumably due to the loss of equipment to mark the cleared lanes).[14] The fact that four gaps were in just one half of one beach sector shows that a lot had "gone right" on this particular stretch of Easy Red, not the least of which was the unusually light—for Omaha Beach—enemy fire. On all the rest of Omaha Beach, only two other complete gaps had been blown. Further, it cannot be chalked up to coincidence that three of these four critical gaps just happened to be made on the very stretch of beach where Co. E's lone boat section had landed and was even then moving to the bluffs almost unopposed. While companies were receiving terrible punishment just a few hundred yards to the east on Fox Green, clearly parts of Easy Red were being spared. Mostly.

The 16th RCT's Follow-on Landings

As noted earlier, Cos. E and F of the 16th RCT were the assault companies of the 2nd BLT. The remaining two support companies of that battalion, G and H, were scheduled to land on Easy Red at 0700 and 0710 hours respectively. Co. G (Wave 5,

H+30) actually came in on target, at the same area LT Spalding's lone boat section from Co. E had landed. Enemy fire was greater at this time, and most of Co. G's casualties that day were lost due to mortars and small-arms fire while crossing the tidal flats to reach the shingle.[15] The 16th RCT S-3 Combat Report records that when Co. G landed, the shingle was 200 yards inland of the *waterline*, and we can assume they had to wade through 25–50 yards of surf to reach that waterline. It is a wonder Co. G lost as few men as it did and was able to reorganize at the embankment as quickly as it did. The company commander made contact with the rear of LT Spalding's section at the base of the bluffs, and the two coordinated their final attack on the crest. Co. G's movement from the shingle had begun by 0730, and it and LT Spalding's section were topping the bluffs by 0800 hours, Spalding heading west to take the WN64 defenses at the E-1 draw from the rear and Co. G moving south on Colleville-sur-Mer. Just as importantly, by 0730 hours Co. G's machine guns and mortars had been emplaced on the beach and stood ready to provide suppressive fire for the next group of infantry landings.

Coming in with Co. G was a provisional antiaircraft battery, which hand-carried heavy and unwieldly .50-caliber machine guns ashore. Between it and a second antiaircraft battery for Fox Green, fewer than a third of their 18 heavy machine guns made it to the beach.[16] According to the 16th RCT's records, only two of these guns made it ashore. The 397th AAA Provisional Machinegun Battalion, to whom these two batteries belonged, claimed five guns made it ashore (apparently none on Easy Red), one of which was knocked out by a direct hit from German artillery. Whatever the actual number, because of lost equipment, these two .50-caliber machine-gun batteries contributed very little to the infantry fight and saw no enemy aircraft to engage.

Co. H (the battalion's heavy weapons company, Wave 6, scheduled for 0710 / H+40) was swept eastward and landed 20 minutes late, again with most of its boat sections landing on Fox Green under the guns of WN62.

The support companies of the 3rd BLT landed on the eastern half of Fox Green at about 0700 hours, soon to be joined by the lost boats of Co. I. The companies were somewhat better grouped than those of Wave 3 but were subjected to the fire of the three strongpoints guarding the E-3 and F-1 draws. Most of these boat sections were reduced to the same impotent state as the earlier troops, who remained huddled at the embankment. Individual elements did retain the initiative, however, and began a long, loosely organized assault on the F-1 draw's defenses, unaware that Co. L was doing the same from another direction.

At about 0720 hours, 102 men, including the advanced echelon of the 16th RCT's command post, landed by LCM. Exactly where they landed has never been determined; judging from the results, it seems they probably came in under the guns of WN62. Upon entering the surf, they promptly lost all their communications gear and suffered 35 casualties on the tidal flats, including the regiment's executive officer who was killed. The opportunity for early, effective command was lost.

By 0730 (H+60 minutes), the two lead battalions of the 16th RCT had landed with most units scattered and only partly effective. Casualties were high. There was no command structure operating ashore and leadership fell to isolated junior officers, NCOs and enlisted men who showed initiative. Not a single strongpoint had been knocked out and not a single exit had been opened. The only bright spot was the small penetration even then being effected by Spalding's boat section and Co. G; their success was apparent to almost no one at that point. The situation would change dramatically in the next 90 minutes.

The regiment had one more battalion to land—the 1st BLT—and its three rifle companies (companies A, B, and C) came in between 0740 and 0755, landing, fortunately, on Easy Red near or through the cleared lanes. The battalion's heavy weapons company (Co. D) was scheduled to arrive in this timeframe but landed more than an hour late. As the three rifle companies came in, German direct fire positions opened up again, giving the Co. G machine-gunners and mortarmen their first solid targets of the day. For the first time, troops of the 16th RCT hit the beach with effective supporting fire that could suppress the enemy, at least to some degree. While the 16th RCT report says they came in under heavy fire, the fact that two of these units suffered very light casualties and were able to maintain organization indicates the fire was not especially effective.

Company C (Wave 10, H+70 / 0740 hours) came in on the same sweet spot at the Roman Ruins as had LT Spalding's boat section and Co. G. Company C blew more gaps through the wire and paused for orders. They were supposed to pass through the positions secured by the 2nd BLT, but with the 2nd BLT "missing" and their objectives unsecured, Co. C hunkered down at the shingle and briefly waited for someone who knew what was going on. When it moved forward shortly thereafter, it followed the path blazed by Spalding and Co. G, reaching the bluffs almost unscathed by Omaha Beach standards.

Company A (also in Wave 10) came in farther west—landing at the gap in the obstacles created by GAT 9 but under the guns of WN64—and launched a frontal attack up the bluffs to seize the strongpoint, which it did with the aid of LT Spalding's simultaneous attack from the rear. Company A, however, lost heavily in the effort.

Company B (Wave 11, H+80) landed behind Co. A, but after sampling the enemy defenses at WN64, thought better of the idea of a frontal attack. It pulled back, moved to its left (to the east) and made it up the bluffs using LT Spalding's path. It, too, took light losses.

The experiences of these three companies—landing within 10 minutes of each other—are instructive. The unit landing at the ruins and using LT Spalding's path sustained small losses, even after pausing in the kill zone at the shingle to wait for orders. The unit that landed in front of WN64 and then moved down the beach to use LT Spalding's path also took light losses. The unit that attacked frontally into the teeth of WN64's defenses predictably took much greater losses. This underscores the fact that the area of the ruins and LT Spading's path to the bluffs was a relatively sure (if not entirely safe) part of the otherwise deadly Omaha Beach.

The other point is that losses for these later landings at the Roman Ruins were considerably lighter than in the period in which Co. G landed. Despite initial chaos and confusion, the fire from ever-increasing numbers of invading troops was building and becoming more effective, while German defenses were being slowly reduced, and the surviving defenders were having trouble coping with the increasing number of targets. As a result, this area became a magnet for other units; Co. H, the remnants of Co. E and other fragments moved along the beach to reach the path blazed by Co. G and the lone boat section of Co. E.

The Initiative Shifts

Fortunately, the rear echelon of the regimental command group, with the commander, landed on this same sweet spot at H+110 minutes / 0820 hours (Wave 13, scheduled for H+95 / 0805 hours, arrived late). Spared the punishment suffered by the first advanced command echelon, it began to bring order from the chaos. Shortly after it landed, word reached the beach that Spalding's boat section and Co. G had cleared a route to the top of the bluffs, and the regimental commander organized movement in their wake. The 1st Division's Advanced Command Post, with the assistant division commander, also landed in this area at H+129 / 0839 hours (Wave 15, scheduled for H+110 / 0820 hours, also arrived late). Due to the success in the vicinity of the Roman Ruins, that stretch of beach quickly became the focus of the division's efforts. By midnight, three more infantry regiments had landed at Omaha beach, all setting foot on the 16th RCT's beaches. Eight of their nine battalions moved inland through the widening gap that had been opened on Easy Red.

Things were beginning to look up at the opposite end of the 16th RCT's beaches as well. By 0800 hours, most of seven infantry companies had landed on Fox Green, with little to show for it except casualties and chaos. But Company L's attack from Fox Red against the F-1 draw's defenses, aided by a mixed force from Fox Green, direct fire from a destroyer offshore and a couple tanks, seized the strongpoint by 0900 hours.[17]

Although the 16th RCT was finally moving off the beach, those on Navy ships offshore were not aware of it. All they could see was chaos and wreckage at the shoreline, sights that made it seem as if the invasion was failing. BG Wyman and COL Taylor, ashore at Easy Red, were busy exploiting the seam up Spalding's draw, but at 0900 hours, even they were unaware of the unfolding successes at the E-1 and F-1 draws.

CHAPTER EIGHT

The Lousy Civilian Idea

"By amphibious we mean a something that can both sail the sea and beach ashore, and generally does neither particularly well."

ANON.

Before examining Capa's actual time on the beach, it is necessary to introduce another character, one that serves as a touchpoint to our narrative at several junctures. It is a ship.

The Landing Craft, Infantry (LCI), was a class of amphibious ship; the larger version of the class (the LCI(*L*)) was used at Normandy and it was designed to carry approximately one company of infantry. It had the virtue of being able to beach and offload its passengers directly ashore (just like smaller landing craft such as LCVPs), as well as cross the open ocean on its own bottom (like larger ships). As with most hybrid designs, it was a construct of compromises and it performed neither role especially well, and yet was an essential part of victory.

As it approached the beach, the LCI would drop a kedge anchor astern. Upon beaching, two steep and narrow ramps would project forward of the bow, by which troops would disembark. The embarked troops were stationed in four compartments below deck and had to negotiate steep ladders in single file to reach the open deck. Burdened with the impedimenta of war and faced with the tasks of negotiating the ladders and ramps, soldiers aboard an LCI found that disembarkation took much longer compared to the smaller landing craft with full-width ramps. When the LCI was ready to retract from the beach, it would use its engines and its kedge anchor to warp itself free off the beach.

As with all beaching craft, the LCIs had flat bottoms, which meant they handled open seas poorly. They were also lightly armed and just as lightly armored. Although they could hold almost 200 passengers, there were no mess facilities for the embarked troops, which meant they had to live off C-rations for the duration of their stay aboard. Many pictures of LCIs during the Normandy landings show evidence of this: boxes of C-rations can be seen stacked on deck, as well as garbage cans with immersion heaters mounted in them (used to wash mess gear). Sanitary facilities were at a premium, and the embarked troops lived a cramped life while aboard. These and many other shortcomings, either perceived or real, earned this class the nickname of the Lousy Civilian Idea, a play on the LCI acronym.

Imperfect as they were, they were also one of the critical innovations which were essential to victory in a war that saw amphibious operations conducted on a scale never seen before or since. At Omaha Beach, LCIs were generally slated to bring in the follow-on infantry regiments, however, a small number of them were fitted into the landing tables beginning about H+65 / 0735 hours when they would bring in mixed loads of troops, most of whom were engineers, medics, or beach control units.

It is one of these craft that intersects the Capa narrative.

Identification

In both versions of his D-Day exploits, Capa said he waded out to a recently arrived LCI(L) (which had medics debarking) and sought refuge on that craft just before it was hit by German shellfire. Capa never explicitly identified which craft it was. We do have statements from three crewmen of *LCI(L)-94*—Motor Machinist's Mate 1st Class (MoMM 1/c) Clifford Lewis, MoMM 3/c Charles Jarreau and MoMM 1/c Niles West—which attest to Capa being hauled aboard that craft while it was beached.[1] Normally this would be enough proof that it was indeed the *94* which carried Capa away.

But of course, nothing in the Capa saga is ever that simple, and once again, it was Capa himself who caused the confusion. Because he pushed the "First Wave with Co. E" myth, a persistent belief endures that he must have landed on Fox Green with the bulk of Co. E. This false lead then caused some, such as Whelan, to conclude that Capa must have boarded *LCI(L)-85*.[2] The *85* did indeed beach on Fox Green—at 0830 hours.[3] It too was hit by German artillery (as well as striking a mine). And making the confusion complete, in *Slightly out of Focus*, Capa referred to his LCI as being in sinking shape, and indeed, the *85* did sink, after transferring its casualties to the *Chase* (documented in a well-known series of photos), whereas the *94* continued working off Omaha Beach for many days and survived the war.

It is worth noting that Capa didn't add the sinking detail until after the war, when he embraced the "First Wave with Co. E" myth in *Slightly out of Focus*.[4] By including the "sinking ship" detail, which seemed to place him on Fox Green with *LCI(L)-85*, Capa appeared to confirm that he was on the same beach sector where virtually all Co. E landed.

As a result, there has been enough confusion over the identity of Capa's LCI to warrant a bit of investigation to clear up the matter. Figure 12 is a detail from Capa's negative 33.

Figure 12. Detail from Capa's Negative 33. (Robert Capa © ICP/Magnum Photos)

Figure 13. LT Gislason's photo of *LCI(L)-94* beached on Easy Red. (Jarreau/National WWII Museum)

Figure 13 is a photo provided by Motor Machinist Mate Charles Jarreau.[5] It was taken by LT Gene Gislason, captain of *LCI(L)-94*, while the ship was beached and unloading troops, about a half hour after Capa's photo.

The obvious point of comparison is the group of tanks. Tanks 2, 3 and 4 in Jarreau's photo (two DD tanks, and one standard tank with a Deep Wading Kit and trailer) are clearly the same tanks as in Capa's photo. In the period between Capa's photo and Jarreau's later shot, there has been some repositioning of the tanks—due to the rising tide—and the #10 tank dozer has moved to the left out of frame. Nevertheless, Capa's and Gislason's photos show the same scene, separated only by time.

By drawing a line (double-ended arrows) in both photos from the pole obstacle in the surf to the three dark dots on the sand dune, we can see that the camera's position on the *LCI(L)-94* is 20–40 yards to the left of Capa's earlier vantage point. This is largely due to the angle at which the *94* has beached (which displaced the LCI's bridge farther to the east relative to the bow). Still, it is apparent the *bow* of the *94* is close to Capa's position when he was on his LCVP's ramp, with the *94*'s bow perhaps just 20 yards east of Capa's position.

Outlined in the dashed white box in each photo is a hedgehog. It is *not* the same hedgehog, but they are in the same row. Because the hedgehogs all sit at slightly different heights in the sand and this row zigzags inshore and offshore a few yards from obstacle to obstacle, we cannot use the hedgehog in Gislason's photo as a yardstick for *precise* measurement of the passage of time, but the difference in tide make it clear that Jarreau's photo was taken after Capa's.

As a result of the foregoing, we have placed the *LCI(L)-94* at the very same place as Capa landed—literally, within just a few yards. These points, coupled with the firsthand stories of Lewis and Jarreau, leave no doubt that the *94* was Capa's ride out.

In an interesting coincidence, the *94* had yet another photographer aboard that day, US Coast Guard Chief Photographer's Mate (CPhoM) David Ruley. As we'll see later, he captured Capa in three separate movie clips as the *94* headed back to the Transport Area. This removes all doubt. All the evidence agrees that the *94* was Capa's ride out.

But how could the *94* have ended up there?

Looking for a Landing Site

LCI(L)-94 was originally scheduled to land on Beach Sector Dog Red at H+70 / 0740, in company with sister craft *LCI(L)-90* (on Easy Green) and *LCI(L)-91* (on Dog White) as part of the 116th RCT's Wave 11.[6] So how is it that the *94* ended up beaching on Easy Red, some two beach sectors and more than 2,000 yards east of its planned target? That's a good question.

We have no official Coast Guard source that addresses this; neither the ship's deck log, war diary nor action reports are available. There are four non-official sources for the *94*'s actions that day, and two shed some light on the matter. One is an article by Mark Johnson recounting his father's ride to Omaha Beach as an Army passenger in *LCI(L)-94*.[7] For this article he had the advantage of interviewing the ship's executive officer (LT(jg) Albert Green) and members of the 104th Medical Battalion that were passengers on the *94*. He also drew on Ambrose's book, which in turn drew on our second source, Charles Jarreau. As noted above, Jarreau, was a crewman on the *94* and he later (much later) gave an oral interview to Ambrose.[8]

USCG photographer Ruley, our third source, provided an account of his D-Day adventures aboard the *94* in the June 1945 issue of *Movie Makers* magazine.[9] Our final source for the *94*'s activities that day is the diary of another crewman, Motor Machinist's Mate 1st Class Clifford Lewis.[10] Unfortunately, neither Ruley's article nor Lewis's diary addresses the change in beaching site.

Fortunately, both Jarreau's and Johnson's accounts addressed the issue and agreed that after witnessing the destruction of *LCI(L)-91* and *92*, the *94*'s captain sought safer waters to the east. Jarreau—who was stationed below decks—said he thought the move was about 300 yards, maybe a quarter mile. Johnson placed the actual landing site correctly (below the site where the American Military Cemetery now stands), but incorrectly said that would be on the border of Dog Red and Easy Green.

Both Jarreau's and Johnson's accounts contain a joker. The average reader probably won't notice the significance of *LCI(L)-92*'s death being slipped into the narrative. *LCI(L)-91* was in the same wave as *LCI(L)-94* and *LCI(L)-90* (Wave 11, H+70 / 0740 hours). *LCI(L)-92*, however, was in a later wave (the sole craft in the 116th RCT's Wave 13 at H+100 / 0810 hours), which necessarily pushes the *94*'s timeline farther backwards.[11] Let's take a moment to trace the timelines of these two lost ships to see how they affect that of the *94*.

The timeline of the *91* is rather well documented in its Action Report and its Report on the Loss of Ship (which contain essentially the same narrative).[12] It beached at 0740 hours, but, due to the rising tide and slow debarkation of troops, it had to keep creeping shoreward. About 20 minutes after initially beaching (about 0800 hours) and with a third of the troops still aboard, the *91*'s forward progress was blocked by a mined obstacle. As it tried to retract from the beach, a teller mine detonated off the port bow, holing the ship above the waterline. After retracting, the captain tried to get LCVPs to offload its remaining troops. Failing this, he then beached again 100 yards west of the original site. It was not until this second beaching, while the remaining troops were debarking, that it began receiving the German artillery fire that set it ablaze and ended up destroying the ship.

If the *94*'s commander based his decision to go east on the spectacle of the *91*'s destruction, then he could not have made that decision until at least several minutes after 0800 hours.

Similarly, the *92*'s beaching is well documented in its Action Report,[13] stating it beached shortly after 0810 hours, and two additional sources are consistent with this.[14] When it beached, the captain brought it in to the lee of the crippled and burning *91*, hoping the smoke from the *91*'s fires would help screen the *92* from German guns. Before debarkation could begin, however, the ship was hit twice in rapid succession, igniting the fire that would destroy the ship.

As a result of this, we must conclude that the *94*'s skipper could not have reached his decision to look elsewhere for a safer landing site until shortly after 0810 hours. This still begs the question, of course, why he hung back for a half hour and did not land when scheduled at 0740 hours, as did *LCI(L)-91* and *-90* of the same wave. Deciding between the risk to his ship and the need to get his troops ashore on the right beach at the critical time in the landing schedule must have been a terrible dilemma.

Once the captain did reach the decision to look for a safer beach, the *94* had to travel roughly 2,000 yards east before finding an apparently safe spot on Easy Red and fitting the ship into the flow of craft heading toward the beach. I'd suggest he could have made this 2,000-yard trip at only moderate speed—at best. OPLAN 2-44, the naval plan governing the operations off the American beaches, dictated the *planning* speed for LCIs was 6 knots during the approach,[15] but the Army landing diagram specified 10 knots.[16] At 10 knots, it would take the *94* about five and a half minutes to cover those 2,000 yards. Add to that time for maneuvering, observation, and the run in to the beach itself, and it is probable the *94* hit Easy Red about 0820–0830 hours. In a following chapter, we'll examine how this timeline fits with Capa's stay on the beach.

The problem is, this 0820–0830 window does not fit with some sources.

Lewis's account, the most well-known version of the *94*'s activity, places it landing on Easy Red at 0747 hours (Johnson appears to have drawn the beaching time directly from Lewis).

The 104th Medical Battalion, on the other hand, put it later:

> At 0840 hours, Lieutenant Charles Giese, litter platoon Commander, with (41) litter bearers, landed and gave first aid to the men on the beach and evacuated them to a point above the high water mark.[17]

That after-action report placed one officer and 41 enlisted men on an LCI having a Navy serial designation of 532, which denoted *LCI(L)-94*.[18] None of that battalion's other load plans matched that combination of personnel, so it appears clear it was Giese and his men aboard the *94*. Johnson's article also mentions Giese as the leader of the 104th's men who were embarked on the *94*.

Ruley's account places the beaching at 0740 hours, as does the after-action report of the 29th MP Platoon:

> At 0740 hours (H plus 70), 6 June 1944, two officers and thirty-four enlisted men, and advance traffic section of the 29th Infantry Division Military Police Platoon, attached to the 116th Regimental Combat Team, debarked from LCI # 94 and came ashore on the Normandy Beachhead in France.[19]

This raises more questions than it answers. Is an official after-action report more reliable than a personal diary? Is the 0740 time cited by Ruley and the MP after-action report merely a parroting of the *planned* landing time? We simply don't know. Nor do there appear to be other critical records available. As noted above, the deck log and war diary of the *94* itself are not available for D-Day,[*] nor is its action report.

---

[*] The National Archives contain War Diaries for the *LCI(L)-94* only for parts of 1945.

The after-action report of the 112th Engineer Combat Battalion is similarly missing (the bulk of the troops embarked on the *94* belonged to this unit; its leadership suffered unusually high casualties and could not exert control of its companies on D-Day, and as a result, it appears, filed no action report).

An hour difference is not inconsiderable. So how to decide?

The losses of the *LCI(L)s 91* and *92* were widely witnessed and well documented, and the formal inquiries and detailed reports required by the Navy for the loss of a ship lend greater credibility to the times they record. Therefore, it is safe to conclude that the *94*'s captain would not have started looking for a safer beach until 0810 at the earliest. From this, a time-and-distance calculation—bound by the laws of physics and common sense—forces us to accept the conclusion that the *94* could not have beached at Easy Red much before 0830 hours.

This means Lewis's time—contained in his contemporaneous diary—for the *94*'s beaching at 0747 hours cannot be considered correct, as it places the beaching more than 20 minutes before the captain would have had reason to even look for a safer landing site 2,000 yards away. While reluctant to discount Lewis's diary entry, it is simply outweighed by the two separate official sets of inquiry regarding the loss of the *91* and *92*. In addition, there is some doubt concerning Lewis's situational awareness, working below decks in the engine room during the beaching. As we'll see later, the *94* actually beached twice that morning, a fact Lewis was unaware of.

Although it is not possible to pin the *94*'s beaching down within a minute or two, it is safe to conclude that it must have done so roughly between 0820 and 0830, at the earliest. As we'll see in a later chapter, one of Capa's own photos captures the arrival of *LCI(L)-94* at Easy Red and confirms the 0820–0830 window.

The actions of the *94* once it beached are just as subject to confusion and conflicting sources, and we will leave an exploration of that topic for a later chapter. For now, suffice it to say that the ship's muster roll did provide one key time. It recorded three crewmen killed at 0850 hours because of enemy action.[20] This took place just after the ship had debarked the last of its troops, and, if Capa can be believed, just after he boarded the craft. This firm time reference casts further doubt on the time Lewis claimed they beached, as it would mean the ship remained on the beach for just over an hour, a wholly unrealistic proposal.

As an ironic postscript to the *94*'s dithering offshore, searching for a safer landing spot, and finally ending up two beach sectors and 2,000 yards away, the ship's captain, Lieutenant Gene R. Gislason, received a Silver Star medal for getting his ship to the *"proper"* beach on the run in.[21]

PART II

Ramps Down

"The Gentiles and Jews who crossed the English Channel on the sixth of June in the year 1944, landing with very wet feet on the beach in Normandy called "Easy Red," ought to have—once a year, on that date—a Crossover day. Their children, after finishing a couple cans of C-rations, would ask their father, "What makes this day different from all other days?" The story that I would tell might sound like this:"

ROBERT CAPA'S INTRODUCTION TO HIS D-DAY NARRATIVE
IN SLIGHTLY OUT OF FOCUS

CHAPTER NINE

Where, Exactly?

"All photographs are accurate. None of them is the truth."
RICHARD AVEDON

Having disproven Capa's "First Wave with Co. E" myth, we are left with two unanswered questions. Just *where* did he land? And just *when* did he land? Let's tackle the first one first.

Easy Red was the largest of the Omaha Beach sectors, over a mile in width. Because enemy defenses were not uniformly distributed along Omaha Beach, it made a great deal of difference where a craft landed. If it landed in front of the E-1 draw, its occupants were dropped into a well-prepared kill zone. If it landed at the far eastern end of Easy Red, its occupants were subject to punishment from the E-3 draw's defenses, located just across the boundary in Fox Green. But, if it beached between the two draws, its occupants would be spared the worst effects of enemy small-arms fire from the defending strongpoints. Such accidents of landing made the difference between life and death on Omaha Beach, between mission success and failure.

As a result, if we want to understand the conditions on the beach when Capa stepped ashore, we must know where he stepped ashore.

Pioneer

Previous efforts to locate Capa's landing spot have been generally led astray by the assumption that he did land with Co. E, which generally started those investigations off in the wrong beach sector. The conclusions, therefore, were generally far off the mark.

An exception to this faulty methodology was the analysis performed by Pieter Jutte, a Dutch researcher and Normandy tour guide. His approach focused on comparing the terrain contours as seen in Capa's photos with the terrain as it stands today. His conclusion was that Capa must have landed in front of the draw on the eastern half of Easy Red, which Spalding's section and Co. G followed to the top of the bluffs. To my knowledge, Jutte was the first researcher to come to this conclusion.

Jutte's conclusion was compelling if for no other reason than the fact that he placed it on the right beach sector. And his comparison of the contour features had much to say for it. I was not, however, convinced. The approach of comparing contour features can be quite accurate when there is minimal tree and bush growth. But when such growth is heavy or changes over time, the subtleties of contour details can be obscured or confused. I saw nothing that indicated Jutte's conclusions were obviously incorrect. But neither did I find it conclusive. So, in 2015, as part of Allan Coleman's *Robert Capa on D-Day* project, I took a fresh look at the matter.

Overlooked Clues

I started by examining Capa's photos taken as he stood in the bow of his LCVP. Despite the bloody and corpse-strewn narrative Capa provided, even a cursory examination of his photos indicated there were few, if any, casualties visible. From this I concluded he had to have landed more or less halfway between beach exits E-1 and E-3. That location was at the outer edge of effective smal-arms range from the defenses protecting the two exits (strongpoints WN64 and WN62, respectively). No other spot on the 16th RCT's beaches was both so free (relatively speaking) from enemy fire, and consistent with the general nature of the bluffs inland. Fortunately, that stretch of beach contained a notable feature, a small walled cluster of ruined buildings, which not only appeared on contemporary maps, but also in some D-Day photos. Some post-landings documents from the 16th RCT referred to these as the Roman Ruins.

From our earlier discussion we know that Spalding's boat section and Co. G had the luck to land in the sweet spot between WN62 and WN64, near the Roman Ruins.[1] In fact, the path these two units blazed to the top of the bluffs passed along the eastern side of these ruins, and then up a slight draw. Those ruins were a prominent feature and show up in several invasion photos, such as Figure 14. So, at this point, my line of reasoning was pointing at the same place as Jutte had identified. Therefore, I focused on the ruins to see if there was anything to link them to Capa's photos. Capa provided the first link.

As Capa was leaving the beach on an LCI, he took two photos of the beach. One photo showed vague outline of structures shrouded in smoke from grass fires, but the second photo clearly showed the structures (Figures 60 and 61, examined in more detail later). They matched the Roman Ruins. That established that Capa was at least in the area of the investigation as his craft left the beach, though it did not specifically establish where he stepped ashore.

The search was then on for more photos of that area to see if I could find similarities with Capa's landing photos. I eventually found a three-photo series taken by LT John W. Boucher (USN) from an LCI as it was beached and as it retracted. The photos were taken on D-Day, and judging from the tide, they were probably taken near

Figure 14. The Ruins on Easy Red. LT Spalding's boat section and Company G landed on the beach in front of these ruins and launched their assault up the bluffs from this location. This photo was taken some time after D-Day. The road in the foreground is not the original beach road but was built by engineers in the days following 6 June. (US Army, *Omaha Beachhead, 6 June–13 June 1944*)

noon. There are enough common features between both photo 1 and photo 2, and between both photo 2 and photo 3, that I could positively anchor all three photos as being taken just to the east of the ruins.

The first photo (Figure 15), aimed about 45 degrees to the starboard of the craft's bow, clearly shows the Roman Ruins in the middle background. Because of the height of the shingle embankment, the lower details of the ruins are not visible (especially the wall running along the eastern side), but the identification was solid.

Note the rear portion of the tank with the deep wading kit on the far left of the picture. The left rear corner of the hull is marked with the number 10, identifying it as tank dozer #10, and therefore the same tank dozer seen in Capa's beaching photos. We can confirm this was a tank dozer as a close examination of the chassis reveals it to be a welded version of the hull, which was unique to the dozer tanks on the 16th RCT's beaches (the other tanks had cast hulls).

The next photo (Figure 16) was taken looking off the port bow of the same craft and shows a group of three tanks. The lefthand tank is a duplex drive (DD) version, with its flotation screen partially lowered. At most, only six DD tanks made it ashore in the 16th RCT's sector. The lighter area at the top center of the rear of the flotation screen is like that seen on one of the two DD tanks seen in Capa's

Figure 15. The Roman Ruins on Easy Red, partially hidden by the shingle embankment, as seen from an LCI about noon on D-Day. At the left edge of the photo is tank dozer #10, which can be seen in some of Capa's beach photos. (LT John W. Boucher, USNR)

beaching photos. (For example, see Figure 12.) The tank on the right is a standard tank with a deep wading. The rear tank is another standard tank, mired in the sand. Behind it is an open armored ammunition trailer, and we can see this tank/trailer combination in Capa's photos as well.[2]

The cumulative details of the tanks shown in Figures 15 and 16, added to their proximity to the Roman Ruins, point to these being four of the same five tanks seen in Capa's photos. The only tank missing is the second DD tank (the one with the life preserver).

Notice the distinctive part of the skyline highlighted in the white outline, as well as the distinctive pattern of vegetation on the hillside.

Figure 17 was taken as the LCI was pulling away from the shore. The camera was aimed straight inland, and the ruins are off camera to the right, at about 45 degrees. The same three tanks are visible, the only difference being that in the interim, the DD tank has pulled up into the sand layer of the embankment. Note the section of skyline highlighted in the dashed white box. Also, the distinctive pattern of vegetation seen in Figure 17 matches that on the righthand side of Figure 16. The slight draw in the hillside in the center of the photo is the route Spalding's section followed to the crest of the bluffs.

Examining the skyline in Capa's negative 32 (Figure 18, which was taken a couple hours earlier), we see the sections of skyline highlighted in the previous two photos match the corresponding sections in this photo. Capa's lower camera position

Figure 16. Taken from the same LCI while beached, this photo shows one DD tank and two standard tanks with Deep Wading Kits. The tank in the rear is stuck in the sand. Note that its M8 ammunition trailer is open and the number of expended shell casings both to the left and right of the trailer. This is an indication of the volume of fire that tanks did provide in support of the infantry. These appear to be tanks 1, 3 and 4 as seen in Capa's and Jarreau's photos (Figures 12 and 13). (LT John W. Boucher, USNR)

Figure 17. A shot of the same tanks as in the previous figure and the bluffs directly inland of them. The ruins are out of frame to the right. This photo was taken a few minutes after Figure 16, as the LCI was retracting; the DD tank has moved up onto the sandy part of the embankment. (LT John W. Boucher, USNR)

Figure 18. Capa's Negative 32, showing the bluffs directly inland from his landing site. Indications are that this is the same group of tanks seen in Figures 15–17, with tank dozer clearly indicated by the number 10 prominently painted at the rear. The ammunition trailer being towed by the tank at the right edge of the film can't be seen in this photo but is clearly visible in other photos taken by Capa. (Robert Capa © ICP/Magnum Photos)

accounts for some minor differences in the skyline, but it is clear this is the same stretch of terrain. Even the pattern of vegetation on the hillside is consistent across all three photos. Although partly obscured by haze, we can make out the draw in the hillside. From Capa's lower perspective in the LCVP, he could not see the beach flats which were in defilade behind the higher shingle/sand embankment. The Roman Ruins are located at the right side of his photo, just out of frame.

These photos definitively place Capa's landing site on the same short stretch of Easy Red as Spalding's boat section and Co. G, though perhaps a hundred yards to the east. As we'll see later, this judgement is confirmed in the photo Capa took while offshore leaving the beach. It shows the Roman Ruins in the same frame as the group of tanks seen both in Figure 16 and in Capa's beaching photos.

This conclusively confirms that Capa landed in the sweet spot. It was just a little east of midway between WN62 and WN64, and as a result was at the outer edge of effective small-arms range for both strongpoints; and with both strongpoints under direct frontal attack, they directed relatively little fire to this stretch of beach. This area would also have lower priority for enemy indirect fire, which necessarily would have concentrated on the ongoing assaults against the beach exits. The site of Capa's landing was, in fact, a seam in the enemy defenses. And that would indeed account for the dearth of death in Capa's photos.

Although most of the two assault BLTs came to grief elsewhere, Spalding's boat section and Co. G had the good fortune to land in this sweet spot and the initiative to exploit it. Gap Assault Teams 9 and 10 (10 was about 50 yards east of the ruins, and 9 about 200 yards west of the ruins) took advantage of the spotty enemy fire to

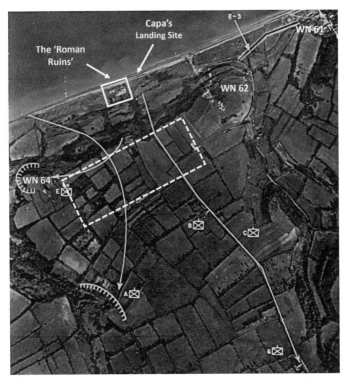

Figure 19. The Roman Ruins on Easy Red in relation to WN62 and WN64. The movements of key units through the gap in the defenses are shown. The dashed box indicates the later site of the American Cemetery. (US Army, *Omaha Beachhead, 6 June–13 June 1944*, with author's annotations)

create their breaches, ensuring easier access for following waves. That good fortune bred more good fortune as most of the 16th RCT's reserve BLT landed in the same area, followed by COL Taylor's landing there as well … and the conditions came together for success.

Capa may have thought he landed in pure Hell—and he certainly portrayed it as such to the public and to posterity—but as far as conditions elsewhere on Omaha Beach stood, Capa's spot on Easy Red wasn't all that bad.

Relatively speaking.

Collateral Damage

This determination of Capa's landing site has fatal implications for much of the Capa mythology, most especially the inventions Whelan added to Capa's descriptions.

Capa did not claim he left the beach on *LCI(L)-85*—which received the damage at Fox Green that would later sink it—but he did observe that unfortunate ship later on D-Day, as it wallowed alongside the *Chase*, offloading casualties before it foundered. Without naming that ship, or claiming he rode on that particular vessel, he noted details of its fate and incorporated them into his own narrative, claiming his LCI was sinking as it raced back to the Transport Area. Whelan chose to accept this point of embroidery as fact and wove it into a scenario that combined several other spurious claims, all with the object of making the "First Wave with Co. E" myth sound plausible, despite the facts. So, Whelan had Capa initially landing on Fox Green where he supposedly took his landing photos. In his Capa biography, Whelan appeared to dodge the issue of which LCI carried Capa away from the beach, merely pointing out that it was listing badly by the time it reached "the mother ship."[3] That, however, was a fairly clear indication he was talking about the 85.

By the time he authored *This Is War!*, however, Whelan was no longer equivocating.[4] He definitively stated Capa landed on Fox Green and then was picked up by the 85. But Whelan's improbable scenario then faced the problem that Capa is known to have returned to the "mother ship" on *LCI(L)-94*. So, he had to somehow rationalize the error involving the 85 with the facts concerning the 94. He invented a second landing on Omaha Beach for Capa. According to the revised narrative, Capa first left the beach on *LCI(L)-85*, but after sustaining damage and before proceeding to the Transport Area, the 85 laid to while fighting fires for 30 minutes then offloaded unwounded troops to LCVPs for transfer to the beach. Which did in fact happen.[5] But then Whelan concluded Capa must have ridden to the beach for a second landing on one of these LCVPs. And then he once again fled to the nearest LCI, which happened to be *LCI(L)-94*.

It is a bizarre concoction and Capa's narratives made absolutely no reference to any of this, except to claim the LCI on which he fled was in sinking condition. All the rest was Whelan's invention in the pursuit of protecting the "First Wave with Co. E." myth. And it falls apart quickly. By Whelan's scenario, Capa's landing photos were made during his first landing on Fox Green. Yet we've proven that those photos were taken on Easy Red. And we've proven that *LCI(L)-94* must have picked Capa up from Easy Red, not Fox Green.

By definitively proving precisely where Capa landed on Easy Red, we've demolished much of the confused and false narrative that has characterized previous analyses of Capa's experience.

Blood and Death Sell

Recall that in the Wertenbaker interview Capa said, "I hid behind some tanks that were firing on the beach." In *Slightly out of Focus* the details became grittier. The tank he hid behind wasn't firing, instead it was "half-burnt," a substitution which made Capa's ordeal sound even more harrowing. So which version was correct?

We can answer that by referring to the group of tanks in the LCI photos above (Figures 16–18). In the preceding paragraphs, I concluded the four tanks in those photos were the same tanks as seen in Capa's photos, the only difference being the absence of the second DD tank. Since all four had moved after Capa's photos to the positions we see them in the LCI photos, clearly, they could not have been set afire as Capa claimed. The only possible remaining tank would be the second DD tank. But that DD tank was up just forward of the embankment, and as we'll see later, Capa never made it far enough to shelter behind it. Furthermore, Figures 16–18 show the entire stretch of beach as seen in Capa's photos. If that second DD tank were knocked out and set afire close to the embankment, then its burning hulk should be there when the LCI photos were taken. And it isn't. When a tank burns, it burns for quite a long time and produces quite a lot of dark smoke. There are no indications in any of Capa's photos—to include the two photos taken as he was leaving the beach—that any of these tanks has been set afire. In addition, LT Gislason, captain of *LCI(L)-94*, took a companion photo to the one in Figure 13 that showed the entire group of tanks. Many had changed positions, and none was on fire.

Clearly all the tanks in Capa's photos were operable, and his assertion that one of them was burned-out cannot be credited.[6] This is just one more instance of Capa hyping up the carnage in his later account.

Vindication

Pictorial evidence leaves no doubt where Capa beached on D-Day. He came in on the relatively undefended stretch of Easy Red beach sector, just to the east of the Roman Ruins.

This analysis, using an entirely different approach, completely validated the conclusions drawn by Pieter Jutte. He got it right.

So now that we know where he landed, the question is *when* did he land?

CHAPTER TEN

When, Exactly?

"The objectivity of a photograph is only an illusion. The captions that provide the commentary can change the meaning entirely."

GISÈLE FREUND, *PHOTOGRAPHY & SOCIETY* (1974)

Establishing Capa's landing *time* is a much more difficult task than was locating his landing site. This difficulty comes not from scarce or contradictory data, rather from the sheer touchiness of the subject. Those who uncritically accepted Capa's fictionalized passages in *Slightly out of Focus* react strongly to anything that implies he did not land as early as he claimed. Ideas that bypass one's critical faculties and become firmly lodged in the brain are usually the ideas that are clung to the most fiercely. So, we'll take a bit more time and effort to examine this topic.

Timeline

To facilitate this discussion, we'll create a timeline for the morning of 6 June. As we develop additional data points, we will add them to this timeline in the hope this will help zero in on an accurate landing time. First, we'll establish the boundary points which set the earliest and latest possible times for consideration.

The earliest time is easy to establish. Since Capa arrived in the invasion area on the *Chase*, he must have landed by means of one of the *Chase*'s landing craft. We know from both Coast Guard and 16th RCT records that the *first* wave of *Chase* landing craft brought in Companies A and C of the 1st BLT, 16th RCT. Both the Coast Guard and 16th RCT records agree that these landing craft and their embarked troops arrived on schedule: 0740 hours.[1] That serves as our initial boundary (Figure 20).

Our latest possible boundary is also easy to establish. We know that Capa was aboard the *LCI(L)-94* when it was hit in rapid succession by two or three enemy shells. While there is some difference of opinion as to *how long* he had been aboard when this happened, there is no question that *he was* aboard at that point. The June 1944 muster roll of the *94* records the casualties from this shelling and records the time: 0850 hours.[2] And thus, we have our latest possible boundary point. Our window of consideration is now just 70 minutes.

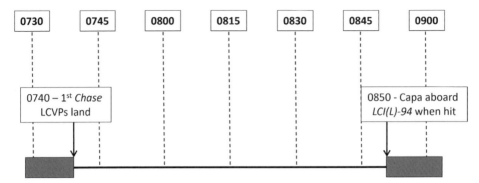

Figure 20. Initial boundaries of Capa's possible time on the beach. (Author)

This end point is also indirectly confirmed by Capa's own photos. One of the pictures he took as the *LCI(L)-94* returned to the Transport Area shows *LCT-305* passing on its run in to shore. The *305* was approaching the beach at 0900 hours, a half hour behind schedule, when it was hit by machine-gun fire.[3] One of Capa's photos (to be examined later) showed the two craft passing each other as the *94* headed to the Transport Area and the *305* headed in. To have these two craft meet where they did and when they did, the *94*—which was limping away from the beach on just one of its two propellers[4]—had to have departed the beach shortly after 0850 hours.

These two boundary points simplify our task. There were only five waves of craft from the *Chase* that were *scheduled* to land in this window, as shown in this next version of our timeline (Figure 21). The boxes for these five waves are outlined in dashed lines to denote their scheduled landing times. Three of the waves (10, 11 and 12) were scheduled to bring in the core of the 1st BLT, 16th RCT: Companies A, B, C and D.[5] The remaining two *Chase* waves, 13 and 15, brought in headquarters elements. Note that Wave 14 is omitted. That wave consisted of 21 DUKWs (2½-ton amphibious trucks) which were launched from LSTs, rather than the *Chase*, so Capa could not have been in this wave.

As the landings did not proceed as planned, we'll modify this timeline to reflect the actual landing times of these waves (Figure 22).[6] We are left with only four waves. Note that Wave 12, carrying Co. D, was badly delayed, and landed at 0920 hours—outside our window of consideration—so it has been omitted from this version of the timeline. Note also that Wave 13 (COL Taylor and the rear echelon of the 16th RCT command group) and Wave 15 (advanced command post for the 1st Division) were each delayed 15–20 minutes.[*]

---

[*] Co. B's beaching time (Wave 11) was listed as a five-minute period. The beaching time for the 16th RCT's rear command post listed as 0815 hours and 0820 hours in different reports, all of which were written by occupants of those two landing craft. For the sake of simplicity, I will use 0820 hours in this work except where the discussion demands greater specificity.

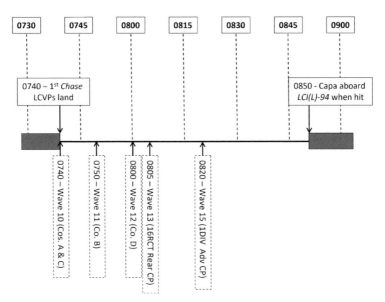

Figure 21. Scheduled landings for USS *Chase* waves on Easy Red. (Author)

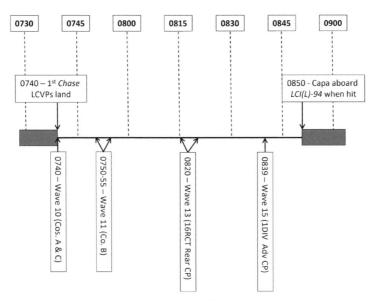

Figure 22. Actual landing times for USS *Chase* waves on Easy Red. (Author)

Recall that while aboard the *Chase*, he mentioned two landing possibilities in addition to the "First Wave with Co. E." They were: 1) landing with Co. B and 2) landing with the regimental commander. Both these options remain in our window of consideration.

The Landing Tables

This would be a good time to step back and see what the operations plans had to say on the matter. The 16th RCT had a civilian news correspondent and a civilian press photographer attached to it for the operation, as well as five photographers of an Army signal unit (Detachment L, 165th Signal Photo Company) (Figure 23). The correspondent was John "Beaver" Thompson, as discussed earlier.[7]

Given that COL Taylor supposedly "invited" Capa to land with his rear command echelon, it is a safe working assumption that Capa filled the 16th RCT's press photographer slot.

A second news correspondent and second press photographer were attached to the 1st Division's advanced command post (which in turn was attached to the 16th RCT "for movement" to the beach and therefore were included in the 16th RCT's landing tables). The 1st Division's news correspondent was Don Whitehead of *The New York Times*. The second press photographer seems to have dropped out, and John McVane, in his 1979 book, said he landed in this serial with Whitehead.[8] However, at this point we can't completely dismiss the possibility that Capa was slotted in this position with the 1st Division's advanced command post.

```
Troops of the 16th CT included:

        Hq & Hq Co, 16th Infantry;
        A-T Co, 16th Infantry;
        Serv Co, 16th Infantry;
        Med Det, 16th Infantry (Less Bn Med Section);
        Air Support Party;
        Det, 1st Sig Company;
        PWI Team;
        Language Interp Team;
        CIC Det and NSFCP;
        1st Engr Bn (Less Co A & B and 1 platoon of Co C);
        37th Engineer Br, (Less Companies AB and C);
        4 Surgical Teams;
        3 Auxiliary Surgical Teams;
        2 Prov AAA AW(S/P);
        1 Platoon, 606th QM Company (Gr);
        Det, 320th Barrage Ballon Bn (VLA);
        197th AAA Bn AW(S/P);
        7th Field Artillery Bn;
        62nd Armd Field Artillery Bn Tankdozers;
        741st Tank Bn (DD) (Less Company B and C);
        Company A, 1st Med Bn;
        Press Photographer and News Correspondent;
        Det L, 165th Sig Photo Company;
        Liaison Party, 231st Brigade, 50th Northumbrian Division;
        Liaison Party, 1st U S Infantry Division;
        Engineer Special Task Force;
        Civil Affairs, and Det, 5th ESB;
        20th Engineer Bn (Less Company A).
```

Figure 23. Extract from the 16th RCT's S-3 Combat Report showing attachment of a press photographer, a news correspondent, and Detachment L. (US Army, McCormick Research Center)

These were the only four slots for civilian members of the press that were included in the 16th RCT's landing tables. We'll proceed on the working premise that Capa filled the 16th RCT's press photographer slot and see how this hypothesis fits with other evidence.

The 16th RCT's landing tables were highly detailed, and identified every separate element assigned to each and every landing craft. The manifest for the LCM in Wave 13 included the news correspondent and press photographer that were attached to the 16th RCT (Figure 24). It's no coincidence that this was the same LCM that was to carry COL Taylor and his rear command echelon. There were only two landing craft in Wave 13: this LCM and an accompanying LCVP. They were from the *Chase* and were scheduled to beach at H+95 / 0805 hours. Apparently Capa was not *invited* to ride in with COL Taylor: he was *ordered* to do so; the landing tables were, after all, an annex of the RCT's Field Order for the operation.

The second media pair was manifested in Wave 15. (Figure 25) This wave consisted of only two LCMs and one LCVP—all carrying the personnel of the advanced command post of the 1st Infantry Division—and it was scheduled to land at H+110 / 0820 hours.[9] As noted in the landing table extract, this media pair was manifested in one of the two LCMs.

One final note about the landing tables. They rule out Capa's option of landing with Co. B, as they make *no* provision for a correspondent among that company's LCVPs. As we've seen in an earlier chapter, while correspondents were allowed to voice their desires to SHAEF as to where they wanted to land, the SHAEF public relations office sent them where they thought best. In the 1st Division, the correspondents arrived aboard ship to discover they had been assigned to very

2160	H/95 min	APA 1	Hq & Hq Co 16th Inf (Incl MPs for Traffic Control and PW)	57	Wey-mouth GWRP*	Easy Red	LCM used
			Ln Py 231 Brig 50 N Div	3			
			Det 18th Inf	1			
			Serv Co 16th Inf	15			
			Hq & Hq Btry 7th FA Bn	9			
			NSFCP	3			
			Btry C 62d FA Bn SP	3			
			H & S Co 741st Tk Bn	5			
			News Correspondent, 16th	1			
			Press Photographer, 16th	1			

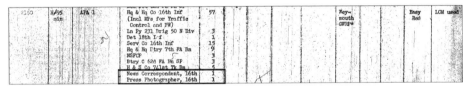

Figure 24. Extract from the 16th RCT's Landing Tables showing a press photographer manifested to land with the rear echelon of the regiment's command group at H+95 minutes. APA 1 was the Field Order's placeholder designation for the attack transport that would carry this unit. The Navy later assigned the USS *Chase* to this requirement. (US Army, McCormick Research Center)

2152	H/110	APA 1	Det Hq & Hq Co 1st Div	25	Wey-mouth GWRP*	Easy Red	LCM used
			Det 1st Sig Co	35			
			Det L 165th Sig Photo Co	2			
			P Corres & Phgr, 1st Div	2			
			[illegible] 29th Div	3			
			OB, 1st Div	3			

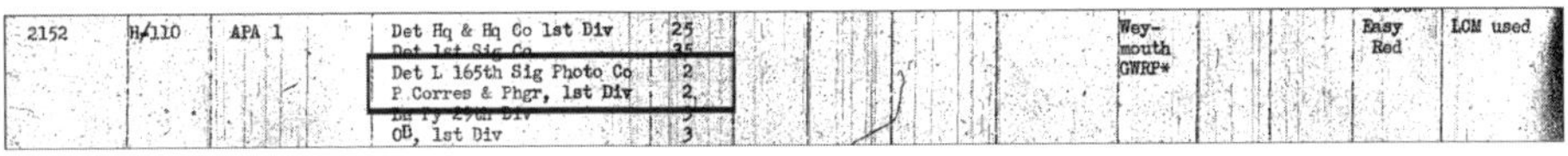

Figure 25. Extract from the 16th RCT's Landing Tables showing a correspondent and press photographer manifested to land with the 1st Division's advanced command group at H+110 minutes. Note also two Army photographers of Detachment L, 165th Signal Photo Company. (US Army, McCormick Research Center)

specific slots, as designated in the landing tables. The painstakingly crafted landing tables dictated an environment in which reporters could not be indulged in their whims to choose their landing craft during movement to the beach. If Capa had made a last-minute decision to ride in with a rifle company, he would have bumped another soldier from the LCVP, depriving the section of a key man, his weapons and equipment. No. A well-rehearsed assault boat section would not be disrupted to suit a photographer's last-minute impulse.

The Reality

These two extracts show what the plans intended for the two press photographers. But did that play out as intended on D-Day?

Fortunately, Capa himself can shed some light on this. Recall that in his interview with Wertenbaker (on D+3) Capa stated, "Just before 6 o'clock, we were lowered in our LCVP and started for the beach."[10] Just before 6 o'clock. This perfectly dovetails with the *Chase's* operations. The *Chase* reported its first boats were lowered at 0536 hours and that it completed lowering the last LCVPs of its first waves by 0601 hours.[11] These waves constituted Waves 10, 11, 12, 13 and 15 in the regiment's landing tables. By comparison, Companies E and F, landing in Wave 3 as the first infantry arriving on the beach, were lowered in LCVPs from the *Henrico* beginning at 0415 hours.[12] So Capa's 6 o'clock comment clearly demolished the "First Wave" myth (just as the issue of being on the wrong attack transport did) and confirms our focus on the *Chase* and its landing craft.

While the lowering time he provided was far too late (by 105 minutes) to be part of Co. E's wave, it was exactly consistent with the lowering time of the LCVP in COL Taylor's Wave 13. So Capa's stated lowering time is right in line with our working hypothesis.

We can double-check this. Major Charles Tegtmeyer (the regimental surgeon) and his medical detachment were manifested in the sole LCVP in Wave 13 (COL Taylor's wave). The detachment's history stated they left the *Chase* at 0600 hours.[13] Also, the *Chase's* Action Report stated that the *last* of its initial rail-loaded* waves was lowered at 0601 hours (referring to the LCVP of Wave 15, the next wave after COL Taylor's). For once, two official reports completely agree with part of the Capa narrative. He, COL Taylor, MAJ Tegtmeyer, and the medics all left the same ship at the same time. Since we know COL Taylor, MAJ Tegtmeyer and the medics were in Wave 13, we have a strong indication that Capa rode in with them on Wave 13, as our working hypothesis states. Note, however, that the last wave from the *Chase*, Wave 15, also had its lone LCVP lowered to the water by 0601 hours, so we can't exclude Capa riding in with that craft.

---

* For rail loading, troops boarded the landing craft while it was still in the davits aboard ship, then the loaded craft was lowered into the water.

But one point needs to be explored. The press photographers were manifested on *LCMs* in both Wave 13 and 15, yet Capa stated he was lowered from the ship in an *LCVP* and his photos taken from the bow of his landing craft confirm it was an LCVP. What happened? There is an explanation for this, and it too points to our working hypothesis of Wave 13. The 16th RCT's medical detachment was manifested in the Wave 13 *LCVP*, but the detachment's history noted they actually climbed down cargo nets into their *LCM*. At some late point in the staging, the decision was made to change the loadout for these two craft, with COL Taylor taking his command echelon in on the LCVP, and MAJ Tegtmeyer and the medics switching to the LCM. Presumably this was to make the command group a smaller target while placing it in a craft more capable of slipping in between obstacles. MAJ Tegtmeyer confirmed this switch in his memoirs, noting that the LCM in which he was embarked followed COL Taylor's LCVP into the beach.[14] Capa's switch from his planned LCM to an LCVP seems to be a clear indication he was part of the same cross-loading adjustments as COL Taylor, MAJ Tegtmeyer and the medical detachment, which indicates he was in Wave 13 with those parties.

This cross-loading helps clarify another loose end. A few years later in his memoirs, MAJ Tegtmeyer stated that his craft left the *Chase* at 0610 hours, a bit later than the *Chase* reported the *rail-loaded* LCVPs were lowered. The LCVPs were held in davits, and the craft were loaded at the rails, then lowered into the water. LCMs, however, were lowered into the water empty, and the troops had to climb down cargo nets to board the craft. It was a cumbersome process complicated by the larger number of troops an LCM carried. Therefore, the LCMs started loading earlier but typically took longer to finish.

Despite this cross-loading, the wave's embarkation and departure were otherwise in keeping with the plan. Their beaching, however, was delayed. When COL Taylor's LCVP arrived off the E-3 Exit, it was met with a hail of fire. They backed off and cruised westward along the beach for several minutes looking for a better landing site, with the LCM following obediently behind. When COL Taylor found a clear run in to the beach, the LCM turned in as well and landed a few yards to its flank. As noted earlier, instead of beaching at the scheduled H+95 / 0805 hours, they touched down at H+110 / 0820 hours.[15]

According to our working hypothesis, this then would also place Capa's landing at H+110 / 0820 hours.

Encounters

In *Slightly out of Focus*, Capa included another passage that supports the Wave 13 hypothesis. When Capa reached the shelter of the shingle/embankment, he found there ahead of him "Larry, the Irish padre of the regiment" and the "Jewish doctor." The "Jewish doctor" was of course MAJ Tegtmeyer. In Chapter XX of his memoirs,

Tegtmeyer described his D-Day landing. It confirms that he landed in the LCM, and that this LCM accompanied to the beach the LCVP that carried in the regimental commander. Tegtmeyer covers in some detail his interactions with the regimental chaplain, Captain Lawrence Deery, during the ride in and while on the beach, so we know these two landed together at H+110 / 0820 hours.

Capa claimed he was the last person off his LCVP, and he described pausing to take cover twice and to snap pictures while working his way up to the shingle. Given this, it would be almost inevitable that Tegtmeyer and Deery reached the shingle before Capa. So Capa's finding these two ahead of him at the embankment is entirely consistent with him landing in Wave 13 from the neighboring LCVP. Even if Capa did not actually make it as far as the shingle (a point to be covered later) he knew that his acquaintances, Tegtmeyer and Deery, were on the accompanying craft, and could easily have woven them into his narrative.

Of course, it is also possible the two *might* still be at the embankment ahead of him if Capa landed with the division's advanced CP in Wave 15, which was also delayed and did not land until H+129 / 0839 hours. However, shortly after landing, COL Taylor strode by and ordered Tegtmeyer and Deery to get up and follow him on his tour of the beach. If Capa landed about 19 minutes after Tegtmeyer and Deery (in Wave 15), then took time at various points before reaching the embankment (as he claimed), there is small chance the doctor and the priest would still have been there to greet Capa. While it is less likely, we can't rule out the possibility Capa came in with Wave 15, though so far Wave 13 fits the evidence better.

We have possible corroboration from another source. In a 1 June 1969 article for the *Chicago Tribune*, John "Beaver" Thompson recounted his landing with COL Taylor on Omaha Beach. While briefly sheltering at the embankment after landing, Thompson described Capa running up to crouch next to a DD tank. This would tend to argue that Capa landed in Wave 13 rather than 15, again, because Taylor quickly gathered his staff—to include Thompson—and moved out. Unfortunately, Thompson's narrative doesn't match Capa's movements as he described them. Further, Thompson's article includes errors that call at least part of his account into question. For one thing, he claims that he and COL Taylor landed at H+60 / 0730 hours—10 minutes before *any Chase* landing craft reached the beach—whereas *all* other accounts from participants place Taylor's landing at least 45 minutes later. For another, he claimed to have been on the USS *Augusta* (CA-31), which he described as the 1st Division's command ship. In fact, the *Augusta* was the First Army command ship, and Thompson was on the *Chase*. And finally, Thompson claimed he warned Capa away from the DD tank as it was a target for the Germans. Just after Capa moved away from the tank, according to Thompson, it took a direct hit that "made the tank a flamer." Suffice it to say that photos taken later by both the captain of *LCI(L)-94* and Capa revealed no burning tanks, while photos of the same area later in the day show all the tanks had moved, proving none had been "made a flamer" during the period Thompson claimed. I suspect some details in Thompson's article, printed 25 years after the events of D-Day, were partly influenced by Capa's autobiography. So, while Thompson's account may support our working hypothesis, the passing of years between the event and his article apparently spawned enough errors that we can't place unqualified faith in any one part.[16]

Nevertheless, at this point, all the evidence seems to support our working hypothesis. The plan called for Capa to land in Wave 13 (or perhaps 15). He debarked from the *Chase* at a time consistent with Wave 13's debarkation (as well as Wave 15's). And he supposedly found ahead of him at the shingle/embankment men who landed with Wave 13.

It seems conclusive that Capa landed with either Wave 13 (most likely) or Wave 15 (less likely). There are, however, other points we must examine before passing a final judgement. Although Capa's photos did not include timestamps, they did include features which will serve our purposes nearly as well: the state of the tide and the height of the shingle/embankment.

A Rising Tide

Figure 26 is taken from Capa's negative 32, which was snapped while he was still on the ramp of his LCVP. The two-tiered nature of the shingle/embankment can be clearly seen, highlighted by the solid-white rectangle. Capa's landing craft has been able to approach close to the shore and the exposed stretch of the tidal flats is just a narrow band, with the surf appearing to be within, perhaps, 20 to 30 yards of the shingle, as highlighted by the dashed rectangle. This narrow band is what the rear echelon of the 16th RCT's command group termed the "7 yard beachhead," their initial impression of the conditions when they beached at H+110 / 0820 hours.

Figure 26. State of the tide as Capa landed on Easy Red, from Capa's Negative 32. The solid white box shows the height of the sand and shingle embankment. The dashed white box shows the extent of the beach not yet covered by the incoming tide. Note the inner row of obstacles in the foreground. (Robert Capa © ICP/Magnum Photos)

Figure 27. State of the tide when lead elements of the 1st BLT landed on Easy Red at 0740 hours. The solid white rectangle shows the height of the sand and shingle embankment. The dashed white rectangle shows the extent of the beach not yet covered by the incoming tide. Note the inner row of obstacles is abreast of the tank dozer in the distance. (US Coast Guard/NARA)

With no gap in the embankment, most of the tanks remained in the surf with their running gear partially protected by the water. The final line of beach obstacles is in the foreground, far behind the incoming tide, and the water level has risen almost up to the gusset plates on the hedgehogs.

We'll compare Capa's negative 32 to a picture taken by Chief Photographer's Mate Robert Sargent (USCG) as his LCVP beached at 0740 hours. His craft came from the *Chase* and carried Co. A, 1st BLT (Wave 10, which also included Co. C, landing farther to the east).[17]

Figure 27 is a detail from a shot he took while standing in the aft of the craft as his troops debarked. Centered in the gap in the obstacles is tank dozer #9, indicating Sargent's craft beached at the lane in the obstacles created by Gap Assault Team 9. This places Sargent's beaching site just a couple hundred yards west of Capa's. Note how much of the tidal flat—highlighted by the dashed white rectangle—is still exposed at 0740 hours. The tide has yet to reach the few obstacles that can be seen (most of the obstacles here were already destroyed by Gap Assault Team 9). As with Capa's photo, a section of the shingle/embankment is outlined in solid white. The discolored shingle layer can barely be discerned as a thin dark horizontal line running behind the turret of tank dozer #9, and the sand tier is the slightly lighter colored band above it; the top of the sand tier is defined by the clouds of smoke.

Also, note that the soldiers are in progressively deeper water the farther away from the landing craft, despite being closer to dry land. This indicates that Sargent's LCVP grounded just seaward of a runnel in the tidal flats. Examining the beach gradient profile and tide table for this stretch of beach, we can locate this runnel and the sandbar just seaward of it.[18] Based on this, Sargent's LCVP grounded on the sandbar approximately 160 yards from the embankment with the soldiers descending into the runnel (which had its lowest point about 125 yards from the embankment and shoaled quickly over the next 20 yards).

Placing Sargent's and Capa's photos together, we can see just how dramatically different the details are. But first we must consider the different positioning of the cameras in the two photos. Sargent was located at the engine cover step just aft of the engine. That placed him about 28 feet aft of the end of the ramp, which can be seen in his photo. Capa, on the other hand, was positioned about 21 feet forward of Sargent's position, at the edge of the bow ramp. To compare the two photos, I have resized them so that figures of infantrymen who are approximately the same distance from the two cameramen are shown approximately the same size. Thus, the two photos can be compared with some degree of accuracy.

All the details common to the two photos indicate Capa's was taken closer to shore and, therefore, later in the tide cycle. The apparent size of the embankment is significantly different, as are the sizes and positions of the tanks, both in relation to the landing craft and the embankment. As noted earlier, the tide tables predict that the distance between the landing craft and the embankment when Sargent landed was about 160 yards, which certainly is consistent with what we see in his photo. By comparison, when COL Taylor's Wave 13 landed at H+110 / 0820 hours, the LCVP would have grounded on a different sandbar about 80 yards from the embankment (again, based on the beach gradient profile, the tide height at 0820 hours, and the LCVP's draft). Capa's photos depict tidal conditions that are much closer to—if not *identical* to—the conditions when COL Taylor's Wave 13 landed, than Sargent's Wave 10.

In my mind there is no doubt that Capa's photos were taken much later than Sargent's, but to convince the doubters we must turn to mathematics. We'll start with the "WRM equation," the standard military method to determine range, given the known width (or height) of an object in the distance. The equation states that

Figure 28. Sargent's photo (left) taken at 0740 hours; Capa's photo (right) taken some time later. The photos have been aligned so that the tops of the embankment are even.

width (expressed here in yards) is equal to the range (in thousands of yards) times the object's apparent width (in mils or milliradians): $w = r(m)$.

We will set up two equations, one for Sargent's photo and one for Capa's, and since we're looking at height instead of width, we'll use "h" in lieu of "w"

$h_s = r_s (m_s)$ and $h_c = r_c (m_c)$

Since the height of the shingle/dune embankment was essentially constant over this stretch of beach, we can set the two equations equal to each other.

$r_s (m_s) = r_c (m_c)$

Next, we divide both sides by m_s to obtain:

$r_s = r_c (m_c) / (m_s)$ ... or, the range in Sargent's is equal to the range in Capa's multiplied by the height in mils of the shingle/embankment in Capa's photo, divided by the height in mils of the shingle/embankment in Sargent's photo.

We cannot determine the measure in mils from these photos, but we can determine their *ratio*. The distance between the top and bottom of the embankment has been marked by a white vertical line in both Sargent's and Capa's photos above. Placing those two lines together, we can determine that the height of the embankment in Capa's photo is more than twice that of Sargent's photo. In fact, the ratio is about 0.25 : 0.11, or 2.27 : 1.0.

Substituting 2.27 into the equation in place of $(m_c) / (m_s)$ results in:

$r_s = r_c (2.27)$

or ... *the range to the embankment in Sargent's photo is more than twice the range to the embankment in Capa's photo.*

Admittedly, this is not a precise calculation, but the two photographers were focusing on action the same distance in front of them, so it suffices to establish a *relative* appreciation for the difference in distances between the two photos: Capa's position was roughly less than half the distance from the shingle/embankment as was Sargent's.

Now let's test this result by comparing it to the data derived from the beach gradient profile and tide tables. If we substitute 160 yards (the derived distance between Sargent and the embankment by the tide tables) for r_s in the equation:

$160 = r_c (2.27)$ and solving for r_c we get $r_c = 160 / 2.27 = 70.5$ yards.

So Capa's photo was taken from a spot roughly 70.5 yards from the shingle/embankment. It confirms what was intuitively obvious by a simple glance. Capa was roughly a bit less than half as far from the embankment when he landed as was Sargent. This is also close enough to our predicted "about 80 yards" for when COL Taylor landed (derived earlier from the tide tables and beach gradient profile) to provide general confirmation.

We know for a fact that Sargent was in the wave that landed at 0740 hours—the earliest of the 1st BLT's waves. And it appears Capa landed at the same general time as COL Taylor's Wave 13. Can we find further proof of this? Let's turn our attention to the other "timestamp" visible in Capa's photos: the state of the tide.

A Rising Tide, Again

In Capa's photos the tide had risen enough not only to reach the *last* row of obstacles, but to cover them almost up to the bottom of the gusset plates of the hedgehogs. Based on the beach gradient profile, from the time Sargent took his photo, the tide must have risen *at least* two feet just to reach the base of the last row of hedgehogs. The hedgehogs themselves were almost 4½ feet high, meaning the tide had a further 18 inches to approach their gusset plates. This means that in the interval between Sargent's and Capa's photos, the tide had risen about 3–4 feet. From 0740 to 0840 hours, the tide was rising at its fastest, about one foot in 11 minutes (based on the tidal charts for that day on the reverse side of the invasion maps).[19] Given that rate and our estimate of a 3–4-foot rise in tide that puts Capa's arrival roughly 33 to 44 minutes later than Sargent's beaching at 0740 hours. In other words, Capa's photos indicate he landed approximately between 0813 and 0824 hours.

Although the preceding analysis would preclude Capa from landing before 0813 hours (Sargent's 0740 hours plus the minimum estimated 33-minute threshold), we'll only block out a 30-minute period as a conservative estimate. In Figure 29, the timeline has been updated to reflect this blocked-out period. The 30-minute period we blocked out necessarily eliminates Wave 10 (Cos. A and C). It also definitively rules out the third landing alternative Capa had considered while still aboard the *Chase*: landing with Co. B. Company B beached between 0750–0755 hours, and the tide could not possibly have come in as fast and far in that time. The 10–15-minute interval since Sargent's photo would have seen only a bit more than a one-foot rise in tide, which could not produce the water level seen in Capa's photos.

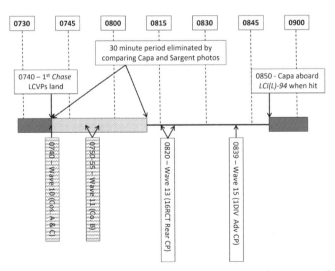

Figure 29. Timeline with 30-minute block added after Sargent's photo, and Waves 10 and 11 eliminated. (Author)

As a result, the only two waves originating from the *Chase* that fall within the period 0810–0850 hours are Wave 13 (because its beaching was delayed from a scheduled 0805 hours to an actual beaching time of 0815–0820 hours) and Wave 15. Recall we eliminated Wave 14 as it consisted only of DUKWs which had been embarked on LSTs, and not the *Chase*.

Returning to the 0813–0824 window we originally derived from analyzing the tide in the two photos, we find it fits with our working hypothesis. In fact, it neatly straddles the 0815–0820 hours beaching time for Wave 13. It would also seem to make a Wave 15 landing less likely.

We have now definitively eliminated two of Capa's supposed landing alternatives: landing with Co. E and landing with Co. B. The only one of Capa's *stated* landing alternatives left is the one that placed him coming in with the rear echelon of the regimental command group, which has been our working hypothesis. In addition to being the last of Capa's alternatives, all the timeline factors point to the same window.

For those familiar with the intricacies of the Normandy planning, it should come as no surprise that this analysis points to Capa landing in one of the two waves specified for a press photographer in the Field Order's landing tables. There is not a shred of evidence that Capa landed outside our window of consideration or with any unit other than the two possibilities specified in the landing tables. This conclusion appears to be rather definitive.

Unreliable Estimates

In preparing this analysis, I made several attempts to use the movement of the *waterline* as an indicator of the passage of time. Having at hand the beach gradient profiles and tide tables, it initially seemed a good line of analysis. It was not. Although those tools did provide the ability to make predictions of the waterline's advance, linking those results to the actual unit combat reports proved impossible in all but one or two cases. For one thing, participants in the landings could only estimate their position offshore when they landed, and these estimates—made hurriedly while under fire—varied widely enough to call their efforts into question. Further, their reports were vague as to whether they were talking about the distances to dry land (the waterline) or the embankment. At best, we can only use the waterline as a very crude estimate, always keeping in mind the vagueness of the statements.

When the LCM of Wave 13 landed at H+110 / 0820, two separate estimates were given by the craft's occupants. The history of the 16th RCT Medical Section reported that it landed about 75 yards from the "*shore*." CPT Ralph, the Headquarters Company commander, reported it was 50 yards from the "*shore*." The difficulty lies in knowing whether the "shore" in these reports referred to the first dry land (i.e., the waterline) or to the shingle/sand embankment (the basis for our WRM calculations).

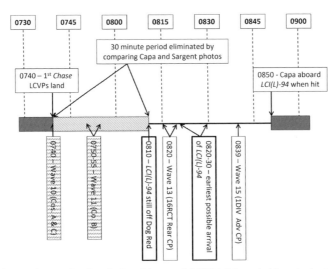

Figure 30. The timeline updated with the addition of *LCI(L)-94*'s probable arrival window. (Author)

Depending on which definition you choose these reports either neatly fit with the WRM calculations, or not. I'll leave it to the reader to decide.

At this point recall our earlier discussion of the *LCI(L)-94*'s beaching time. Because the *94* was still off Dog White at least until 0810, it could not have beached at Easy Red before 0820 hours, and possibly as late as 0830 hours. Based on those conclusions, we'll add two additional points to our timeline (Figure 30). The first marks the *94*'s presence off Dog Red at 0810 hours. The second marks a 10-minute window (0820–0830) which indicates its likely arrival time at Easy Red. The latter will be a key benchmark window when we examine Capa's debarkation photos in the next chapters.

Past Performance

To summarize, all the evidence points to Capa landing between 0810 hours and 0830 hours. Of the three landing alternatives Capa said he considered, the only possible remaining option was landing with COL Taylor in Wave 13. Capa did not mention landing in Wave 15 as a possible option, but this analysis cannot rule it out—though it seems far less likely. Not a single bit of evidence contradicts a Wave 13 (or, less likely, a Wave 15) beaching. It is only Capa's version of events in *Slightly out of Focus* that claims a First Wave landing, and that version is notably not supported by his contemporaneous Wertenbaker interview.

Those who are heavily invested in Capa's own tales of derring-do may recoil in horror at the suggestion Capa landed not in the first wave, but in Wave 13, or, worse, Wave 15. But it should come as no surprise. As noted previously, Capa's record of invasion-day participation is not impressive. He missed the Dieppe Raid. He missed the North Africa landings. Although he did cover a reinforcing airdrop of the Sicily invasion, it was only as a ride-along and not until D+2. Capa then missed the Salerno landings. He did make the Anzio landings, but while he implied that he landed with the commander of the Rangers, he actually landed at least several hours after H-Hour. He evaded jump school, thereby disqualifying himself to jump at Normandy. After the Normandy invasion, he was offered the opportunity to participate in the 82nd Airborne Division's next operation, but he was "not available" when the division was alerted and locked down for Operation MARKET GARDEN. It was not until the British crossing of the Rhine with Operation VARSITY—just six weeks before Germany surrendered and two weeks after the Rhine had already been breached at Remagen—that Capa arrived early in an assault (in this case a parachute jump). Notably, he came in on the same plane as the regimental commander of the second regiment to drop, which tends to support the idea that he landed with the regimental commander on Easy Red, too.[20]

The wonder isn't that Capa landed so late on Omaha Beach. The wonder is that he landed as early as he did, as it was wholly inconsistent with his wartime conduct up to that point. Given what we now know of his actual conduct during the war, it seems incredible anyone would believe the "First Wave with Co. E" story in the first place.

CHAPTER ELEVEN

Easy Red at 0830 Hours

"I never saw the rear of an army engaged in battle but I feared that some calamity had happened at the front—the apparent confusion, broken wagons, crippled horses, men lying about dead and maimed, parties hastening to and fro in seeming disorder, and a general apprehension of something dreadful about to ensue; all these signs, however, lessened as I neared the front, and there the contrast was complete …"

GENERAL OF THE ARMY W. T. SHERMAN

Proceeding on the basis that Capa arrived about 0820 hours, let's focus on the specific conditions at the specific spot in front of the Roman Ruins when he arrived. Although some of this will repeat parts of our earlier narrative, the focus of this chapter will be on the impact of enemy fire on the stretch of beach where Capa landed.

The 7-Yard Beachhead

Lieutenant Spalding's platoon and Co. G had already broken through German defenses atop the bluffs and set out on their respective missions, though word of their success was just filtering back to the men on the beach when COL Taylor (and Capa) arrived. On its way off the beach, Co. G had policed up and taken with them at least parts of the two wayward boat sections from the 116th RCT. In their wake they had left a narrow but clear path off the beach. Co. G's support weapons were still in action in the vicinity of the embankment, attempting with some success to suppress enemy direct-fire weapons sited in WN62; certainly, losses to enemy direct-fire weapons among follow-on landings were lighter after Co. G's support weapons went into operation.

With most of the gap assault teams decimated and the tide covering many of the obstacles, landing craft of following waves were having difficulty determining where it was safe to land. A growing number of landing craft were milling offshore. Gap Assault Teams 9 and 10 had succeeded in completely blowing the equivalent of four gaps through the Easy Red beach obstacles, though apparently only a 100-yard-wide portion was marked and easily visible to landing craft milling offshore. This lone "safe" lane began to draw heavy traffic. Most of the LCTs due in on Wave 8 had been waved off by beachmasters, however, as there was no room on the narrow beach for the vehicles they carried. As a result, a good deal of heavy equipment was not landed, which in turn prevented key follow-on engineer elements from accomplishing their missions. The equipment that had been landed was largely useless, being unable to cross the shingle, and would soon be drowned out by the rising tide.

While smaller craft continued landing, conditions conspired to make some of the units they carried ashore combat-ineffective. Coming in at H+30 / 0700 hours with Co. G in Wave 5 was the provisional antiaircraft battery allocated to Easy Red. It brought in by hand nine M1921 water-cooled .50-caliber machine guns. Or at least tried to. At over 120 pounds, the weapons were too heavy to easily manhandle through the 50 yards of surf and carry under fire across the 200 yards of exposed tidal flats. There are no records as to how many of the nine machine guns in this battery made it to the embankment and went into action on Easy Red. Though there is little record of their contributions, the 397th AAA Provisional Machinegun Battalion noted that three of the 18 guns supporting the two 16th RCT's beaches were given to the infantry, and one gun manned by the air defenders was knocked out by a direct hit while preparing to cover the advance of the infantry.[1] It is possible one or two guns added their firepower to Co. G's heavy weapons. Nevertheless, most of the men of this unit, rendered weaponless and impotent, gravitated to the embankment. They remained there not through a fear of advancing, but because lacking the tools of their trade, they had been made redundant. Absent rifles and mine-clearing equipment, they could not even move forward into hostile country as improvised infantrymen. They were not so much pinned down at the shingle, as they had nothing to do and nowhere else to do it until the tide ebbed and they could try to salvage their weapons from the surf.

Similarly, Co. A of the 81st Chemical Mortar Battalion (with eight 4.2-inch mortars carried in on eight handcarts, and ammunition carried in on eight more carts) came in at 0720 hours in the same ill-fated Wave 7 as the regiment's advanced CP.[2] (A second mortar company, Co. C, was due to land at this time on Fox Green but was unable to land until 1500.) Company A lost several of the carts carrying the extremely heavy (330 pounds each) and unwieldly mortars. The commander was mortally wounded before he could reach the beach. The company reorganized at the shingle and much of the equipment was salvaged later in the day, but they remained confined to the "7-yard beachhead" for the initial hours until the beach flats were cleared sufficiently to permit them to move forward and establish firing positions. In the meantime, the company's idle personnel added to the impression gained by later arrivals that the initial assault waves were still pinned down.[*]

Many of the engineers were in the same state, either because equipment in Wave 4c was late or mis-landed, or because the LCTs of Wave 8 could not land.

---

[*] Despite the company's problems and enforced idleness for much of the day, two of its members earned the Distinguished Service Cross on 6 June.

The situation was exacerbated by the loss of the engineer battalion commander, executive officer and operations officer, which eliminated leadership for the unit. So, the men remained at the embankment where later arriving waves mistook them for assault units still pinned down. An LCI with a mixed load of engineers, medics and signal troops arrived at H+65, and, unable to move onto the beach flats, they too remained huddled at the embankment. Between H+65 and H+110, 34 DUKWs—18 carrying artillery pieces and their gunners—were scheduled in, almost all of which swamped. Many of their surviving artillerymen made it to shore, but with no equipment. Again, lacking the necessary tools of their trade, they remained in the shelter of the embankment.

The commander of the 741st Tank Battalion arrived in Wave 13 with COL Taylor at 0820 hours; until then there had been no command presence on the beach to coordinate the actions of the surviving elements of the three tank companies. Several of the tanks that had succeeded in making it ashore were by then knocked out or immobilized. The survivors fought where they thought best or happened to land. Remarkably, Capa's debarkation photos captured no fewer than five surviving tanks within a hundred yards of his LCVP. A brief motion picture clip showing Capa's landing site at the time he was ashore shows a sixth tank (a DD tank) as part of this group; it was located out of frame to the left of Capa's debarkation photo set. Finally, an additional photo Capa snapped as he was leaving the beach on *LCI(L)-94* showed a seventh tank (a standard tank) atop the embankment just a hundred yards down the beach to the west. As a result, about half the surviving tanks on the entire 16th RCT frontage were located within spitting distance of where Capa landed. His landing site was the one place on the 16th RCT's beaches that was well supported by the big guns of the armor battalion.

The regiment's reserve battalion, the 1st BLT, had landed largely intact and most of it had been reorganizing at the embankment. Company A landed near exit E-1 and took the initiative to attack the WN64 strongpoint. Between Co. A's frontal attack and Spalding's concurrent attack from the rear, WN64's defenders were fully occupied. They had neither time nor weapons to spare for targets in the vicinity of the Roman Ruins several hundred yards down the beach. From that time on, troops landing at the Roman Ruins encountered little or no fire from either directly ahead on the bluffs (cleared by Co. G and Spalding's boat section) or from the western flank (where Co. A and Spalding's boat section were reducing WN64).

Meanwhile, Co. G's advance toward Colleville would soon have a similar effect to the east. Cutting behind the German command post controlling the strongpoints defending the E-1 and F-1 exits, Co. G's advance on Colleville disrupted German communications as well as efforts to supply the strongpoints' dwindling ammunition stores.

Company C and the 1st BLT's command group landed close to Capa's beaching site. The 1st BLT's original mission was to pass through the 2nd BLT and seize objectives two miles beyond the beach, but with no sign of the badly dispersed

2nd BLT or indications that its initial objectives had been captured, Co. C paused temporarily at the shingle awaiting orders, in the meantime blasting five additional lanes through the wire obstacles so they'd be ready to move when orders came. Meanwhile, Co. B landed behind Co. A, but after encountering enemy mines and fire, pulled back, and headed east toward the "safe" route inland at Capa's landing site, and would follow Company C when it climbed the bluffs.

By 0830 hours, the conditions at Capa's landing site were deceptive. Three separate waves of infantry (LT Spalding's section, Co. G and Co. C) had landed. The first two had moved inland and the third was moving (or about to, the time of its movement off the beach was not recorded), soon to be followed by Co. B as it sidestepped to the ruins. It was one of the few spots on the entire length of Omaha Beach where such success was unfolding. And yet, curiously enough, each arriving wave gained the impression that the previous waves were still pinned down and had failed to advance off the "7-yard beachhead." In reality, it was primarily the supporting units, deprived of equipment and hence the ability to perform their tasks, which remained in the partial shelter of the embankment. The infantry on Easy Red had largely advanced successfully; it was, mostly, the hapless support troops that gave the mistaken impression that the invasion had foundered at the shingle.

The classic case of this is found in the report of Co. A's landing. It reported that when it landed, the initial assault waves were still pinned down on the beach. Due to mis-landings, no infantry had landed there before Co. A arrived, only support elements. As GEN Sherman observed 80 years earlier, the impressions gained at the rear of a battle are very misleading.

When the rear echelon of the regimental command group arrived at H+110 / 0820 hours (Wave 13), several factors came together: the commander was on scene and could personally influence the action. News came of the penetration of the bluffs by Spalding's section and Co. G, and Companies C and B of the reserve BLT were on hand and ready to move or were converging to the site. Presented with the opportunity and having the means at hand, the regimental commander exploited the penetration and started the process of clearing the jam on the beach. In short order, Companies C and B were over the bluffs, the regimental CP was established at the foot of the bluffs, and two follow-up regiments had been ordered to land on Easy Red.

But how much of this would Capa have recognized? Probably none of it.

Beyond the Viewfinder

When COL Taylor passed by, gathering his staff behind him and ordering units to exploit the penetration, Capa remained motionless. Although it was Taylor— accompanied by his staff—who walked past and ordered Deery and Tegtmeyer to get up and follow him, Capa apparently failed to notice Taylor. In *Slightly out of*

EASY RED AT 0830 HOURS • 107

Focus he stated that Deery and Tegtmeyer "were the first to stand up on the "Easy Red" beach." It is difficult to believe Capa missed Taylor and his command group as they stopped to collect Deery and Tegtmeyer and moved on.

Indeed, this is our first clue that Capa may never have made it to the shingle. Had he been there in the company of the surgeon and chaplain, it is doubtful he would have told a story so completely at odds with reality. It is even more difficult to believe that Capa could think the first men to stand up on the beach were the chaplain and doctor, especially since men had been fighting on the beach for two hours by that time. But such are the oddities in Capa's versions of history.

His inertia—or fear—prevented him from perceiving that things were somewhat better than they first appeared. As a result, he limited his own situational awareness to the "7-yard beachhead." His entire perspective of the landings was a perfect example of Sherman's description of apparent calamity. He saw only those who could not advance, either due to death, wounds, lack of equipment, lack of orders or lack of will. He seems to have screened out all indications of success or progress. No mention of the tanks firing (at least in his book; in his interview with Wertenbaker, he did note they were firing). No mention of Co. G's supporting weapons in action. No mention of COL Taylor calmly walking upright past him, gathering men in his wake. No mention of nearby infantry units who were together, organized, blowing gaps through the wire or advancing inland.

Ruley, the Coast Guard cameraman aboard *LCI(L)-94*, provided a view that stands out in stark counterpoint to Capa's. While the *94* was beached within yards of Capa, he was alerted by another seaman that a demolition charge was about to go off just past the shingle/embankment, as marked by a purple smoke grenade that had been ignited to warn nearby troops. Much to his chagrin, Ruley missed the shot. It is obvious, however, that Ruley had witnessed yet another gap being cleared for troops to pass through and off the beach. Capa, who was ashore—or at least sheltering in the surf—completely missed this action or its implications. Oddly, Capa, "the Greatest War Photographer in the World," missed what a Coast Guardsman noticed.

One of the problems with combat photography is that press photographers very seldom truly accompany the riflemen in the lead ranks.[3] As a result, much of the work produced by them focuses on the rear areas, documenting the accurate but rather misleading "apparent calamity" in the wake of the battle. As press photographers in WWII were, after all, almost entirely civilians, one can understand their reluctance to wander near a swarm of indiscriminate bullets. Such constrained coverage resulted in a highly distorted view of the battle, yet few people appreciate this inherent distortion. Press photographers in general, and most particularly in the first hours at Omaha Beach, restricted themselves to the rear area of the invasion—usually some distance offshore. In Capa's case it was the area of the tidal flats and shingle (if he got that far), which happened to be a prepared enemy engagement area. And so, his visual record on the beach is limited, focusing on wrack, ruin and apparently helplessness under fire.

There were no photographers there to capture Spalding cresting the bluffs or attacking WN64. No one to memorialize in pictures Co. G's assault on Colleville. Not a single photograph of the lone tank that fought its way through the E-3 draw. No. With the sole press photographer present on the beach unwilling to move forward and looking for a quick way out (as was proper given his mission that day), the photographic record he left us merely documented the depressing chaos in the *wake* of the attack. It is a perspective that is accurate in some respects, but not representative of the unfolding success at the Roman Ruins.

Indeed, Capa's personal perspective was even more distorted. A cursory glance at his photos betrays his misplaced focus. Except for his initial photos from the ramp of his LCVP, all his remaining beach photos are focused not on the actions of the assaulting units at or beyond the shingle, rather they are all angled more or less backwards, offshore. If his camera's viewfinder is any indication, once he found himself in the surf, he was not the least bit interested in the progress of his "old friends" of the 16th RCT as they fought their way inland. It would seem he spent his whole time focused offshore—from which direction he was seeking rescue. Such were Capa's blinders.

In fact, the dynamic was even more overwhelming. Where Sherman's "apparent calamity" would normally be spread and dispersed over a large area behind a normal battlefield, on Omaha Beach at 0830 hours all of that was compressed into a very narrow stretch. The dense concentration of this "apparent calamity"—packed into the "7-yard beachhead"—could well have been overwhelming. And given Capa's previous experiences, it probably was just that. Recall that his only previous assault experience was the initial walk-over at Anzio six months before; and even there, he had landed hours after the assault waves.

All these factors, each reinforcing the next, conspired to make Capa and his camera fairly unreliable witnesses to history. There were obviously extenuating circumstances. Many others, including trained and experienced soldiers, were also initially overwhelmed by the scenes they encountered on the beach. The division had not seen combat since the Sicily campaign had ended the previous August, a peaceful interlude of almost 10 months. Omaha Beach was certainly not a gentle reintroduction to combat for the division's veterans, and it would have been worse for the division's many unblooded replacements. Nevertheless, it is important to recognize that these biases and limitations *are* present in Capa's work that day.

A Reckoning of Blood

To fully understand the context of Capa's stay on the beach, we need to take a moment and challenge one of the most widely held misconceptions of D-Day, and that is the "Bloody Omaha" reputation.

Yes, it was a bloody, costly operation. If you had the poor luck to be in certain small units, it was more than bloody, it was almost a massacre. Yet by WWII standards, it was far from unprecedented. At Tarawa, *one* division of Marines lost over 1,000 men killed in four days of fighting—against an island-bound enemy that could not be reinforced and included no panzer divisions. By comparison, at Omaha, a corps of *four* Army divisions, the division-sized Engineer Special Brigade Group and all the corps-level units combined lost 1,225 men killed in seven days of fighting—against an enemy drawing on mobile and armored reserves hundreds of kilometers away.* Yes, it was costly, but in a war that saw 405,000 American dead in 3½ years of fighting—the vast majority of them in the last 11 months of the conflict—it was not the unique bloodletting that popular history would have us believe.[4]

More germane to this discussion, however, is the uneven bloodletting across the five-mile length of Omaha beach. I've previously alluded to the relatively "light" casualties around the Roman Ruins. It is time to prove this assertion by reviewing the fate of the units that landed there. But first a word of caution.

Most figures for casualties among the 16th RCT are drawn from the regiment's own casualty report. The problem is that the casualty reports normally covered two- or three-day periods. The first casualty report submitted after 6 June covered the period from 0630 hours on 6 June through 1200 hours on 8 June (Figure 31. "Dagwood" was the 16th RCT's codename).[5] In other words, the commonly cited figures for losses on D-Day reflect 53½ hours of fighting—not the 17½ hours of D-Day itself. Furthermore, the figures for losses include those who were missing and believed to be stragglers. They must, therefore, be reduced by the return of 129 men who were listed as missing in the 8 June report but had rejoined the regiment in the next three days—which would reduce the casualty total by just over 13 percent. As a result, the cost of D-Day proper has been rather inflated. But even if we focus only on the casualties suffered on 6 June itself, the lethality of the *beach* is still overestimated; a significant number of casualties suffered on D-Day were lost beyond the bluffs in fighting to secure inland objectives. While these losses may rightly be counted as part of the cost of securing the D-Day beachhead, for our purposes—assessing the lethality of the beach sector where Capa landed—those figures are misleading and distort an appreciation of the actual context.

After the war, the John Hopkins University Operations Research Department, under contract with the Department of the Army, tallied the casualties for the 16th RCT on a day-by-day basis.[6] While these figures still included casualties suffered beyond the bluffs on D-Day, they at least tried to separately identify the 6 June casualties and provide a better baseline. It is these figures which I have generally used below. Figures for units not belonging to the 16th RCT, such as the 81st Chemical

---

* The actual losses at Omaha are a hotly debated topic even today. Rather than get embroiled in that issue, I have merely quoted the figures cited in Omaha Beachhead to provide a rough approximation.

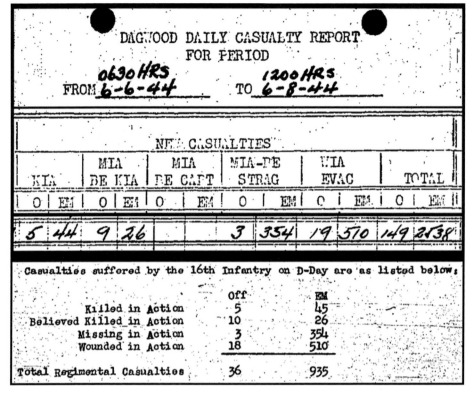

Figure 31. Reported casualties for the 16th Infantry Regiment (not including attached units). Top: 16th RCT initial casualty report covering the first 53½ hours after H-Hour. (Note: the "Total" column shows present for duty strength at the end of the reporting period.) Bottom: Casualty figures as reported in the "CT16 S-3 Combat Report" incorrectly attribute all casualties suffered in the 53½-hours period as happening just on D-Day. (US Army, McCormick Research Center)

Mortar Battalion, are drawn from those units' own reports. The losses among the major units landing at the Roman Ruins follow.

Gap Assault Team 10 (39 men). The first non-tank troops ashore here, they received no enemy fire at all during their initial 20 minutes of work. Although the enemy did engage them following their first gap-clearing detonation, they nevertheless were able to perform their mission and more. Although they took heavy casualties, they still suffered some of the lightest losses among the gap assault teams on Omaha Beach.

LT Spalding's boat section (approximate 32 men) landed next and lost just three men reaching the foot of the bluffs and two more seizing a toehold atop the bluffs. Only one of these five casualties was fatal.[7]

Co. G's corrected casualty figures for D-Day show 49 casualties (rather than the 60–64 commonly cited). This number was reduced to 45 by the return of stragglers. Roughly 20 of the 45 casualties—40 percent—were suffered in fighting beyond the bluffs or from friendly naval gunfire which struck the unit later that day in Colleville. That would mean about 25 men were lost prior to cresting the bluffs. Of these 25, an unknown number were lost when one of the six LCVPs capsized offshore, *not due to enemy fire.* To put this in context, Co. G's authorized strength was 193 officers and men. As with the other assault units, its strength had been beefed up to 222 men in anticipation of casualties, and a further 17 men had been attached from specialty units (medics, naval gunfire spotters, etc.) for a total of 239. The six LCVPs carrying in Co. G held 200 men according to the landing tables (183 from Co. G and 17 attachments). The 39 remaining Co. G men who could not ride in on the initial six LCVPs—the overstrength echelon—came in later in the day with various support waves. So, Co. G's losses prior to attaining the bluffs, and including those resulting from the capsized LCVP, amounted to 12.5 percent of those landing in the six LCVPs, or about 10.5 percent of the company's total strength including attachments. These are not inconsiderable losses, but they certainly are not excessive for an assault landing on a fortified coast. And they most definitely are not as horrific as most Omaha Beach narratives portray.[8]

Co. A, 81st Chemical Mortar battalion, (approximately 90 men), *which spent the entire day at the shingle/embankment or on the beach flats,* lost just two men killed and one wounded.

Co. C, 16th RCT, (approximately 231 men) suffered just 13 or 14 casualties (two different figures are cited) for all of D-Day, to include significant fighting beyond the bluffs, according to the Johns Hopkins study. These light casualties included those taken when one LCVP took a direct hit. (By comparison, the Dagwood initial report reflected 21 casualties for the first 53½ hours after adjusting for the return of a single straggler in the following reporting period.)

Company B, 16th RCT, (approximately 233 men) had one craft take two hits and sink. Nevertheless, it, too, took just 14 casualties for all of D-Day, including fighting beyond the bluffs, according to the Johns Hopkins study. (By comparison, the Dagwood initial report reflected 26 casualties for the first 53½ hours after adjusting for the return of 21 stragglers.)

Wave 13 (approximately 128 men) beached, and its troops made it to the shingle/embankment *without losing a man.* The regimental Medical Section (embarked in this wave) spent the entire day between the waterline and the bluffs, constantly exposing themselves as they collected and treated casualties, and lost just one man, wounded, for the day.

This short summary includes roughly 1,000 men landing before the Roman Ruins. Of these, fewer than 100 became casualties, and a very large proportion of these were suffered not on the beach, but in fighting beyond the bluffs or in craft that foundered offshore, not from enemy action. Since these units were assaulting Hitler's dreaded Atlantic Wall in a high-risk amphibious operation, and so much had gone wrong during the landing, these are surprisingly light losses.

More importantly than the lower casualties, however, is the fact that units landing before the Roman Ruins were able to maintain organization, exercise effective leadership and rapidly take the initiative, excepting only those units which had lost their equipment and were forced to inactivity.

The relatively light losses near the Roman Ruins stand in stark contrast to those suffered a short distance away. Co. A, 1st BLT landed beneath the guns of WN 64 which guarded the eastern side of the E-1 exit and launched a frontal attack on that strongpoint. Despite unexpected assistance from Spalding's section, which attacked that strongpoint from the flank about an hour later, Co. A lost 64 men on D-Day, 45 of whom were hit just trying to cross the antitank ditch on the beach flats below the strongpoint.

I am not implying that the area near the Roman Ruins on Easy Red was a bucolic paradise. The increasing volume of landing craft drew the attention of some of the surviving Germans and their remaining weapons (though their positions were coming under steadily increasing pressure from direct assaults). Much confusion and disorganization reigned, and many men remained inert under cover. Nevertheless, it was one of the least dangerous stretches of beach at that time. Enemy fire came in waves, waves that not surprisingly coincided with the arrival of each new wave of landing craft, or momentary gaps in the billowing smoke from grass fires that helped shield the men from German observed fire.

Many first-hand accounts focused on the shelling, which is usually the primary cause of casualties. But the regiment's Medical Section, operating in the draw beside the Roman Ruins, reported that of the many causes of casualties (mines, artillery, mortars, machine guns, etc.), "the greater [number] of dead resulted from bullet wounds through the head" which it attributed to snipers,[9] but just as likely was due to the fact that the head was the only part the men exposed over the top of the embankment. This is revealing. As the area was at the far end of effective small-arms range from WN62, casualties from small-arms fire would typically be a smaller proportion of the total suffered. And yet they exceeded casualties caused by artillery, which is normally the largest killer on the battlefield.

That means the German indirect artillery fire must have been primarily directed elsewhere along the beach, especially to support the defenses at the beach exits. This is confirmed by a report from the German 352nd Artillery Regiment at 0730 hours, which stated that their fire was concentrated on targets between WN61 and WN62 (the two positions defending the E-3 exit).[10] So Capa's landing site, midway between the E-1 and E-3 exits, received much less indirect fire by comparison. A similar pattern held true for the larger-caliber direct-fire guns, such as the two 75mm guns in WN62. While they could bear on Capa's landing site, their fire was reserved for lucrative targets, such as LCIs, LCTs and LCVPs, rather than small groups of soldiers.

Even when shells were on target, the results of fire were generally not as effective as most histories have portrayed. At least in part, this is because the calibers of enemy direct-fire artillery were generally smaller than popular reports claimed. There were only two 88mm guns among all the Omaha Beach defenses, one at each end of the beach, and the 88mm gun nearest to Easy Red was knocked out by one of the tanks as early as 0710 hours. Among the five strongpoints covering Easy Red, Fox Green and Fox Red beach sectors—a length of over 3,000 yards—the direct-fire guns included the single 88mm gun, six obsolete 75mm or 76.2mm field artillery pieces employed in the direct-fire mode, five 50mm antitank guns and two 37mm guns.[11] So not only were half the defenders' large guns just 50mm or smaller, but most could not bear on the area in front of the Roman Ruins. And of those that could, many were dedicated to covering target sectors elsewhere, especially those immediately in front of the beach exits or the strongpoints themselves. Finally, many of the guns that could bear on the area of the Roman Ruins had been knocked out by the time Capa landed.

Hits from larger-caliber guns could prove disastrous, as *LCI(L)-85*'s damage on Fox Green in front of WN62 demonstrated. But with such a high proportion of lighter-caliber guns, lethality was less than it could have been. One LCVP took a direct hit as it neared the beach, but had only two casualties, indicating the shell came from a light piece. *LCI(L)-94* was on Easy Red for 30 minutes and was not hit until it had debarked its troops and was retracting. Capa's description of the captain, crying and covered in the gore of his "assistant," and the assertion that the craft was listing as they raced to reach the "mother ship" before sinking, made for a good, scary read, but in fact, the *94* made at least two more trips to the beach ferrying troops that day, and worked the beach for several more days. It did not sink, and in fact, suffered as much materiel damage (although no casualties) from crashing through obstacles as from hits by enemy guns. Despite claims that the *94* was hit by 88mm shells, the only enemy gun still in action that could bear on the *94* was the one remaining 75mm field artillery piece shooting in the direct-fire mode from a concrete bunker in WN62 to the east.

By the time Capa landed, the volume of fire *at this stretch of Easy Red* was comparable to what the 16th Infantry Regiment had faced many, many times before in North Africa and Sicily. Not only could individual men move, but entire units were moving through this fire.

Believing What You Don't See

An appreciation of the relatively light enemy fire at the sweet spot on Easy Red is important to our understanding of Capa's pictures. For decades popular interpretation of his photos has dictated that we are witnessing helpless men hopelessly pinned down under murderous enemy fire. And while such carnage certainly did prevail over much of Omaha Beach, it did not at the Roman Ruins on Easy Red. And it is not evident in Capa's photos. It has only been the context in which his photos have been presented that has misled us and caused us not to see what is plainly shown in his images.

In a later chapter we will examine proof of this in Capa's own photos. None of these photos shows the windrows of corpses rolling with the waves at the waterline, as Capa claimed. Despite the lurid descriptions of blood and death at every turn, the photos bear witness to the simple fact that Capa landed at a lightly defended sector of Omaha Beach.

CHAPTER TWELVE

One Hundred Forty Minutes in an LCVP (and Nothing to Show for It)

"Wherever there is light, one can photograph."

ALFRED STIEGLITZ

The SHAEF Public Relations Division had developed a comprehensive list of suggested/desired photo subjects it wanted on D-Day. The list was organized both by service and by phase of the operation with the intent to ensure comprehensive coverage and to minimize duplication.[1] For the phase beginning with landing craft leaving the transport ship until they neared to beach, the list included these subjects:

e. MOVING IN FOR ASSAULT

(1) Sighting of enemy coast as you approach.
(2) Any craft blowing up as they hit shore.
(3) Shots of naval barrage if laid down across beach.
(4) Expressions of men in your boat as it heads toward shore … tense, smiling.
(5) Shots of OIC and helmsman.
(6) Dive-bombers … any near misses …
(7) Enemy fire … explosions of mines, etc.

Capa was surely aware of this list of suggested topics. His pictures of embarkation and time aboard the *Chase* closely adhered to the point-by-point guidance for photos during that phase. His shots of troops sunning themselves on deck through the last glimpse of England picture followed the photo guidance perfectly. Capa knew what was expected of him, both generally as a seasoned war photographer and specifically as a still photo pool cameraman.

So why did he apparently fail to take a single photo during this phase?

One of the most intriguing questions of the Capa D-Day saga concerns the complete lack of photos prior to his LCVP grounding at Easy Red. No pictures of grim men eating their final breakfast before the invasion. No shots of assembly and final inspections. Nothing of the activity aboard the *Chase* as the landing craft were loaded. No offshore photos from an LCVP showing the bombardment. No views of rocket-equipped LCTs shelling the beach. Nothing to capture the tension-packed moments in the LCVP as men steeled themselves for combat, or the danger-fraught final run in to the beach. Not even a shot of neighboring craft swarming to the shore. As incredible as it seems, we have absolutely no photographic evidence that Capa captured a single shot of any of these riveting moments.

Not one.

He did capture the scenes of troops being peacefully ferried to their transports in Weymouth Harbor, exactly as the SHAEF PRD memo instructed. And yet he saw no value in scenes approaching a very hostile shore at a pivotal moment in history?

What responsible combat photographer would have neglected that part of the story? Similar shots of these very same scenes were a staple of D-Day still photography. Chief Photographer's Mate Sargent's fame was assured precisely because of the shots like this he took as Wave 10 approached the beach and landed. Indeed, Capa's only photos of the Sicily invasion consisted solely of these kinds of pre-jump shots which he took when he rode along with the paratroopers. Yet are we to believe Capa didn't think to snap a single photo prior to the ramp dropping on 6 June 1944? That doesn't sound like an experienced war photographer at all.

Out of Order

Those who have read *Slightly out of Focus* may be confused by this discussion. In that book, there is a Capa photo of embarkation (Figure 32). That photo shows an LCVP suspended at deck level from the aft port davit station, with a soldier boarding the craft (an example of rail-loading). The numerals on the LCVP identify the craft as "PA26-26," or LCVP #26 from APA-26, the *Chase* (the P is hidden behind the rope fender). In the background can be seen another attack transport, several smaller landing craft, and a couple of other ships on the distant horizon.

The caption placed the time as "early on the morning of D-Day."[2] On the facing page Capa described the early morning pre-embarkation activities, his embarkation onto an LCVP and his approach to the beach. The reader may be forgiven for assuming Figure 32 was taken before Capa left for the beach. Whether the placement of this photo was done with the intention to deceive the reader, or was due to simple inattention by editors, it had succeeded in convincing some readers that Capa started taking his D-Day photos at the very outset of the landing.

From our recent discussion, however, one problem is immediately apparent with this photo. Sunrise on 6 June 1944 was 0558 hours. Since Capa stated he left the *Chase* shortly before 0600, and since this landing craft is just beginning to be loaded (as evidenced by the lack of heads visible in the craft), then this photo would have to have been taken 10–20 minutes before sunrise. And that is not speculation. Recall the *Chase's* Official Action Report states that the last of its initial rail-loaded LCVP waves was *lowered* by 0601 hours.

We must ask: would there have been sufficient light for this photo before dawn—0558 hours—on an overcast day? The initial response might be to point to the darkness of the photo and agree that it could very well have been taken at dawn. But this is deceptive, as the darkness appears due more to the shot's exposure and being backlit, than due to low ambient light.

Coincidentally, this tableau was also captured by a Coast Guard photographer (Figure 33). The "26" painted on the LCVP's engine hatch indicates this is again a *Chase* LCVP. The identification as LCVP #26 is confirmed by several distinct details common to both photos: the arrangement of cables on the engine hatch is identical (outlined in the solid

Figure 32. Capa's photo showing troops boarding an LCVP on 6 June 1944. (Robert Capa © ICP/Magnum Photos)

white box), as is the knot in the vertical rope (in in the solid black box), and the exact placement of the boat hook (in the double white box). The only difference between the two shots (aside from the angle) is that now the LCVP is nearly full of troops.

Whereas Capa's photo was taken from the LCVP's bow, the Coast Guard photo was taken from the stern, and we can gain a more accurate appreciation of the ambient lighting. It is obvious from this view that these photos were not taken before—or near—sunrise, rather taken well after sunrise and under overcast conditions. A cursory examination of the shadows cast by the helmets on the soldiers' heads indicates that this picture was taken when the sun was well above the horizon—which rules this out as being taken anytime close to Capa's 0600 hours departure from the *Chase*.

Getty Images also holds a copy of this image and credits it to Gallerie Bilderwelt; its caption claims that the craft is on its *second* trip of the day "after the assault in the morning." This supports Capa's statement in *Slightly out of Focus* that when he returned to the *Chase* after his beach excursion, "the last wave of the 16th Infantry was just being lowered."[3] In *This Is War!* Whelan also concluded this photo was taken after Capa's beach excursion and he was back aboard the *Chase*.[4]

Figure 33. A Coast Guard photo showing the same boarding scene that Capa captured in Figure 32. (US Coast Guard/NARA)

For the moment we will accept this "second trip" explanation and delay further discussion of the photo until later. Suffice it to say that it is clear from the lighting that Capa's rail-loading photo was *not* taken before his landing.

Light Matters

Capa appears not to have taken a single D-Day picture until he stood on the ramp of his LCVP as the troops stepped ashore. In his *Slightly out of Focus* version of the event, he appeared to try to indirectly justify this glaring failure without calling attention to it. On the run in to the beach, he stated, "It was now light enough to start taking pictures, and I brought my first Contax camera out of its waterproof oilskin. The flat bottom of our barge hit the earth of France."[5] Keep in mind that in this narrative, he claimed he landed at 0631 hours with the first wave. If we believe this passage, then: 1) he took *no* photos before landing, and 2) the reason was insufficient daylight.

We know Capa did not land at 0631 hours. He landed at 0820 hours, which was just over 3 hours after first light* (0516 hours) and almost 2½ hours after sunrise (0558 hours). With Capa boarding his landing craft at virtually the same moment as sunrise, we can accept poor lighting as an excuse for a lack of photos at that stage. It does not, however, provide an excuse for the lack of photos showing last-minute preparations below decks; one of the three cameras he carried that day could have been prepared for indoor lighting. And it most certainly does not excuse the complete lack of photos for the near 2½ hours he rode in his LCVP before landing. Certainly, Coast Guardsman Sargent had enough light between 0730–0740 hours to shoot his famous pictures of the approach to the beach and the landing of Wave 10. So Capa cannot use poor lighting as an excuse for his lack of photos during his ride to the beach 40 minutes later.

But if insufficient lighting was not an excuse, why do we not have a single photo prior to his LCVP hitting the beach? Even if A. D. Coleman, Ross Baughman, Rob McElroy and Tristan da Cunha had not conclusively disproven the Darkroom Accident fable (which they did do), it would be too much to believe that an accident destroyed every frame prior to the critical first shot on the ramp of the LCVP yet spared all the remaining shots on the same roll of film. There simply has to be another explanation for the absence of photos for the dramatic early stages of Capa's D-Day.

The Missing 28

Capa's first debarkation photo is exposure number 29 from a roll of 38 exposures; that leaves us with three questions: 1) were there ever 28 frames on that roll of film before his first shot on the ramp of the LCVP, 2) if there were, what could have been on those 28 negatives, and 3) why is there no surviving evidence of those 28 negatives?

The first of these questions might seem odd, as most people are used to film coming in prepackaged cassettes with standard numbers of negatives. But one theory has it that Capa's supply of film came in longer rolls that were not prepackaged in cassettes. In this scenario, the photographer would cut lengths of film from the large roll and wind it on spools to fit his requirements. This was an actual practice used by some photographers. If Capa did this, the start of a roll in his camera could be any number that happened to be at the end of the larger roll he took it from. In other words, negative 29 would be the first frame of the roll he self-loaded and there simply would not be negatives 1–28 loaded in his camera. So, it seems that could be possible.

It quickly runs into two problems, however. The right side of negative 38 shows a wider dark border, which indicates the end of the roll of film. So Capa was working

---

* Defined as beginning of Civil Twilight, when the sun is 6° below the horizon. Times used here and throughout the plans, execution and later reports are GMT+2, or British double daylight savings time. There was no need to reset clocks for a new time zone between the UK and operations afloat or ashore.

with a roll limited to 38 exposures, not a longer roll. In theory, he still could have cut down a standard-length roll and used only the last 10 frames, but that would mean he intentionally embarked on his most important assignment having limited his camera to 10 shots. That simply defies belief. Whatever his faults may have been, there is nothing in his background that suggests he would do something so unprofessional.

The second problem is that we know he was using the standard prepackaged film cassettes. The proof of this goes back to Rob McElroy's investigation into the Darkroom Accident fable. Part of that fable points to the off-center placement of the images on the film strip. The images are far enough off center that they cross into the row of sprocket holes on the bottom of the film. Originally the theory held that the off-centered images were a result of the high heat in the drying cabinet causing the emulsion to slip downward. McElroy destroyed that explanation, noting that the film was dried vertically, so if there was any emulsion slip, it would slip along the long axis of the film, not in the direction seen on the negatives. He went on to prove that the offset images were due to the Kodak film cassettes Capa used. They did not fit perfectly in the Contax camera, and the slight free play permitted the cassettes, and the film, to shift slightly downward, resulting in offset images when exposed.

Capa's D-day photos show this typical offset pattern, which means he used the standard prepackaged film cassettes. Which in turn means he wasn't custom-loading his film, so the film in his camera could not have started at frame 29.

That then takes us to the second question: what could have been on those 28 negatives? There are just two possibilities. The first is that he took 28 photos of activity on the *Chase* prior to the beginning of the landing operations. But all his surviving prelanding pictures are paired with pages of caption notes for those rolls of film. Which leads us to the second possibility. The only period he failed to fill out pages of caption notes was during his excursion to the beach and back, which implies those missing 28 negatives were exposed during that same period: specifically, from the time he left the *Chase*, until the ramp of his LCVP dropped and he snapped negative 29. So, the simplest and most obvious explanation is that exposures 1–28 were in all probability taken that morning between loading and landing, most likely in the last hour before landing, when light would be sufficient and the exciting drama of the ride to beach was building. At least that seems to be what Friar Occam's razor would have to say on the matter.

But do we have anything in Capa's narrative that can shed light on this question? Not directly, but we can make a logical inference.

Getting Wet While Holding a Raincoat

Recall Capa's colorful description of joining the assault on Hitler's fearsome Atlantic Wall with his Burberry trench coat draped over his arm (contained in both his accounts). On its surface the idea of hitting the beach in the first wave (as Capa claimed) of an assault on a hostile shore with an expensive new trench coach in hand is just plain odd, and most people tend to dismiss this strange detail as just another bit of Capa eccentricity. But I suggest it's more than that. From the moment the LCVPs shoved off, the troops aboard were showered by spray from the sea, as well as less pleasant liquids from seasick men. Long before any of them even took their first step off the landing craft, they were cold, thoroughly wet, and extremely miserable. So … why did Capa's Burberry remain stylishly draped over his arm, rather than doing its proper job of keeping him dry? In a spray-drenched setting, why was he not wearing his Burberry and instead elected to leave it draped over his arm?

The answer seems obvious. To a professional photographer, what one item is more important than even his physical comfort? His camera, of course. The most logical explanation for not wearing his trench coat was that he was using it to shelter his camera from the sea spray. Which would mean he had at least one camera out of his leather camera bag and out of the camera's waterproof wrapping, ready for use. This was what he advised the soldiers of the 165th Signal Photo Company to do when he spoke to them during their training.[6] From this it is logical to assume that if he had it out, then he was prepared to use it, and almost certainly did use it during the movement to the beach.

But if that were the case, then it would be fair to ask why did he not mention using his camera aboard the LCVP in either of his versions of that day? To answer this, we can only point out that his Wertenbaker interview also neglected to mention his taking pictures from the ramp of the LCVP when it grounded, yet we have five photos that prove he did. In fact, according to that account, he didn't even begin taking photos until he reached dry land, which his photos also disprove. Capa simply did not provide a very complete narrative for Wertenbaker. As for *Slightly out of Focus*, by the time he wrote that, whatever had happened to the missing 28 had taken place three years previously, and I believe Capa merely crafted his later tale to fit the few existing photos that had survived the Darkroom Accident story, which by that time was firmly established.

Sacrificed?

So, if the missing 28 photos *were* exposed during the run in, what happened to them? That's a good question.

Could it be that the lost 28 photos were a sacrifice to the "First Wave with Co. E" myth? Being buried back in Wave 13 (or even 15), his pictures prior to landing would have plainly revealed he was nowhere near the first wave. Instead, shots of the run in would have shown a host of craft preceding him to the beach. Capa's paltry total of 7, 8, 9, 10 or 11 landing pictures (take your choice among the various claims), if taken from back in the pack of the landing order, would be greatly devalued. While they would still have historical value, they would have marginal immediate value in terms of magazine sales, and that was the metric *Life* cared most about. Having just a few shots which could be passed off as first wave photos would have far greater publication punch than many more shots that revealed their intrepid photographer landed much later and under far less sensational conditions. In addition, shots during his 2½-hour run into the beach clearly would have shown far too much daylight over an extended period for an event that he claimed took place just a half hour after sunrise.

It is time to again confront a truth too many wish to ignore. Capa's beach photos are not only technically poor but show very little of real interest. The sole reason they have resonated through the years is the false representation that they were taken in the first wave of the assault and under terrible German fire. Having stripped away both deceptions, his photos are revealed as rather average work which show minor glimpses somewhere to the rear of the advancing forces. That which imbued his photos with false drama and impact, when peeled away, leaves a body of work that paled in comparison to other photographers that day.

Editors know how to package and present photos so that they achieve maximum effect; that is after all, their job. It's possible *Life*'s editors (whether in London or stateside) realized that they had a remarkable marketing advantage: they had the only photos taken *on* any American invasion beach by a *civilian* correspondent before noon on D-Day. They may have played that advantage as fully as they could. Presenting Capa's unremarkable photos as having been taken under extraordinary circumstances—the First Wave myth—transformed them in the eyes of *Life*'s unwary readers, and, as it turned out, to history. The excising of photos from the run in (which were duplicated anyway by other D-Day photographers such as Wall, Sargent and Brandt) would be a small price to pay to achieve the Pygmalion-like transformation of Capa's landing photos.

There is another possible explanation to be considered. We've discussed earlier the vigorous efforts to maintain the FORTITUDE deceptions. It may also be possible that his shots during the run in were sacrificed to the censor's red pen. They simply may have shown too much of the invasion force.

It is, therefore, my conclusion—and admittedly not a proven fact—that he must have exposed 28 negatives on 6 June, during his trip from the *Chase* to the beach. No photographer worth his salt would have failed to document that spectacle. This conclusion also explains why he arrived at the beach with just a quarter of a roll of unexposed film left in his camera. It is the only remotely logical explanation for this set of strange circumstances. The fact remains, however, that we have absolutely no evidence of what was pictured in those initial 28 frames. Nor do we have any solid evidence of what might have happened to those 28 frames, whether they were sacrificed to the "First Wave" myth, cut by a censor, or suffered yet a different fate.

Nevertheless, this is the most reasonable explanation for the facts. Given this, I'll proceed on the assumption (unproven, but probable), that Capa arrived at Easy Red with 28 exposed frames in his camera that documented at least part of the trip from the *Chase* to the beach.

CHAPTER THIRTEEN

Capa on the Beach—In His Own Contradictory Words

"I believe in equality for everyone, except reporters and photographers."
MOHANDAS GANDHI

"Will not the caption become the most important component of the shot?"
WALTER BENJAMIN, *A SHORT HISTORY OF PHOTOGRAPHY*

As with the rest of his D-Day legend, his time *on* the beach is rife with contradictions and questions. At the heart of this confusion are his two principal versions. In neither version did he allude to his role in the still camera pool, or the need to return to the UK as soon as humanly possible. So, he had to come up with plausible excuses for leaving the beach.

Wertenbaker's Interview

As noted earlier, in the Wertenbaker interview Capa stated that after debarking from his landing craft, he made his way to the cover of "some tanks that *were firing on the beach*" (emphasis added).[1] He waited there for what he estimated to be 20 minutes, then, realizing that the tanks were drawing fire, he made his way to the beach (by which he apparently meant the shingle/embankment). "It was very unpleasant there and, having nothing to do, I start shooting pictures. I shoot for an hour and a half and then all my film is used up." At that point he fled to a nearby LCI that was discharging troops. Presumably the idea that he had "used up" all his film provided the rationale for Capa to seek safer places; he'd done his job, had no more film to shoot, so there was no reason to stay (he did not mention the need to get his film quickly back to London). It was the lack of film, not a lack of courage that prompted his flight. Between the time it took to work his way to the tanks, the 20 minutes behind the tanks, the time it took to work his way to the embankment and the 90 minutes taking pictures there, this version has Capa spending a good two hours on the beach before fleeing. At this point he hadn't mentioned the First Wave myth, and frankly gave a time for departing the *Chase* consistent with COL Taylor's Wave 13. By this reckoning, he must have left the beach at about 1020 hours, based on the conclusion he landed in Wave 13 with COL Taylor's command post. But if Capa's timeline here is correct, the movement of troops off the beach would have been well underway by 1020 hours, a movement he could not have missed. In addition, the follow-on 18th RCT was landing about that time, a major movement Capa also seemed to have missed. Finally, it would have been high-water stand at this time, but photos taken from the craft that took him from the beach prove high tide was at least an hour away. As a result, his assertion that he stayed that long on the beach is not credible—a conclusion that fits with our previous information that he was already aboard the *LCI(L)-94* when it was hit at 0850 hours.

According to this version, the only point at which he took photos was at the shingle. He failed to mention taking pictures from the ramp of his landing craft, despite the evidence of his own pictures showing he did so and made no mention of the coxswain booting him off the ramp. There was no mention of sheltering behind a hedgehog or taking pictures there, and no mention of taking photos while sheltering behind the tanks. Nor is there any mention of running into the regimental chaplain, surgeon, or fellow correspondent Jack Thompson once he reached the shingle.

Capa's claim that he continued taking pictures until he *had used all his film* is extremely curious, as Wertenbaker noted Capa took just 79 pictures "of the fighting on the beach." Seventy-nine photos are very close to the 76 pictures Capa might have squeezed out of two rolls of film (assuming he managed to get 38 exposures from a roll with a nominal 36 exposures, as we know he did with the roll for the "Magnificent 11" photos). So, Wertenbaker's comment seems to indicate that Capa only used two rolls on the beach (apparently including the missing 28 exposures in that tally). Are we supposed to seriously believe that Capa arrived to cover THE major invasion of the war, but took so little film with him on his adventure? That is simply not credible, especially considering his following sentences in which he revealed that upon boarding the LCI he changed film in his cameras and began shooting more pictures. And he did take several photos on the LCI as it returned to the Transport Area. So, he still had fresh film when he left the beach. This indicates the "no more film" excuse for leaving the beach was not true. Perhaps he only meant that he used up the initial roll of film in each of his two cameras? But if that is so, why did he not change film on the beach and continue photographing?

The confusion that characterizes this version of his landing appears to be quite genuine. In a 19 July 1944 letter to his brother, he wrote: "Cornell, please write how my pictures were, I do not know what I was taking, what got lost and how are the ones which got printed."[2] From this it seems he was badly rattled and not fully aware of his own actions or the events taking place around him.

Slightly out of Focus

In his memoirs published three years later (1947), Capa told another version, one chiefly differing in the inclusion of fanciful detail, and one that painted a far bloodier environment.[3] One cannot escape the conclusion that Capa "sexed up" this landing narrative to make for a more sensational book.

In this version, he began shooting with one camera on the ramp of his landing craft, got booted—literally—off by a sailor, then took shelter behind an obstacle and continued shooting pictures. His photos do not, however, show that he snapped any pictures while sheltering at an obstacle. He then made his way to the shelter of a (now) burned-out tank, but in this version made no mention of taking pictures there or of tanks firing. He then moved to the shelter of the shingle, where he switched to his second camera and continued shooting. Having finished the roll in his second camera, he reached for a replacement roll but ruined it before he could load the camera. Shortly thereafter he was overcome by fear and fled to a nearby LCI.

By this accounting, he shot—again—at most two rolls. This would total not more than 50 exposures, or not more than 76 exposures, depending on whether you include the missing 28 photos. And yet, he claimed his total of shots while on Easy Red was 106, which would have to include a third roll of 35mm film, a roll he never mentioned in his narrative while on the beach.

Notably, in his own book Capa quietly omitted the claim that he spent almost two hours on the beach; in fact, he gave no indication at all how long he spent there. He also dropped the claim that he used up all his film while on the beach. As far as we know from this version, he only exposed the original roll in each of his two cameras and ruined a third roll. In this version, he didn't run out of film on the beach; he frankly ran out of courage.

Also in this version, Capa introduced his encounter with the regimental chaplain and surgeon, but again curiously omitted any mention of Jack Thompson, who, riding in on the same LCVP with COL Taylor, was almost certainly Capa's fellow passenger. And although Thompson later noted Capa's presence on the beach, Capa did not reciprocate.

This version also introduces another curious detail. As he approached the beach, he stated, "It was now light enough to start taking pictures, and I brought my first Contax camera out of its waterproof oilskin." Ignoring for the moment the disingenuous comment about the light conditions and focusing on the oilskin, at first glance this seems a perfectly normal precaution to have his camera safely tucked away in a waterproof cover during a landing. But curiously, he made no mention of an oilskin wrapping in the Wertenbaker interview, and it wasn't part of the advice he gave to the men of the 165th Signal Photo Company. There is no proof, but to me it appears to be a detail he fabricated later—along with the deceptive comment about light conditions—to explain why he took no photos during the ride to the beach.

And finally, in this more harrowing version, Capa's LCI had become a sinking ship which he was fortunate enough to leave before it sank.

As I said before, nothing about the Capa legend is simple.

Confused Counts

There are some aspects common to both his landing narratives. In both versions, as his craft was en route to the beach, they encountered returning craft that had landed the first wave of troops; in light of this, it is strange that the "first wave" myth can endure. And both versions included the curious detail that he landed with his elegant Burberry raincoat over his arm, which he quickly discarded. Both versions included the tale of the soldier who "saw" his mother waving his insurance policy. As in the Wertenbaker version, Capa's memoirs repeated the claim that after boarding the LCI he reloaded "both cameras" with fresh film and resumed taking pictures, at least 11 of which we know survived the supposed "Darkroom Accident."* Beyond that, few details match between the two versions. He even quotes himself differently as he mutters under his breath (*"Mon vieux,* this is not so good" vs. the Spanish phrase *"Es una cosa muy seria,"* i.e., "This is a very serious business").

And again, the two versions cannot even agree as to how many pictures Capa took and how many survived. In the Wertenbaker version, the interviewer appended the comment that Capa took 79 photos "of the fighting on the beach," of which only *seven* survived. In Capa's own book, he summed up the day's work by saying he took 106 pictures on Easy Red, of which only *eight* survived. Whether the surviving total is seven (Wertenbaker) or eight (Capa), neither tallies with the number of shots on the digitally recreated contact sheet—which shows nine, not including the "Face in the Surf" picture (which would be number 10) or the additional photo John Morris (his photo editor in London) claimed existed (a number 11?).

Both Wertenbaker's version and Capa's version seem to agree that he used only two rolls of film ashore on D-Day (despite Capa's spurious claim of 106 pictures). The simple fact is that two rolls of film (one of which began at frame 29) is an astoundingly small number of shots for the coverage of the pivotal battle on the Western Front. And the confusion is only compounded by the fact that there is no evidence whatsoever of film from his second camera on the beach.

Myth Busted

Yet even these modest claims are doubtful. The excuse given for the small number of "surviving" photos has been that all the rest—however many that might have been—were ruined in a darkroom accident by a hapless intern (variously identified

---

* These include five photos which were printed in the 19 June 1944 issue of *Life* and one in Wertenbaker's *Invasion.* More on the latter later. The fact that *Life* printed as many photos of Capa *after* he left the beach (five photos) as they did of his combat shots (again, five photos) reflects the reality that there were very few shots on the beach to choose from.

as Dennis Banks or Dennis Sanders). But research by Coleman, McElroy and da Cunha has definitively proven that this explanation is simply not technically credible. Their research is so convincing that even Morris—the man who had originated and pushed the Darkroom Accident explanation for 70 years—finally acknowledged that Capa must not have taken more than a dozen or so shots on Omaha Beach—possibly with just one of his cameras.[4]

That was an explosive development, one that forces a complete reevaluation of the Capa saga. What set of circumstances could have resulted in the "Greatest War Photographer in the World" fleeing the scene of the best story of his life, after taking so few photos? Was it a lack of courage? Lack of film? Or the need to get his film back to London as quickly as possible? Or a combination of these?

Could Morris's belated conclusion be correct? We have already shown that Capa could only have spent 30 minutes—at the maximum—ashore on Easy Red. Morris's admission would seem to indicate that Capa spent an incredibly brief part of that time snapping those 10 shots. That seems hard to believe, especially since nine photos of three separate scenes were snapped in rapid succession.

Yet when we examine Capa's own film, we find support for the conclusion that he spent only a few brief moments taking pictures. We can judge just how brief by comparing the water height on the most shoreward row of hedgehogs in his first set of photos and his last photo. Figure 34 is a detail from Capa's negative 32, one of the initial series of five shots taken quickly in succession in the brief moments he stood at the ramp of his LCVP. Figure 35 is a detail from Capa's negative 38, the last known shot he took on the beach. Prominent in each shot are hedgehog obstacles in the same obstacle row. There is virtually no difference in the height of the tide between the two shots. And, indeed, when examining all Capa's shots we find this holds true, even when considering the minor variations caused by dying waves as they roll in and recede. What does this tell us? Plenty, actually.

Figure 34. Detail from Capa's Negative 32. (Robert Capa © ICP/Magnum Photos)

Figure 35. Detail from Capa's Negative 38. (Robert Capa © ICP/Magnum Photos)

From our previous discussion of the tides, we know that during the brief time Capa was in the surf or ashore, the tide rose a foot about every 11 minutes. Despite this rapid rise, there is no meaningful difference in the levels of the tide between Capa's first set of photos (Figure 34) and last (Figure 35) photo. Indeed, what little rise in tide evident in Figure 35 can arguably be attributed to the visible dying surge of water from an incoming wave. If Capa spent anything more than just a few minutes taking pictures, there should have been a substantial difference in water levels.

To put this in perspective, Figure 36 is a detail of the photo taken by LT Gislason from *LCI(L)-94*. At the time this photo was taken, the ship was still offloading troops and, according to Capa's narrative, he had not yet boarded. That places this photo sometime before 0850 hours (when the ship was hit by German fire). Note the hedgehog highlighted in white. It is in the same row as those shown in Figures 34 and 35, and just a few yards from them. The height of the water on the hedgehog in Figure 36 almost covers the entire obstacle. Figure 34 was taken at 0820 hours when Capa's LCVP beached, Figure 35 was taken some time after that, and Figure 36 was taken at least a few minutes before the *94* was hit at 0850 hours. The marked difference in tide height between Figures 34 and 36—separated by only 20–25 minutes—is obvious, clearly indicating how fast the tide was rising. By comparison, the difference in tide levels between Capa's first set of photos, Figure 34, and his last photo, Figure 35, is negligible.

Figure 36. Detail from Figure 13—a picture taken aboard the *LCI(L)-94.*

There is only one possible explanation for the apparently static water level between Figure 34 and 35: very little time passed between Capa's arrival on the beach and the time he stopped taking pictures. With the Darkroom Accident fable discredited, and lacking any evidence at all that he took photos from the vicinity of the embankment, the logical conclusion is that Capa spent a very, very short time taking pictures. Based on the difference in tide—certainly less than half a foot—it seems Capa must have spent fewer than six minutes using his camera.

We now have a better handle on how Capa spent his limited time ashore. His entire stay on the beach was something less than 30 minutes—between his landing at 0820 and when he was aboard the *94* as it was hit retracting from the beach at 0850, during which, it appears, he spent fewer than six of those minutes actually taking photos. And even that seems generous.

Let's now turn to the beach photos themselves and see what we can learn from them. In outline, the 10 photos consist of three sets of shots (each focusing on a separate scene) and one individual shot. Although Morris claimed there was one more, there is no evidence for it, and therefore it cannot be analyzed here.

- The Debarkation Set. Includes five photos taken from the ramp of his LCVP, focusing on debarking troops heading for cover (negatives 29–33).

- The Engineer Set. Includes two photos showing a group of engineers apparently preparing an obstacle for demolitions (negatives 35 and 36).

- The Face in the Surf. One photo showing a lone soldier struggling in the water. No original negative exists for this photo, so it is assumed to represent negative 37 which is missing in the digitally recreated contact sheet.

- The Obstacle Forest Set. Includes *two non-sequential*—but nearly identical—photos showing a very dense swath of beach obstacles (negatives 34 and 38).

CHAPTER FOURTEEN

The Debarkation Set

"If your pictures aren't good enough, you aren't close enough."

ROBERT CAPA

The first five photos (negatives 29–33, Figure 37) were taken as Capa stood in the open bow of his LCVP and show the troops of his craft wading toward shore shortly after they debarked. In the middle distance there is the concentration of armor that we discussed earlier. There are two duplex drive tanks in the center, identifiable by the canvas floatation screens (which are still partly raised) and their single chimney-like air duct. One DD tank is faced away from the camera, and the second is broadside facing to the left (east) and has a distinctive white life preserver hanging on its flotation screen. There are also three "standard" tanks, identifiable by the wide, twin air ducts which are bolted to the engine compartment; the ducts are part of the "deep wading kit" and can be identified by the forward-curving tops. The tank on the far right still has its ammunition trailer attached. The second standard

Figure 37. Capa's first set of five photos showing troops debarking. (Robert Capa © ICP/Magnum Photos)

tank—just to the left of the DD tank with the life preserver—may also still have its ammunition trailer, but the troops clustered behind make verification impossible. As noted previously, the third of these three standard tanks—tank #10—is actually the tank dozer supporting Gap Assault Team 10; these three tanks were supposed to land four minutes before their teams, and the large numerals painted on the dozer tank were used to guide the gap assault team into the same stretch of beach. Because of the angle of the tank and soldiers clustered around it, the dozer blade is not visible.

As we also discussed earlier, Capa claimed one of these five tanks was "half-burnt," but that is exaggeration. Tanks that have been set afire burn for extended periods, producing thick black smoke. Nothing of that sort is noticeable in this series of photos, or in photos shot of this area later in the day. A tank might have been immobilized, though, and even temporarily abandoned, but photos of this area later that morning indicate it must have been fixed or re-crewed as all five of these tanks were repositioned a couple hours later.

Just beyond the farthest tanks can be seen the shingle/embankment, which, at this time, has not been breached by dozers and still prevents the tanks from moving inland. The darker and lighter bands of the shingle/embankment can be seen. Troops are sheltering at each band, but the ones on the upper portion are most noticeable due to their contrast with the lighter color (highlighted in white, Figure 38). It is likely, though impossible to prove, that the troops sheltering against the lower, darker band are men from units that have lost their equipment, such as the mortar and antiaircraft companies that landed there earlier. Their primary concern would be safety. Similarly, the men higher up on the embankment are likely "still in the fight," either firing back at German positions or preparing to move through the

Figure 38. Detail of Capa's Negative 31. (Robert Capa © ICP/Magnum Photos)

gaps in the barbed-wire obstacle at the top of the sand. These could include some of the men from Co. G, which placed its machine guns and mortars there (between 0700–0730 hours) to provide covering fire for the rest of the company as it moved inland. Or it is possible they are men from Co. C, 1st BLT (Wave 10 / 0740 hours), which may still have been awaiting orders before heading inland.

Because the embankment was higher than the beach flats behind it, we can't see any troops that may be moving inland at this time. The most we could expect to see is individual men crossing the top of the embankment in single file through a gap in the barbed-wire obstacles. Noted military historian Brigadier General S. L. A. Marshall observed, "Here as elsewhere on D-Day, movement was not made by 'charges.' Each section of 20 to 30 men tended to advance in an irregular column, sometimes in a single file, and was often checked by a burst of enemy fire or the discovery of mines."[1] Because of the embankment, we don't see even that.

The primary focus of this set, however, is the group of soldiers who have just exited the landing craft and are making their way toward shore. A glance at these photos confirms that these soldiers are *not* from one of the assault infantry companies. As several observers have noted, none of the specialized weapons or equipment the assault troops carried can be seen in the photos. No bazookas, no machine guns, no mortars, no Bangalore torpedoes, no flamethrowers. Instead, the most common equipment in the photo consists of bulky, oddly shaped, hand-carried bundles or satchels; they appear to be M1944 cargo packs or similar bags. This looks exactly like a group of staff personnel burdened by awkward non-combat loads. This is also exactly what we would expect to see carried by the various headquarters personnel that came ashore in the two waves that we postulated for Capa.

While Capa and others (such as MAJ (Dr.) Tegtmeyer) provide bloody descriptions of the troops being decimated while landing, that is not depicted in these shots. There are no splashes from incoming small-arms fire, or explosions from artillery. Only in negative 31 (Figure 38, above) can we see any indication of weapons fire, and that is a faint dust or smoke cloud which *appears* to indicate the right-hand DD tank has fired its main gun. There are men prone in the surf—most behind or near obstacles—and others are seen falling. Whether they are wounded, merely tripped, or have had a failure of courage cannot be determined. Still, their postures do not convey the sense of death or serious injury which combat veterans readily recognize. Nor can you see the rows of corpses that were supposed to be floating at the waterline. Not a single one, in fact. Which is amazing, given that this is almost two hours into the landings. As other photos attest, the many dark shapes floating in the surf are discarded life belts, not corpses.

Reinforcing this impression of *relative* calm is the number of men continuing to make their way upright to the shingle. Even those who have taken shelter behind tanks do not give the impression of sheltering from active, effective fire to save their lives from imminent death. They give the impression of men who automatically

Figure 39. A detail of Capa's Negative 32, showing troops taking momentary shelter behind a tank. (Robert Capa © ICP/Magnum Photos)

sought cover, not because they had to, but because it seemed natural to do so. They look like they have taken the opportunity to prudently pause behind the tanks while they look around to get a feel for what's going on. Which is a perfectly natural instinct when entering a dangerous situation, but when the source of danger is not yet apparent.

Another analysis suggested that the men sheltering behind the nearest tank (#10, in Figure 39) indicate that this part of the beach was primarily under fire from WN64 (to the west, or right), rather than WN62 (to the east, or left), and concluded that Capa's landing site is farther west than we have determined in this article. The logic underpinning that conclusion was that far more men are sheltering on the left side of the tank, so the danger must be coming from the right. That analysis dates to before Capa's landing site was definitively located, and flies in the face of the fact that the Roman Ruins was closer to WN62. The simple reason that more men are sheltering on the left side of the tank is that side of the tank was twice as long as the vehicle was wide. There was simply more room for shelter.

In fact, both the left side and rear of the tank could only provide shelter against fire coming from directly ahead on the bluffs. The men on the left side of the tank are exposed to any oblique fire coming from WN62, out of frame to the left. And those men sheltering at the rear of the tank are exposed to any oblique fire coming from WN64, out of frame to the right. Since men are sheltering in both spots, it indicates they are not receiving fire from either location. And since the bluffs straight ahead were, by that time, cleared of enemy by Spalding's section and Co. G, this indicates the men are not currently under effective enemy fire, rather they just automatically sought shelter as they got their bearings.

How do we reconcile what we see in these photos with the various descriptions to the opposite? Capa's view was very narrow, and Easy Red was a large sector. Both the accounts of carnage and the pictures of relative calm and safety might both be accurate, being separated merely by a few score yards or a few minutes. Combat is like that.

Part of the answer also probably lies in the nature of the defense. Sustained fires simply could not be placed on all sectors of the beach all the time. For instance, in the two hours between the beginning of the invasion to Capa's landing, a single enemy machine gun firing at its sustained rate of fire could theoretically fire almost 20,000 rounds. Resupplying that gun, and the dozens of others deployed there, would be a significant problem, and local ready magazines could not hold that much ammunition. The problem was equally daunting for larger-caliber guns with their much bulkier rounds. As a result, fire discipline had to be maintained, and fire had to be reserved for lucrative and priority targets. Certain sectors, in front of the beach exits for example, would have a high priority for coverage, whereas Capa's sector of Easy Red would be of lesser immediate concern to the defenders. In addition, larger-caliber guns would reserve their fire for selected, high-value targets, such as larger landing craft. So, a small stretch of beach like Capa's part of Easy Red might see virtually no incoming fire for extended periods, and then suffer surges of fire, usually coinciding with the arrival of larger landing craft. Meanwhile, a stretch of beach a hundred yards away that had been getting pounded might suddenly experience a pause.

We can find proof of this in the official records. The 16th RCT's report of the actions on D-Day has this to say about the landing of the rear echelon of the regimental command group in Wave 13:

> At H+110 ramps of the LCVP and LCM (comprising CP personnel) were lowered. The craft had been under enemy artillery fire and MG fire on the way in. There was no fire when personnel waded only a short distance, waist deep, because the tide had risen. … When the last man exited the LCM, the craft was brought under fire.[2]

This passage almost exactly describes Capa's experience—and reinforces the conclusion that Capa did land in the LCVP mentioned in the quote. It also perfectly explains why Capa could take several pictures from the ramp of the landing craft, while fully exposed yet undisturbed by enemy fire. It also explains why those troops apparently are not subject to incoming fire. It would seem Capa got his initial photos just before German attention was drawn back to his beach sector as "the last man exited the LCM." The LCM followed the LCVP into shore and, with many more troops aboard, would take longer to get the last man off. The after-action report of the 16th RCT's Headquarters Company covering this incident is very similar, with another key point added:

> The rear CP Group, in one L.C.V.P. and one L.C.M., left the "Chase" at approximately 0615 hours, and proceeded towards the beach. At about 0815 hours the ramp was lowered. The boat

was about 50 yards from the shore. The boats had been under some artillery and machine gun fire on the way in, but as the ramp was lowered there was no fire immediately. The men went off orderly, into the water, waist deep. All equipment was gotten off. As the last few men were getting off, the L.C.M. was brought under fire, but no one was hit. There was no sand bar to cross, such as the Advanced Group experienced, and the distance to the beach was much shorter, due to the fact that the tide had risen considerably.[3]

"... but no one was hit." To repeat, this was precisely the LCM in which MAJ Tegtmeyer arrived, and was just a few yards away from the LCVP in which Capa arrived. And yet no one was hit. This report was written by CPT Ralph, the Headquarters Company commander himself, the man responsible for his company's personnel accountability and casualty reporting, and apparently also the Army troop commander for that LCM. It was written within 10 days of the landing, when memories were fresh. If he said no one was hit, we must believe it, and in turn question the more dramatic descriptions of Capa and Tegtmeyer, which were written a few years later.

Ralph's description of the *advanced* CP's landing—which took place an hour earlier and apparently some distance to the east—*does* mention "there were dead and wounded all over, on the beach, in the water," but he makes no mention of such details where the *rear* CP landed an hour later. Nor do Capa's photos show it.

It is a testament to the power of narrative—and perhaps the general public's naiveté as well—that Capa's bloody tale has convinced us for seven decades that his pictures depict something that quite clearly is not evident in those photos. There isn't a single indication of the many corpses rolling with the waves at the waterline in Capa's photos, yet we have long ignored the evidence of our eyes—even of Capa's own photos—and blindly accepted his highly exaggerated description of gore and death.

As alluded to above, MAJ Tegtmeyer provided an excellent example of the unreliability of first impressions. In his book, he devoted several paragraphs to graphical descriptions of the bloody mayhem surrounding him on the beach, and the near certain death that awaited anyone who exposed himself. There is an explanation for MAJ Tegtmeyer's graphic perspective. Within moments of landing, he was whisked away by COL Taylor and thrust into the carnage on some of the bloodier stretches of the regiment's beaches. He can be forgiven if, in later years, his impressions *after* landing may have colored his recollections of the debarkation itself. Nevertheless, from the moment MAJ Tegtmeyer rose to follow COL Taylor, he and his entire medical section moved throughout the hell on the beach and worked on casualties while fully exposed for the remaining 13 hours of daylight. And as already noted, *they suffered only a single casualty themselves* (one man wounded). This shows how powerfully misleading the initial shock of combat can be, and how quickly a good commander can shake men out of it.

CHAPTER FIFTEEN

The Engineer Set[1]

"Photography deals exquisitely with appearances, but nothing is what it appears to be."
DUANE MICHALS

Capa's five shots from the bow of his landing craft would prove to be fully half of his tally of known D-Day beach photos, yet he had not even stepped into the surf at that point. That was about to change. In *Slightly out of Focus*, Capa claimed that his departure from the landing craft came because of a boot in the rear from the boatswain,* who mistook his pause while taking pictures as a reluctance to debark.

For the moment, we'll skip his next photo (negative 34) and examine the two-photo Engineer set that includes negatives 35 and 36. These photos were taken at some point after his enforced debarkation and before reaching the shingle (if he ever got that far). The focus of the set is a group of men lying prone around one of the steel hedgehogs. One of the figures is often identified as a corpse. Slightly to the right rear is another hedgehog with at least one man partially obscured by that obstacle. In the center rear are a log ramp obstacle and a pole obstacle. Two men are at the pole obstacle in the first photo; in the second photo, the second man has moved to the right and is barely visible between the left and center arms of the right hedgehog. Behind these are three (Figure 40) and four (Figure 41) landing craft heading into the beach.

There's a bit of confusion as to where Capa was when he took these photos. In the Wertenbaker interview, he claimed he started taking photos

Figure 40. Capa's Negative 35. (Robert Capa © ICP/ Magnum Photos)

* Presumably he meant bowman.

only *after* reaching the shingle, but his pictures show just the opposite; we have photos from in the surf, but *none* at the shingle. In *Slightly out of Focus*, he claimed to have taken pictures while behind a hedgehog, while sheltering behind a tank and while at the shingle. We have no evidence that he took any photos from the shingle, but it is possible this Engineer set was taken from behind either a hedgehog or a tank. Let's see if we can determine which.

Figure 41. Capa's Negative 36. (Robert Capa © ICP/Magnum Photos)

All Capa's photos of the beach show a single row of slightly staggered hedgehog obstacles. A brief clip of motion picture film of this area taken by Coast Guardsman David Ruley shows an oblique angle of this same area and confirms there is not a second row of hedgehogs (examined in more detail in the next chapter). These hedgehogs are visible in every single photo Capa took while in the surf, and it is clear he was *forward* of the obstacles when he took the photos. Judging from those pictures, he was perhaps 15 but certainly not more than 20 yards forward of the hedgehogs. The only point offering cover in that area was tank dozer #10, and that appears to be where he sheltered while taking his five photos in the surf. As we'll see later, we can definitely place him there when he took the Face in the Surf photo, so it is safe to say that was also his position when he took the Engineer set.

This disproves his assertion that he stopped and took pictures in the shelter of a hedgehog. He may have briefly paused behind one of those obstacles, but the consecutive numbers on his negatives means that he took no intervening photos between those he took on the ramp and those he took at the tank dozer. The only way this part of his narrative could be true would be if he used his second camera while sheltering behind a hedgehog. While he did have two Contax cameras with him, not a single negative from a second roll has ever surfaced. With the Darkroom Accident myth debunked, that catchall explanation for missing photos vanished. The lack of photos taken at the hedgehogs indicate none were taken there.

Creative Captioning

As noted earlier, after Capa left the beach early that morning on *LCI(L)-94*, he and his film eventually made it back to Weymouth; Capa sent the film by courier to *Life's* offices in London, without explanatory notes. Captioning the images was left to those who had never witnessed an amphibious assault, much less the Omaha Beach landings. So, it fell to assistant associate editor Dennis Flanagan in the New York office to create captions for these photos, based on background information contained in *The New York Times* article (which originally printed a pool version of the photos) and Flanagan's own observations of the photos.[2] By the time that film reached the *Life* offices, the ordeal of Omaha Beach was beginning to be known. A cursory glance at negative 35 appeared to illustrate precisely that theme. As a result, *Life*'s Flanagan penned the following caption when that photo was printed in the 19 June 1944 edition of the magazine:

> Men in the second wave also take cover until all their boats have come in. Behind them men are jumping into water up to their necks. Their heads can be seen just above surface. Combat engineers cleared lanes through obstacles farther off shore so that boats could get in.

And with this piece of inventive fiction coming from the pen of a stateside staffer, that interpretation of the photo became cemented in the popular imagination, whether it was true or not. Knowing no better, the American public accepted it as gospel for more than 70 years.

This narrative was echoed by scores of later books and articles on D-Day. With so few photos available to illustrate the initial landings from the beach perspective, Capa's photos were used almost indiscriminately to illustrate a wide variety of Omaha Beach topics, with little attention paid to relevance or accuracy. Lacking other sources of photos, they became the still photo equivalent of B-roll footage. Even the Army's official history of the Omaha landings (*Omaha Beachhead, 6 June–13 June 1944*) fell into this trap. It included negative 35 and provided it with this caption:

> The obstacles were used as shelter by assault troops facing the task of crossing the tidal flats under full exposure to enemy fire, but the delay often resulted in heavier losses. Landing craft in the background are having trouble in the outer obstacles.[3]

The problem with the "men pinned down in the surf" narrative was that while it was true at many points on Omaha Beach—especially in front of the heavily defended beach exits—we've proven that Capa himself landed at a stretch that was under relatively light fire. As noted earlier, this fact led to that section of beach being the springboard for one of the decisive advances on D-Day. So, when Flanagan added a caption that was accurate in the *macro* sense—but inaccurate for that particular scene—he condemned the photo to misinterpretation for decades to come.

Let's take a fresh look at Capa's negative 35 (Figure 40), free from the bias of the captions. First, we'll make a 3D recreation of the men in the shot and their relative positions. (Figure 42)

Now, taking this model, viewing it from above, and orienting it in relation to the shoreline (Figure 43), an important fact becomes obvious. Only one of the men (#2) is positioned so the hedgehog will protect him against frontal fire from the beach (the solid white arrow). The top man (#1) is just too far back for the hedgehog

Figure 42. A 3D recreation of Capa's Negative 35. (Author)

to be useful as shelter. And neither of the two men on the right (#3 or #4) is covered by the hedgehog.

The situation is even worse when taking the dashed white arrows into account. Those arrows indicate the direction of fire coming from the nearest German strongpoints (WN62 and WN64). The arrow on the right (from WN62) represents the major source of the fire directed on this section of the beach throughout the morning. Yet, as the arrow indicates, not a single man is covered by the hedgehog from this fire. So, the men in Capa's negative 35 clearly are not seeking the shelter of the hedgehog, as the traditional interpretation would have us believe.

Which begs the question: if they weren't seeking shelter, just what were they doing? With three of the men

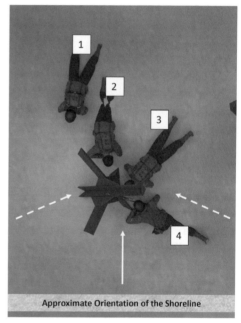

Figure 43. An overhead view of the 3D scene from Figure 42. (Author)

arrayed in a spokes-in-a-wagon-wheel arrangement, it seem clear they are concentrating on something. And it isn't unreasonable to guess the top soldier (#1) is observing or even supervising them. But again, what is the object of their interest?

The popular interpretation of these two photos has long been challenged by amateur historians who understood the significance of some minor details they contained, and to my knowledge, Pieter Jutte provided some of the earliest and best observations on the internet. By enlarging negative 35 (Figure 44), we can see several important clues. The first is a curious downward facing white arc on the front of the helmet worn by man #1 (outlined by the half circle). This insignia was a European Theater of Operations standard helmet marking, indicating the wearer was an engineer. We can also see the same crescent on the helmet of man #3. Because this second arc is partially obscured by an object running diagonally in front of it (a rifle?) the symbol might initially escape notice.

As two of the four men are engineers, and as all four seem to be focused on the same task, we can assume men #2 and #4 are most likely engineers as well. Given the phase of the invasion (within the first 120 minutes after H-Hour) and a bit of knowledge about the landing plan for the 16th RCT's half of Omaha beach, we can safely conclude these men belong to the Engineer Special Task Force, and most likely Gap Assault Team 10, which had landed in on this stretch of beach almost two hours earlier.

Returning to the enlargement, we discover evidence to support this theory. Within the three solid-lined rectangles can be seen a thin line stretching across the entire photo and passing through two hedgehog obstacles. There are only two likely explanations for this line. The first is that it might be "field wire," the two-strand communications wire used for field telephone networks. Many of the invading troops carried spools of this wire; in fact, such a spool can be seen in Sargent's photo (Figure 27), apparently left behind in the LCVP by an overburdened or flustered soldier. But commo wire would not be strung through the surf.

The second explanation is that this is Primacord, the WWII-era generic term for detonation cord. Primacord was not affected by water, so engineers could use it to link multiple charges in the surf to detonate them simultaneously. This was the standard detonation method used by engineers on D-Day. The fact that the line in negative 35 goes from obstacle to obstacle—where the charges would be—fits perfectly with the employment of Primacord.

Figure 44. A highlighted detail from Capa's Negative 35. (Robert Capa © ICP/Magnum Photos)

Figure 45 is a still taken from a US Army training film showing an engineer team preparing beach obstacles for demolition. Note the soldier highlighted in the solid-lined box unspooling Primacord from obstacle to obstacle.[4] Other soldiers are rigging explosive charges to the individual obstacles. Those charges would then be connected to the main ring of Primacord, which would be used to detonate all the charges at once.

The demolitions charge most used by the gap assault teams on Omaha Beach were Hagensen (or Hagenson) charges (Figure 46).[5] These were two pounds of C2 plastic explosive stuffed in a rectangular canvas covering. The charge had straps and hooks to fasten it to an obstacle, and a short length of Primacord, to connect to the main ring of that had been strung between obstacles.

To destroy a hedgehog-type obstacle, the demolitions plan called for two Hagensen charges to be placed on opposite sides of a gusset plate where the three legs were joined. Now that we know what to look for, we can see some of these charges in three of Capa's photos, negatives 32, 34 and 38 (Figure 47 shows two of those pictures).

The action captured in Capa's negatives 35 and 36 now takes on an entirely new aspect. These are not infantrymen under withering enemy fire, too afraid to move

Figure 45. Engineers prepare beach obstacles for demolitions during training. The figure highlighted in solid white box is unspooling Primacord, and lengths of it can be seen the dashed white boxes. (CriticalPast)

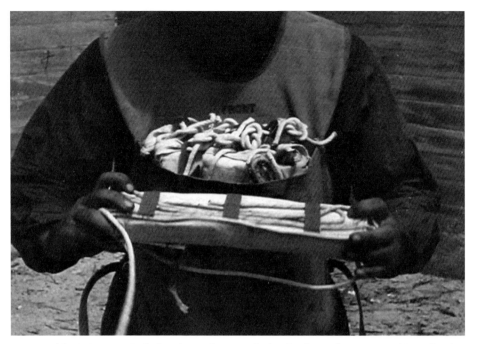

Figure 46. A Hagensen Pack demolition charge in the hands of a combat engineer. (CriticalPast)

and seeking the slim cover of an obstacle. Instead, they are engineers doggedly going about their dangerous task of clearing obstacles. While they have taken the commonsense precaution of lying down to avoid needless exposure, they are not seeking shelter to any degree that prevents them from doing their job, and certainly are not using the obstacle as cover from enemy direct-fire weapons. These are men grimly persevering in the face of danger, not cowering from it.

Even a close look at the "corpse" reveals a different take. He is propped up on his elbows, and his head, though lowered, is not buried in the surf or sand. In fact, he appears to be concentrating on something just below his face. Further, we see what just might be part of the engineer helmet marking, dim, indistinct and partially obscured, but there. Far from being a corpse, it is more likely that this man is focused on some task—such as priming the detonation system—while his companions look on. That is, after all, why they came to that stretch of Normandy sand.

Now turning our focus to the two men at the pole obstacle in the center background (Figure 44, outlined in the circle), we recognize another fact. They are not sheltering behind the obstacle, either. They, too, appear to be combat engineers preparing an obstacle for demolitions. Ensign Karnowski was the Navy officer in charge of the Naval Combat Demolitions Unit element within the Gap Assault Team 10.[6] He noted in his report that as the tide rose, he and LT Gregory (the Army officer commanding the Gap Assault Team) swam out to the remaining obstacles

Figure 47. Details from Capa's Negative 32 (left) and Negative 34 (right) showing Hagensen Pack demolition charges fixed to hedgehog obstacles. (Robert Capa © ICP/Magnum Photos)

that had been partially covered by water and destroyed them one at a time. The two men at this pole obstacle may well be these officers.* Indeed, many of the details in Capa's Engineer set fit perfectly with Ensign Karnowski's sketch of Team 10's actions that day (Figure 48), to include Team 10's tank dozer #10. The black box on the sketch highlights Karnowski's note, "LT Greg Army while water was 6 ft deep."

Capa's Engineer Set clearly shows an organized engineer operation as it performs exactly the task it was sent to Normandy to do. And now that we know what to look for, the results of their efforts are obvious. Only two seaward obstacles remain standing; the scores of obstacles that should have been there are gone; they've already been demolished. The Army's caption stated, "Landing craft in the background are having trouble in the outer obstacles." But this does not seem to be the case. Instead, they have a remarkably obstacle-free run in to the beach until the last row of obstacles. And the LCVPs have definitely moved between photos, indicating they are not hung up on obstacles or foundering.

As noted earlier, all this was due to the efforts of Gap Assault Teams 9 and 10, which blew the initial four complete gaps on East Red. Most attention is normally focused on the leading tank and infantry units, but these two gap assault teams were the unsung heroes of Easy Red in particular, and Omaha Beach in general. With two-thirds of the initial gaps on all Omaha Beach being blown on Easy Red alone, one can easily understand how this quickly became the critical route to the beach for follow-on craft.

At this point, a glance back at Sargent's photo of the 1st BLT's landing (Figure 27) is revealing now that we are sensitive to the condition of beach obstacles. Sargent's photo is remarkable for the absence of such obstacles. A few scattered obstacles can

---

* The Army commander, 1LT Gregory, was severely wounded by shrapnel within an hour of Capa's landing and died on the beach. Ironically, he was wounded not in midst of his extremely dangerous task, but after Team 10 was forced to cease work by the rising tide and had taken shelter among the dunes.

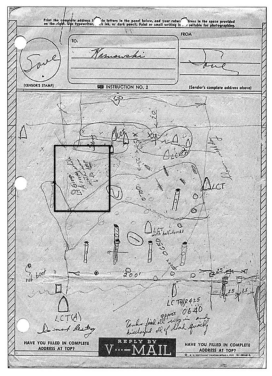

Figure 48. A hand-drawn sketch of Gap Assault Team 10's initial demolitions on Easy Red. The sketch was made by Navy Ensign Karnowski, who led Naval Combined Demolitions Unit 45, which was part of Gap Assault Team 10. (Courtesy of the US Navy Seabee Museum, Port Hueneme, CA.)

be seen in the distance, roughly at the distance of the tank. Between the tank and the landing craft, however, there is just one intact obstacle. There should have been several rows of obstacles in that area, but in their place are merely numerous bits of debris, the remnants of the blown obstacles. At the waterline we can see one of the rubber boats the engineers used to float in their demolition supplies from their landing craft. And of course, the tank in the picture is tank dozer #9, which assisted Gap Assault Team 9 in clearing its lane. Thus, we have pictorial evidence of the success of the two gap assault teams on Easy Red.

As luck would have it, Capa landed on the eastern half of Easy Red, where Team 10 was going about its vital business, and it seems he captured them at their work.* Unfortunately, Capa did not recognize what he was witnessing, apparently overwhelmed as he was by the shock of the landing. Nor did the *Life* staffer who

---

* Although upwards of 200 additional engineers had landed in this vicinity by the time Capa arrived, it is fairly certain the engineers at work in Capa's photos are the men of GAT 10. The Hagensen charges were specially developed for use by the gap assault teams, and they were the only units issued them. Since the engineers pictured are employing the GAT's Hagensen charges, and performing the tasks of the GATs, we can safely assume these are LT Gregory's men.

then captioned the photos for publication; and to be fair, no one could have expected him to. As a result, the heroes of Teams 9 and 10 were not properly recognized for decades.

GEN Sherman's observation regarding the "apparent calamity" of the rear areas proved all too true. The first incorrect impression can easily dominate and distort subsequent perception. Even when looking directly at men doing their job, the shocked observer—or cameraman—may not be able to see what he sees.

Of course, this final effort of the engineers on the last row of obstacles may have been delayed. The cluster of troops seen passing through obviously would have prevented the engineers from setting off the demolitions. Which explains why Capa didn't mention any explosion on the order of what the engineer's blast would have produced. Further, photos Capa took leaving the beach show a high proportion of the obstacles of the last row still peeking above the higher tide. Nevertheless, this does nothing to diminish the critical contributions of these engineers.

One final comment should be made regarding Ensign Karnowski's hand-drawn sketch. Team 10's tank dozer and the two standard tanks with it came in on *LCT(A)-2425*, as shown at the bottom right of the sketch. All three are evident in Capa's photos. Another LCT(A) is shown landing at the bottom left of the sketch, well within 200 feet of *LCT(A)-2425*'s beaching spot. In the first waves, LCT(A)s were only used to carry tanks and tank dozers. If Karnowski correctly identified the LCT as an LCT(A) variant, his sketch would indicate that two more tanks and another tank dozer beached very close to Capa's landing spot. On the other hand, with three DD tanks in the near vicinity (the two DD tanks visible in Capa's photos and a third DD tank we'll identify in the next chapter), it seems these must be the three DD tanks that were landed directly on the beach. That LCT saw its first DD tank sink when launched offshore and decided to carry the remaining three DD tanks it had aboard directly onto the beach.* The only other DD tanks to reach shore in the 16th RCT sector were the two that survived the swim in, but we can rule them out due to the presence of the third DD tank. So, the second LCT(A) (a modified LCT-5 design) in his sketch might have been a misidentification of the LCT-6 type craft that carried the three DD tanks directly to the beach. At this point we can't make a better guess.

---

* The LCTs carrying in the duplex drive tanks each had four tanks embarked. The LCTs carrying in the non-swimming tanks only had three tanks embarked: two standard tanks and one tank dozer.

CHAPTER SIXTEEN

The Face in the Surf

"One photo out of focus is a mistake, ten photos out of focus are an experimentation, one hundred photos out of focus are a style."

ANON.

The next photo is the iconic "Face in the Surf" shot that shows a lone soldier prone in the water. Not only did it grace the cover of Ambrose's D-Day book but was also chosen as the cover for the 2001 edition of Capa's own *Slightly out of Focus*, as well as countless other collections of Capa's works. Ironically, it is the one image for which the original negative did not survive.

Figure 49. The "Face in the Surf," believed to be Negative 37. (Robert Capa © ICP/Magnum Photos)

Mistaken Identity

Over the years, several D-Day veterans (or their relatives on their behalf) have come forward to claim that they were the man in the picture. The current "most likely" candidate for the Face in the Surf is Huston Riley.[1] Riley came in on boat section 2, Co. F, 16th RCT—one of the "special assault teams"—which put him in Wave 3 and placed his landing on the eastern half of Fox Green. No fewer than 12 assault boat sections from Wave 3 were intermingled in this stretch: three from Riley's Co. F, 16th RCT, five from Co. E, 16th RCT, and four from Co. E, 116th RCT. Riley's claim as the man in the photo is in turn based on Capa's claim that he came in on the first wave with Co. E, 16th RCT. At first glance this would make his claim seem reasonable, with almost all Co. E, 16th RCT mis-landing where Riley landed and at roughly the same time. His story also includes an intriguing detail. As he foundered wounded in the surf, Riley remembered two men coming to his aid, dragging him to safety; one was a sergeant, the other had a camera around his neck and press insignia on his shoulder. It seems conclusive.

But it quickly falls apart. As we've demonstrated at some length, Capa landed almost two hours later than Riley, and on Easy Red. The proposition that Capa ended up *ahead* of Riley on *Fox Green* is not credible. As with almost all the claimants to the Face in the Surf, Riley's claim is predicated on one or more aspects of Capa's legend, aspects which are not true. Hence the claim cannot be true. It is merely a parasitic legend that has attached itself to the host legend.

In Riley's case we have a further problem. Riley claimed he saw a press insignia on his rescuer's uniform. Capa did not wear press insignia on his combat uniforms. A search of photos of the man turns up just one picture of Capa wearing a service uniform with correspondent insignia on his shoulder and overseas cap (as he posed before Mont-Saint-Michel during a bit of tourist travel after the Normandy breakout). But there are no pictures of him wearing that patch on his field uniforms or while covering actual combat. Pictures of him in Tunisia, during the race across France, and just before the jump across the Rhine, also show he did not wear the combat correspondent's patch on either helmet or jacket. In fact, many correspondents did not wear it on the grounds that distinctive insignia merely made one a more attractive target.

More to the point, *Life* photographer David Scherman snapped a shot of Capa wearing his field jacket aboard ship on 7 June when he arrived back at Weymouth. It has no correspondent insignia at all, nor does his helmet. (Figure 50)

Small, incorrect details like these often creep into otherwise unverifiable claims to bolster their believability. It isn't normally done with intent to deceive; it's usually an unconscious effort to flesh out fragmentary impressions with details that would be present if the mistaken belief were actually true. Still, once revealed to be false, they only discredit the original claim.

Figure 50. Capa (left) aboard ship at Weymouth upon arriving back from Omaha Beach on 7 June—with no press insignia on his field jacket or helmet. (David E Scherman/The LIFE Picture Collection/Shutterstock). AP photographer Harry Harris (right) with the war correspondent insignia on his helmet and shoulder. (AP/Alamy)

If Riley were at least partially correct—that his rescuer had a camera around his neck—then there is a more likely explanation. Two members of Detachment L of the 165th Signal Photo Company landed on the 16th RCT's Fox Red beach sector, beyond the eastern limits on the intended landing areas.[2] If there is any truth to Riley's account, then his misguided boat team would have had to land farther east than records indicate, but it still would have required Riley to remain foundering in the surf for an hour before his rescue.

Although unlikely, it is not impossible. Under heavy enemy fire, many troops in the first wave found that trying to cross the 250–300 yards of open beach flats was less than attractive and decided that discretion was the better part of valor. As a result, many went prone in the surf and crept forward with the rapidly incoming tide. If Riley was wounded, this would have been an entirely rational option, and might explain why he was still in the surf an hour later when an Army cameraman helped rescue him. Except ... Riley's account does not indicate he spent that much time in the surf before being rescued.

Nevertheless, there is no explanation that sees Capa—who landed on Easy Red at 0820 hours—pulling Riley out of the surf on Fox Green where he landed almost two hours earlier.

False Impressions

Beyond the popular obsession to identify the man in the image, superficially the shot is not otherwise memorable. It is merely a man in the surf. The shot is so badly blurred that little can be discerned. It does, however, bring to mind Capa's trick to make an image appear to have more action or drama than is actually there: blur the exposure.* Negative 37 is the only image of the ten so badly blurred. Of his other shots, only his very first (Negative 29) shows much blurring at all, and not very much by comparison. Is the blurring in Negative 37 a result of Capa's growing, paralyzing fear? Or is it Capa falling back on his photographer's kit bag of tricks to add a little drama to an otherwise bland photo?

Other than that, the image tells us little. We can't tell if the soldier is wounded (his face shows no sign of serious injury), has simply tripped or if he is pinned down. Without any obvious clues, the observer projects his own feelings or his own bias onto the image. Or … the observer, unconsciously seeking a handle for the moment, internalizes the context provided by the caption, without a moment's pause to question the accuracy of that caption. And so it is that three generations have been led to believe they are witnessing the kind of unmitigated disaster and horror that took place in the landings before, for instance, the D-1 exit at H-Hour, rather than the far less lurid scene before the Roman Ruins at H+120.

Yes, this photo/caption pairing is *that* misleading.

But let's take a second look at the photo. Beyond the soldier, there is one gem overlooked by most observers. There are three hedgehogs, two log ramps and a single pole obstacle (the blurring makes some double images). The intriguing item, however, is the blurred image on the top right edge of the shot. The object is some distance seaward and must be one of the various types of landing craft. We can quickly rule out the smaller types—such as LC(A)s, LCVPs, LCMs and LCTs—as they did not have the height apparent in the blurred image. Of the remaining two beaching craft, the LCI and LST, we can rule out the latter as none beached or even approached this close to shore on D-Day. That leaves the LCI as the only remaining possibility.

In a remarkable coincidence, we have film taken *from* that very same LCI at virtually the same moment.[3] A. D. Coleman discovered a brief motion picture clip in the documentary *Beachhead to Berlin*. It showed an LCI beached at an angle to the shore, discharging its troops. Allan recognized the tank in the center rear of

---

* Capa told a fellow correspondent O. D. Gallagher in the Spanish Civil War that, "If you want to get good action shots, they mustn't be in true focus. If your hand trembles a little then you get a fine action shot." Kershaw, p. 43.

Figure 51. A frame captured from the film clip identified by A. D. Coleman. (NARA/Internet Archive)

the film as the same tank dozer #10 captured in Capa's beach photos. Recall it was behind this very tank that Capa was sheltering when he took the Engineer set of two photos.

Examining the two photos (Figure 52), we realize that this is not merely a matter of one item appearing in two different pictures. Rather, it is a case of two photographers taking pictures of one another at *almost* the same moment.

Below is a detailed comparison of the two images. On the left is Capa's Face in the Surf photo, and on the right is the frame from the movie clip. The white highlights identify the obstacles common to both images. Those four obstacles clearly are a match—though viewed from *almost* exactly reverse angles. There is some difference in the reverse angles because the LCI was still approaching the beach in Capa's photo, but moved forward and was beached when the shot was taken from the LCI. Regardless of minor differences in angle, identical obstacles confirm Coleman's identification of the scene.

A cursory look at the tide levels in both Capa's photo and the LCI's movie clip indicates the two images were taken within a very few minutes of each other. The question, then, is which photo was taken first? In Capa's photo, the LCI is not discharging troops—none can be seen in the water. Either the LCI is still approaching the beach or has finished debarkation and is retracting from the beach. Can we determine which is the case?

Figure 52. Capa's "Face in the Surf" photo (left) and a frame from *Beachhead to Berlin* (right) showing troops debarking from *LCI(L)-94*. Taken just minutes apart, they show reverse angles of the same scene.

The chances are low that two LCIs landed at the exact same spot at Easy Red during the very few minutes Capa was there, and we know Capa fled on *LCI(L)-94*, so it is probably the *94* in the background of the Face in the Surf. We know that the *94* had a motion picture cameraman aboard, Chief Photographer's Mate David Ruley. In a 1945 article in *Movie Maker* magazine, Ruley related his D-Day adventures aboard the *94*. The article included a group of six stills that had come from the 1945 Coast Guard/Warner Brothers movie *Beachhead to Berlin,* and which were attributed to Ruley's D-Day camera. One of those includes the scene we see in Figure 51.

With the common and nearly indiscriminate use of generic stock footage to illustrate events, attributing that film to Ruley could be open to question, but we can confirm that this clip did come from his camera aboard the *94*.

Coleman also discovered a second clip in the documentary, taken from the bridge of an LCI.[4] It is not otherwise remarkable except for a very distinctive stack of field ration boxes on the forward deck. That stack is identical to the stack of boxes seen in one of LT Gislason's photos taken aboard *LCI(L)-94*—right down to the random, jumbled orientation of several of the boxes (Figure 53, outlined by the solid white rectangles). Confirming this identification, two Stokes basket litters can be seen leaning at equally identical and random angles at the bottom right of each image (within the dashed white rectangles). Clearly both Gislason's still photo and this movie clip were taken aboard the *94*, which means this movie clip was indeed Ruley's. This is the first link in a chain of identification.

Next, by comparing frame grabs from the two movie clips (Figure 54), it is apparent that all the details in structure, deck fittings and rigging appear identical, which indicates, as a minimum, that the two craft shown were part of the same sub-class or series of LCIs. There are also two small, unique details common to both frame grabs involving the piles of rations. The first (outlined in the solid white rectangle) is the side of the top box where it rests against the shield; it is at the same angle to the shield in both photos. The second detail is the open top flap of the lower left box (outlined in the dashed white rectangle). In the photo on the right, that flap

Figure 53. Detail from LT Gislason's still photo showing *LCI(L)-94* as it was beached on Easy Red (left) and a frame from *Beachhead to Berlin* taken aboard a previously unidentified LCI (right). Note the exact same stacking of boxes highlighted in the solid white squares and the same stacking of Stokes litters in the dashed white squares. (The National WWII Museum, NARA/Internet Archives)

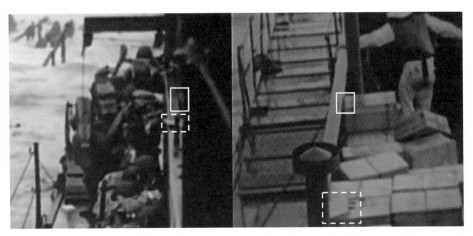

Figure 54. A comparison of the details in the two movie clips discloses that it is the same landing craft in each clip. (NARA/Internet Archive)

is partially open and is hanging loosely over the box top. In the photo on the left, the flap is bent backwards so that it rests on the shield, apparently blown there by the wind.

To strengthen this last point of identification, we refer back to Gislason's photo taken during debarkation and compare it to the two movie frames. (Figure 55). Gislason's photo shows the box lid was blown open, just as the still from the beached clip shows. Since these common details involve the rather sloppy, semi-random stowage of consumable deck cargo, rather than cookie-cutter configuration of the craft itself, it would stretch the limits of reason to believe two identical LCI's would have their deck cargo stacked identically—right down to the random angles and randomly opened box flaps. It's safe to say both film clips were taken from the same LCI.

Figure 55. Connecting the dots. Left: the half-open box flap during the clip at sea. Center: LT Gislason's photo showing the box flap blown open while beached. Right: the open flap during the beaching film clip. All three images came from the same ship, *LCI(L)-94*. (The National WWII Museum)

Between these four images we have firmly established a chain. Gislason's photo showing the *94*'s deck cargo proves it is the same craft as shown in the similar film clip. A comparison of the two film clips proved they came from the same craft—the *94*—and must therefore be Ruley's work. And the reverse angle film clip proves that the LCI is the same as in Capa's Face in the Surf photo. Therefore, the LCI in Capa's shot then must be the *94*.

This answers the question raised above: was the LCI in Capa's photo just arriving? Or was it retracting after debarking its troops? Since that craft is the *94*, Capa's photo must show its arrival. If the *94* were retracting, Capa could not have captured this photo, as he was aboard the *94* as it retracted. (In a later chapter we will revisit this conclusion in light of additional evidence, but for now we will proceed on the basis that the LCI must have been arriving.)

Earlier we estimated the *LCI(L)-94*'s timeline would have permitted the ship to beach on Easy Red no earlier than 0820 hours, and most likely before 0830 hours. We can now validate that analysis. We have determined Capa spent at most six minutes taking pictures after landing at 0820 hours. Since the tides in Capa's photos are essentially identical to those in Figure 51, then it follows that the *94* beached within this very narrow window.

Independent Confirmation

The frame from Ruley's debarkation film clip contains a couple of other interesting points, which, though not relating to Capa's Face in the Surf photo, provide support for conclusions reached in earlier chapters.

Beyond tank dozer #10 is a large dark shape. The size and shape indicate it is a tank; given the time the shot was taken, no other vehicles of that bulk would have been ashore. The tall thin object rising above the tank is the chimney-style engine air duct that was unique to the 741st Tank Battalion's duplex drive tanks, and given how much of that duct is exposed, that DD tank's flotation skirt must be completely collapsed. This tank, being to the east of tank dozer #10, would have been out of frame to the left of Capa's debarkation set of photos. Both Capa's ramp photos (taken before Ruley's clip) and Gislason's last photo (taken after Ruley's clip) show the other two DD tanks in the same positions at the shingle on the right side of tank dozer #10, so this new DD tank cannot be one of those original two. This proves that in addition to the five tanks in Capa's beach photos (one tank dozer, two standard tanks with deep wading kits and two DD tanks), there was a sixth tank—a DD version—in the immediate vicinity of Capa's landing site. Given that there were only five—perhaps six—DD tanks on the entire range of the 16th RCT's beaches, the presence of three of those in proximity at the Roman Ruins tends to confirm this was the beaching site of the one LCT that brought its three DD tanks all the way into the shore, as we suggested at the end of the last chapter. (Later we will find proof of a seventh tank in another photo.)

With six tanks identified (so far) within 100 yards of Capa's landing site, and with Co. G's machine guns and mortars also present, this reinforces our conclusion that this section of the beach was exceedingly well supported by suppressive fire, at least by comparison to other sectors of the 16th RCT's beach. This is confirmed by

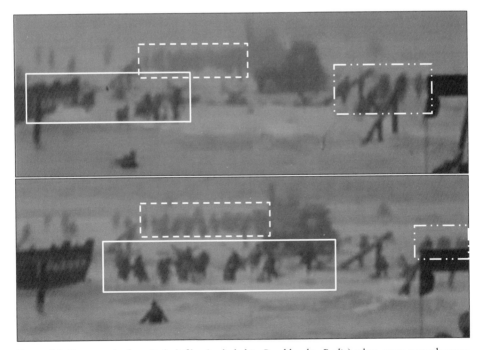

Figure 56. Frame grabs from Ruley's film (included in *Beachhead to Berlin*) taken seven seconds apart. Note the unimpeded movement of troops ashore. (NARA/Internet Archive)

the figures in the background. In Ruley's actual movie clip we can see two groups of men (LCVP boatloads) moving rapidly through the surf to the shore (Figure 56). A third large group is moving behind the newly discovered DD tank, which itself is moving at a walking pace toward the shingle/embankment. In addition, it appears the men are debarking from the *94* without noticeable interference from enemy fire. The vast majority of men visible are upright and moving. Contrary to the impressions given by Capa's photos, very few are sheltering behind the beach obstacles and there's no evidence that troops are pinned down. Again, enemy fire on this part of Omaha Beach was unusually light by the standards present elsewhere.

And this brings us full circle to my assertion earlier in this chapter that Capa's Face in the Surf picture has been presented to seven decades of viewers in a false context. The wider-angle view presented in the movie clip—taken precisely during the period Capa claimed he and his Face in the Surf soldier were supposedly pinned down—shows troops in large numbers upright and moving through the surf. Quite clearly and quite simply, Capa's Face in the Surf photo is something of a fraud. While accurate in the small view—showing a soldier struggling in the surf—it completely misrepresents the context of what was happening beyond the narrow boundaries of Capa's viewfinder. It is a colossal irony, therefore, that this misleading photo has become the iconic visual representation of the actual horror taking place at other parts of the beach.

Of course, this photo is not a fraud in the legal or even, perhaps, the moral sense. In fact, when *Life* published the photo, its editors were almost certainly under the impression that their caption and context were generally accurate. This photo appeared to perfectly illustrate what little they could infer from Capa's experiences that day. They probably were not able to know better, and Capa's failure to provide caption notes left those editors guessing. With no better understanding, it is no wonder they submitted to the urge to make their coverage appear as spectacular as possible. And publications that followed over the next 75 years merely repeated the errors.

For a historian, however, a better understanding is imperative. The hype generated by a publication to boost circulation must not substitute for fact. Lurid misrepresentation of photos cannot be permitted to erase from history the actual conditions at this pivotal point, both on this beach sector and in the larger sense.

Whatever emotions Capa's photo may evoke, the rational mind must realize that it's being misled.

CHAPTER SEVENTEEN

The Obstacle Forest Set

"A photograph is usually looked at—seldom looked into."

ANSEL ADAMS

This two-photo set is the most troublesome of the D-Day series.

At first glance, it seems little different from the rest of Capa's beach photos. The images show a general view looking eastward along the beach and are angled slightly offshore of his position. The images are filled with a veritable forest of obstacles with dozens of soldiers sheltering among them. Because the two photos show the same scene, I have lumped them together as a single set, but the two photos are not sequential. They represent negatives 34 (which we skipped over earlier) and 38, and therefore are separated by negatives 35 and 36 (the Engineer set) and the missing negative 37 (presumed to be the Face in the Surf photo).

Although the two photos are framed a bit differently (negative 34 is pointed almost parallel to the shore) they show essentially the same scene. Most of the soldiers visible in the two photos are in nearly the same positions.

There are a couple of noteworthy details contained in these photos that bear discussion. During our analysis of the Engineer set, we noted that Hagensen Pack demolition charges were visible in three of Capa's other photos. Both photos of

Figure 57. Capa's Negative 34. (Robert Capa © ICP/Magnum Photos)

Figure 58. Capa's Negative 38. (Robert Capa © ICP/Magnum Photos)

Figure 59. Detail from Capa's Negative 38. Hagensen Packs (demolitions charges) are highlighted in solid white. Highlighted in dashed white are two faint lines (difficult to see in this resolution) which appear to be detonation cord linking the charges. Note the soldier's helmet just below the left Hagensen Pack. It shows a horizontal white band, the standard helmet marking for an MP. (Robert Capa © ICP/Magnum Photos)

the Obstacle Forrest set show Hagensen Packs emplaced on hedgehog obstacles, as Figure 59 demonstrates (outlined solid white).

Also, here again we can see—very faintly—a line running between the obstacles (highlighted in dashed white). Seeing this line in conjunction with the Hagensen Packs attached to those obstacles confirms our earlier conclusion that this is detonation cord. This, again, is evidence of an organized engineer effort. To set up a ring main system like this requires several men working as a team, performing multiple tasks: running and stringing the detonation cord, placing charges individually on a dozen or more obstacles, and priming the firing system.

Note also the Military Policeman in the photo (identified by the horizontal white band on the helmet just below the left Hagensen Pack). While Capa was on Easy Red, MP presence was limited. Some MPs landed with the ill-fated advanced command group for the 16th RCT at H+50, but that group landed farther east. Sixteen MPs were scheduled to arrive on Easy Red by LCI at 0735 hours, along with members of the 37th Engineer Battalion, but it is not certain they landed on time or at the Roman Ruins. A number arrived aboard the LCM in Wave 13 that accompanied Capa and COL Taylor ashore at 0820 hours, and it beached just to the east of Capa's LCVP, which is exactly the area in which the MP in negative 38 is located.[1]

Although most soldiers are taking cover in the obstacle belt, both photos show men casually standing erect. In negative 34 there is one man, and possibly a second, at the far right of the image in the distant background. Only a close examination can spot him. In negative 38, however, there are two obvious men in the center of the image, standing between a pair of log ramp obstacles. They are looking out to sea, apparently unconcerned about the possibility of enemy fire. The groups of sheltering soldiers at that point do not seem to have changed, so it appears these two men have walked into frame since the first photo of this set was taken. Enlargement of this second photo suggests the right-hand standing figure has the horizontal bar on the rear of his helmet marking him an NCO, although this is uncertain.

The posture of these standing men provides important context to the rest of the scene. Without these erect figures in the two photos, it is easy to believe the troops are pinned down by murderous enemy fire, just as the traditional interpretation of Capa's photos holds. But with men standing in both photos, it gives an altogether different meaning. Now the soldiers among the obstacles are merely prudently seeking cover until they can advance. Perhaps they are waiting for orders, or until a demolitions team detonates a charge at the shingle to clear a gap through the barbed-wire obstacle. The casual posture of the two erect men indicates that neither they nor the soldiers in the photo are under effective fire.

Understanding how the two erect figures in the center of negative 38 completely change the impact of the photo, it isn't hard to guess which negative *Life* chose to include in its 19 June 1944 issue. If you've been paying attention, you will have guessed that they chose the photo which gave the direst impression. And you would be correct. *Life* printed the photo *without* the two erect figures; they chose negative 34, with the small standing figure barely noticeable in the distance. Perhaps not so coincidentally, when printed in that issue, the brightness of this one photo was increased far beyond any of the other nine in the article, so much so that the standing figure in the distance became an indistinct blur. Once again, apparent reality was determined by editorial selection. This distortion by means of selective illustration was repeated by Whelan in his *This Is War!*, in which he included the picture from negative 34 and omitted that from 38.[2] To understand the correct context, recall that at almost exactly this same time, Ruley was filming this same stretch of Easy Red, and his film showed groups of men freely moving upright to the shingle.

The final point to note involves the landing craft visible in the two photos. On the far left of Figure 57 is an LCVP which is retracting, as evidenced by the ramp which is being raised. However, framed within the largest log ramp (left center of Figure 57) is a second LCVP, and a third LCVP, faint and farther away, just to the right of it. These two craft are also visible in Figure 58, with the third LCVP much more visible in that photo. These two LCVPs were not visible in the Engineer set and are significantly farther east than the LCVPs that were visible in that set. (See Figure 59's enlargement for a better view of these two landing craft.)

Neither of these two LCVPs seems to have altered positions between the two shots. The center LCVP almost certainly has not moved and is even in the same canted position in both shots. The right LCVP may have moved a small amount, but the slight change in the position of Capa's camera has also changed the relative positions of other points of reference. Significantly, neither of these LCVPs has its ramp lowered. In addition, they are sitting directly amongst the breaking surf, a dangerous position due to the threat of broaching. Recall that these two photos were separated by negatives 35–37, and the time it took to set up and snap those three photos. Yet these two craft remained motionless. The logical conclusion is that these two craft were hung up on obstacles, which, if true, indicates they came in outside the lanes cleared by Team 10. Although pictures Capa took while leaving the beach do not appear to show wrecked LCVPs in the immediate area, both Ruley's film and one of Gislason's photos show a foundered LCVP in this area; it may very well be one of the craft we see here.

Sequencing

One curious point about the Obstacle Forest set is that the two negatives—34 and 38—are not sequential. Sandwiched between them are the Engineer set and the Face in the Surf, which, though lacking an identifiable negative number, logically is normally placed as negative 37. And that's odd.

When Capa saw a scene he liked, he took multiple sequential shots of it, as illustrated by his other sets at the beach. And yet here he took one single shot of a scene (negative 34), then interrupted his attention to take a two-photo set of a different scene (negatives 35 and 36) and an individual photo of a third scene (negative 37), then returned to his first scene for one last shot (negative 38). What was so urgent or eye-catching about engineers lying around a hedgehog that it distracted him from his subject in negative 34? And while the image of the Face in The Surf was enough to catch his interest, it represented a significant change in focus. Negatives 34–36 and 38 were all pointed generally offshore and to the east, whereas the Face in the Surf was about 90 degrees to the left, or generally offshore to the west. Why didn't he take more than one shot of the Face in the Surf, as he did with all his other landing photos? And what was so compelling about the scene in the Obstacle Forest set that it immediately ripped his attention back from the Face in the Surf? And finally, why is the quality of the Face in the Surf photo so much worse than that in the photos immediately before and after it? The man in the water certainly was not going anywhere so quickly that Capa couldn't take a moment to focus properly. This entire sequence makes very little sense.

Capa claimed in both versions of that day that he used both of his Contax cameras. Is it possible that the 10 images at the beach came from two separate rolls of film? The best way to prove or disprove that possibility would be to examine the original contact sheets that were submitted to the censors on 7 June. But that's a problem; those have never turned up. Whelan discussed a second contact sheet for these photos in *This Is War!*, stating it came from the International Center for Photography (ICP) archives, and suggesting it was originally made by someone in Magnum's studios in the late 1940s.[3] He noted that this contact sheet had Capa's photos printed out of order, with D-Day photos intermixed with photos from D+2. Whelan's *This Is War!* included an image not of this second contact sheet, but of a third. This contact sheet included only the nine Capa landing photos and their sequence had been rearranged in the proper order of the negative numbers. This third version of the contact sheet was a digital recreation. Just to thoroughly confuse the matter, ICP provide yet a fourth contact sheet in 2014—again digitally recreated—in response to a request from Coleman. This final contact sheet differed from the previous version in two respects. First, negative 38 was shifted to the right to highlight the empty spot which the missing negative 37 should occupy. Second, in the *This Is War!* version, the tape used to affix the negatives in place obscures the top and bottom margins of almost all the negatives. In the 2014 version, this tape is not visible.

Although the original Magnum contact sheet included nine negatives, apparently one (negative 31) was subsequently lost;* the archives now hold only eight negatives. As a result, the contact sheet used by Whelan in *This Is War!* and the contact sheet ICP provided to Allan Coleman included only eight original negatives, and a photo of negative 31 taken presumably from the Magnum contact sheet. Further, none of these include the Face in the Surf photo, or the negative for one additional exposure Morris claimed he saw.

Because the one constant in Capa's narratives was that he exposed one roll from each of his two Contax cameras during the landing, I was attracted to the possibility that his surviving photos came from two separate rolls of film. It would certainly explain the odd sequence of images. In that scenario, Capa would have exposed negatives 34–38 in a burst of five photos of the Obstacle Forest, just as he had done with the burst of five photos from the ramp of his landing craft. By that logic, negatives 35–37 came from the second camera, with the two engineer photos being the end of a similar four- or five-shot burst, and the Face in the Surf being the first of a two-photo set that ended the roll. To check this possibility, I examined the edges of the negatives. Although there were similarities in gross features of the adjoining negative edges, it seemed to my inexpert eye there were too many fine-edge discrepancies to rule out the possibility of a second roll.

Fortunately, a much better qualified man than I provided a definitive analysis: French photographer Tristan da Cunha.

As mentioned earlier, Tristan joined A. D. Coleman and Rob McElroy in their effort to disprove the Darkroom Accident fable. He obtained film produced in that period of the same manufacturer and type used by Capa. He then exposed a roll, developed it, and subjected it to excessively high temperatures in a drying locker. The emulsion did not melt. In a stroke, Tristan definitively proved that the story John Morris had pushed for decades was technically infeasible. Tristan then went a step farther. He subjected another exposed roll to a saltwater bath for 36 hours before developing it, to test the theory that seawater could have accounted for the

---

* Not to be confused with the lost negative for the Face in the Surf (negative 37?), for which we have no evidence other than reproductions of the original print.

loss of Capa's film.* Although there was some minor degradation, it could not have resulted in the scope of damage Hicks referred to. It was the final nail in the coffin for the two explanations put forward for the supposed loss of Capa's film.

Tristan's work went beyond this, however. He artfully reassembled the film strip from the images on the several contact sheets. The edges fit. All the photos came from the same roll of film. This means that the odd sequencing of scenes must have reflected the chaotic workings of Capa's mind under the stress of the moment, and nothing more.

So, the mystery of the second roll of film remains. Did he use his second camera while ashore? If so, what became of the film?

Distortion

Tristan provided another important insight.† Negative 38 shows significant distortion along its left side. Prints from that negative are normally cropped to remove the distortion, so the flaw is only apparent when looking at the negative. The defenders of the Darkroom Accident point to that distortion as proof that the emulsion ran due to excessive heat in the drying locker.

But Tristan recognized the flaw for what it actually was. The distortion resulted from the film not lying flat when it was exposed. The metal film cartridges of the time tended to bind as the film approached the end of the roll. The increased force used to advance to film could cause the film to warp slightly rather than lie flat. That in turn caused the distortion when the negative was exposed. And that is apparently exactly what Capa did. He used a standard 36 exposure roll of film, but his negatives show he advanced the film for two additional exposures (negatives 37 and 38), which placed excessive tension on the film.

Tristan's reconstruction of the film strip revealed that this distortion was actually present to a minor degree along the right edge of negative 36 and was undoubtedly present and increasing on the missing negative 37 until it matched the degree of distortion seen on negative 38.

Moving On

This concludes our discussion of Capa's stay on Easy Red. Despite a few unresolved questions, significant points have been clarified. We've been able to definitively pin Capa's specific landing site down to within a few yards, and within a short window of time. This proves once and for all that Capa could not have landed on Fox Green

---

* In a 10 June congratulatory cable to Capa, *Life*'s Managing Director Wilson Hicks ascribed the loss of the film to damage from seawater. *Life*'s 19 June 1944 spread featuring Capa's photos implied this as well.

† Da Cunha's excellent analyses can be found at https://tdacunha.com/robert-capa/.

or anywhere with the First Wave, and thereby also demolishes some of the claims for the identity of the Face in the Surf.

An examination of his Debarkation set also sets the record straight concerning the carnage Capa described on the beach. It simply is not present in his visual record. On the contrary, his pictures—and those of other photographers at the same spot and at the same time—reinforce the belief that the sweet spot on Easy Red was exposed to *relatively* light fire.

We've also been able to take a fresh, unbiased look at the Engineer set, and realize that for years the action pictured has been misunderstood or misrepresented by publications and readers alike. In much the same manner, we've stripped away the hyperbole and placed the Face in the Surf photo in more accurate context. And finally, by identifying the upright figures in the Forest Obstacle set, we've put that scene in its proper context as well.

Most importantly, we've laid the foundation for the conclusion that Capa did not intend to step ashore that day, and only ended up there by mischance. His rapid flight was the only way he could successfully fulfill the demands of his job as a pool photographer. Whether his flight was given impetus from fear is as irrelevant as it is understandable.

PART III

Beat Feet to the Fleet

"Even in the middle of a war a news photographer has to worry about getting his hot negatives back to the processing point while they are still news. He also likes to beat the official Army cameramen. Probably the greatest competition of that kind occurred during the invasion of Normandy, when each of more than 100 military and civilian photographers was determined to get his pictures back to London first."

BERT BRANDT, ACME NEWSPICTURES. AS A MEMBER OF THE US ARMY STILL
PHOTO POOL AT OMAHA BEACH, HIS D-DAY PHOTOS WERE THE FIRST
CIVILIAN FILM TO MAKE IT BACK TO LONDON.

CHAPTER EIGHTEEN

Day Tripper

"Scoops depend on luck and quick transmission …"

ROBERT CAPA IN *SLIGHTLY OUT OF FOCUS*

The Wrong Question

One of the many curious aspects of the D-Day legend is Capa's flight from the beach. The confusion on this point can be laid directly at Capa's feet as he gave two different reasons to explain his flight: lack of film and later, lack of courage. Given Capa's reputation as the "Greatest War Photographer in the World," neither of these explanations seems particularly convincing.

As for the matter of his courage, a close examination of Capa's wartime escapades—one which strips away his self-glorifying exaggerations and fabrications and focuses on independently verified accounts—shows that he was seldom as far forward or in as much danger as he liked to claim. As his "fictionalized" account of parachuting into Sicily demonstrates, it seems Capa's exploits were often more fanciful than factual. Another example is his claim of being pinned down under fire for hours when he snapped the "Falling Soldier" picture, which we now know to be a staged photo taken far behind friendly lines. This is a topic we'll examine in a bit more detail in a later chapter. For the present it suffices to note the inconsistency in his brave-sounding claim that he sought out the point of danger by landing with Co. E in the first wave, but then actually fled like a scalded cat after a few minutes on the beach with a follow-on wave.

Steadfast bravery in the forefront of battle was not part of Capa's actual history. So perhaps the question is not "why did he flee the beach?" Rather it should be, "why should we believe he was supposed to be on the beach in the first place?"

To the Far Shore—or Just Short of It

Virtually every aspect of Capa's two versions of his D-Day saga has been embellished, to say the least. Whether it be the unit he claimed to have landed with, the time he landed, the conditions on his beach sector or his picture-taking activity on the beach, the facts have contradicted him at every turn. His narratives are fraught with fiction. And yet the only reason we believe he planned to go ashore is because he said so. That's certainly not reason enough. So it is that we must reconsider whether Capa ever intended to step off his LCVP.

Nothing about his role within the still photo pool indicates he should go ashore. He wasn't included in the amphibious training course that the assault correspondents who would go ashore had to attend. His editor expected to hear from him early D+1, which he could not do if he went ashore on D-Day. So why is there this persistent belief he intended to follow the troops inland on D-Day?

As the pictorial record makes clear, civilian press photographers did not land in the initial waves of amphibious operations in WWII. Consider the 39 major amphibious landings in MacArthur's Southwest Pacific Theater of Operations, the dozen or so in Nimitz's Central Pacific Theater, and the five major American landings in the Mediterranean Theater. Of this impressive total, civilian press photographers captured none of the beach activity of the initial waves. None. Why? Because they did not land in the initial waves of amphibious assaults. The few photographic examples of soldiers ashore early in a landing were snapped by Army Signal Corps cameramen, not civilian correspondents.*

There were good reasons for this. It was a deadly war, and correspondents were, after all, civilians. The correspondents who voluntarily placed themselves in the actual front lines—such as Jack Thompson jumping in with paratroopers in North Africa and Sicily—were rare. Those who were killed that far forward—such as Ernie Pyle—were, fortunately, even more rare. Although 54 correspondents accredited to American forces died during the war, at least a third died not because of enemy action, rather due to reasons as varied as plane accidents, vehicle accidents, friendly air attacks and even a heart attack.[1]

And assault landings posed unique challenges for correspondents. In the days following a landing, the normal means of getting copy to the rear and onto the wire simply weren't available. Text and voice stories might be able to use a radio to get them back to a bureau, but photographers were out of luck. Their photos could not be released until cleared by a censor, and censors couldn't review film until it was developed. And, of course, there was no lab to develop the film on the beachhead. That meant a photographer had to have his film physically carried out of the invasion area to get it back to his bureau, a task that was a significant hurdle and would entail major delays.

It's important to remember that Capa was in the ground forces still photo pool. The mission of that pool was to get the first photos of the invasion back to London as quickly as possible. From there, selected pool photos of American forces would be

---

* For example, the famous photos of Rangers seizing French coastal artillery fortifications during the Operation TORCH landings in North Africa were taken by Phil Stern, a Signal Corps soldier assigned to the Rangers.

sent to Washington, D.C. by radiotelephoto for immediate release. With luck, they might even make the late editions of the west coast papers on 7 June. In addition to radiotelephoto, a twice-daily courier plane was scheduled to take larger batches of film to Washington. Speed was vital, and stepping ashore wasn't going to improve your chances of getting your film back quickly.

As D-Day approached, the odds against the still photo pool got a bit worse. The invasion plans made provisions for a naval dispatch boat service. Its mission was to provide a high-speed courier shuttle between command ships offshore and the UK. Among their other duties, SHAEF counted on these boats to transport press material: "Every effort will be made to expedite the forwarding of press, radio and magazine copy, radio film [sic] recordings and photographic material. This material is authorized to be handled via official dispatch boats."[2] Beginning the afternoon of D-Day, the dispatch boats were supposed to make five runs a day.[3] But it was not to be. The boats were nine British seaplane tenders (small harbor motor launches), but it was discovered their materiel condition was so poor that necessary repairs precluded their availability for the first week after D-Day.[4]

A last-minute effort was made to expedite the return of film from the beaches. On 2 June the SHAEF Public Affairs Division requested authority to send a Major Ulman to the American beaches to pick up film and return it to London.[5] MAJ Ulman was to arrive at either Omaha or Utah Beach (at his discretion) by 1030 hours on D-Day to collect film, then report to USS *Augusta* (command ship for the Western Naval Task Force, lying off Omaha Beach) by noon. It's unlikely Capa or the other still photo pool cameramen were aware of this initiative, as it arose after they were locked down with their units, and possibly already aboard their transports. And in the end, it doesn't matter. In a 15 June message to the War Department, the Public Affairs Division reported Ulman's mission was a failure; he was unable to contact any photographers, Public Affairs officers, or message centers.[6] The failure of his task may be due to the fact that the orders directed the commander of the Naval Dispatch Boat Service to provide Ulman transportation to Normandy—the same dispatch service that didn't have any serviceable boats. That problem was underscored by the fact that Ulman had to travel back to the UK aboard one of the attack transports, not a dispatch boat.

So as the day of invasion neared, Capa, Brandt and Landry (the three remaining members of the still photo pool) faced the prospect that there was no reliable system to get their photos back to the UK, unless they carried them back themselves. In these circumstances, the advice given to them by the coordinator of the still photo pool (Charles Smith, International News Photos) must have carried special weight. In fact, the suggestion "that it would be okay if any of them saw a chance to rush back to London with their own negatives and thus beat the official Army courier system" sounds more like a thinly veiled directive.

At this point Landry quietly dropped out of the narrative for a while. His D-Day experiences were not recorded, and the only film we have of his appears to have been shot on D+2. There is no definitive evidence pointing to Landry's assault role. As noted earlier, the corps commanding the Utah Beach landings hadn't made provisions for embedding correspondents, so the landing tables for that beach do not list a press photographer, or any other correspondents. According to Whelan's vague description, Landry was tasked to cover the paratroopers,[7] but as we've discussed, Landry had avoided jump training, so if Whelan were correct, he might have been relegated to crossing the Channel by ship along with the paratroopers' vehicles and non-jumping echelons. Whelan further stated Landry landed in the "first wave" at Utah Beach but provided no support for this. It is probable that Landry was aboard the LCT carrying the press support team for Utah Beach. That LCT caught fire in mid-Channel and returned to the UK and as a result they did not land until D+2. I have dealt elsewhere with the military urban legend that claims Landry's film and that of others was dropped overboard by a careless officer. Suffice it to say that D-Day film exists for every cameraman known to have actually stepped ashore that day. There is neither film nor evidence Landry landed on D-Day.[8]

As a result, SHAEF's still photo pool hopes would depend on the efforts of just two men: Capa and Brandt. They were assigned to the same division,* were assigned to adjacent assault regiments, and were embarked on ships carrying the same troop load for their respective regiments (the support battalion and regimental rear command post element). In short, they had identical missions. Not only that, but both men were sent to the 1st Division's headquarters together during the marshalling. The still photo pool effort had come down to a head-to-head duel, with each photographer keenly aware of the stakes. The winner would be the man who chose the fastest way to get his film back to London.

The "be first" imperative must have figured largely in Capa's mind for other reasons as well. By the time the Normandy invasion came around, Capa's record was notably lackluster for a man who billed himself as the "Greatest War Photographer in the World." He'd missed the Dieppe Raid. He'd missed the North African landings and, later, his photos of the battle of El Guettar—a critical victory for the US Army as it rebounded from the Kasserine Pass defeat—had taken almost three months to get to his publisher, by which time they were old news. He missed the surrender of Axis forces in Tunisia which ended the North Africa campaign. He missed D-Day for the Sicily landings (his round-trip flight with the paratroopers was two nights later). He missed the capture of Messina, which ended the Sicily campaign. He missed the Salerno landings. While Capa's later telling of the Anzio landings implied

---

* Brandt was assigned to the 116th Regimental Combat Team, which was an organic part of the 29th Division, but during the initial phases of the landings the 116th RCT was attached to the 1st Division to ensure unity of command.

he wanted to accompany that assault, the fact is that he had been scheduled for Anzio without his knowledge even as he was trying to wrangle a transfer out of that theater of operations. In *Slightly out of Focus*, he claimed his landing craft was lowered into the ocean at midnight,[9] implying he was going to land in the pre-dawn assault waves. He actually landed at least five hours after H-Hour (and perhaps as many as 18 hours depending on the interpretation of the caption notes he provided for his photos) by which time it was clear the landing was unopposed.* By his own admission, he'd already been fired twice by *Life* and had quit once, and had been fired by *Collier's* on the very eve of the Sicily landings.[10] Getting picked up by *Life* again after the Sicily landings couldn't mask the fact that his accomplishments in the war had not been remarkable. His contract with *Life* would be up in July, a month after the Normandy landings, yet he hadn't filed a photo assignment for *Life* in the past four months (the Anzio coverage in January 1944). Though Capa became a sainted figure later, his reputation in mid-1944 was certainly not as stellar as many would like to believe today. His photos had been featured in several fine photo spreads, but nothing that truly stood out from the pack of other war photographers. His greatest work up to then was his "Falling Soldier" picture, which, as we now know, was faked. In fact, up to this point, no news organization had valued him enough to hire him as a staff photographer; he had always been relegated to work on a contract basis.

Capa needed a win. He needed the first photos from the Big Event: the invasion of Normandy. And he wasn't going to get them by *staying* on the beach. In fact, just stepping on the beach could prove fatal, both literally in terms of his life, and figuratively in terms of getting his film back. As explained previously, once a reporter—or photographer—stepped ashore, for all practical purposes, he was subject to the same "no rides off the beach" stricture as every other man, regardless of the greater latitude granted to photographers. The reality is that Capa would be just another guy in an olive drab uniform whose rearward movement was supposed to be halted at the waterline. Unable to leave the beach himself, his film would be subjected to the highly questionable channels for couriering press products. Even if the naval dispatch boat service had appeared as planned, getting film quickly off the beach to those boats would have been a hurdle.

---

* Whelan said Capa landed at daybreak (W/RC, p. 205); sunrise was approximately 0727 hours and H-Hour was 0200 hours. Whelan offered the excuse that it was too dark to take pictures when the assault waves went in, so there was no use for Capa to land with them. While that was true, it also meant that when he eventually did land, he was hours behind the assault troops and in no position to photograph them. Capa's caption notes, however, state that "In that late evening we arrived on the beach." Since H-Hour was at 0200 hours, this would seem to indicate he landed late on D-Day, not early. His caption for the next photo stated, "In the early morning the troops are getting up from their first bivouac on the beach." That description can only apply to the morning of D+1, as the activity of the assaulting waves in the early hours of the landing cannot remotely considered a bivouac.

Failed Efforts

The difficulty in getting press material off the beach is best illustrated by the experience of the Omaha Beach press support team and its correspondents, who landed at various times on D-Day. Both the team's two radios and the wire recording machine were lost in the surf, which meant they had to rely on the courier system. As copy from the reporters (such as Jack Thompson with COL Taylor of the 16th RCT, and Don Whitehead with the 1st Division's assistant division commander) piled up, the team's two lieutenants were having no luck getting the copy off the beach. LT Brightman tried to get carbon copies to the USS *Augusta*,* but since he could not leave the beach himself, he had to entrust it to the coxswain of a landing craft. It was never seen again. LT Fuller and Tommy Grandin (Blue Network) took another set of copy and tried to hitch a ride on Navy craft directly back to England. They failed; the "no rides off the beach" orders foiled them. They made another effort on D+3, loaded down with additional copy and film. This time they ran into two correspondents accredited to the Coast Guard aboard a beached landing craft, and with the aid of one of them, LT Fuller and Grandin were finally able to wrangle a ride off the beach in a boatload of casualties. It was not until the early hours of 10 June—D+4—that they reached London with their copy and Grandin could get on the air. For his efforts, LT Fuller was threatened with court martial.[11] His offense? He had "violated the strict rule about going off the beach and back to England, had encouraged and actually assisted war correspondents to go with him."† Getting media products off the beach in the first week of the invasion was difficult, to say the least.

As a result, the only people who got their stories out quickly were those who trusted in their own devices. Wright Bryan got his eyewitness story from within his drop aircraft on the air soon after his plane landed back in England. Robert Reuben, parachuting in with the 101st Airborne, hit the ground and sent off by carrier pigeon a preprepared story with the electrifying dateline of "Normandy" that was delivered at Dover. Before stepping ashore, Captain Herman Walls, commanding the 165th Signal Photo Company, sent off two carrier pigeons with film of the crossing and the approach to the beach. Landing at 1130 hours, Wall spent an hour photographing the beach activity. Shortly thereafter, a shell burst traumatically amputated part of his leg, broke his arm, and killed SGT Peter Paris, a *Yank* reporter. Wall applied a tourniquet to his own leg, passed out and was evacuated from the beach some hours later. Aboard a British destroyer he underwent a second (medically conducted) amputation to clean up the initial wound. Throughout these ordeals, Wall refused to

---

* The *Augusta* (CA-31) was a *Northampton*-class cruiser. During the landings, Gen Bradley and his staff were embarked on it.

† Given the near mutiny among the press corps about the inability to get their copy filed, the idea of court martialing the one officer who had succeeded in getting the products back was soon discarded.

let go of his camera and film, surrendering it only the next day to an Army Pictorial Service representative in the UK. The film contained "thirty-five perfect negatives of excellent quality." This was the first film actually *from the beach* to be received in London, beating both Brandt's and Capa's, even though Wall's photos from the beach were taken a few hours after Capa's.[12] Sergeant Richard Taylor, with Detachment L of Wall's company, landed at Fox Green in the 16th RCT's area, and took the only motion picture film shot on the beach during the first hours of the invasion. Like Wall, he was wounded and evacuated, taking his film back with him, ensuring an early delivery to the censors.[13]

Although those events lay in the future as Capa mulled over his D-Day plans, they illustrated what he already knew. Getting film off the beach and back to the censors and a lab would be a major hurdle. And frankly, it was a needless one. The Army Signal Corps photographers were there to follow the troops during the initial stages of the fight. The still photo pool just wanted some shots of troops splashing ashore for the front pages of papers back home. And the civilian photographer correspondents of the pool didn't need to get their feet wet for that.

And Brandt knew that, too, which is why he merely rode to the beach on a landing craft and immediately returned to his attack transport for the trip back to the UK. Although he claimed he went ashore,[14] there is no evidence he did, and at best, all he could have done was step briefly into the surf, then hop back into the craft that brought him in. While admitting Brandt's film beat his own to London, Capa sourly noted that Brandt "had never left his boat, never touched the beach," and Capa was undoubtedly correct. Brandt never pretended he was going to follow his regiment as it fought ashore. He was quite clear that he planned to return to the UK as soon as possible rather than cover the fighting beyond the surf.* The fact that he left his baggage and all his photographic kit, except his Rolleiflex camera, aboard his transport attests to this.

Given the unofficial competition to make it back first with photos of the invasion, it's difficult to believe that Capa did not intend to follow Brandt's lead. Or, more properly, follow *his own* lead, which Brandt was copying. If you recall Capa did much the same thing for the Sicily invasion; he merely rode along with the paratroopers, photographed their actions in the plane, then rode back with the aircraft for the express purpose of getting his photos back as quickly as possible. SHAEF scheduled broadcast journalist Wright Bryan (NBC) to use the same procedure with the 101st Airborne Division's 6 June D-Day drop.[15] There is every reason to believe Capa intended to repeat the tactic he had used before, and which two others were using for the same operation.

Whelan's notes for the preparation of his book include this passage:

---

* See his quote at the beginning of Part III.

> When Capa went in on D-Day, what he probably mainly wanted were not only exciting action pix but also pix that would quintessentially show the first Allied troops landing in France. Once he had those pix, the rest of the day's action was probably not too important to him. He wanted to get his pix back to London as quickly as possible.[16]

Whelan was undoubtedly correct. So, there is no reason to believe Capa ever planned to step ashore and drop his film off at a yet-to-be-established film-collection point in the hopes an unspecified courier chain would ensure that film made it back to London in a timely fashion.

John Morris, Capa's London photo editor, stated that he expected Capa's film immediately. To underscore this point, Morris told a gripping tale of his anguished wait for Capa's film, the supposed Darkroom Accident that ruined almost all his film, and then the delays and obstacles that nearly prevented Capa's "surviving" film from getting into a pouch for air delivery back stateside to meet the deadline for *Life*'s next issue.[17] Much of this tale is obviously a dramatic invention, and it neatly avoids mentioning that some of Capa's photos were sent stateside the same day via radiotelephoto for the press pool's use. Still, Morris's tale makes it clear he fully expected to receive Capa's film—and if we literally accept Morris's tale, he expected to hear from Capa himself—within 30 hours of the first troops hitting the beach. Given the nearly immutable laws of amphibious landing screw-ups, that was an incredibly unrealistic expectation, *assuming Capa intended to step ashore.* Did Morris's expectations reflect a complete naiveté concerning military matters in general and amphibious operations in particular? Or was it a realistic expectation based on knowledge that Capa never planned to step off his landing craft, but rather intended to conduct a "drive-by" photo shoot and return by the first fast ship? In other words, was Morris totally clueless, or was he making reasonable assumptions based on a less ambitious photo assignment for Capa?

Morris does not come off looking very well even in his own telling of these D-Day events, as we'll examine in more detail in a later chapter. So, it might be easy to write off Morris's expectations for early film arrival to his cluelessness. Yet it would seem the editor of the still photo pool (E. K. Butler, AP) had the same expectations, having pestered Morris throughout the day on D+1 for photos. Butler was neither as young nor as inexperienced as Morris, so if he were expecting early photos, then it seems likely he knew something.

At this point one might suspect that Morris's and Butler's expectations were based on knowledge that MAJ Ulman would be couriering film back from the beach on D-Day. But this seems highly unlikely. For one thing, Ulman's mission was very much a last-minute affair, with the idea being floated in the SHAEF staff only on 2 June, which was at least three days after Capa and the other correspondents had been whisked away and locked down in the assembly areas. Further, Ulman's mission merely had the objective of ensuring rapid transfer of film from a ship off the coast of France to a harbor in the UK. And that leg was the least problematic for a photographer landing on the invasion beaches. The real problem would be how to rapidly get that film off the beach and to the right command ship while under nearly impossible conditions. In other words, Ulman's mission did not address the real crux of the problem for a photographer on the beach. So Ulman's mission would not have reduced the risk inherent to Capa landing with the 16th RCT.

More to the point, Ulman's destination was not known; his orders specifically left it to his discretion whether he went to Utah or Omaha Beach. Even if Morris knew which beaches his photographers were headed to, he still would have had no clue which beach Ulman would choose as his destination for his D-Day film collection. So Ulman's mission could not have been the basis for Morris's and Butler's expectation for the early arrival of Capa's film. Ulman could just as well have chosen Utah Beach. And yet, nowhere in Morris's dramatic retelling of the Capa Saga do we hear him waiting with bated breath for Landry's film from Utah Beach (he wouldn't have known about Landry's problems for a couple days more). If we can believe anything of Morris's account, he expected early film from only one of his photographers: Capa. And finally, Ulman was directed to report to the USS *Augusta* off Omaha beach by 1200 hours for transport back to the UK; if Capa had intended to go ashore and stay there, he couldn't have expected his film to get back to the *Augusta* by noon unless he carried it off the beach himself, which again, was the most problematic link in the chain.

Morris's tale indirectly indicates he was aware that Capa's mission as a still photo pool correspondent would require his return on the first returning convoy. That much would be clear given the nature of the photo pool assignment, even though neither Capa nor Morris had any foreknowledge of the assault's location or which unit Capa would accompany.

Unfortunately, Morris here, as usual, undermined his own credibility. While preparing her manuscript, Jozefa Stuart interviewed Morris years earlier.[18] In that interview he stated that Capa definitely had not intended to return to England. This simply does not square with his later versions of the Capa tale in which he expected to hear from Capa early D+1 and expected Capa's film at the same time. Neither of these could have happened if Capa landed with the 16th RCT. And Morris should have known that. I suspect Morris told Stuart that to bolster Capa's First Wave story but did not realize how it contradicted parts of his own narrative.

The bottom line is this. The simplest, safest, most reliable and most expeditious plan would be to cover the landings without stepping ashore, and then bring his products directly back to the UK with the fastest available returning transport. That is what his job as a pool photographer demanded. That was what fellow pool photographer Bert Brandt did. That was what broadcast journalist Wright Bryan did with his observations. Morris may have lacked experience in covering war, but Capa did not. Further, given his hard-learned lessons about quickly getting photos back (his failure to get his El Guettar photos back, for example), he would not have planned to fail on D-Day.* He would have planned to personally hand carry his film to the UK. Nothing else could have provided even a reasonable chance of getting the photos back to Morris in the time expected and beat Brandt in the process.

Tyranny of Time, Space and Schedules

The typical reader of *Slightly out of Focus* might not appreciate the practical constraints facing Capa if he dared step ashore.

The only certain way to get back to the *Chase* would be to hitch a ride on one of the *Chase*'s own landing craft. The problem was that after Capa's Wave 13 landed, there was only one more wave of *Chase* landing craft in the early landings, and that was Wave 15 due to land just 15 minutes after Capa. Assuming he could talk his way aboard one of those craft (two LCMs and one LCVP in that wave), that still would only leave him 15 minutes on the beach, a fairly absurd plan. Worse, Easy Red was over a mile wide, and there was no way to know in advance where along that length of beach Wave 15 would touch the sand. After the *Chase*'s initial LCVPs returned to the ship two (from Wave 10) were sent to the USS *Anne Arundel* and four to the USS *Dorothea L. Dix* to assist their unloading.† But even if those ships sent them back to the same beach, it would be the same problem: there was no telling where along that long stretch of beach they would land. It isn't likely Capa would risk everything on such improbable coincidences. And *Chase*'s final wave of landing craft, carrying various "overstrength" detachments was slated for Fox Green, not Easy Red where Capa was both scheduled to land and did land.

Recall that his LCVP was lowered into the water just before 0600 hours, and it was scheduled to beach just over two hours later, at 0805 hours. He would have had no idea what speed limits the OPLAN specified for the various types of landing craft in the boat lanes, so the best he could do to determine how long the return trip would take was a ballpark estimate based on how long the ride in took. The return ride might take a bit less time (not being limited to the deliberate rate of movement governed by the landing schedule), but that would be offset by the likelihood that the craft that picked him up wouldn't belong to his transport, and hitchhiking between ships would require more time. So, assuming the ride back would take a similar two hours, then he had to figure the round-trip travel time alone—not counting time on the beach—could take a bit more than four hours. And that posed a problem.

The naval sailing instructions dictated the planned movements of the attack transports, which formed the first and fastest convoy due to return after H-Hour. By 1040 hours, the *Chase* was to have finished offloading its troops and was scheduled

---

* The pictures he shot of that battle for *Collier's* took three months to reach New York.
† They were transports, not attack transports, and carried fewer LCVPs.

to start hoisting its landing craft back aboard as they returned, and then reposition farther offshore to await the first convoy back to the UK. So Capa was faced with a narrow window in which to fit all his activities. And since those activities included not just taking pictures, but also trying to finagle some ad hoc series of rides off the beach and back to the *Chase*, then he would have been setting himself up for failure. Capa simply could not afford to step ashore and still have a realistic chance to get his photos back before anyone else.

It was an impossibly brief window to both cover the land battle and to reliably convince some landing craft's commander to disobey orders and take him off the beach. Capa's famous charm and glib tongue normally would have had a very good chance of convincing someone to look the other way and break a rule or two. But the invasion beaches of Normandy were far different from a smoky pub where booze, charm and time were Capa's allies. Amidst the mayhem of an invasion, under fire and with no time to schmooze, Capa's charm would be of little avail. In this context, where landing craft touched down and were gone in a matter of seconds, Capa could not have based his planning on his ability to charm a coxswain.

In the event, he landed 15 minutes late, cutting his margin ashore even more thinly. By any reasonable standard, he would have missed his ride back to the UK were it not for three unexpected factors. First was his impulse to flee the beach after an unexpectedly brief time ashore (as we'll see, it wasn't more than 15 minutes). Whether this was due to panic or running out of film, neither would have been part of his planning for a brief stay ashore. Second was the appearance of *deus ex machina* in the form of the misguided *LCI(L)-94*, miraculously whisking him away far sooner than anyone could have reasonably expected. Recall our previous analysis showed he spent fewer than six minutes actually taking pictures during this period, so it must be he spent the rest of his 15 minutes ashore seeking a landing craft to rescue him. Despite those two providential factors, Capa still didn't return to the *Chase* until sometime between 1030 and 1100 hours (as we'll see in a following chapter) by which time the *Chase* was already *supposed* to be wrapping things up.

The third factor was the *Chase's* delayed departure. Losses among LCTs delayed unloading of the *Chase's* cargo. Then, the arrival of the fatally damaged *LCI(L)-85* delayed the *Chase* as it offloaded the *85's* troops and crew. And finally, due to the failure of the Gap Assault Teams, most of the larger landing craft carrying the reserve regiments were unable to beach. So, at 1200 hours the *Chase* and other transports were ordered to send all available LCVPs back to Easy Red to ferry troops from the larger landing craft through the obstacles and to the beach. As a result, the *Chase* couldn't start recovering her craft until 1430 hours. But Capa's personal planning for D-Day could not have predicted any of this.

And that's the problem in a nutshell. If Capa had indeed intended to land with the troops, he would have been facing an impossibly tight planning window to return to the *Chase* and would have had to do it despite orders prohibiting stragglers from catching rides off the beach. That is neither a rational nor reasonable plan for a man who needed to get his film back as soon as possible, both for his own purposes and to satisfy the Public Relations Division's and Morris's expectations. Whatever his faults may have been, we should not assume Capa planned to fail.

When speaking of his photos of the battle for Troina in Sicily, Capa himself said that "scoops depend on luck and quick transmission."[19] We must conclude Capa never intended to leave the LCVP. The only hope he had to beat Brandt was if he did the same as Brandt: stay on his landing craft as the troops debarked, snapping what photos he could during those brief moments.

Just a Quick Stop

Capa's own photos provide evidence which tends to confirm this conclusion. The last man off his landing craft was a noncommissioned officer, as was standard during landings. The job of this tail-end sergeant was to ensure everyone exited, with all their weapons and equipment, and did so as quickly as possible. The longer it took troops to leave the landing craft, the more danger they were in. The fact that negatives 29–33 all show the tail-end sergeant ahead of Capa indicates that Capa was not counted among the passengers who were going ashore. Otherwise, the NCO would have herded him off with the rest of the crowd.

But is it possible that Capa arranged for the sergeant to ignore him so he could pause at the break of the ramp to take photos of the troops debarking, after which Capa would then exit? Not really. LCVPs were made of wood with ¼-inch thick armor on the ramp and sides,[20] which was barely sufficient against small-arms fire. While debarking troops under fire on a hostile shore, they were at their most vulnerable with their ramps down. Recall that COL Taylor's LCVP (with Capa embarked) aborted its initial run in to shore after witnessing the fire and carnage on the beach. It then cruised westward along the beach looking for a site where it could make it into the shore. Even then, on the final approach to the beach, it was subjected to machine-gun fire. Although that machine-gun fire slacked off briefly while the troops were exiting, the crew would not have been in a mind to loiter, stationary with its ramp down, just to indulge a photographer's whims.

A look back at Coast Guard CPOM Robert Sargent's photo shows the reality of assault landings (Figure 27). The last man is hardly off the ramp and the crew has already begun to raise it as the craft reversed. In fact, the last man is hardly noticeable because he is already mostly obscured by the rising ramp. Lightly armored landing craft such as these LCVPs simply did not tarry under fire with their ramps open. They started raising the ramp immediately and began retracting as quickly as they could. That is, after all, why the 16th RCT's medical section had such trouble getting landing craft to accept casualties;[21] the landing craft would not wait until a litter party could make its way out to it.

No. The more rational explanation of what we see in Capa's own photos is that he did not expect to leave the landing craft, and further, that the troops he was with did not expect him to, either, as indicated by the tail-end sergeant leaving him behind. Capa merely took advantage of the final moments the ramp was open to photograph the troops wading towards shore.

The next logical question, then, is why *was* Capa afforded the time to capture at least five photos from the ramp? The film in his Contax camera had to be manually advanced for each shot, and while this would not have taken much time in an absolute sense, in the relative time environment of combat, those seconds would have seemed like an eternity. A good estimate is that Capa's five photos spanned the time it took heavily laden men to move some 20 yards in thigh- to knee-deep surf.

The crew of the LCVP may not have realized that Capa intended to stay aboard for the ride back to the *Chase*, and even if they did, they could not have imagined he'd endanger them by fouling the ramp for several seconds. Remember that this craft was COL Taylor's, and the brass he had on his collar meant the LCVP's crew was focused on his whims and fancies. While Capa's importance is now greatly exaggerated, under fire off Omaha Beach he was very much a non-entity in the grand order of things, and a mere fly on the wall within that particular LCVP. Capa would have been completely overshadowed by the colonel, majors, captains and sergeant major, and his ability to persuade, much less direct, the LCVP crew would have been negligible. The crew probably had little to no idea what Capa intended to do, and while under fire, most certainly couldn't have cared less. Unless it endangered them.

As a result, it is entirely likely that the crew of the LCVP was momentarily nonplussed to see a lone "soldier" remaining on the ramp of their craft, taking photos. This confusion gave Capa a few extra seconds to take his shots, and the crew of the LCVP was only spurred into action by the resumption of enemy fire (which, as CPT Ralph noted, occurred when the last man of the nearby LCM exited). Capa expected to stay right there until the ramp was raised and the boat safely returned to the *Chase* with early film of the landing, exactly as CPOM Sargent had done 40 minutes earlier at the same beach sector in another *Chase* LCVP. The only difference is that Sargent remained at the rear of the LCVP for his shots while Capa advanced to the ramp.

Not Loaded for Bear

In the small matter of Capa's film supply, we find further evidence that he planned a quick return to the *Chase*. Recall that in the Wertenbaker interview, he claimed he kept shooting pictures on the beach until he had used up all his film (supposedly 79 pictures). In *Slightly out of Focus* he shot two rolls of film and ruined a third. While that version didn't claim he ran out of film, the point was clear that he carried very little film with him that day. Morris seems to have been painfully aware of this hole in the Capa narrative. For decades he tried to explain away Capa's lack of film by blaming it on the baggage limit of 125 pounds. That is a ridiculous excuse. How much would a dozen more rolls of 35mm film weigh? Simply put, the film Capa took with him that day would suffice only for the briefest window of picture taking. And that's proof he didn't intend to step ashore.

Compare his trivial supply of film with that carried by SGT Reuben Weiner, a photographer with the 165th Signal Photo Company, who jumped into Normandy with the 82nd Airborne Division.[22] He carried in both a Leica still camera and an EYEMO movie camera (with its supply of lenses), 12–15 rolls of 35mm film for the single Leica, and 15–20 100-foot rolls of film for the EYEMO. This film supply was intended to carry him through the 24–48 hours it was expected until linkup with forces coming in over the beach. This was in addition to his full load of combat gear, weapon, rations, etc. And he carried onto the aircraft an additional 40 pounds of parachute and reserve chute.

Or consider Jack Lieb (*News of the Day*), who landed late 6 June on Utah beach. He carried a 35mm motion picture camera, and carried ashore such an adequate supply of film that it took eight days to exhaust it.[23]

Why did Capa supposedly take with him to the beach only a small fraction of the film that SGT Weiner or Jack Lieb carried? Either he planned on taking an absurdly small number of photos over the next few days ashore … *or he wasn't planning to go ashore at all*. It's clear that as experienced a war photographer as Capa was, he did not come to the Normandy beaches prepared for anything but the briefest of visits.

Accidental Tourist

So, given all of this, how did he come to be crouching in the surf behind a tank? It may well be he was indeed booted (literally) off the ramp by a crewman who was impatient to retract. That was his humorous description of his debarkation in *Slightly out of Focus* (though there is no mention of it in his Wertenbaker interview). But just because it is a humorous description does not make it less likely. During an opposed landing, the crew was not going to simply sit there waiting to be hit by enemy fire as Capa continued to shoot frame after frame. They had done their job, delivered their troops to the beach, and it was time to leave before their luck ran out. Given this, the boot to the rear anecdote seems very plausible.

And this also may explain why Capa had the time to take his five debarkation photos. When the coxswain saw a lone "soldier" standing on the break of the ramp, not exiting, it would take a few moments for him to order the bowman to take care of it, and a few moments for the bowman to make his way forward and facilitate this "soldier's" debarkation by means of a size 11 boot.

Alternatively, the resumption of enemy fire may have forced his departure. Per CPT Ralph's account, there was a brief pause in the enemy machine-gun fire as the troops debarked, but it resumed shooting after the last man stepped off the ramp of the neighboring LCM. And in the Wertenbaker interview, Capa noted that they heard "some popping around our boat, but nobody paid any attention" as the craft approached the beach but made no mention of being under fire as the troops exited. It was only after he was in the surf that he noted men falling. So, both accounts indicate that they were not taking effective fire when they initially beached. (It was only in Capa's later, sexed-up version of the narrative that the landing craft was under fire as it unloaded the troops.) In this brief initial period of calm, Capa's pause to take several pictures—standing erect on the threshold of the open bow ramp—seems far more reasonable than doing the same under heavy fire. When the Germans found the range again moments later and shattered the brief calm, the exasperated coxswain may well have simply thrown the engine into reverse and gunned it to retract from the beach. Capa, with his eye to the viewfinder, would have been caught off balance and stumbled forward, down off the ramp. Or he might well have automatically dived for cover and accidentally ended up in the surf.

So Capa's reflexive dive for cover, the bowman's boot or the coxswain's sudden effort to retract—or perhaps a combination of all three—probably resulted in Capa's departure. Regardless, all the evidence indicates Capa's arrival in the surf was totally unplanned and unexpected.

And sudden turns of deadly events can quickly unnerve a man. In this scenario, the debilitating fear that supposedly came over Capa would appear much more understandable. He would have been thrust into a situation which was unplanned, unexpected and without a quick way out. Not only were his chances of rapidly getting his film back to London apparently dashed, but he was suddenly facing a degree of mortal danger he hadn't envisioned. His undignified flight to *LCI(L)-94* therefore was probably as much motivated by the need to quickly get his film out (as little as there was) as it was by pure unanticipated fear stemming from a totally unplanned arrival in the surf.

Pacing

Let's look at the state of Capa's cameras, specifically his rate of film expenditure. His first picture from the ramp of the landing craft was exposure 29, and his last picture before entering the surf was exposure 33. That meant he had exposed the vast bulk of the roll on the approach to the beach and had only five shots left at the end of his Debarkation set. Does that fit with a man who is intending to land? Would a professional, seasoned war photographer really plan to land with so few unexposed frames in his camera? No. It is far more reasonable to conclude he was busy exhausting that roll of film because he'd reached the climax of his trip, and the imminent raising of the ramp would draw a curtain on the scene. His pattern of exposures indicates that the culmination of his coverage would be the moments of debarkation, and he paced his exposures accordingly.

One could point to his second Contax camera and suggest he reserved the film in it for use on the beach. But it is at least as likely that he was reserving that roll of film to document the ride back from the beach.

This conclusion, that Capa's personal landing was unplanned, neatly explains an oddity we touched on earlier. Recall that we have evidence of Capa taking only five photos after leaving his LCVP. Curiously, none of those photos captures actions ashore, which would have been his sole purpose for landing. None of those five photos was directed toward the enemy positions. And none of them showed anything of the assaulting soldiers at the shingle/embankment. Every one of those five photos was oriented toward the water. His focus in the brief moments ashore was clearly riveted on the direction from which rescue would come. And despite evidence of several landing craft having beached within yards of him during his stay, not a single photo documented troops charging ashore towards him. It's hard not to conclude that when those landing craft arrived, he was more interested in trying to hitch a ride than capturing their landings with his camera.

Fear Factor

This hypothesis—that Capa never intended to exit the landing craft—also helps to explain his careless and unabashed discussion of his cowardice in later years. As the man who revelled in the title the "Greatest War Photographer in the World," it might very well have raised awkward questions had he remained on the landing craft and never stepped ashore, just as had Brandt. A brief stay on the beach (which no one would realize was accidental) would serve to enhance his cultivated reputation for bravery. And the fit of cowardice neatly explained his rush to leave the beach, whereas the lack of film excuse (which he abandoned in his *Slightly out of Focus* version) would beg the question, why hadn't he brought more? At any rate, his frank admission of cowardice, coming from a man with a reputation (largely self-generated though it was) for bravery, and who claimed to have *volunteered* to land "in the first wave with Co. E," would be quickly excused and forgiven by the vast majority of the reading public who could only thank God they didn't have to be on Omaha Beach that day, and were impressed he chose to be there.

At this point it is necessary to refer to Capa's interview with Wertenbaker three days after D-Day. During this interview Capa made not a single reference to being overcome by uncontrollable fear. There was not a single word devoted to his trembling hands which ruined a film change, his need for a shot from his flask to calm his nerves, or his talk with a psychological casualty back aboard ship, in which the two vied for the status of worse coward. Capa may well have been overcome by fear, but he did not put that explanation forward until three years later, when he needed to explain his bailing out on the First Wave with Co. E. Better to admit to understandable fear than to admit the much less heroic nature of his actual job that day.

It was likely well after the landings that he realized his accidental arrival on the beach could be turned to his benefit. He could finally take credit for participating in an opposed assault landing, hopefully enhancing his rather sorry record in that respect. His fit of cowardice, which was no doubt at least partially true given the unexpected debarkation, elicited sympathy and compassion while also neatly covering and deflecting questions about how he intended to get his film back in the first place. And, of course, the bloody details he invented for the *Slightly out of Focus* version added justification for his conduct.

And this tactic worked. The panic attack detail, which was only added in the following years, neatly diverted readers from raising otherwise obvious questions about the contradictions and logical failures of the saga.

The Dispatch Boat Service

There is one last option we need to briefly consider. Let's assume that Capa was aware of the plans for the Dispatch Boat Service, and, not knowing it would fail to materialize, had decided he could spend several hours ashore taking pictures, and still get his film back to the USS *Augusta* in time for the evening courier boat back to the UK. The dispatch boat would then bring his film back to the UK many hours before any transport ship could possibly arrive.

The problem with this assumption is that as the day unfolded, Capa made no effort at all to avail himself of the dispatch boats. Neither did Brandt. The fact that neither Brandt nor Capa even tried to send their film back with a dispatch boat indicates that they were either not aware of this option or were aware that it had fallen through. In either case, it could not have factored into Capa's plans in any manner that would permit him to consider actually going ashore on D-Day.

Beyond this, it is interesting to note that both photographers were not simply intent on personally getting their film back to the UK as soon as possible, but both were intent on doing so aboard the *same* assault transports on which they had crossed the Channel to Normandy the previous night. Neither man left the beach on a craft belonging to the ship on which they crossed the Channel. Capa left on *LCI(L)-94* and Brandt's Omaha Beach photo shows he was aboard an LCT.[*] Both men had to finagle rides back to their respective attack transports. This point has implications which we'll examine in a later chapter.

---

[*] In the May 1945 *Popular Mechanics* article ("I Cover the Battlefront," p. 82) Brandt stated he came in on an LCT, and since he did not actually go ashore, he must have begun his trip back on the LCT he arrived in. LCTs were not part of the transports' organic boat complements. They were merely tasked to report to a transport, receive cargo for the beach, and after landing it report to whatever transport next required an LCT.

Back to the Burberry

Previously we briefly touched on the absurdity of Capa assaulting Hitler's *Festung Europa* with his new, expensive overcoat draped across his arm. A Burberry was an item especially unsuited for the combat environment one would meet during the early hours of an amphibious invasion. One thing a combat photographer does not need while running, dodging and jumping for cover is something that encumbers one of his arms when his camera requires both hands to operate, and while he also has to keep the strap to his camera bag from slipping off his shoulder. That's too many things to juggle under fire and doesn't make sense. But with the realization that Capa did not intend to step ashore, the Burberry detail does begin to make sense.

It is difficult to convey just how miserable it was to ride to the beach in an LCVP. They were flat bottomed, which was necessary for beaching, but also made stability at sea marginal. Their flat bow ramps, which were necessary for rapid debarkation, made for very blunt bows. Instead of slicing through waves, they slammed into them with all the finesse of a barn door through a plate-glass window, causing sheets of cold Atlantic seawater to cascade into the craft. The engines and pumps were less than one could hope for, so as the craft shipped water, the troops often had to use their helmets to bail just to stay afloat. Within minutes of being lowered into the water, the occupants were generally at least partly soaked by cold water and remained so for the next two hours. It was an experience only made worse by the fact that they were packed in so closely that they could hardly move to ease cramped muscles.

So, in these wet conditions, we are supposed to believe that Capa kept his one waterproof piece of clothing ... draped across his forearm? Previously we speculated that the missing 28 negatives were exposed during the ride from the *Chase* to the beach. It's the most likely explanation for Capa arriving at the beach with just the last part of a roll left to shoot. Subject to continual drenching every time his craft struck a wave, it's obvious he needed to protect his camera as best he could. Which is where his Burberry came into play. It was not a pointless fashion statement that merely made it more difficult to work his camera: it was a makeshift, but important, means of protecting his camera between shots.

By comparison, John MacVane had also boarded the *Chase* with a trench coat, but as he began to seriously think through what he would experience during the landing, he decided it was impractical and abandoned it before he left the ship.[24] He was not carrying a camera that would need to be protected on the ride in; he was equipped with a waterproofed wire recording machine stowed in a backpack. As a result, he recognized the absurdity of bringing a trench coat. On the other hand, Capa, not intending to step ashore but needing to use his cameras on the ride in, would have found his trench coat very useful in protecting his camera between shots aboard his LCVP.

The Right Answer to the Right Question

So, it would certainly seem Capa had no intention to do more than capture the moments of debarkation and return to the *Chase*. I submit this is the most logical—if not the only—explanation for the many contradictions, inconsistencies and technical questions we have observed in this survey of Capa's D-Day saga. This explains why he landed with so few rolls of film. It explains why he landed with so few unexposed frames left in his camera. It explains the presence of the otherwise ridiculous Burberry. It explains why he fled so precipitously. And it explains many other troublesome details.

Most vitally, it explains the major problem: how could Capa have reasonably expected to get his film back to London in the time required. By now, even the most diehard Capa fan must acknowledge the distinct possibility—if not certainty—that Capa never intended to step ashore, and that he only ended up there by accident. But this is not the extent of the evidence suggesting Capa did not intend to land. As this analysis continues, we'll examine other factors which support this contention:

But right now, it is time for Capa to scamper up the ramp to the illusory safety of *LCI(L)-94*.

CHAPTER NINETEEN

Flight

"Don't pack up your camera until you've left the location."

JOE MCNALLY

As with every other aspect of his saga, Capa's two narratives aboard the *LCI(L)-94* conflict. Unlike those other aspects, we have much more corroborating evidence for this stage of his saga.

His two versions of the flight to the *94* do contain some similar details. He saw the craft land and discharge medics (Capa claimed they had red crosses painted on their helmets, but in Gislason's photo the red crosses are on arm brassards) and decided to head for it. After the last medic debarked, Capa claimed he caught the attention of the crew and climbed aboard. But the two versions include notable differences.

In the Wertenbaker interview, he climbed aboard the *94* and began changing film. As he was doing this, the ship's pilothouse was hit, and he was covered with what he at first thought were "feathers" but turned out to be the kapok stuffing from life jackets shredded by the blast. He noted the captain crying and covered in his "assistant's" gore, and then confused, he boarded an LCVP. In this account, he made no mention of going down into the engine room or taking any pictures while aboard the *94*.

In the *Slightly out of Focus* version, the LCI was hit just as he reached the deck, where he was covered by the "feathers" and noticed the captain crying and covered in his "assistant's" gore. Then Capa went below decks to the engine room, dried his hands, and changed film in *both* cameras. Going back on deck, he then took "one last shot" of the beach as they departed, and "some shots of the crew giving transfusions on the open deck." A barge came alongside to take off casualties and he took no more pictures as he was busy helping with the stretchers.

Other Voices

There are four crewmen who can shed light on Capa's actual actions: Motor Machinist Mate 3rd Class (MoMM 3/c) Charles Jarreau, MoMM 1/c Clifford Lewis, MoMM 1/c Niles West and CPhoM Mate David Ruley.

Jarreau's position on the ship has been a matter of some confusion, and bears clarification. Photographs of D-Day, including one used in this analysis (Figure 13), were donated to the National WWII Museum in his name. They were taken from the open conn of the ship, leading some to conclude Jarreau took them himself and therefore was on the bridge during the beaching. But these photos were taken by LT Gislason, the ship's captain, who was an avid amateur photographer. In his interview with Ambrose (some five decades after the event) Jarreau stated: "I had pictures that he [the captain] took actually going on the beach with his own camera." Despite this disclaimer, and despite Jarreau stating his beaching station was in the auxiliary steering compartment, Ambrose placed Jarreau above decks. Apparently, Ambrose misread this line in Jarreau's interview, "And one of the guys we picked up was Frank Capa [*sic*], the *Life* photographer, and the poor fellow, he was there in the water, he was holding his cameras up to try to keep them dry, trying the catch his breath." When Jarreau used the pronoun "we" he was clearly referring to his ship picking up Capa, and not that he was personally involved in the effort. Nevertheless, by the time the incident made it into Ambrose's book, he gave Jarreau credit for personally spotting Capa in the water. Another author took it a step further, claiming Jarreau was "struggling to lift wounded aboard when he spotted Capa."[1]

Jarreau was in fact stationed in auxiliary steering, just as he stated in his interview. Auxiliary steering was at the extreme aft of the ship, below the main deck. There was a small deck hatch Jarreau could (and did) stick his head through. But the superstructure blocked his view to the front of the ship, and with his head just inches above the steel plates of the main deck, he could not see the surface of the ocean within some 30 yards of the ship. Simply stated, it was physically impossible for him to see anyone struggling in the water at either of the bow ramps. And he most certainly was not in a position to help fish anyone out of the water.

Lewis's account did not mention Capa by name, but his diary stated, "A *Life* photographer came aboard our ship from the beach and was soaking wet. He came into the engine room to get dry." As Capa was the only *Life* photographer on Omaha Beach at that time, it is certain he was the rescued photographer. And the engine room detail confirms that Capa did go below.

West recounted, "I remember Capa coming down to the engine room to dry his film, so nervous he was smoking cigarettes in both hands."[2] The detail of Capa's nervousness and two-fisted smoking tends to support his admission of blind panic in *Slightly out of Focus*. ("I paused for a moment. And then I had it bad … I did not think and I did not decide. I just stood up and ran for the boat.")

Ruley's film shows he used his motion picture camera both from the open conn and from the boat deck to film the landing. From the latter position he captured a close-range sequence of troops heading down the port ramp (Figure 51). As a result, he was in the best position of the three crewmen to observe and report on the *94*'s actions that day. He was also in the best position to possibly see Capa come aboard, but, unfortunately, did not mention that incident. Oddly enough, Ruley did not mention the world-renown Capa being aboard the *94* at any part of his narrative, despite having Capa hold his slate board at one point (nor did Capa mention Ruley, for that matter). Fortunately, as we'll see, his film was more forthcoming.

Three of these men touched on the *94*'s beaching, but all had different takes of the episode.

Lewis's diary entry stated:

> We disembarked our troops and started out when the Skipper noticed we had fouled an LCVP with a line and started back in to assist them. At that moment 3 shells burst into the pilot house and exploded killing 3 of my shipmates and wounding two including an officer.

Jarreau's account was rather muddled and did not mention retracting and heading back in. He stated the ship narrowly missed a mine on an obstacle, but an LCVP cut in front of them, hit the mine and sank. In another passage he described the ship getting hit by three rounds of 47mm shellfire but did not link it in time with the withdrawal from the beach. Given what we now know of German weapons in the strongpoints, the shells must have come from the one surviving 75mm gun in WN62 that was covering this part of Easy Red.[3] Jarreau also claimed that 20 embarked troops were killed or wounded in the shelling, but this is not substantiated by any other reports, or Ruley's film, and is probably a product of a confused memory.

Again, neither Lewis (in the engine room) nor Jarreau (in auxiliary steering) was in a position to see these events. Ruley probably provided the most reliable description. Not only was he on the bridge where he could see the action and witness the captain's orders, but his account was recorded within a year of the event:

> After we had disembarked about a hundred troops, the tide, which was very strong, started to swing the ship in toward the row of mined obstacles. The skipper, seeing a clear space down the beach, backed off and ran down opposite an obstacle whose mines had been detonated. He drove the ship over this and over two rows of hedgehog obstacles. This maneuver was a big help to the troops, and it aided me in getting a medium shot of them fighting on the beach. Until then I had taken nothing but long shots, besides some footage of the troops disembarking and wading ashore in the water. These soldiers were under machine gun fire, but, because of our close positions, more of them succeeded in getting to the beach.
>
> Just as the last of the troops had gone down the ramps and into the water, the ship was hit three times in rapid succession by an antitank gun from a shore battery on the beach. Two of these hits were made in the pilot house and our steering gear was put out of commission as well as the bridge communication system. Our helmsman and also two other seamen were killed. Three were wounded.[4]

Ruley's account fits perfectly with the photographic record and, in fact, explains a nagging question. The video clip showing troops initially debarking from the *94* (Figure 51) places the ship 50–75 yards west of the point that the *94* finished its debarkation process as seen in LT Gislason's photo (Figure 13). We now have an explanation for that shift of location: it was necessary to retract and beach again to compensate for the tide's easterly current.

One of Ruley's later film clips also shows some of the damage the ship suffered from the shells.[5] The impact on the port side of the pilothouse confirms the shot came from a gun located in the direction of WN62 (defending the E-3 draw, to the east of Easy Red). Ruley's account of smashing over two rows of hedgehog obstacles also perfectly fits Capa's Debarkation set, which shows a staggered row of hedgehogs (easily confused as two rows) still intact at that point. And it fits with LT Gislason's photo, which shows the *94* beached with its bow just penetrating this row of hedgehogs.

The only apparent discrepancy in Ruley's account is his claim that three crewmen were wounded. The ship's muster roll indicates only two crewmen were transferred to other ships for treatment, and, as we've seen, Lewis only mentioned two wounded. It's possible, however, that a third seaman was lightly wounded and did not require evacuation.

Lewis estimated they left 50 minutes after beaching, but his figure is confusing. For one thing, he placed the *94*'s beaching at 0747 hours, at least 20 minutes before it even began the search for an alternate beaching site (which eventually brought it to Easy Red between 0820 and 0830 hours). In addition, his 50 minutes (which would be 0837 hours) would have the ship already departed 13 minutes before we know the ship was hit at 0850 hours. West thought they stayed an hour and neither Jarreau nor Ruley addressed it.

As discussed in an earlier chapter, all we know with any degree of certainty are three times. The first is a 10-minute window which is the soonest the *94* could have arrived at Easy Red: 0820–0830 hours. Second, Capa himself landed between 8015 and 0820 hours and, as we've determined earlier, spent only about six minutes snapping pictures after stepping ashore. One of these shots captured the *94* arriving towards the end of his brief picture-taking effort, which confirms the calculation that has the *94* beaching in the 0820–0830 hours window. The third time comes from the *94*'s muster roll, which provides definite, contemporary evidence that the ship was hit at 0850 hours by enemy fire, an event Capa claimed he was aboard to witness.

This provides us some reliable time windows for both the *94* and Capa. With the *94* beaching in the 0820–0830 hours window, the ship could only have spent 20–30 minutes before being hit. But the ship was not beached all that time, as this 20–30-minute window also includes the time necessary for the LCI to retract and beach a second time farther east as a result of the shifting tide. Further, there is some confusion whether the *94* was already retracting when it was hit or was still on the beach.

Similarly, Capa's stay on the beach could have been a maximum of just 30–35 minutes; from 0815–0820 hours window when his LCVP beached, to 0850 hours, when the *94* was shelled. From this outside figure we must subtract however long he was aboard the *94* before it was hit, a point about which his two versions leave some doubt.

The Several "One Last Pictures"

Next, let's take a look at Capa's own photographic record of his flight to see how it compares to his narratives. In the Wertenbaker interview, Capa merely stated that after boarding the LCI, he started to change film when the ship was hit. After that, "Then things get slightly confused. I was, I think, exhausted." He made no mention of taking pictures aboard the LCI.

In *Slightly out of Focus*, however, Capa said that after the ship was hit, "I went down to the engine room, dried my hands, and put fresh films in both cameras. I got up on deck again in time to take one last picture of the smoke-covered beach." But Capa rarely took just a single picture of a scene. He was what Willy Ronis would derogatorily term a "photographic machine gunner," that is a cameraman who would just take a series of rapid shots hoping to capture one good one. And his time aboard the *94* was no exception.

The ICP archives hold contact sheets that were created after Magnum acquired the rights to Capa's works from *Life*. These contact sheets contain not just Capa's D-Day film, but also pictures shot after he returned to Normandy on D+2. The sheets are clearly missing many of Capa's shots, and their order on the sheets is somewhat random and jumbled. But the sheets do include many hitherto unpublished Capa photos and permit us to draw conclusions about his total picture tally after he left the beach. In fact, it seems certain he took no fewer than 60 photos during this time.

And so, it is no surprise to discover Capa took at least four and possibly six "One Last Pictures" of the beach

Though seldom recognized today as one of Capa's shots, Figure 60 was published in *Life*'s 19 June issue, part of a seven-page spread of Capa's D-Day work. Outlined in dashed white is the distinctive section of skyline we previously used to identify Capa's landing site. Outlined in solid white are the smoke-shrouded Roman Ruins.

Figure 60 appears to confirm the additional (sixth) tank at the point where Capa landed (the third DD tank also seen in Figure 51). In addition, it shows a seventh tank atop the embankment at the far right of the image. This is probably one of the two standard tanks that landed with tank dozer #9 and Gap Assault Team 9 a couple hundred yards to the right of Capa's beaching site. We can't tell from this picture whether this tank was operational or knocked out at this time

Figure 61 is a second Capa "One Last Picture" image.[6] Note that by examining the alignment of obstacles in these two photos we can determine this photo was taken just

Figure 60. Capa's "One Last Picture," as published on page 28 of *Life*'s 19 June 1944 issue. (Robert Capa © ICP/Magnum Photos)

Figure 61. A second photo taken by Capa as *LCI(L)-94* left the beach. (Yves Cordelle and ICP/Magnum)

a few moments *earlier* in *LCI(L)-94*'s withdrawal than Figure 60. This is confirmed by the exposure numbers on the negatives. These two images (Figures 60 and 61) also provide critical evidence as to why the enemy fire was relatively ineffective on this sector of Easy Red. Both show a fairly thick wall of smoke wafting parallel to the shore. That smoke would have a screening effect, interfering with the defenders' ability to observe and target the invaders. This also helps explain why fire varied in intensity; the Roman Ruins were almost entirely obscured when Figure 60 was taken but were much more evident moments earlier in Figure 61. Eddies in the wind or variations in the strength of the flames would change how thick the smoke was.

Troops hidden by smoke one minute would find themselves exposed to German observation and fire the next.

These two photos show the *94* was pulling away from the beach while Capa was taking these pictures. Although the aggressive cropping of the original image has distorted our perception somewhat (Figure 60 shows only about a half of the original image), it is clear the LCI was fairly close inshore when these photos were taken, and that the ship must have gotten underway just a few minutes before. The low camera position relative to the sea indicates Capa was standing on the main deck. The ladder leading up from the engine room led to a cross passageway that opened to the main deck on both port and starboard sides, just forward of the fantail. Based on the changing view between the two shots, the LCI was moving eastward and was in the middle of a turn away from the beach toward the Transport Area, with Capa shooting off the ship's starboard side.

Encounter

As the *94* headed back to the Transport Area, Capa took six more photos of traffic in the boat lanes. At least two of these were facing generally east, off the starboard side of the ship. One shows virtually nothing, just one or two craft in the far distance. The second shot captured *LCT-305* shortly after it began its run in to the beach. This photo, too, was on page 28 of the 19 June *Life* issue (Figure 62). The *305* was sunk by the enemy later that morning. The camera's height confirms that Capa is still on the main deck shooting from the starboard side. In addition to the *LCT-305* heading inshore, there is another LCI leaving the beach, and a few smaller craft in the distance. There is also what appears to be a landing control ship at the far-left edge of the frame, and its position would mark the general location of the Line of Departure.

LCT-305 was carrying elements of the 197th Anti-Aircraft Artillery Battalion and was scheduled to land on Easy Green at H+120 / 0830 hours. Due to congestion on the beach, it was held at the Line of Departure and, depending on the source, only neared the beach at 0900 hours, when its bridge was hit by enemy fire.[7] Given its heading and wake, the *305* was clearly on its run to the beach when Capa took this photo placing the encounter somewhat before 0900 hours.

LCI(L)-94 was hit at 0850 hours, and Figure 62 places the *94* at least 2,000 yards off the beach before 0900 hours. Even accounting for some inaccuracies in recording times, it indicates the *94* could not have been much delayed by the shelling it suffered at 0850 hours, otherwise it simply could not have made it back to where we see it during its encounter with the *305*. The ship must have remained under power and underway in the wake of the shelling, and its crew must have immediately implemented backup steering and communication measures and continued its withdrawal from the beach virtually uninterrupted, with but a minute or two delay.

Figure 62. Capa's photo of *LCT-305*, as published on page 28 of *Life*'s 19 June 1944 issue and in Wertenbaker's *Invasion*. The ill-fated *305* (which was lost later in the day) began its run to the beach at 0900 hours, 30 minutes late. (Robert Capa © ICP/Magnum Photos)

A Lot of Nothing

The next Capa "after the beach" photo that was included in the 19 June 1942 *Life* issue is a full-page shot showing another view from the withdrawing *94*, this time with the camera pointing westward. There probably were more shots taken in this direction, as the three succeeding negatives are missing (which would total 12 photos since boarding the *94*). Again, Capa appears to have been on the main deck, shooting this time from the port side. For our purposes here, it adds little to our understanding of Capa's timeline, and serves only to document the existence of another Capa D-Day photo. In fact, the photo shows so very little that would inform or interest the reader that it is curious the magazine devoted a full page to it.

Figure 63. Page 29 of *Life*'s 19 June 1944 issue, showing Capa's view to the west from the withdrawing *LCI(L)-94*. Although one other LCI can be clearly seen heading into the beach, there is almost nothing else of interest in the photo. (Robert Capa © ICP/Magnum Photos)

Although probably unnoticed by the average reader, a German intelligence analyst viewing Capa's photos would be struck by how very little of the scope of the invasion is evident in these images. A few tanks. A couple score soldiers. A hazy, indistinct cluster of men and machines on a short, grainy stretch of beach. No progress is evident beyond the dune line. And finally, we have these two photos of the seaward approaches that manage to capture fewer than 10 watercraft, all of which were the smaller classes of ships present.

This seems to continue an odd trend we noted earlier. We would expect Capa's *beach* photos to show little. The soldier's horizon at the water's edge is normally short and narrow, and this is reflected in Capa's beach shots. But offshore it was another matter altogether. The horizon was much farther and the view much wider. His photos at this point should have shown much more. The Navy stated it had over 1,500 boats, craft and ships of all types off Omaha Beach alone. In fact, the Normandy landings were among the largest amphibious landing in modern history.[*] Yet Capa managed to capture none of this awesome display of power in his photos. How could this be? It's a question we'll hold for later.

Loss of the Port Ramp

After taking his previous 12 images near the fantail of the ship, Capa made his way forward along the port side of the main deck, where he encountered another photo opportunity. Lewis's diary account of the *94*'s landing that day included this passage: "and [we] were now high tailing it out minus the port ramp which had to be cut away." He didn't explain why it had to be cut away. It might have gotten hung up on one of the beach obstacles or it may have been damaged by enemy shellfire. Unfortunately, even Graham, whose duty position was at the ramps, made no mention of this problem.

Capa's photos seem to provide verification of Lewis's comment, as the next photo on the contact sheets is a previously unknown image of four crewmen on the port side of the deckhouse. It isn't clear what they are doing, but it appears they are hauling on a line and that line would seem to be leading to where the port ramp would normally be. The line isn't visible, but it seems logical to infer it from the postures of the crewmen.

Based on Lewis's comment, it is likely this photo captured the crew struggling with the damaged ramp before it was finally cut away. From what little can be seen, it appears the *94* was headed back to the Transport Area and based on the fact that the *94* has already passed *LCT-305*, it would seem the struggle with the port ramp lasted at least 10 minutes before it was cut away shortly after that photo was taken.

---

[*] The landings in Sicily rivalled those in Normandy, depending on how you measure "largest."

Based on the contact sheets, it is likely the next two images also captured this scene, but they are missing.

Photographing the Photographer

From the main deck Capa climbed a ladder up to the boat deck, where he ran into a fellow cameraman. As noted previously, among the crew of the *94* was Coast Guard CPhoM David Ruley, a motion picture cameraman. In the leading frames of one of his D-Day reels, we see Capa holding the slate board for Ruley.[8] For anyone who doubts this identification, it should be noted that this was filmed *after* the *94* had discharged its troops, and the only man left aboard wearing an Army uniform was Capa. The clip contains a couple very interesting points. The first thing we notice is that there is absolutely no sign of the shredded kapok stuffing that supposedly covered him because of the shelling. It is remotely possible that while drying himself and changing film in the engine room he was meticulous enough to remove every last trace of the kapok debris; but it is also incredibly unlikely.

Second, he not only looks completely dry, but quite dapper. During his brief stay on the beach, Capa claimed to have lain prone in the surf, crawled on his belly ashore, made a futile effort to dig a foxhole and finally waded out to the LCI.

Figure 64. Capa holding Ruley's slate aboard the *LCI(L)-94* as it returned to the Transport Area. (CriticalPast)

And yet there is minimal—if any—evidence of that in his appearance. Even his fingernails are clean.

Capa's combat uniform consisted of wool pants, a wool shirt and a cotton/poplin field jacket with a flannel lining. Nothing in that ensemble would dry very quickly or repel dirt, sand or mud. To be that grime-free, Capa could not have engaged in the beach activity he claimed.

And to be that dry, Capa would have had to spend far more time in the engine room than would have been possible if he did board just before the ship was hit. In fact, in *Slightly out of Focus*, he claimed that as he headed to the LCI, "every wave slapped my face under the helmet," which, if true, meant he would have been thoroughly immersed and completely soaked to the skin. And LT Gislason's photo (Figure 13) confirms the water was that deep. So how did Capa come to be so neat, clean and dry in Ruley's film? He had just boarded when the ship was hit at 0850 hours, and then went below to the engine room. About 10 minutes later he photographed *LCT-305* as it passed, but his four "One Last Pictures" of the beach prove he'd been above decks for the majority of that 10 minutes. How had Capa managed to dry off and clean up so thoroughly in only a couple minutes? It's a question we'll leave for later.

The reel of film that began with Figure 64 also showed the crew treating one of their casualties (Figure 65). Capa also captured this same scene with his camera (Figure 66), resulting in the fourth "after the beach" photo included in *Life*'s 19 June

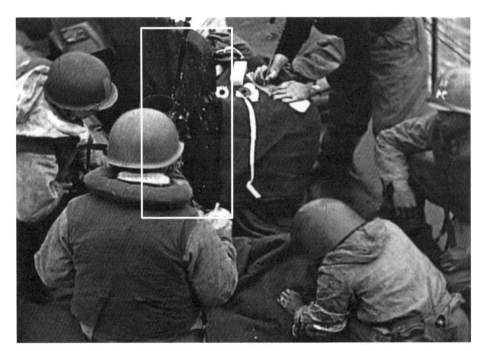

Figure 65. A still from Ruley's film. This clip shows the same scene as one of Capa's shots (Figure 66) and was apparently taken a few minutes after Capa's. (CriticalPast)

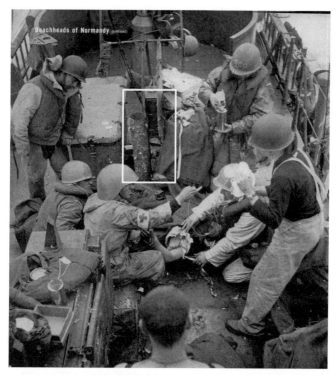

Figure 66. Shown on page 30 of *Life*'s 19 June 1944 issue, this Capa photo captures the crew of *LCI(L)-94* as they treat one of their own casualties, mortally wounded Seaman 1st Class Jack DeNunzio. (Robert Capa © ICP/Magnum Photos)

issue. Capa's position was almost identical to Ruley's, both shooting from the level of the open conn and just above the stricken pilothouse. Ruley's position on the bridge was just a few feet to the left (when looking aft) of Capa's position. Although some of the figures have moved to different spots, it is clear it is the same scene.

Both images show the *94*'s Pharmacist Mate 3rd Class Henry Pilgrim tending to a casualty. *Life*'s caption incorrectly indicated the craft was an LCT (*Life*'s editors seem to have used "LCT" as a catchall term for any landing craft). The caption indicated that Pilgrim (a medic) was a medical officer, which was also incorrect. The wounded crewman pictured was Seaman 1st Class Jack DeNunzio; he had both legs and part of his abdomen taken off by the shells.[9] He died a soon after being hit, despite the crew's efforts. *Life* considered the gory photo interesting enough to devote nearly a full page to the shot.

The scene is on the boat deck just aft of the *94*'s pilothouse and forward of its number 2 gun mount (visible at the top of the photo). The pilothouse took at least one of the enemy shells, and the booby hatch just out of frame to the right was the site of the other known shell's impact.

Wertenbaker's *Invasion* contains a second, nearly identical Capa shot of this scene. In fact, the contact sheets show Capa took at least six more photos of this scene. Judging from the numbers of the negatives, he probably took three more of that scene, but those negatives are missing. We do know that by the time he took a shot of the next scene, he'd already taken 24 total pictures since boarding the *94*.

An additional detail should be noted in these photos: the shredded kapok stuffing evident in both Figure 65 and 66. It is the white flecks outlined in the white rectangles. Another Ruley clip taken in the following days showed that fragments from the hit to the booby hatch sprayed across the boat deck from right to left (as viewed in Figures 65 and 66). In the process, they shredded the life jacket of at least one crewman, resulting in the kapok debris. At first glance, that would seem to confirm Capa's claim that he was covered in "feathers" by the hit. But a closer look reveals that the kapok debris was limited to a very small area, and did not extend far enough to cover Capa, who was supposedly down on the main deck when the hits occurred.

Transfer at Sea

In the next stage of Capa's flight, we run into the familiar conflict of detail. In both his versions, Capa claimed the wounded from the *94* were transferred to an LCVP and he went with them. The LCVP then transferred them to the *Chase*. Lewis's diary made no mention of the LCVP, rather merely mentioned that the wounded were put aboard the *Chase* and the dead put aboard an LST. Jarreau's interview makes no mention of transferring casualties; he merely recalled the *94* returning to an attack transport which he thought was the *Leonard* (he probably was referring to the British Landing Ship, Infantry *Prince Leopold*, which was one of the transports for the western end of Omaha Beach, where the *94* started its day).[10] West's account doesn't address this at all. The muster roll for the *94* states one wounded crewman (Quartermaster 3rd Class (QM 3/c) David Anthony) was transferred to the USS *Chase*, and a second wounded crewman (LT(jg) Francis Mead) was transferred to the USS *Dorthea Dix* (anchored in the second row of ships in the Transport Area, just seaward of the *Chase*).

In *Slightly out of Focus*, Capa claimed he took no more pictures because he was too busy lifting stretchers. This is hard to credit. Capa had made a career of standing aside, recording the agony and death of others for money and fame, without getting involved to aid the victims. It is a bit much to expect that he came so far out of character at this point.*

---

* This brings to mind Hemingway's anecdote of the time he was pinned down in a ditch under fire, while his friend Capa watched his predicament for two hours from a close-by position of safety, hoping, Hemingway believed, to be able to capture the famed author's death or wounding on film. (SOOF, p. 178) Their friendship never fully recovered from the incident. (Kershaw, location 1727)

In his Wertenbaker interview, he said that after the LCI was hit and the captain was covered in his assistant's gore, things then got confused, explaining that he was exhausted. When the LCVP came for the wounded, he merely went with them. No description of bearing stretchers or having the presence of mind to take photos as his job may have required.

Ruley's film can help clear this up (Figure 67). One brief sequence shows our old friend LCVP 26-26 (i.e., LCVP #26 from APA-26, the *Chase*; see Figure 32) maneuvering its starboard side along the *94*'s port side.[11] A stretcher is barely visible in the LCVP, but another clip shows this was strapped closed and no casualty was aboard at this point. The crew of the *94* can be seen in the right foreground struggling to lower a Stokes litter (a basket litter) to the main deck. In it is QM 3/c Anthony, who was wounded by the shell to the pilothouse. Surprisingly, at the port bow of the LCVP we see a familiar figure: Robert Capa. He boarded the 26-26 even before the casualty did. Perhaps the excuse for this moral faux pas would be that he intended to capture the scene on film, and he is indeed holding his camera in his right hand.

To confirm this identification of Capa, note the rather unusual placement of the canteen to the front of Capa's left hip. Canteens were normally worn to the rear, but Capa had a habit of wearing his to the left front, possibly because in that position it helped keep his shoulder-slung camera bag from swinging forward. Referring

Figure 67. A still from Ruley's film showing Capa aboard LCVP 26-26 while awaiting transfer of QM 3/c Anthony. (CriticalPast)

Figure 68. In another Ruley sequence, QM 3/c Anthony was lowered into LCVP 26-26. In the last frames of the clips, Capa stepped forward and grasped one corner of the litter. (CriticalPast)

to Figure 50, we see Capa the next day in Weymouth in the same gear, with his canteen in the same position.

The final Ruley clip featuring Capa focused on the transfer of QM 3/c Anthony into LCVP 26-26, a difficult task given the state of the sea. The 26-26 had sheared off and turned about since the previous clip, indicating how long it took to get that stretcher into position. With its port side along the *94*, Capa's position in the bow was initially out of frame. But in the last few frames of the clip (Figure 68), Capa stepped forward and grabbed one corner of the litter. In this picture, Capa's leather camera bag is visible, slung off his left side. So, it seems Capa did help out with at least that one stretcher.

We can find further verification in Capa's own photos. The contact sheets show that Capa took at least three photos from within LCVP 26-26 as Anthony's litter was being manhandled into the craft. Figure 69 is one of those.[12] He was standing at the bow of the LCVP when he took all three photos. After taking that picture, he apparently moved to the aft of the craft where we see him appear in Ruley's film (Figure 68) to grab one corner of the stretcher.

Capa was at least partly accurate when he said he was helping with stretchers. However, he seems to have rather exaggerated his humanitarian assistance when he re-spun the tale for *Slightly out of Focus*, as the clip goes on to show the LCVP pulling away with only the one stretcher case aboard. In fact, that version became especially fanciful at this point. He implied the entire crew was evacuated: "An invasion barge

Figure 69. A previously unpublished Capa photo taken from within LCVP 26-26 as the crew of *LCI(L)-94* transfers QM 3/c Anthony. (Robert Capa © ICP/Magnum Photos)

came alongside and took us off the sinking boat. The transfer of the badly wounded on the heavy seas was a difficult business." As the *94* was never in danger of sinking, we have here a striking example of how freely he tended to fabricate details.

In the background of this photo, just below the cathead, can be seen two vertical masts supporting one of the distinctive trusses for the USS *Ancon*'s antenna array. Interestingly, in one of the images on the contact sheet, a censor has marked out those distinctive features; apparently that photo was "passed for publication as censored," but there is no evidence it was ever published. The *Ancon* was the last ship on the eastern end of the attack transports, in the shoreward row, and the *Chase* was anchored just to the west of it. At the time of this casualty transfer, the *94* was positioned between the two rows of ships in the Transport Area. And this fits with the disposition of the wounded, both going to ships immediately nearby: QM 3/c David Anthony going to the *Chase*, a couple hundred yards to right of the camera's position, and LT(jg) Mead going to USS *Dorothea L. Dix* (AP-67), in the second row of transports, directly seaward of the *Chase*. This photo also establishes that Capa remained aboard the *94* until the ship reached the Transport Area—some

13 miles from the beach—and within just a few hundred yards of both the *Chase* and the *Ancon*.

LCI(L)-94 was assigned to naval Assault Group O-2, which was charged with landing the 116th RCT on the western half of Omaha Beach. Most LCIs in this group were directed to return to that group's attack transports after their initial beachings to assist further unloading. But four of the LCIs, including the *94*, were instructed to report to the Naval Officer In Charge of Omaha Beach for further instruction.[13] The NOIC Omaha Beach was aboard the *Ancon*, so the *94*'s presence off the *Ancon*'s starboard side at this point fits perfectly. This positioning tends to confirm the belief that Capa either didn't know about the fast dispatch boat plan or knew that it would not be available for D-Day. The fact that he made his way to the *Chase* instead of the *Ancon*, even though both were within a couple hundred yards, indicates he saw the *Chase* as his best option for getting his film back quickly.

Figure 69 and its two mates raise the number of known Capa's after-the-beach shots to at least twenty-seven. Oddly, one of the negatives for this scene is flipped horizontally on the contact sheet, which may confuse the casual observer.

The stretcher photo provides another benchmark. One of Ruley's clips was filmed as the *94* approached the transports from the beach. That clip shows the *Chase*, and between the *94* and the *Chase* is the stricken *LCI(L)-85*. Figure 69, taken after the *94* lay to on the far side of the *Chase*, established that Capa was still aboard the *94* when it encountered the *85*. That was Capa's first sight of the *85*'s damaged condition and the image would stick in his mind for future use.

Dressing Down

Before leaving the *94* with Capa, we should examine his combat gear as seen in Ruley's photo. Or rather the lack of that gear. Based on our earlier conclusion that Capa never intended to step ashore, it comes as no surprise that Ruley's film shows he was not equipped for service ashore.

Capa was extremely vague in describing his load for the assault. He merely said, "They fixed a gas mask, an inflatable lifebelt, a shovel, and some other gadgets around me, and I placed my very expensive Burberry raincoat over my arm." That is a very short list, even accounting for the "other gadgets." Missing are a long list of items needed for even just a few days ashore with a unit. These would include a helmet, a pistol belt, an assault vest, which contained or had attached to it, meat can (mess kit) with cover, three K rations, three D rations, a canteen, canteen cup, canteen cover, toiletry kit, field sweater, raincoat, spare underwear and socks, bedroll, blankets, shelter half, poles, pegs and dozens of minor items ranging from water purification tablets to seven boxes of matches per man. Hung elsewhere about him would have been a first aid kit, gasmask, gas brassard and, of course, his camera bag.

Some of this equipment would have been brought ashore later with baggage. There was no need for his bedroll, wool blankets, or shelter half on D-Day, for example. Nevertheless, he would have been left with a respectable amount of gear hanging about him for the assault.

Of all that, we can see but four items in Ruley's film: a helmet, a pistol belt, a canteen and what appears to be an empty entrenching tool cover (the pouch on his right rear hip). Oddly enough, an entrenching tool was not among the items SHAEF ordered to be issued to correspondents,[14] but correspondent Jack Leib's motion picture film from the staging at the Press Training Center shows other correspondents packing entrenching tools with their gear, so we can assume they were added to the equipment list. The entrenching tool cover tends to lend credence to at least part of Capa's description, which said he had a "shovel" fixed to him. It might also lend credence to his claim that he tried to dig a foxhole on the beach but hit stones and threw away the shovel. We have no evidence, however, that Capa ever reached the shingle, and much that indicates he simply could not have.

It can be argued that Capa's absence of field gear in Ruley's photos has a simple explanation: when he boarded the 94, Capa might have simply shucked off his combat gear, as he thought he no longer needed it. Yet it is the very fact that Capa still has the entrenching tool cover and canteen on him in Ruley's film that tends to disprove that idea. When wearing the assault vests (troops of the 16th RCT had been issued these in lieu of the standard haversack), the entrenching tool was attached to the top of the vest's pack, high on the back between the shoulder blades, as innumerable D-Day photos attest. Similarly, the canteen was attached to the bottom rear of the assault vest. If Capa had been equipped with combat gear, the entrenching tool cover and canteen would have remained attached to his assault vest when he shucked it off. Yet in Ruley's film we see Capa wearing both of those items attached instead to his pistol belt.

And why would he have taken the time to unfasten his entrenching tool cover and refasten it to his pistol belt before shucking off his combat gear. This would be an entirely pointless effort … *since it was empty*. Similarly, he would also have to take the time to unfasten his canteen and transfer it to his belt, a rather pointless effort being back on a ship with fresh water.

Beyond this, if we are to believe Capa, at this point he was still contemplating the possibility of returning to the beach and did not give up on this idea until after reaching the *Chase*. If he were still contemplating a return to the beach that day, there would have been no point in partially disassembling his gear when he shucked it off, as he would have to reconfigure it again before his second landing. Furthermore, logically he would have had to take his combat gear with him when he left the 94. It is not, however, present in either his own photo (Figure 72) or in any of Ruley's clips showing the interior of LCVP 26-26 as it pulled away.

So, we have no evidence of Capa ever having the necessary field gear with him at any point on D-Day. Further, what minimal gear he is wearing is configured in a manner that argues against him ever having a full set of gear that day. Which once again supports the conclusion he did not plan to go ashore. But that leaves one obvious, dangling thread. If he were not planning to go shore, why did he have an entrenching tool cover attached to him? That would imply he had an entrenching tool *in* the cover at some point, and an entrenching tool was only useful ashore. Right? Well, that isn't necessarily true.

The troops had been fed a large farewell meal early on D-Day. They then were confined to a small landing craft for two or more hours, during which they were facing bowel-wrenching—literally—prospects on a hostile shore. It is a simple fact of nature that some of those bowels could not be controlled. LCVPs had no bathrooms. When the urge hit—as it was bound to for at least one or two men of every boatload—you had limited options. You could separate your helmet from the helmet liner, then defecate in your helmet and throw the waste overboard. This, however, had the less than desirable side effect of ending up with that tainted helmet right back on your head. Or you could defecate onto the blade of your entrenching tool, then use the shovel to throw the waste overboard.

Of course, if you were Capa, and not planning to go ashore—and therefore having no need of an entrenching tool there—you simply tossed the entrenching tool overboard with the waste, rather than carry the tainted shovel on your hip for the rest of the day. Whether it was Capa himself who used his entrenching tool thusly, or he nobly donated it to the cause of a stricken man who would need his own shovel ashore, is not important. This is the practical explanation as to why a man who otherwise did not carry a set of field gear would have an empty entrenching tool cover on him when he reached the *94*. Bringing an entrenching tool along was a very sound precaution for a long ride on a boat with no bathroom.

Compounding Errors

At this point we must pause for a moment to address errors contained in Whelan's *This Is War!* As a loyal champion of Capa's legend, Whelan was from time to time faced with the problem of reconciling Capa's claims with the evidence. That usually resulted in greater confusion as Whelan had to invent improbable circumstances to make sense of it all. Capa's movements from the beach is such an instance.

Because Whelan accepted Capa's claim that he landed with Co. E, he mistakenly placed Capa on Fox Green beach sector where almost all of Co. E did land. Thus, when seeking a candidate LCI for Capa's flight from the beach, he seized on *LCI(L)-85*, which beached there and was severely shelled. The *85* beached at 0830 hours and it too carried medics among its embarked troops. Given that Whelan was working from an incorrect foundation, his choice of the *85* must have seemed a reasonable decision to him.

The problem was that Whelan also knew that Capa was taken to the Transport Area by *LCI(L)-94*. How to explain Capa being on two LCIs? He seized on a passage in the *85*'s action report for an answer. After the *85* had retracted from the beach, it still had several troops aboard, some of which were transferred to LCVPs to be taken back to the beach. Whelan took this fact and married it to Capa's statement that he transferred from his (unnamed) LCI to an LCVP.[15] He then concluded that this LCVP *took Capa back to the beach* with the other troops from the *85*, and it was there, during a *second* landing, that Capa sought refuge on a *second* LCI, the *94*.

That scenario is absurd. When the *85* first beached, it did so in water too deep for the troops to debark. No one left the ship at this point. The *85* retracted and beached a second time, detonating a mine that split open the void tank. The starboard ramp failed to lower, and the ship was hit by approximately 25 shells. Only about 50 troops were able to go down the port ramp before it was hit and blown off the ship by enemy shellfire, leaving most of the troops stranded aboard. The *85* retracted again and stood offshore to transfer most of its remaining troops to LCVPs. At no time in this sequence would Capa have had the chance to board the *85*, even if he were on this, the wrong beach sector.

Whelan's assertion that Capa landed twice and was taken off the beach twice by two different LCIs was simply editorial fantasy concocted to reconcile contradictions in a story that was also part fantasy.

At this point in our narrative, Capa is safely aboard LCVP 26-26, and not so coincidentally, headed back to the very same ship he left three hours previously.

CHAPTER TWENTY

Early Boarding[1]

"To me, photography is the simultaneous recognition, in a fraction of a second, of the significance of an event."

HENRI CARTIER-BRESSON

The last chapter left us with some very curious points which have not been resolved.

The most obvious points revolve around how Capa could have reappeared above decks looking so dry and clean after such a brief stint in the engine room. It doesn't make any sense.

But beyond that, there are several other minor discrepancies. In both narratives, right after the "feathers" detail, he mentions the crying captain who was covered in his "assistant's" gore. How could Capa have seen that? The captain was two decks above him, on the open conn, and all the casualties were one deck above Capa, either in the pilothouse or on the boat deck, and none of them, nor the captain, would have been visible to Capa on the main deck.

And why did Capa take so little notice of the shell hits? In the Wertenbaker version he merely noticed "a slight shock." In the hyped-up *Slightly out of Focus* version, he simply "felt a shock." Neither of these are convincing descriptions of field-gun shells hitting the ship, especially since—if we are to believe him—he would have been very close to the site of those hits when they impacted. No loud detonation. No flash of fire. No rain of shrapnel. It's very odd.

And what of the kapok? In both Ruley's film and Capa's own photo, the kapok debris field was very small and certainly did not extend beyond the boat deck. So how is it that Capa, a deck below and shielded by the pilothouse, got covered in kapok debris?

Something is seriously wrong in Capa's narratives, and his dapper appearance in Ruley's film points to the key flaw: Capa could not have been so dry if he boarded just before the ship was hit.

Let's review the sequence he gave in *Slightly out of Focus*. As he reached the deck, the ship was hit once, he paused to wonder why he was covered in feathers, he observed the captain crying and covered in gore (which would require him to go two decks higher on the ship), then went three decks down to the engine room, changed film in two cameras and returned above decks to get his two "One Last Picture" photos as the ship pulled away. And, though he didn't explicitly state it, Ruley's film showed he dried off and cleansed himself of kapok debris in that short interval. This sequence poses a major time-and-space problem.

To understand this problem, let's examine the context. At the point where *LCI(L)-94* beached the second time, the obstacle belt was just a bit less than 100 yards deep, based on the invasion map's obstacle overlay. The *94* itself was just over 50 yards long, and its bow was beached abreast of the inner edge

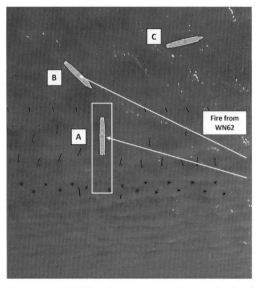

Figure 70. *LCI(L)-94*'s movements during the brief moments of its withdrawal after its second beaching. (Author)

of the obstacles, as illustrated by LT Gislason's photo (Figure 13). In other words, the ship needed to retract only 50 yards before its stern was clear of the obstacle belt and it could start turning. And we have a good idea how quickly it covered that distance, based on the statements of two crewmen.

Boatswain's Mate 1st Class Marvin Graham was on duty at the boarding ramps. He stated, "We were off the beach and almost clear of all obstacles, when two hits from a field gun caught us."[2] Ruley, the Coast Guard cameraman, stated, "Just as the last of the troops had gone down the ramps and into the water, the ship was hit three times in rapid succession by an antitank gun from a shore battery on the beach."[3] The two accounts seem to differ as to exactly where the ship was when it was hit, with Graham placing it almost clear of the obstacles. If we take Ruley literally, it was still beached. The key points, however, are that: 1) the ship was either about to retract, or was in the process of doing so, and 2) the two (or three) hits came in rapid succession.

As noted earlier, one of Ruley's post-D-Day films sequences indicate where two of the shells impacted on the ship. One impact was at the boat deck level on the port face of the booby hatch leading into the pilothouse. This meant the ship was facing almost directly toward the beach when it was hit on the port flank by the surviving gun in WN62 to the east. That places the ship somewhere in the box labelled A in Figure 70. The second impact was on the front face of the pilothouse at the edge of one of the forward portholes. The impact appears to have been almost directly perpendicular, meaning that at that moment, the ship was facing almost directly at the gun in WN62. In other words, it had already completed a roughly 45-degree turn, with its stern moving to the west (starboard) and its bow angling to the east (port) (Point B in Figure 70.) Since the ship had completed that much of its initial turn between two hits that happened "in rapid succession," that tells us very little time elapsed while the ship made this delicate maneuver.

One of those hits knocked out several circuits, to include steering from the pilothouse. However, that damage did not delay the ship's withdrawal. Graham's account continued:

> I ran back to the steering engine room when the skipper [Gene R. Gislason, Lt. USCGR] yelled to me that the electric steering gear was out. Cody [Matthew Cody, MoMM2c] was already down in the compartment. We changed over to hand steering. This switch took only a few seconds, then the ship swung around and was out of danger.

So, if Capa was above decks when one or more shells hit (point A or B), then he had only a minute or two before he had to have been back on deck to take his "One Last Shot" of the beach pictures (point C). And in that very brief interval, he had to find his way to the engine room, smoke two cigarettes (per West), dry his hands and change the film in two cameras (per Capa himself). And his clothes had to dry off from his total immersion and he had to pick off all the kapok. Moreover, he had to have time to master the panic attack that led to his unceremonious flight, at least to the degree that he could resume taking well-focused pictures.

And we have already indirectly confirmed how unforgiving this timeline was. Recall that the *94* passed *LCT-305* a little more than 10 minutes after the *94* was hit at 0850 hours. Since almost all those 10+ minutes were consumed by the time it took to travel from point C to where it met *LCT-305*, something less than 3,000 yards offshore, then Capa would have had just a few brief moments below decks to accomplish all that he claimed between points A and B, and point C.

And that is clearly impossible.

The Other Option

So … where does that leave us?

Up to this point, based on his narratives, we have assumed he boarded when the last of the troops had debarked, and just before the ship was hit. But no one recorded the time Capa boarded, and we've only pegged it to 0850 hours because Capa tied his boarding to the shell hits. Knowing that he played fast and loose with virtually all other details so far, let's see if we can find a more reasonable explanation.

We've already identified an earlier boarding opportunity. Recall that Ruley stated the *94* interrupted its first debarkation because the tide was sweeping it towards a mined obstacle. As a result, it halted debarkation, hauled up its ramps, backed off the beach and nosed in again about 100 yards farther east. Was Ruley correct in this detail?

Yes, he was. Ruley's account of two beachings for the *94* was confirmed by LT(jg) Coit Hendley. Hendley was the captain of the ill-fated *LCI(L)-85* on D-Day. With his ship a loss, Hendley was attached to the flotilla staff and while there, he compiled an account of the flotilla's LCIs on 6 June.[4] It stated in part:

> The story of the LCI (L) 94 was much the same as that of the other two ships of her wave. On her first beaching she managed to disembark approximately 100 of her troops under light artillery fire and the ubiquitous machine gun fire.[5]
> The rising tide was pushing the ship into a thicket of mined stakes. The ship backed off and went about 100 yards to the west to try again. Going into the beach this second time, the ship ran over a ramp type obstacle that was not topped by mines and two rows of hedgehog obstacles. The remainder of the troops were put ashore.

Hendley confirms Ruley's account in all but one detail. Hendley had the *94*'s second beaching to the west of its original site, whereas Ruley placed it to the east. Lieutenant Gislason's Figure 13, showing the *94* beached at its second site, confirms it was to the east, as Ruley stated.

We now have two embarkation opportunities for Capa, and since the latter (at about 0850 hours) is plainly impossible, let's examine the former. Assume for the moment that Capa moved to the ramp at the first beaching site and waited for an opportunity to board. When the flow of debarking troops was interrupted as the ship prepared to retract and reposition, Capa scrambled up. With ramps that took notably longer to raise and no one to stop him until he reached the top (unlike as it would be on an LCVP), Capa could make it to the deck unobstructed, where he could plead his case to an unexpectedly receptive audience: a shutterbug-captain (Gislason) and a fellow member of the D-Day photographic mission (Ruley). And that's assuming, in the middle of retracting, the captain had time to even notice Capa's arrival on deck. So, is the earlier boarding opportunity plausible?

Well, right away this option seems to fit one point. Recall earlier when we observed that Capa's photo taking seemed to stop almost as soon as he spotted *the 94* in the background of his Face in the Surf picture (negative 37; he took just one picture more). Having spotted possible rescue in the viewfinder, Capa quickly changed from stranded photographer to refugee, and the abrupt end of his picture-taking merely reflected it. And so, he started moving to the *94*'s first beaching site. This makes far more sense than the alternative, in which he passed up the first chance to board (not knowing there'd be a second beaching). And if he passed up that first boarding opportunity, it poses the very awkward question as to why he didn't pull out his second camera and take pictures during the roughly 15–20 minutes more he had to wait for the unexpected second boarding opportunity, instead of huddling uselessly behind the tank dozer.

The early boarding option explains other discrepancies. Boarding at this juncture, Capa would enter the engine room at least 15 minutes earlier than the standard narrative allowed. Thus, he would have been below decks when the shells hit, and not subjected to a rain of kapok debris. That in turn explains his dapper, kapok-free appearance in Ruley's film. And an earlier boarding time would afford Capa at least 15 additional minutes in which to dry off in the 120° temperature of the engine room,[6] which would explain his dry appearance in Ruley's film. An early boarding, with the tide one or two feet lower,[7] might also mean Capa wasn't immersed as high as his chin, which could also help account for his dry upper torso in Ruley's clip.

When the shells hit at 0850 hours, an early boarding would find him still down in the engine room. With Capa two decks below and a couple bulkheads aft of the impact points, their detonations would have been greatly muffled, especially with the sound of the ship's eight diesel engines at his side.[*] Under those conditions, if he noticed a shell hit at all (and he apparently didn't notice at least one of them) it would have seemed very much like the "slight impact" he mentioned, rather than the violent detonations that killed three and wounded two (or three?) others. Indeed, the slight impact he mentioned might even have been the ship hitting an obstacle as it ran onto the beach the second time, and not shells hitting the ship.

Capa probably wasn't even aware that there had been two beachings, since the two crewmen in the engine room with Capa weren't aware of it. West didn't mention it, and Lewis gave a garbled account of a single beaching and an abortive attempt to go back in to help an LCVP. Even Jarreau didn't mention it; his view from the aft steering compartment was a bit better than those down in the engine room, but still very limited and he gave an even more garbled account than did Lewis. So, if West, Lewis and Jarreau were unaware of a second beaching, we can hardly expect the badly shaken Capa to have had better situational awareness.

A More Likely Scenario

I believe we have proven that Capa's account is impossible if we assume he boarded at the end of the *94*'s second beaching. The timeline simply doesn't allow for all he claimed he did or must have done. On the other hand, if he boarded at the end of the ship's first beaching, virtually all the objections to his narratives are explained or mooted.

So, this is what I suspect happened.

Based on the evidence of his photos, and his limited time ashore, Capa made it no farther than to take shelter behind tank dozer #10, the spot from which he captured the "Face in the Surf" photo. Seeing *LCI(L)-94*'s first beaching, he quickly

---

[*] It isn't clear if the propeller was damaged (which would require four of the engines to be disengaged) before Capa boarded, or during the final retraction.

ceased his picture-taking. It was approximately 100 yards from Capa's position behind the tank dozer to the *94*'s first beaching site. Ironically, the *94*'s second beaching site would be almost exactly where Capa was huddled, but not knowing it would have to reposition, he moved to where the *94* was initially debarking troops. With fewer than a hundred yards to cover, he had time to reach the *94*, even having to slog through calf-deep surf. And there he waited until the flow of troops down the boarding ramps stopped as the ship prepared to retract and relocate. He then boarded.

However, merely boarding the ship was no guarantee of safety, especially above decks, and we can expect that a man as badly shaken as was Capa would seek cover below decks. To this we can add the assumption that the professional photographer in him wanted to see to his cameras and film (whether drying it or changing it), which reinforced his urge to head below decks. But how to get there?

The hatches to the troop compartments would have still been congested with soldiers coming up on deck to debark. The first hatch into the deck house, however, would have been free of embarked troops; conveniently, it led to a ladder down into the engine room. Capa naturally would have taken it, for safety from small-arms fire and incoming shells, for comfort (to dry off) and to look after his cameras.

Once he arrived in the engine room, he would have had 15 to 20 minutes to dry off in the 120° heat and regain his composure. And being below decks when the ship was hit, he couldn't have been covered in kapok. These two points explain why he looked so dry and clean in Ruley's film (Figure 64). His presence in the engine room when the ship was hit, amid the roar and vibration of the eight diesel engines, explains why he only noticed one shell hit, which seemed like nothing more than a slight shock.

After the ship had retracted the second time and the engine room had received orders to "steam ahead," Lewis was relieved from duties in the engine room—his station during beaching operations. This meant that the ship had completed its landing and the disembarkation of its troops, and that probably was the signal to Capa that the ship was turning away from the beach, and it was safe to come back up from the engine room. Once on deck, he took his two "One Last Picture" photos, followed by his photo of *LCT-305* and the photo of the offshore craft to the west.

A nearby ladder then took him up to the boat deck and the scene of the crew treating a dying crewman. If Capa did see the bloodstained captain, it was likely at this point. None of the casualties were in the open conn, where LT Gislason was when the ship was hit. But later, with the ship out of danger and headed away from shore, Gislason would have felt it was safe to momentarily leave the conn and check on the casualties. Any blood on Gislason would have been transfer blood from contact with the casualties down on the boat deck (rather than splatter from the impacts). Capa, arriving late on the scene, jumped to the wrong conclusion, or simply exaggerated the details.

At some point while on the boat deck, Capa and Ruley encountered each other, and Capa obligingly held Ruley's slate board as seen in the latter's film clip. Ruley's film shows that he had filmed the landing both on the boat deck and in the open conn. Taking advantage of his permission to access the conn, Ruley probably took Capa up there with him. From that vantage, the pair took their shots looking down at the crew working on the casualty on the boat deck (Figures 65 and 66). Lieutenant Gislason isn't in either of those images, which suggests that he, too, was back up in the conn by the time they took their shots. It is perhaps an interesting insight into the minds of cameramen covering momentous events, that neither our photographer nor our cinematographer ever acknowledged the other's presence in their accounts of that day, despite their obvious proximity and interaction.

Capa could not resist embellishing this simple sequence of events. As was common for him, he borrowed details from—or simply inserted himself into—scenes others had experienced. So, he saw the kapok debris field and made himself a victim of it. Later, he photographed sailors struggling to transfer a stretcher down to an LCVP, and he inserted himself into the process, exaggerating his role. And of course, having seen *LCI(L)-85* limping along in sinking condition, he appropriated those details for his account of his own ship.

And that, I believe is the most likely scenario that can be sifted out of Capa's vague and conflicting narratives. I won't claim this scenario is correct in all its details. It is, after all, a result of balancing well-established facts with a great number of accounts that are partly accurate, partly doubtful and sometimes plainly wrong. Nevertheless, I suggest that it is the most likely sequence of events as we understand the facts today.

Reloading

One minor point needs to be noted, if not resolved. In the Wertenbaker interview, Capa said he "started to change my film" when the shell hit, presumably disrupting the act. Because he was covered in "feathers" at that point, he couldn't have been below decks yet. He did not mention finishing the task, nor did he mention whether he was changing film in one or both of his Contax cameras. And he never mentioned going down to the engine room, though we have two witnesses that he did.

In *Slightly out of Focus* he offered a different version: "I went down to the engine room, dried my hands, and put fresh films in both cameras." In this version he was, again, above decks when the shell covered him in "feathers" but hadn't started changing film.

Lewis and West also gave different versions of the same scene. Lewis simply said Capa came down to get dry. West said Capa came down to dry his film, while smoking two cigarettes at the same time.

So why do these discrepancies matter? There might be a couple of reasons. First, it goes back to his credibility when he discussed why he left the beach. In the

Wertenbaker interview, he left because he'd used up all his film. And yet in both accounts he claimed to change (or at least started to change) film once he was aboard the *94*. So, he couldn't have run out of film, unless he just meant he'd exhausted the roll in his camera. And that interpretation fits with his version in *Slightly out of Focus*. Before fleeing to the *94*, he said his wet hands had ruined one fresh roll of film he was trying to load. And even during panicked flight, he said he rationalized it by the thought, "I'm just going to dry my hands on that boat," which, coupled with his previous comment, seems to imply he would finish changing film after the needed hand drying.

The question of motivation is largely irrelevant, however. As discussed earlier, he wasn't supposed to be ashore, and likely ended up there in error and was justified in flight. It was only the heroic but untrue fable that he planned to go ashore with Co. E that forced him to come up with a plausible excuse for needing to leave the beach at the first opportunity.

The second reason that it might matter is a question of what Capa didn't say. Why was reloading his cameras in the engine room such a central feature in *Slightly out of Focus*, when he completely omitted any reference to changing film thereafter? As we'll see later, from the time Capa boarded the *94*, he would change film at least four more times in the next three hours, including two times on the *94* *after* he came up from the engine room.

In the final analysis, therefore, it isn't necessary to determine exactly what he did down there, and it's probably impossible to do so anyway. For all the witnesses and their accounts, they merely painted a hopelessly contradictory picture. The point is that none of the succeeding film changes required a trip to the engine room. It seems increasingly clear the film change was merely a pretext for Capa to seek shelter in the bowels of the ship until it got off the beach.

The recognition that Capa had to have boarded *LCI(L)-94* at the end of its initial beaching brings his experience on the beach into much clearer focus. He wasn't there for the two hours he claimed in the Wertenbaker interview. And he wasn't even in the surf for the roughly 30 minutes between his Wave 13 LCVP's beaching time (0820 hours) and the hits on the *94* as he supposedly boarded (0850 hours).

No. Likely, he was ashore—or rather crouching in the surf—for as little as 15 minutes. In the absolute sense it is not a negative reflection on Capa that he was there so briefly. He should never have been ashore in the first place, and there's no reason to fault him for leaving as soon as possible. He was trying to fulfill his mission to get his film back as quickly as possible.

Where this *does* reflect poorly on Capa comes as a result of his compulsion to falsely paint himself in a heroic light, deciding to land with a first wave unit with the toughest assignment. In this context, his actual time on Easy Red serves only to diminish his credibility and stature.

CHAPTER TWENTY ONE

Chase, Again

"... we are there with our cameras to record reality. Once we start modifying that which exists, we are robbing photography of its most valuable attribute."

PHILIP JONES GRIFFITHS

In both versions of his saga, Capa then ended up right back on the *Chase*, the same ship from which he set out a few hours earlier. Such agreement between versions of Capa's own tale is rare, yet the proof is simple. *LCI(L)-94*'s muster roll shows Anthony was then taken to the *Chase*, which, after all, was LCVP 26-26's mother ship. And, since Ruley's clips showed Capa aboard 26-26 with the wounded QM 3/c Anthony, then Capa ended up at the *Chase*, too.

Perhaps it is fitting then that history has made its best effort to contradict him on one of the few occasions when he was both consistent and correct. History insists instead that Capa returned to the *Henrico*. Both Magnum Photos[1] and the International Center for Photography[2] state that Figure 71 was taken by Capa aboard the *Henrico* (along with 11 nearly identical, seldom seen shots). There is no explanation for this. Capa's descriptions of his D-Day exploits never mentioned returning to the *Henrico*. Even Whelan agreed it was the *Chase*.

Just to confuse things more, Sam Fuller, who we saw earlier falsely putting himself and Capa aboard the *Henrico*, said Capa returned to the USS *Thurston* (AP-77) for the trip back the UK, landing at Portsmouth.[3] Fuller supposedly got these details during a post-war evening of drinks and reminiscing with Capa. We know the Portsmouth detail is wrong; he wasn't the only American to confuse Portsmouth with Portland (the latter was in Weymouth Bay, the start and return points for the Omaha attack transports). And the *Thurston* detail is also clearly wrong.

Life's editors, stuck with the job of captioning photos for which Capa did not provide caption notes, merely described it as a hospital ship in its 19 June edition.[4] It was not. There were no hospital ships off Omaha Beach that day. Instead, specially equipped LSTs were the primary casualty evacuation means. But given that censors would not have permitted publication of the ship's actual identity, we can forgive this minor error in captioning.

Figure 71. Shown on page 31 of *Life*'s 19 June 1944 issue, this Capa photo was taken after his return to the *Chase*. The caption provided by Magnum Photos states, "Omaha Beach. June 6th, 1944. The first victims of the landings, on board the US boat 'Henrico.'" (Robert Capa © ICP/Magnum Photos)

Something in this scene must have captured Capa's fascination, because the 12 photos he took of the scene are far more than he took of any other scene. Either that, or he felt there was nothing else of interest and he just wanted to finish off the roll. In fact, this was the final roll he shot on D-Day, and it brought his total after leaving the beach to 60 images.

Here again Capa was vying with Coast Guard photographers for the same pictures. A Coast Guard motion picture clip includes a close-up of this same scene, showing a corpse on a stretcher being lowered by a crane to the same group of sailors seen in Figure 71.[5]

Still, there are differences between Capa's two versions of his time back aboard the *Chase*. In the Wertenbaker interview he noted the casualties aboard the *Chase*, that men were administering transfusions and that he took "a lot of pictures."[6]

In the *Slightly out of Focus* version, Capa stated he began taking pictures again once he boarded the *Chase*. In this telling, the sailors (now blood soaked), were sewing corpses into white sacks.[7] As is consistent with the two narratives, the *Slightly out of Focus* version is bloodier and more replete with corpses. In this case, at least, the more sensational narrative appears to be the more accurate; about half the casualties visible are already in body bags, and it appears the sailors are in the process of placing the rest of the corpses in bags.

Connecting the Dots

Neither of his two accounts specifically mentions the subjects of the additional photos he took aboard the *Chase*, but three scenes he described do appear in his film. Figure 71, of course, illustrates the handling of the fatalities, but two other scenes preceded it. In *Slightly out of Focus* he mentioned in passing that upon arriving back at the *Chase*, "the last wave of the 16th Infantry was just being lowered." It appears Capa captured at least one photo of this. Recall that the LCVP to which Capa transferred *from LCI(L)-94* was the 26-26. Now refer to Figure 32, the LCVP Capa photographed being rail loaded. It was also LCVP 26-26. When examining Figure 32 earlier, I concluded that the photo did not capture the initial assault troops boarding for the dawn attack, as many sources have insisted. Instead, it had to have been snapped several hours after sunrise, based on the apparent position of the sun in the companion photo Figure 33 (taken of the same scene from a different perspective, by a Coast Guard photographer). And now we've shown that Capa arrived back on the *Chase* on the very LCVP seen on both Figures 32 and 33 and did so several hours after sunrise.

The contact sheets complete the sequence for us. They include a previously unknown image of LCVP 26-26 as it was hoisted back aboard the *Chase* (Figure 72). Capa is standing in the craft, towards its aft, and his camera is focused on the crew passing Anthony's litter across to the crew of the *Chase*. Thus, we have visual proof of both Anthony and Capa returning to the *Chase*. This photo is labelled exposure 9, and the negative for Figure 32 is labelled exposure 11 of the same roll. So, the sequence of events started with LCVP 26-26 hoisted aboard and Anthony's litter passed to the crew of the *Chase* (Figure 72), then the last wave of troops began boarding the 26-26 (Figure 32) followed by the last troops boarding the craft (Figure 33).

We've connected the dots.

Normal procedures were that once an LCVP had been lowered to the water, subsequent waves for that craft would be embarked using net loading, not rail loading. But given the stretcher case that was aboard the 26-26 with Capa, they probably decided it would be easier to hoist the 26-26 back aboard to remove the casualty. Other D-Day photos show the same procedure: LCVPs hoisted back aboard ship to unload the wounded (though with larger landing craft, only the stretchers themselves were winched aboard). And once 26-26 was back in the davits, it seems they took the opportunity to rail load it with troops of the last wave. According to the 16th RCT's Landing Tables, these were the excess personnel of the "overstrength" echelon

Figure 72. Capa's negative 4-C-9 showing LCVP 26-26 hoisted back aboard the USS *Chase*. The litter with QM 3/c David Anthony is being transferred to the *Chase* for treatment and evacuation to the UK. (Robert Capa © ICP/Magnum Photos)

(i.e., those men who could not fit in each company's initial allotment of six LCVPs for the assault).[8] They were the last elements scheduled to leave the *Chase* and six LCVPs were allotted to the task as part of Wave 19 (scheduled to land H+250 / 1040 hours). They were also more than an hour and a half late departing the *Chase*. Having just climbed out of the 26-26, Capa was in the perfect position to capture an embarkation shot which the dawn's poor light had precluded when he himself boarded shortly before 0600 hours.

It also provides some indication of the time Capa arrived back aboard the *Chase*. The *Chase*'s deck log and Action Report agree that all embarked troops and cargo had been unloaded by 1100 hours (unloading was behind schedule). Since Capa captured at least this one LCVP being loaded, we know therefore that he had to be back aboard the *Chase* sometime before 1100 hours.

We can check this conclusion. The distance from the beach to the Transport Area was approximately 23,000 yards, and the planning speed for LCIs in this area was 10 knots. In theory, *LCI(L)-94* should have reached the vicinity of the Transport Area in a bit less than one hour and 10 minutes, or about 1000 hours if it started shortly after 0850 hours when it was hit. But given that the *94* was partly crippled and operating on a single prop, it must have taken a bit longer. Using our previous estimate of a maximum of 8 knots, it would have taken at best 90 minutes. It then took some time to lay-to and transfer Capa and the casualties to LCVP 26-26—which Ruley's film shows took several minutes—and additional time for the LCVP to reach the *Chase* and be hoisted aboard. So, in all probability Capa couldn't have arrived back aboard the *Chase* before 1030 hours.

That narrows Capa's arrival back on the *Chase* to about a 30-minute window between 1030 and 1100 hours.

The Death of the *85*

In *Slightly out of Focus,* Capa also made a brief comment that "sailors were hoisting stretchers from sinking barges alongside" the *Chase.* This was more hyperbole; the *Chase* had several LCTs alongside, which had been part of the first two waves to land and had returned to load more vehicles from the *Chase.* There was, however, only one sinking craft alongside the *Chase.*

LCI(L)-85—the source of so much confusion in Capa's saga—was on scene to mix things up once again. In previous chapters we covered the *85's* ill-fated beaching attempts. It then stood off the beach about 200 yards and succeeded in putting out the fires, but the flooding could not be controlled, and the ship began listing. All but about 30 able-bodied troops who were still aboard were transferred to LCVPs for landing. The *85* then limped back to the Transport Area where Capa, aboard the *94,* passed the *85* as it neared the *Chase.* Once on the *Chase,* Capa again saw the *85,* but from a much closer distance.

During this phase of Capa's saga, Whelan discussed in detail only those photos which were included in *Life's* 19 June issue. However, the contact sheets show that Capa took several shots documenting the damaged *85,* taken from the deck of the *Chase,* four of which are on the contact sheets. Two images show the *85* approaching the *Chase,* and two show the LCI alongside. Figure 73's view is nearly straight down and shows a very limited portion of the LCI's decks. Its focus is a casualty with a medic attending to him. The other three shots of this sequence were taken from farther aft on the *Chase* and show more complete views of the *85.* There are several negatives missing in this range, and it is probable he devoted many of them to this scene.

The *85* had come alongside the *Chase* to transfer casualties and the troops that had not been able to land. It also sought assistance to fight the flooding. The Action Report for the *85* indicates it came alongside the *Chase* at "about 1200" hours and pulled away by 1330 hours.[9] The *Chase's* reports, however, place the *85* mooring alongside at 1115 hours and casting off at 1240 hours.[10] It was at some point during this period that Capa photographed the ship.[11] The *85* finally capsized at about 1430 hours.

Figure 73. Capa's photo of *LCI(L)-85* alongside the USS *Chase*. (Robert Capa © ICP/Magnum Photos)

In *Slightly out of Focus*, Capa described the retreat of his own LCI thusly: "Our boat was listing and we slowly pulled away from the beach to try to reach the mother ship before we sank." As noted earlier, the *94* took no hits below the waterline,* was not listing and was in no danger of sinking. It made a couple more runs between the Transport Area and the beach that day and continued to work the beach area for several days thereafter.

Obviously Capa was so impressed by the ordeal of the *85* that he sought to incorporate it into his own tale for the sake of dramatic impact. It is worth recalling that Capa was frank in admitting that *Slightly out of Focus* was not overly constrained by a strict adherence to the truth. The facts need not interfere with a good story. Unfortunately, Whelan did accept these fictional points as fact and tried to weave the *85*'s actual activities into Capa's movements, which has caused no end of confusion ever since.

It must be noted that as with his previous sets of D-Day photos, Capa's picture of the *85*'s ordeal was again neatly duplicated by ubiquitous Coast Guard photographers. They captured several additional photos and a brief motion picture clip of the

---

* It damaged a propeller and shaft when it smashed over a submerged obstacle on its second beaching.

stricken *85*, taken during this same period and from a virtually identical vantage point. Whelan speculated that one of these was a Capa photo, but so far there is no proof one way or the other.[12] The fact that Whelan could not match that photo to a Capa negative—or even a type of camera Capa used—underscores the confusion that remains about Capa's body of work after leaving the beach.

Exhaustion and Recovery

According to the account in Wertenbaker, Capa became confused while still aboard the *94*, attributing it to exhaustion, and when an LCVP came by to take off the wounded, he went with them. Once back aboard the *Chase*, he took "a lot of pictures," then lay down, asking to be woken in an hour. Somebody threw a blanket over him. When he woke, the ship was on its way back to England.

Slightly out of Focus changes this sequence. It was only later, when he started taking pictures on the *Chase,* that "Things got confused …" There is no mention of confusion or exhaustion aboard the *94*. Nor is there any mention of lying down to take a nap or asking to be woken in an hour aboard the *Chase*; instead, he apparently just blacked out. Sometime later he woke up in a bunk, naked, no dog tags, but with a note on his neck stating he was an exhaustion case. Conveniently—if not entirely credibly*—his camera bag was nearby, despite both him and his roommate having been stripped of clothing and equipment. Capa and the other man, another "exhaustion case," then engaged in a debate to see who was the greater coward. None of this was even hinted at in the Wertenbaker interview.

The claim that he was stripped of clothing and equipment is an odd invention, as motion picture film of casualties from the *Chase* being offloaded in Weymouth of 7 June show none of the wounded had been stripped of their clothes; they wore the same clothing they had on when wounded. Scherman's photo of Capa taken on 7 June back at Weymouth (see Figure 50) also contradicts Capa. That photo was taken on an LST which Capa had boarded to return to Normandy. Clearly, he was not actually in the casualty chain of evacuation for exhaustion cases. In fact, in the second nearly identical photo Scherman snapped, Capa looked rather jovial and showed no effects of his recent bout of exhaustion.

Further, in those photos he was outfitted in the same manner as he was in Ruley's film clips: cotton-poplin field jacket, wool pants and wool shirt, and helmet. He's even wearing the distinctively placed canteen. His shirt is too obscured to see any details; however, Scherman's photo shows that the left shoulder and breast of Capa's field jacket still bore the marks made by the strap of his camera bag on D-Day.

---

* As CPT Wall had experienced, cameras and film in the possession of casualties were to have been placed in the classified courier bags, secured by the ship's company and sent to London. Wall kept his only by dint of pitching a big enough fit. Capa was unconscious, but supposedly the crew made no effort to secure his film, which was by default classified at that point.

Since he retained his same minimal field gear (helmet, pistol belt and canteen—the side with the entrenching tool cover is hidden) and wore the same field jacket, then obviously he hadn't been stripped of his clothing and gear. In *Slightly out of Focus* Capa claimed he changed clothes, and Scherman's photo tends to support that. What can be seen of his wool pants shows no indication of the previous day's ordeal, perhaps indicating he had been able to change into clean pants. Coast Guard attack transport ships did not keep stores of Army clothing, so if Capa did change clothes aboard the *Chase,* he must have had access to his baggage and that he had left it stowed aboard the *Chase* during his jaunt to the beach. The packing list for 1st Division troops landing on D-Day did not include spare pants or shirt, and excess baggage for those troops had been loaded into two LCTs for later delivery.[13] So, if Capa changed clothes as he claimed (and as Scherman's photos suggest), then his baggage was not loaded on LCTs with that of the landing force, and indicates, once again, he never intended to land.

In Scherman's photo, Capa, who was prone to a heavy five o'clock shadow, was also clean shaven; he'd had access to toiletries and been able perform personal hygiene overnight. All in all, he presented a far better appearance than the rest of the bedraggled survivors who stumbled ashore at Weymouth on 7 June (as seen in film showing survivors and casualties arriving at Weymouth that day).[14] One can only conclude he returned not just to the *Chase,* but to the baggage he temporarily left aboard that ship on D-Day, fully intending to return.

Before moving on, let's revisit his canteen. Given the odd placement of that canteen and what seems to have been a greater need to have it always about him than even his camera bag, one is led to suspect it was filled with something more potent than water. Based on the canteen's cap, Capa was carrying a silver-colored aluminum M-1910 canteen. He did say he brought alcohol along on D-Day, but claimed it was in the "silver pocket flask" he supposedly bought at Dunhill's. It is fair to speculate that the silver Dunhill pocket flask detail was an exaggeration designed to add stylish flair to his stories, and that he smuggled his booze along with him as many generations of soldiers have done, hidden in plain sight in his canteen.

Film Cache

When Capa arrived back in the UK and delivered his film, he passed along more than just the D-Day film. He also passed along the film he exposed aboard the *Chase* during the staging at Weymouth and during the night crossing of the Channel *before* D-Day—i.e., during the period 3–5 June. This included three rolls of 35mm film, based on the comments in his surviving caption notes (the Troops Sunning roll, the Last Glimpse of England roll and the Briefing to Invasion roll) as well as an unknown number of negatives from his Speed Graphic. These numbers exclude the packet he sent before sailing which were already in the censor's hands in London on

D-Day. When the *Chase* returned to England on D+1, this film, showing staging and Channel crossing, was placed in his packet for London along with his D-Day film. The question is, where was that film while Capa was taking his excursion to the beach?

I believe there's no chance he would have taken that exposed film with him on his D-Day excursion. Even a short jaunt to the beach that did not entail landing would expose that film to the dangers of water damage, sinking of the craft, enemy fire and a host of other mishaps. By leaving his pre-invasion film aboard the *Chase* on D-Day, Capa would have guaranteed that at least part of his take would make it back to the UK, no matter what happened to his camera bag—or him—that day. So, odds are that Capa left the exposed film aboard the *Chase* when he boarded his LCVP on D-Day.

And we have an indication that this is what he did. Capa's caption notes for a roll of Contax 35mm film exposed on D-1 described the troops having their last look at the British shore as they sail for the invasion (the Last Glimpse of England roll). At the bottom of the second page, sandwiched between the caption notes and instructions for developing the film, Capa later added a cryptic line: "Film like everything got wett by landing [*sic*]." This is important. The caption notes were for a roll of film he exposed aboard ship *after* sailing (during the night Channel crossing) but *before* the landings. Yet his "wett" comment is clearly a *post-landing* addition.

Whelan unaccountably tried to claim that this wetting of Capa's gear happened during his transfer from the *Chase* to the *Henrico* before setting sail from Weymouth.[15] But we know that Capa *did not transfer* between ships and remained on the *Chase* throughout. The page of caption notes with the "wett by landing" comment could only have referred to a dunking on D-Day, not a ship-to-ship transfer in an English harbor. Because this page of caption notes—and the others filled out *before* D-Day—survived and did not get soaked, it could not have accompanied him into the surf, where his "film like everything got wett." He must have left his exposed film and its accompanying pages of caption notes back on the *Chase*. And the fact that he had to include the "wett" note on an already used page of caption notes strongly indicates his supply of blank caption notes had been ruined by the water during the landing. The absence of caption notes for any film he used on D-Day supports this conclusion. As we'll see, he had plenty of time during the morning hours of 7 June back in Weymouth to fill out the necessary pages of caption notes—*if* he had any that were still usable.

If, as he claimed, he planned to land and stay ashore with the invading troops, his pre-invasion products should have been dropped into one of the classified film pouches, sealed and placed in the custody of a ship's officer. But his "wett" comment shows he had access to this material after returning to the *Chase*, indicating he never relinquished it to a Coast Guard officer. This means he left those pre-invasion products someplace he could retrieve them, such as his baggage. Which, again, means he intended all along to return to the *Chase* after his LCVP trip.

By Chance the *Chase*?

This also explains the "coincidence" by which Capa ended up back on the *Chase*. The casual reader of Capa's saga may have missed the significance of this, but the attack transports were not the primary casualty evacuation means. According to the naval plan, "b. LSTs will provide the major casualty lift from the far [Normandy coast] to near shore [the UK]."[16] In support of this, designated LSTs received an augmentation unit of 21–23 medical personnel and necessary equipment. No fewer than 24 LSTs arriving off Omaha Beach were charged with this duty on D-Day, with 10 of them present during the period of Capa's flight. LCIs were the primary vehicle for ambulatory cases. The 15 attack transports were the third evacuation priority, and to be used only "as the military situation permits." They received no special medical augmentation. Once the operation was underway, the provisions of this plan were largely carried out as directed. The vast majority of casualties were treated and evacuated via LSTs. Even when British "hospital carriers" (smaller converted ferry boats) became available starting D+1, almost 80 percent of casualties still came out via LSTs.[17] Only 560 casualties went out on the various attack transports *for both Omaha and Utah,* though many more uninjured survivors were evacuated to the UK by way of the attack transports.

Further, the *Chase* was not a "mother ship" to *LCI(L)-94*, so there was no evacuation-related consideration that would call for the *94* to seek the aid of the *Chase*. And yet it did.

But Capa was not a casualty. So why are we discussing casualty evacuation procedures? It comes down to the question of why LCVP 26-26—a *Chase* landing craft—had been hailed in the first place. If it had been hailed for the primary purpose of getting the wounded to the prepared casualty-receiving ships (with Capa then merely a hitchhiker), then the 26-26 should have gone to one of the LSTs that were just a few hundred yards away in the second line of ships in the Transport Area. Not only were these the designated receiving ships, but their bow doors made cross-handling of stretchers much, much easier.

In other words, with 10 LSTs immediately available as primary casualty-receiving ships off Omaha Beach that morning, Capa instead ended up coming back to one of 15 tertiary receiving ships. And not just any of them. He came back to *the very same ship on which he arrived.* We can believe this was incredible, random luck—ending up back on the correct one out of dozens of possibilities. Or we can believe the 26-26 was hailed for the primary purpose of getting Capa back to the *Chase*, with the wounded Anthony then being a hitchhiker.

Let's return to an earlier oddity that we noted but did not explain. In Ruley's clips showing LCVP 26-26, Capa was the first man to board the 26-26, before even the casualty. That's something of an ethical faux pas in the combat world. We also saw that the *94*'s crew was unprepared to transfer Anthony to the 26-26 even though Capa was already aboard. In fact, they hadn't even gotten him on a stretcher yet, and preparations took so long that the 26-26 had to sheer off and come back minutes later for the stretcher transfer. That suggests the 26-26 was initially hailed for the express purpose of helping Capa get back to his attack transport, and the decision to transfer Anthony was an afterthought.

I suggest this was not random luck that brought Capa back to the very same ship. Rather, Capa made his way back to his original ride because that is exactly where he intended to return had his day gone as planned, and therefore where he had stowed his kit and his exposed film.

Capa's arrival back on the *Chase*—contrary to both the dictates of the OPLAN and statistical probability alike—reinforces the conclusion that he had planned to return to the *Chase* early on D-Day, and that he never planned to leave his landing craft at all.

CHAPTER TWENTY TWO

Camera Confusion

"Not everybody trusts paintings but people believe photographs."

ANSEL ADAMS

If the camera is the primary tool of the photographer, then it is strange how carelessly Capa handled the topic in his stories. Granted, his storytelling was more focused on spinning "ripping yarns" than on technical descriptions of his gear, but one would still expect a certain level of attention paid to the instruments of his livelihood. Unfortunately, this was not the case. His cameras were treated almost as stage props, mentioned only in passing as if to add a small detail to complete the scene. This seemingly careless facet of his narratives leaves us with a couple points that require some clarification.

Speed Graphic

The Speed Graphic was perhaps the most well known of the iconic "press camera" type (see Figure 50, right side). Those unfamiliar with the name are still probably familiar with the camera from older movies showing news photographers popping flash bulbs in their Speed Graphic cameras as they covered crime stories. The Speed Graphic was a versatile camera which could produce high-quality images. It was a staple in the kit bag of most professional photographers, and many of the most popular images of the 1940s, 1950s and 1960s were taken by Speed Graphic cameras.

The Speed Graphic was extensively used by civilian war photographers and military combat cameramen in World War II. Joe Rosenthal used one for his famous image of the Marines raising the flag over Iwo Jima, and a photo of the men of the 165th Signal Photo Company shows half of them holding that camera. Despite this, the camera was bulky, slow and a bit complicated to use in fast-moving action environments, which is why many war photographers preferred Contax or Rolleiflex cameras for combat conditions. Nevertheless, good photographers ensured they had a variety of tools to meet the conditions they might encounter, which is why Bob Landry, Bert Brandt and Capa all had a Speed Graphic or similar "press cameras" in their gear.

While aboard the *Chase*, Capa took several photos of coxswains being briefed on a depiction of the boat lanes drawn on the floor of the ship's "gym" (an empty cargo hold). There is neither a contact sheet nor an original page of caption notes for this roll of film, but Whelan said it was taken with Capa's Rolleiflex.[1] And this is confirmed by the back of one of those photos; the title is Invasion Preparations and is listed as Capa Rollei 1. Whelan then stated Capa switched to his Speed Graphic camera for a close shot, which showed one Army and two Coast Guard officers squatting in front of a wall covered with reconnaissance photos. Coleman examined the surviving negatives held by ICP and confirmed there were a number taken using the 4 × 5 format film of the Speed Graphic.

Despite this, there is debate whether Capa had taken his Speed Graphic along for the invasion. The question generally arises from the belief that Capa had planned to go ashore with the 16th RCT on 6 June. Capa believed that a war photographer should only take the most necessary gear on a shoot to avoid being needlessly loaded down. Following this logic, he would have had no need for his Speed Graphic ashore on D-Day and would have left it behind. This argument is buttressed by the film clip of Capa aboard LCVP 26-26, which shows the camera bag he wore that day was too small to hold his Speed Graphic. Indeed, there is general agreement that Capa could not, and did not take his Speed Graphic on his jaunt to the beach that day.

The question is, where did he leave it? Those who believe Capa was going to remain ashore with the 16th RCT suggest he left his Speed Graphic back in the UK, possibly to be sent forward to Normandy with either the baggage of the 16th RCT or with the baggage of the press camp. But how to account for the photos aboard the *Chase* which he took with a Speed Graphic? One suggestion is that he must have borrowed one from a Coast Guard cameraman aboard the *Chase*. It is a plausible argument.

I would suggest a different explanation, however. Capa had been selected to cover the invasion, from marshalling to the initial moments of the landings. This would potentially involve taking pictures in a wide variety of environments, to include the Press Training Center, the 1st Division base camps, the invasion marshalling camps, embarkation, aboard the *Chase,* during his excursion to the beach and finally on the return trip to Weymouth. Given this, he would have packed his entire photography kit—or at least as much as he could, given the 125-pound baggage limit—to ensure he had the right equipment for the varied conditions he would likely encounter. So, when he needed a Speed Graphic aboard the *Chase*, he simply used his own. When it came time to board his landing craft early 6 June, he took only his camera bag and the cameras he felt he'd need in the next few hours, leaving the rest of his 125 pounds of baggage aboard the *Chase*. He intended to reclaim his baggage when his landing craft returned him to the *Chase* later that morning.

So which explanation is correct? Or at least most likely? To answer that we turn back to Bert Brandt. As noted earlier, Brandt's mission that day was identical to Capa's, and the two had been together both at the Press Training Camp and the 1st Division headquarters during the staging for the invasion. As the two men were embedded with the same division and operating under the same baggage handling provisions, there's good reason to believe their gear was organized and handled in similar fashions.

We know Brandt took his Speed Graphic camera aboard his attack transport (USS *Charles Carroll*). Before the landings, Brandt was pictured hamming it up with soldiers and sailors aboard the *Carroll*. In one photo he stands in the center of a group of GIs, overburdened by a variety of combat and photographic gear. Part of that gear included his Speed Graphic camera clutched in his right hand, and its large carrying case—which was the size of a small suitcase—in his left.[2] Neither the Speed Graphic nor its case would have been practical aboard a landing craft on the way to the beach on D-Day, but that photo proves he took that gear with him when he boarded the *Carroll*. On the morning of 6 June, he left his bulky gear aboard the *Carroll*, and took only his Rolleiflex (his preferred camera for action shots) to document the landings from his LCM. After his drive-by photo shoot of the beach, he returned to the *Carroll* and the rest of his gear. Upon his return to the UK with his film, he was whisked away to London for an interview. Some days later he returned to Normandy and was pictured on the beach after landing, drying his camera gear. His Speed Graphic camera case was again at his feet.[3]

Although Brandt didn't intend to use his Speed Graphic during his foray to the beach, he nevertheless kept as much of his photographic kit as close to him as possible during his various travels incident to the invasion, as there would be more photo opportunities at hand than just those during the early hours of 6 June. And there is every reason to believe Capa would have behaved in a similar fashion. As a result, it is reasonable to conclude Capa took his own Speed Graphic aboard the *Chase*, along with the bulk of his photographic kit, and he used his own camera to snap the photos contained on the 4 × 5 format negatives.

Having concluded that Capa left his bulkier photographic gear aboard the *Chase*, as well as most of his personal gear, we have yet another indication he did not intend to go ashore with the 16th RCT on D-Day. His nonessential gear was back aboard the *Chase* because he intended all along to return to the ship. Just as Bert Brandt had done over at the *Carroll*.

Contax or Rolleiflex?

Up to this point, our discussion has proceeded on the assumption that Capa's photos on *LCI(L)-94* and back on the *Chase* were taken using one of his two Contax cameras. This assumption is based on his *Slightly out of Focus* narrative in which he specifically mentioned using his two Contax cameras while ashore. In fact, Capa never mentioned carrying anything but his two Contax cameras during his D-Day adventures. Neither his own *Slightly out of Focus*, Wertenbaker's *Invasion* nor Kershaw's *Blood and Champagne* even hinted at there being a Rolleiflex along on Capa's excursion to the beach.

Quite the contrary, Capa's two narratives would seem to indicate he used his Contax cameras exclusively on his D-Day excursion. He specifically mentioned pulling out a Contax camera on the LCVP as he neared the beach and mentioned using both of his Contax cameras while on the beach. Once he boarded the LCI as he fled, he "put fresh films [*sic*] in both cameras," then went back on deck and started taking pictures (per *Slightly out of Focus*), from which one would logically infer he was still using those Contax cameras while taking pictures aboard *LCI(L)-94*.

Whelan contradicted this, indicating Capa used his Rolleiflex once he boarded the LCI and while back aboard the *Chase*. In his *Robert Capa* biography, Whelan merely mentioned the Rolleiflex in a footnote, stating, "In addition, the images that Capa had shot with his Rolleiflex before and after the actual landings survived intact."[4] But that comment falls far short of proving Capa used his Rolleiflex while aboard *LCI(L)-94*. Whelan was more emphatic, however, in *This Is War!*, stating that, "Capa shot that picture [Figure 66, the corpsman treating the wounded aboard *LCI(L)-94*] with his Rolleiflex, which he used exclusively until he stopped photographing for the day."[5] Whelan also included an image of the negative for the photo of the last troops boarding LCVP 26-26 (Figure 32), which was the same format as a Rolleiflex.

But Whelan had so much wrong about the Capa D-Day saga that it's fair to ask whether we should blindly accept his word for it. For instance, he seems to have had a rather poor grasp of Capa's photo take during this period. With just a single exception (Figure 32) he discussed *only* those scenes used in *Life*'s 19 June issue and seemed totally unaware of several duplicate Capa photos which we have identified in this analysis. Nor did he appear aware of the additional scenes which were not included in the *Life* spread: the photo of the casualty transfer between the *94* and LCVP 26-26 (Figure 69), and the photo of the *85* alongside the *Chase* (Figure 73). As noted earlier, Whelan also cited another photo of the sinking *LCI(L)-85*, taken from the *Chase*, which was included in a New York paper's 9 June edition,[6] and suggested it was "possibly" one of Capa's. The fact that Whelan could not tell if it was Capa's or not is evidence that he was working from an incomplete collection of film and was well aware of it.

And indeed, that was the case. When *Life* transferred the rights for Capa's images to Magnum in the late 1940s, only a scattering of his D-Day negatives survived either the censor's red pen or *Life*'s filing system. The images that did survive were gathered, arranged in a rather disjointed sequence, and from them several contact sheets were created. This is an important point. None of the original contact sheets created by Morris's London laboratory survived, and the contact sheets that do exist were made from an incomplete set of surviving negatives.

The result is a surprising level of confusion regarding just what Capa did photograph. There are several Capa images that have never been released beyond their inclusion in difficult-to-view, recreated contact sheets. There are several never-released duplicate shots of scenes, to include no fewer than four pictures of one scene. ICP held one unlabelled image which they did not know was a Capa image.[*] And based on the negative numbering system on the surviving negatives, fewer than half of the photos Capa took after leaving the beach have been accounted for.

But one thing is clear. All the surviving negatives on those recreated contact sheets—from the time Capa left the beach—are clearly the square format of the Rolleiflex's 120 film. But does that mean he did not use his Contax cameras at all during this phase? Well, the contact sheets show that the several "one last shots" of the beach were all taken with the Rolleiflex, and since these were his first photos taken after boarding *LCI(L)-94*, it would seem he did transition to it at that point. And the complete absence of 35mm negatives would support that.

Once again, the visual record can help us. Figure 64 contains a small surprise. That frame came from the Critical Past enhanced film reel, which was slightly cropped. By combining that frame with the corresponding frame from the NARA version of the film, it is possible to determine that there were three camera straps around Capa's neck at that moment. Each of his camera straps, whether on a Contax or Rolleiflex camera, had two adjustment buckles, one on each the left and right chest. In Figure 74 four buckles are visible, indicating two cameras. Also visible is a third strap. No buckle is visible for that strap, presumably because it has been adjusted so the camera will hang low enough not to interfere with the other two cameras. It's also possible to determine that one of the buckles is a prong style. His Contax cameras used friction buckles, and only his Rolleiflex used the prong style. This proves that after coming topside from the *94*'s engine room, Capa was wearing two Contax *and* one Rolleiflex around his neck.

Why would a cameraman in combat conditions encumber himself with three cameras dangling from his neck? It seems to directly violate Capa's own maxim that a war photographer should operate with the minimum gear possible so he could move quickly. Nevertheless, Capa himself bears witness to the fact that he did this from time to time. While relating an incident during the Battle of the Bulge when

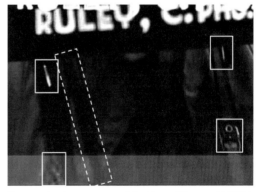

Figure 74. A composite of the Critical Past and NARA frames showing the four buckles for two camera straps (solid rectangle highlights) and an additional strap (dashed highlight).

---

[*] Figure 69; it is not on any of the recreated contact sheets, and it was only when I paired it with Ruley's film that they acknowledged it was Capa's.

he was momentarily mistaken for a German by American soldiers, he claimed, "When they were close enough to make out the three German cameras around my neck, they became very happy GIs. Two Contax cameras and a Rolleiflex—I was the jackpot!"[7] So our identification of three cameras around his neck while aboard the *94* is not out of character for the man.

But why? Why did he change the film in his Contax cameras if he didn't intend to use them soon? Why did he keep them out, ready for use if he didn't intend to use them in the next few minutes? Why not take the opportunity in the engine room to stow them back in his camera bag, especially since he'd pulled out his Rollieflex? All of this argues for the possibility that he did use his Contax cameras after leaving the beach.

The short note Capa supposedly included with his film packet to his editor on 7 June seems to support this. It said, "John, all the action's in the 35 millimeter."[*] Would that "action" not include the shots he took on the *94* or on the *Chase*? Surely the inshore shots of the beach would be included in "the action"? As would the photo of the mortally wounded *LCI(L)-85*? And the casualties on both the *Chase* and the *94*? That interpretation would seem to indicate he used his Contax cameras after leaving the beach. And yet …

There isn't a shred of evidence that he did. No photo. No negative. As with the roll of film from his second Contax on the beach, there is nothing to even hint that he took any photos from his Contax once he left the beach.

Counting Rolls

In *This Is War!*, Whelan included the *Life* 19 June pages showing Capa's five after-the-beach photos. Whelan only discussed two of them in any detail and mentioned in an aside that he took "a few" shots of a third scene (the casualties aboard the *Chase*). He completely avoided any mention of how many photos Capa's took after he left the beach. We don't know why he passed over this obviously important point.

Knowing he exclusively used his Rolleiflex makes our task of assessing Capa's photo-taking activity much easier. The 120 film for the Rolleiflex came in standard holders of 12 frames. From the marginal notes on the surviving negatives, we know he used film from five rolls of film. Three of his rolls show images for exposure 12 (including the last two rolls he used that day). It is safe to conclude the remaining two rolls were also fully exposed.

These five rolls prove Capa took no fewer than 60 photos after he left Easy Red beach sector. Whelan had access to these same contact sheets. Why didn't he simply do the math and reveal Capa's total?

---

[*] We have only John Morris's word that such a note existed or its contents. And his description of its message has varied over time.

And this brings us back to a point raised earlier. Capa made it quite clear that upon boarding *LCI(L)-94*, he went down to the engine room to change film … *in the two cameras he would not use for the rest of the day*. Yet he never once mentioned the four times after that when he changed the film in his Rolleiflex. And that would include two film changes while still aboard *LCI(L)-94* after coming up from the engine room. Odd, indeed.

Scaling Back

If Capa had three cameras around his neck while standing on the boat deck aboard the *94*, Ruley's last scene of Capa in LCVP 26-26 shows he had downsized by the time he clambered into the LCVP. In Figure 67 we see only one camera around Capa's neck. Presumably he decided it would be wise to minimize the number of dangling devices before he attempted the acrobatic act of jumping into the sea-tossed LCVP.

There has some question as to which camera it is. In some cleaned-up versions of Ruley's film, several points seem to mark it clearly as a Rolleiflex. In other versions of the same film, those cues are simply not discernable, and may have been artifacts of the enhancement process. To my mind the evidence in that clip was not conclusive enough to render judgement. It may seem unlikely that Capa would have used his Rolleiflex—which required him to look down through the viewfinder—while trying to take photographs in a bucking LCVP, but it is not impossible. Brandt's use of his own Rolleiflex while aboard a landing craft on D-Day demonstrates that. On the other hand, if Capa switched to his Rolleiflex under those conditions, it would give weight to the idea that he really did run out of 35mm film while sheltering behind tank dozer #10.

But now that we have access to the contact sheets, any doubts are resolved. He took at least four photos from within LCVP 26-26, and all the negatives are 120 format—as they are for every photo he took since he boarded the *94*. The camera on his neck while he was in LCVP 26-26 is obviously his Rolleiflex.

The Second Contax

As discussed earlier, there isn't a shred of evidence that Capa used his second Contax during his D-Day excursion to the beach. In fact, in the interview he gave to Wertenbaker, Capa never mentioned a second camera. He only said he took pictures for an hour and a half. It is only in the fictionalized *Slightly out of Focus* version that he claimed he used a second Contax on the beach. That's a very slender reed upon which to depend for those who insist he used both cameras on the beach.

Sam Fuller, who provided us false and confusing testimony about the USS *Henrico*, once again provides evidence which is probably just as false and confusing. But it might contain a grain of truth, too.

As noted earlier, after the war Fuller ran into Capa and was invited to Capa's house for drinks. They naturally ended rehashing the war in general and D-Day in particular. Fuller recounted a story Capa told him during that reunion. Capa claimed he spotted a German officer atop the bluffs, standing boldly, hands on hips, shouting orders to the men behind him. Capa was able to pick out the German at that distance because he was using his "telescopic" lens, which he also supposedly used to take pictures of the German.[8]

The anecdote is clearly false. The very few German officers who were anywhere near there were sheltering in bunkers or trenches hundreds of yards to either the left or right flank. And by the time Capa landed, the bluffs to his front were almost certainly already cleared by Spalding's boat section or Co. G. In fact, if there was anyone standing up there at that time, it was most likely an American officer or NCO chivvying troops over the crest. Fuller was wrong about Capa returning to the UK on the USS *Thurston* (AP-77),* and he is undoubtedly wrong here, as well. In addition, there is no photographic record of this second roll, or from a camera equipped with a telephoto lens that day (and the tired excuse that it must have been lost in the Darkroom Accident doesn't wash anymore).

However, if Capa did have a telephoto lens on his second Contax, it might explain why there was no film from it. His photos from the landing craft and from behind the tank dozer focused on subjects relatively close to his position. He was never able to focus on long-range subjects. So, he simply had no need to use his telephoto-equipped camera—*if* it was so equipped.

It is an interesting bit of speculation, but it is just that. There are instances of Capa wearing two Contax cameras with one equipped with a telephoto lens, but we don't have any evidence Capa had a telephoto lens on his second camera on 6 June. Whelan stated he did, but that seems to have been based solely on Fuller's anecdote, which was based on a war story Capa told over drinks. That isn't the gold standard for evidence.

Fuller's account of their evening included another interesting item, although it is a bit of a digression. He teased Capa that he didn't see him on the beach, and that the only correspondent they heard about landing with them was Jack Thompson.[9] Recall Fuller was the green-faced, seasick man standing ahead of MAJ Tegtmeyer in the LCM, and that Capa claimed he sheltered at the shingle embankment with Tegtmeyer. Fuller was probably nearby as well, since he exited the LCM just before Tegtmeyer. Yet Tegtmeyer never mentioned meeting Capa, and Fuller clearly stated he did not see him either. Although Fuller is far from a complete or reliable source, his account does seem to indicate Capa never made it out of the surf.

---

* The USS *Thurston* was present in the Transport Area.

CHAPTER TWENTY THREE

Return to the Near Shore

"The whole point of taking pictures is so that you don't have to explain things with words."
ELLIOTT ERWITT

As a postscript to Capa's D-Day movements, let us touch a moment on his return to England. It should go without saying that this stage of Capa's saga is again wrapped in confusion and contradictory accounts.

The Capa saga has him arriving back at Weymouth the morning of 7 June 1944 (D+1), where he dropped his film in a courier pouch. Capa only said he "docked" that morning and delivered his film;[1] he wasn't any more specific than that. Initially, Whelan was vague about the time of Capa's arrival. In his Capa biography, he didn't bother trying to pin down this delivery time to the morning or afternoon; he simply said Capa arrived that day.[2] Later, in *This Is War!*, in which he generally adhered more closely to the Capa fabrications, he adopted Capa's "morning."[3] And that's very curious. A central mystery in the saga is the unexplained delay in getting that film to Morris at his London office. Yet Whelan made no effort to determine when the film was handed off, which would determine how long that delay would have been.

To shed some light on this, we turn to the records of the USS *Chase*, on which Capa arrived in Weymouth. From its official report and its war diary, we know the *Chase* did arrive in Weymouth that morning, anchoring in the roadstead at 0536 hours as part of a returning convoy of attack transports.[4] It did not dock or tie up at a pier, however, meaning no one could get off the ship until harbor craft arrived. Which was something of a problem.

Most attack transports were finished with their Normandy roles after their D-Day sorties; at that point follow-on convoy requirements shifted to LSTs and merchant marine ships. As a result, there was no urgent operational need envisioned to quickly service these attack transports on their return. Further, with the arrival of so many attack transports in the same convoy, what little service support that was available was stretched thinly.

This difficult situation was made worse by the loss of DUKWs in the sea off Omaha Beach. Those DUKWs were supposed to have been the primary casualty evacuation means from the beach, and they were to return casualties to the LSTs specially equipped for handling casualties. The LSTs were capable of beaching on the shore in Portland Harbor and it was planned they would do so and directly offload their patients to waiting ambulances. But with so many DUKWs lost, Navy and Coast Guard landing craft were pressed into service when they could be persuaded to take aboard the wounded from Omaha Beach. These landing craft naturally tended to carry their cargo of casualties back to their own ships, since they were required to return there for follow-on tasks anyway. This tendency was reinforced by a Navy directive that stated casualties taken by troops while embarked in small landing craft should be taken to the crafts' mother ships. So, the attack transports arriving back at Weymouth were carrying far more casualties than had been anticipated, and the few harbor craft that could ferry the wounded ashore were at a premium.

As a result. it wasn't until 1045 hours (five hours after anchoring) that HMS *Queen Empress* came alongside to take off the 322 dead, wounded and survivors the *Chase* had aboard.* The *Queen Empress* began life as a Clyde River side-wheel paddle steamer, and served in WWI as a Royal Navy troopship and then as a hospital barge during the Russian intervention.[5] Although it had been returned to civilian service between wars, it was back serving the Royal Navy in WWII, this time as an auxiliary vessel. By May 1944 she was in poor condition and in the process of being laid up but was nevertheless pressed into service to help with the returning D-Day convoys. Transfer of casualties and survivors from ship to ship is a difficult and time-consuming process, and the *Queen Empress* was not able to pull away from the *Chase* until 1245 hours.

So, it would seem that Capa's first opportunity to get ashore would have been a bit more than seven hours after the *Chase* dropped anchor.

The modern reader, accustomed to the privileges and deference afforded today's media, might protest that surely some special provisions would have been made by the ship's captain to get Capa and his film to shore more quickly, perhaps by using one of the *Chase*'s LCVPs to taxi him to a dock. But that was not the case.

Recall that the SHAEF Public Relations Division had dispatched Major W. A. Ulman to Normandy on D-Day for the sole purpose of personally couriering film from the invasion. Originally the plan was for him to report to the USS *Ancon*, where he would be picked up by the Dispatch Boat Service for travel back from the invasion area, but that service failed to materialize on D-Day. As a result, on D-Day the Navy arranged for MAJ Ulman to hitch a ride back to the UK on an attack transport. Coincidentally, the attack transport he hitched a ride on was the *Chase*, which, after all, was anchored right next to the *Ancon*. The 6 June 1944 deck log for the *Chase* noted that at 1515 hours, COL. W. A. Ulman, U.S. Army, reported aboard for transportation per the authority of Commander, Western Naval

---

* The deck log of the Samuel Chase mistakenly described the *Queen Empress* as a tug.

Task force memo, dated 6 June 1944. The difference in rank is accounted for by the fact that Ulman was promoted to lieutenant colonel on 1 June 1944, a point the clerk in Public Relations Division seems to have missed when he requested Ulman's orders on 2 June.

So, by mid-afternoon of D-Day, both Capa and the Public Relations Division's special film courier were on the same ship just off Normandy, about to return to the UK.

Ulman was travelling on special high-priority SHAEF orders, which, as we've just seen, were further amplified by a directive from the Western Naval Task Force headquarters. Despite this "juice," according to the deck log Ulman did not disembark from the *Chase* until 1044 hours. In reality, that would have been the time he signed out with the officer of the deck. The ship had been at anchor for a bit more than five hours at this point, and it is unlikely that it suddenly made an LCVP available for Ulman's use. With the *Queen Empress* coming alongside just a minute later at 1045 hours, it is safe to conclude that Ulman signed out with the officer of the deck in preparation for boarding the *Queen Empress*. And the *Queen Empress* did not depart the *Chase* until 1245 hours.

All of this begs an obvious question. If Capa and Ulman—the special film courier—were aboard the same ship, why didn't Capa simply pass his film off to Ulman and be done with it?

Capa probably wasn't even aware Ulman was aboard. Ulman was supposed to have returned via the special Dispatch Boat Service, so his arrival aboard the *Chase* would have been unplanned and unexpected, and likely would have gone unnoticed to a fatigued Capa, who had probably passed out by then anyway. The *Chase* had a crew of almost 500 and berthing for almost 1,500 embarked troops (space that was occupied by only the 322 survivors, wounded and dead). In a ship that large, it is probable that neither man knew the other was aboard. And this seems to have been the case. As discussed earlier, in a 15 June cable SHAEF's public Relations Division noted that Ulman's D-Day mission had been a failure; he had been unable to contact photographers, message centers or public relations officers. And this seems definitive evidence Capa did not meet Ulman, much less pass his film off to him.

Capa's account in *Slightly out of Focus* would seem to indicate he took his film ashore himself. After being greeted on the pier as a hero by the stay-behind correspondents—at least in his telling of the incident—he supposedly turned down an offer of a flight to London for a broadcast interview, and instead dropped his film off in a "press bag" and returned to the beachhead a few hours later on the first boat available. A Press Message Center had been established in the Red Barracks, near Nothe Fort, Weymouth, to receive and courier film back to London, so Capa probably dropped his film off there if he wasn't met on the quay by a courier.

Readers who paid attention to Capa's narrative in *Slightly out of Focus* might be excused for asking the perfectly reasonably question: how did Capa escape the casualty evacuation and treatment system? He should have been hustled off the *Queen Empress* and into an ambulance. But no. As a combat exhaustion case, he was apparently not only allowed to simply walk away from evacuation process without so much as a cursory medical examination but was miraculously recovered to the extent he could return immediately to the combat zone. It doesn't sound right, does it?

I suggest the entire "exhaustion case" anecdote was merely a plot device to lend credence to his cover story for returning to the UK. While his job required him to return immediately, the tale he told in *Slightly out of Focus* was that of the heroic cameraman invading the Continent with the first wave of troops. Panic may have been his excuse for dashing to the *LCI(L)-94*, but he also needed a plausible reason for not taking another LCVP back to the beach when the panic subsided. While aboard the *Chase* he stated, "this was my last chance to return to the beach. I did not go." Shortly thereafter, he says he passed out, providing the sympathetic reader a reason to excuse his failure to return to his comrades on the beach. It wasn't a lack of will or courage. The poor guy was just physically incapable of going.

But Capa quickly discarded the casualty plot device, much as at the outset of his saga he quickly discarded the plot device of landing with Co. E. It served the purpose of impressing the unwary reader, and having accomplished that, was not permitted to interfere with the story proceeding in a completely incompatible direction. As a result, Capa made no further mention of his experiences among the casualty evacuation system. He doesn't mention transferring to the *Queen Empress* with the other casualties. Nor did he mention how he escaped from the medical system, which would have whisked him away to a base hospital in the UK for evaluation and treatment. Capa seems to have simply transcended the situation and transformed himself from psychological casualty into a reinvigorated invader.

Once again, we see Capa's dramatic exaggerations undercut by his own narrative.

Whether Capa's film left the *Chase* in Ulman's hands, in Capa's hands as a correspondent or in Capa's hands as a casualty, the *Queen Empress* was the earliest opportunity for a ride to shore, and it didn't depart the *Chase* until 1245 hours. That would put Capa stepping onto the Weymouth quay about 1300 hours, and accounts for a good deal of the delay in getting his film to London.

The film did encounter a delay, arriving in London between 2100 and 2130 hours, depending on which version of Morris's stories you choose to believe. So, the 1300 hours disembarkation time means it would have taken about eight hours for Capa's film to get to London. The delay is especially inexplicable since, according to Capa, he had the opportunity to fly to London, as Brandt and his film had done. His refusal to take advantage of the opportunity must have resulted in a large part of the delay that nearly caused his film to miss the next *Life* deadline. If that offer had been made to him, his refusal would not reflect well on his professionalism. However, the claim that he was offered a flight might have just been a face-saving effort to place himself on an even plane with the man who scooped him.

After the film was dropped off in Weymouth, someone from there called Morris's office to let him know the film was on the way. Depending on which version Morris told, that happened either at 1800 hours or 1830 hours. Assuming Capa dropped off his film shortly after 1300 hours, it raises a couple of questions. Was the film dispatched shortly after it was received at Weymouth, and the call was delayed five or more hours? Or was the film not dispatched until about 1800 hours, and the call was put through just after it was dispatched? Either delay—the dispatching of the film, or the phone call—seems excessive. The distance between Weymouth and London is less than 140 miles by road, so an express motorcycle courier should have been able to cover that distance more quickly, even given traffic conditions caused by the massive convoys heading to the ports. And five hours to get a phone call through is equally unlikely. Unfortunately, this aspect remains a mystery.

Dockside Encounter

In its 26 June issue, *Life* ran an article detailing the D-Day exploits of several of its photographers. The paragraphs credited to David Scherman (assigned to the US Navy's still photo pool)[6] recounted his experience aboard an LST on D-Day and its return to an unidentified harbor in England. That account had him poised inside the bow doors as the LST docked back in the United Kingdom, ready to capture the first view of activity on the pier once the bow doors opened. Instead, once the doors opened, there was Capa, waiting to capture a photo of the first wounded to come off the ship. A potentially dramatic photo opportunity ended up being nothing more than two photographers poised to snap shots of each other.

In his book, however, Whelan stated that Scherman claimed the *Life* version was incorrect: that instead it was Capa in the ship and he, Scherman, on the dock; that the event took place in Portsmouth, not Portland Harbor; and that it took place the evening of 6 June.[7]

Scherman's account is rife with obvious errors. Clearly it did not take place on the evening of 6 June, as the *Chase* didn't arrive until the next morning. Further, the *Chase*'s deck log and narrative report of the landings state it arrived at Weymouth, then moved to the adjacent Portland Harbor. Scherman's ship was *LST-317*, and according to its deck log it moored alongside the Hard #2 dock on the Portland "hards"* at 1107 hours on 7 June. So, the records of both ships involved contradict the version Whelan got from Scherman and confirm the meeting could only have taken place on 7 June and in the Weymouth/Portland Harbor area.

---

* Embarkation hards—or hardened beach areas—were constructed at numerous ports on the southern coast of the UK. They were essentially slipways which were stiffened by mats of linked concrete blocks which could support the weight of beached landing craft. Portland Harbor's hards could accommodate two LSTs with three more tied up at the adjacent dock.

Other aspects of Scherman's version also appear unlikely, if not incorrect. The detail of the bow doors opening seems to tie the incident to an LST-type ship. Attack transports such as the *Chase* did not have bow doors; LSTs did. If the two men were on the opposite sides of a set of bow doors, then it would seem most likely that it was Scherman arriving on *LST-317*. Scherman's photos are concrete evidence that he was on an LST for D-Day. Further, the *Chase* anchored in the harbor; LSTs could nose into the "hardstands" where they were able to directly load or discharge cargo and troops through the bow doors. So, the details of Scherman's version seem to contradict all known facts. The facts seem to point to Scherman standing inside the bow doors as they opened, with Capa waiting on the shore. In other words, it seems the *Life* version must be correct and Whelan's wrong.

Whelan obtained Scherman's version during an interview in preparation for his Capa biography. Scherman's tale must have raised red flags for Whelan, too, and his notes show he subsequently telephoned Scherman to verify the notes he had taken. Scherman did verify them, and Whelan included that version in the book.[8] So it would appear Whelan captured Scherman's comments accurately. Whelan had second thoughts on the matter and in his later *This Is War!*, he revised his conclusion, and correctly had Capa returning to Weymouth/Portland, not Portsmouth. But if we dismiss Scherman's obvious errors as to the port and date, should we not also dismiss his memory of who stood where?

It may be, however, that Scherman's story does have some truth to it. For one thing, it is difficult to believe that Capa managed to get off the *Chase* at Weymouth in time to get his film to a courier, and then travel to the Portland hards by the time Scherman's *LST-317* opened its bow doors when it arrived at 1107 hours.[9] Recall that Capa, aboard the *Queen Empress,* could not have reached the Weymouth docks until about 1300 hours.

On the other hand, the reverse is possible. It is possible that with *LST-317* mooring at the Portland docks just after 1100 hours, Scherman could have travelled the five miles to the Weymouth docks by the time the *Queen Empress* arrived from the *Chase* at roughly 1300 hours. In this scenario Scherman would indeed have been waiting on the dock as the forward (not bow) doors of the paddle wheeler opened to discharge casualties. And Capa could have been there inside the doors waiting to take a picture of activity on the dock as they opened.

Of course, this begs the question: why would Scherman leave the activity at Portland Harbor, where literally dozens of LSTs were beaching, discharging casualties and embarking the next wave of invaders, just to travel to Weymouth to watch a paddle wheeler that was only discharging casualties? The explanation may be simple. Scherman had to go to Weymouth to deliver his film to the Press Message Center at Red Barracks and, as a pool photographer, he would have rushed there as soon as possible after landing to drop off his D-Day film. After dropping off the film, he was just a couple hundred yards, across the channel, from the Weymouth quay, where casualties from the attack transports were being unloaded, affording Scherman more picture-taking opportunities. And so it was that Capa and Scherman most probably did meet as the *Queen Empress* docked and opened its forward door. This appears to be the only scenario which even partly reconciles Scherman's memory of events and what we know of Capa's movements.

As noted previously, there are D+1 film clips showing the *Queen Empress* docking at the Weymouth quay and discharging casualties to a row of waiting field ambulances.[10] The litter cases were taken off first, followed by the dead in white body bags. The ambulatory cases, being last to get off, are seen milling about on deck in many of the clips. Unfortunately, neither Capa nor Scherman can be seen in any of the clips.

First by a Nose

Let's pause for a moment to examine Bert Brandt's return from Normandy. His ship, the attack transport USS *Charles Carroll* (APA-28) had repositioned to the outer Transport Area off Omaha Beach in preparation for sailing back to the UK and was anchored there next to the *Chase*. The *Carroll* recorded being underway for Portland Harbor at 1951 hours on 6 June.[11] Fifteen minutes later the *Chase* recorded it was underway at 2006 hours, indicating they sailed in the same return convoy. Similarly, the *Carroll* reported it was anchored off Portland Harbor (i.e., in Weymouth Bay) at 0518 hours on 7 June; the *Chase* reported it had anchored at 0536 hours, 18 minutes after the *Carroll*, confirming that they arrived in the same convoy.

And here is where luck seemed to favor Brandt over Capa. At 0730 hours, the HMS *Exwey** came alongside the *Carroll* to take off casualties. This was three hours and 15 minutes before the HMS *Queen Empress* came alongside the *Chase*. The *Exwey* cast off from the *Carroll* at 1045 hours, which was probably the earliest time Brandt could have left the ship for shore. So, Brandt was probably already headed to shore with his D-Day photos as the first harbor craft was coming alongside the *Chase*, and two full hours before the earliest that Capa's film could have left the *Chase*.

That neatly coincides with Capa's comment in *Slightly out of Focus* that Brandt (Capa did not deign to mention his name, but his identity is obvious) "had returned two hours earlier. ... He was now on his way to London with a terrific scoop."[12]

By the mere happenstance of Brandt's ship being positioned earlier in the same convoy, his film was able to reach the Press Messenger Center first, and by that narrow margin won the laurels. As a result, *Life* would have to find a new angle to hype Capa's pictures.

---

* Misspelled in the *Carroll*'s deck log as Exmay. Like the *Queen Empress*, it was a shallow-draft paddle-wheel ship built in 1888 and converted for use as a minesweeper.

Strike a Pose

At this point Capa is just about to temporarily pass out of his own D-Day saga. The attack transports had done their job and would not be involved in carrying the endless stream of reinforcements to France. That job was left to the LSTs and cargo ships. Having delivered his film in Weymouth, Capa hopped an LST in nearby Portland Harbor for one of the next convoys back to Normandy. Presumably it was on this LST that Scherman took the photo of Capa looking weary after his D-Day adventure (Figure 50). As noted earlier, Scherman also took a second, almost identically posed shot, except in this one, Capa was smiling slyly; the knitted brow and fatigue had disappeared and the charm had reappeared. The two photos were taken just seconds apart, judging from the ash on his cigarette. Given the nearly instantaneous transformation, you must wonder, which was the genuine emotion, and which was the pose assumed for the camera?

Whichever was the genuine emotion, if one of those pictures was going to get published, it had to portray the "correct" feeling. So, it comes as no surprise that *Life* chose to print the one with the grimmer expression. This was a perfect example of selecting a photo because it portrayed the "right feeling," whether it was accurate or not. It's also the same justification for honoring the "Falling Soldier" photo despite its acknowledged fabrication. Editorial selection can and will determine which perspective you see, often based on criteria having nothing to do with accuracy.

Capa's return on the LST was also confirmed by a photo taken from the super-structure of that LST, loaded with troops and vehicles, heading to the Normandy coast.[13] Unfortunately that photo is usually incorrectly captioned, claiming it was taken on 1–5 June, prior to D-Day. That's obviously wrong as his photo clearly shows an LST, whereas he was aboard an attack transport—the *Chase*—during that period.

Not Dead Yet

As a parting shot to Capa's presence in our analysis, we turn to one last bit of sensational exaggeration. He informed the reader that upon reaching the press camp behind Omaha Beach on D+2 (8 June) he found a wake in progress in his memory. Supposedly, some unnamed sergeant had seen his corpse floating in the water, and with Capa missing for 48 hours he was not only declared dead, but the censors had already released his obituary.

This is so absurd that it is amazing he had the courage to put it into print. It is even more incredible that it has been uncritically believed by so many. Soldiers were not declared dead simply because they were unaccounted for and someone thought he saw their corpse. That person would be listed as missing in action until the living man was located or his mortal remains were recovered. Since Capa had just hand-carried his film to the UK on 7 June (to the apparent relief of those running the

SHAEF still photo pool) it defies belief that the SHAEF Public Relations Division (who both owned the still photo pool and held the correspondents' obituaries) would release his obituary in the belief he'd died the previous day, on 6 June! Furthermore, even if he were confirmed dead, his obituary would not have been released until his next of kin had been notified, which in the wake of D-Day could take weeks. And the fact that no paper or weekly magazine ever printed that obituary should make it clear this ridiculous anecdote is false. Finally, we've already seen how poor communications were for the press between the beachhead and London in the days following 6 June, so it is absurd to think the other correspondents in Normandy could have been so well informed about goings on in London.

Capa's *Slightly out of Focus* vaguely placed this reunion in the barn of a Norman farmhouse. Whelan, however, unaccountably placed this reunion in the French city of Bayeux, which was about eight kilometers inland of the British Gold Beach.[14] Which poses a problem. When Capa arrived back in Normandy, he again landed on Omaha Beach. Along the shoreline there had been a narrow and tenuous linkup between Omaha and Gold beaches late 8 June, but there was no road connection until the next day. Neither Capa nor the rest of the First US Army press corps could have made it into Bayeaux on 8 June.

So, we temporarily come to the end of Capa's part of his D-Day saga, and on the very same note as we began it: faced with conflicting information, exaggeration and fabrication, through which we must sift to find the slivers of truth. Or at least, make a good guess at what that truth may be. Nevertheless, this analysis has gone far to explain the puzzling delay in Capa's film reaching London. At least seven hours were taken up merely getting his film off the ship and into the hands of the Press Message Center. But there still seems to be an unaccounted period from about 1300 hours to 2100–2130 hours. If he had gotten off the *Queen Empress* about 1300 hours, where was his film during that period? For that, we'll have to pick up the threads of Morris's saga.

CHAPTER TWENTY FOUR

Film Follies

"Most newspaper readers, knowing that the invasion going was tough and that dead Germans were more important than live news, were reasonably content with the papers' big headlines and voluminous coverage."

TIME, 19 JUNE 1944

With Capa's film safely ashore, our attention shifts to follow its journey onward.

After Capa's film was dropped off at the Press Message Center (or into the hands of one of its personnel who may have met him coming ashore) someone there called Morris's London office several hours later to tell say, "Capa's film is on the way. You should get it within an hour or two." Morris said this was "at 6 PM" according to the earlier Jozefa Stuart interview but placed it "at about 6:30 Wednesday evening" in later versions of the story.[1] Whatever the time, the call ended his agonized wait for news of the film. Morris never claimed to have taken that call himself, much less spoken directly with Capa, although retellings in print and online have carelessly added many extraneous details.

Whatever conversation there was, between whomever was on each end of the line, it did nothing to inform Morris of just what had happened to Capa on D-Day or explain why his film was late. Morris first claimed he "had negatives in hand"* at 9:30 Wednesday PM, according to the Jozefa Stuart interview, but later changed it to "around nine" in other retellings.[2] So it arrived in a window roughly 2½ to 3½ hours after the call.†

Neither of Capa's versions of events mentions a note included in the film packet, nor did Whelan's 1985 *Robert Capa*. Whelan's notes from his interview with Morris for that book, however, say that as Capa was still in a state of shock, the film packet included a brief handwritten note that just said "here it is."[3] Whelan decided not

---

* Presumably he meant the film had arrived by then, and not that he personally had the developed negatives in hands.

† In his narration for *Time*'s 29 May 2014 video, the 98-year-old Morris said that the film packet *arrived* at his office at 1800 hours. Although undoubtedly an error, it illustrates the difficulty in verifying facts in this saga.

to use that assertion in his 1985 book, but did include it in his later work *This Is War!*[4] Morris further claimed that Capa had not intended to return to England, but provided no indication why he thought that.[5] That is almost certainly not true. While neither Capa nor Morris may have initially known the specific unit Capa would accompany, both knew he was a member of the still photo pool. And the pool coordinator had made it very clear in his "suggestion" that they bring their film back themselves to expedite its delivery. So, it is a mystery why Morris would claim Capa, contrary to the plans, hadn't intended to return to England. One suspects Morris added this detail in later years to support Capa's fanciful assertion that he intended to land with the invading troops on D-Day.

By the time Morris penned his own memoir in 1998, Capa's brief note had become downright wordy: "A scrawled note said that the action was all in the 35-millimeter, that things had been very rough, that he had come back to England unintentionally with wounded being evacuated, and that he was on his way back to Normandy."[6] It appears Morris attempted to shore up this hole in his original narrative by introducing the additional phrases to that note's content when he penned his own memoir. That note has not survived and we have only Morris's word that it even existed, or what might have actually been in it. In fact, from this point on, Morris's versions of events are our only first-person account, and they did not publicly surface for decades and then varied in the retellings, casting doubt on their accuracy. There are no contemporary records or corroborating testimonies from other characters in the drama.

Morris also provided conflicting versions of what the packet contained. His most well-known version (*Get the Picture*) states there were "four rolls of 35-millimeter film plus half a dozen rolls of 120 film (2¼ × 2¼ inches) he had taken in England and on the Channel crossing."[7] But 16 years earlier he provided Jozefa Stuart a different tally: two rolls of 35mm and four of 120.[8] Curiously, in neither account did he mention any Speed Graphic film.

Whatever the formats and number, they had finally reached London. And it is at this point that Morris—our sole narrator—began omitting a tremendously important part of the story.

Secrets, Safeguards and Indiscretions

Morris implied Capa's film was delivered directly to *Life*'s London office, but this was not the case. As noted in a previous chapter, undeveloped film was presumed to be classified as secret. As a result, when exposed film arrived from the field, it was not delivered to the news bureau for which the photographer worked, rather to the SHAEF message center at the British Ministry of the Interior.[9] There a censor would immediately review the pages of caption notes that accompanied the film to determine how the film would be handled. If the caption notes indicated no particularly sensitive material, the film would retain the presumptive secret classification and be sent to the news agency's lab. After developing, the film, two copies of the prints and contact sheets would be returned to the MoI where censors would normally either pass the film for publication or mark out any offending details with a red pen. In the latter case, the prints would be stamped "passed for publication as censored." Clearance by the censors effectively removed the secret classification of the film. From there the film was returned to the agency's lab where edits would be made (if necessary), additional prints made for the photo pool and for the news agency's home office, then it would be packaged for flight to the US.

On the other hand, if the caption notes indicated the film included top-secret material, the film was handled with much tighter security. It could either be sent to a military lab for developing, or it could be placed in the custody of an officer who would maintain control of the film as it was taken to the news agency's lab, where he would oversee its processing with a bare minimum of lab technicians present. The custody officer would then take the film and all its products back to the censors at the MoI for censorship review. If the developed film did contain top-secret material, the censors would retain the offending parts of the film as well as corresponding prints and contact sheets. Any photos judged to be acceptable for release were sent back to the bureau, possibly with minor directed edits, for final prints and preparation for dispatch.

The censors had a wide variety of items they were looking for, from the relatively minor to the most critical. For example, in Figure 4 we can see the censor's ink marks indicating background harbor details that needed to be obscured before the photo could be released. In Capa's embarkation photos we can see where unit patches have been similarly eradicated as was the distinctive roofline of the Pavilion on the Weymouth quay. The censors were guided in their task by a document referred to as the "Censor's Bible," which would eventually grow to over 200 mimeographed pages. The most critical items on the censor's list for D-Day, of course, were things that might reveal the true scope of the invasion.

Recall once more the double bluff the Allies were playing. To protect the Normandy landings, the Allies had convinced the Germans by various devious means that the main invasion would be aimed at the Pas de Calais and launched by Patton's phantom army. To carry off that bluff, the real invasion would be portrayed as a diversionary operation designed to draw German strength from the Pas de Calais. So the Normandy landings had to appear *almost* as if they were the real invasion, but had to be just unconvincing enough that German intelligence analysts would "see through" the first layer of deception (that they *were* the main landings) and believe the second layer of deception (that they were a diversionary operation), thus protecting the base layer of truth (that they were indeed the main effort). Despite the fragile nature of this circular deception, and despite the scope of the fighting that soon unfolded in Normandy, the FORTITUDE SOUTH deception worked for several weeks,[10] and was succeeded by FORTITUDE SOUTH II on 19 July.[11] Hitler maintained the forces guarding the Pas de Calais largely intact. In fact, between 6 June and 8 July, German strength at the Pas de Calais actually increased from 19 divisions (six field divisions and the rest limited employment divisions) to 22 divisions (11 field divisions and the rest limited employment). Even after the American breakout from the beachhead on 28 July, which prompted Hitler to release more divisions from the Pas de Calais, he refused to denude that coast.[12]

In the immediate wake of D-Day, the most important potential leaks the censors were sensitive to included: 1) any *unauthorized* press report indicating there would or would not be further invasions (to avoid ruling out a Pas de Calais invasion); 2) any indication of the actual forces involved in the landings (to mask the size and quality of the units involved); and 3) any details of the Mulberry artificial harbors (to keep the Germans in the dark about allied resupply capabilities, which, lacking a natural harbor, would otherwise limit the operation to a minor invasion). Memoranda from both Churchill and Eisenhower stressed the vital importance of guarding these three subjects, as did numerous other documents.[13]

The few "leaks" that were permitted were closely controlled and were designed to further the FORTITUDE deception. *Life's* 19 June 1944 issue included the (authorized) tease that the Allies had additional armies they could commit to the drive on Cherbourg, "or into other landings along the invasion coast." And its 26 June 1944 issue contained the following statement: "General Bradley estimated that the Nazis had 16 divisions in the line with a total force of 60 divisions in France. General Eisenhower, in a report, said more allied landings could be expected." That sentence, not surprisingly, was preceded by one noting Allied airstrikes in the Pas de Calais.

Within this framework, the media was allowed to provide coverage of the long-awaited Second Front after D-Day. After all, this was how the main landings would normally be covered in the press, and what the Germans would expect to see. But the media would not be allowed to provide concrete evidence to substantiate the scope of the landings. The Germans would be allowed to hear the trumpeting in the press, but not be allowed to stick their noses too far under the tent. German open-source intelligence—Allied and neutral newspapers arriving in Berlin via embassies in neutral countries—would provide evidence of a far less powerful invasion force than was the actual case. As a result, hopefully, they would conclude the Normandy landings were more noise than substance, reinforcing the belief that the full weight of the invasion would come ashore at the Pas de Calais in mid-summer. The censors were the first line of defense against a zealous media accidentally giving the game away.

Sins Coming Home to Roost

Some correspondents could be a greater worry than others, and Capa did not have a particularly good record in the ETO when it came to security. In late 1942, it was he who took the photo of a bombardier in the nose of a US Army Air Forces B-17 at an air base in the UK; that photo accidentally showed the top-secret Norden bombsight. Not bothering to pass his film through the air base censor, Capa instead dropped his film into the hands of his editor (at the time he was working for the UK *Illustrated* magazine), who in turn had the film cleared by the nearest convenient censor. Unfortunately, that censor was in the British Royal Air Force and was not sensitive to the status of the US Norden bombsight. *Illustrated* magazine had already printed 400,000 copies of the issue with that photo on the cover before the error was spotted. The offending copies were recalled and destroyed, at what must have been substantial cost. Although Capa escaped formal censure by the ensuing inquest, the incident delayed his accreditation for several months (a fact he "altered" in his autobiography).[14] The incident also undoubtedly gave him a rather bad reputation with the censorship community.

And it is doubtful John Morris's stock was very high among the censors, either. Morris obtained a set of photographs of the devastation caused by Allied bombing of Berlin. The photos supposedly came via diplomatic pouch from Stockholm, and Morris didn't bother to detail how he obtained the classified photos from diplomatic sources. While claiming he knew there were slim chances of getting the photos past the censors, he nevertheless gave it a try. The censor confiscated the entire packet. While Morris attempted to pass it off as something akin to a fraternity prank when he told the story to the media crowd that hung out at the Dorchester Hotel, it was in fact an incredibly irresponsible thing to do for the London photo editor of a major American weekly magazine.[15]

Bureaucracies are famously humorless and have notably long memories. This is doubly so when a bureaucracy is charged with enforcing secrecy. Both Capa's actual transgression and Morris's attempted transgression were the stuff that would fester in the forefront of the censorship community's corporate memory.

So, it was into this very sensitive censorship environment, and with a rather poor reputation with the censors, that Capa's film arrived late on D+1—without caption notes. What exactly happened there no one knows, and no one probably ever will. All we know is the result. Only a small number of pictures have survived from the four—or two?—rolls of 35mm D-Day film Morris claimed he received. What could account for its disappearance? The traditional explanation of the Darkroom Accident has been demolished, so we must look for another culprit.

It seems increasingly likely that somewhere in the censorship process it was decided Capa's photos showed far too much of the size and scope of the invasion to risk being released. And if his film did show evidence of those top-secret matters, the censors had the power not only to stop release of the offending photos, but to retain the negatives, all prints, and the original contact sheets which contained images of the offending photos. And that's a key clue, for not one original contact sheet for Capa's D-Day film has survived. Images of contact sheets that show his D-Day pictures, such as that in Figure 1, are post-war recreations using the surviving negatives.

Changing Truths

Which brings us back to the overlooked but very curious omission in most versions of the Morris saga. In his later retelling of the story, he crafts the tale to make it appear the film came to him "around" 2100 hours, not from the MoI, but directly from Weymouth, and then it went directly to his lab. Soon thereafter Hans Wild called on the interphone to say the shots looked fantastic, but "a few minutes later" Dennis Banks came to break the bad news that the film was ruined. From the time it arrived until the bad news was received, it all seemed to have happened in a very short time, certainly less than a half hour.

But he told much a different story in his earlier Jozefa Stuart interview. While the sequence was the same, the timeline was longer. Suspiciously longer. In this version he received the film at 2130 hours but provided a rather vague—and much longer—time for Dennis Banks reporting the bad news "at about midnight or 1 o'clock." Which is odd. In that interview, Morris was specific when talking about all other times that day: when his office got the call from Weymouth (1800 hours); when he received the film (2130 hours); when he took the film to the censors (0700 hours); when the censors released the film (0845 hours); and what time he had to get the film delivered for shipment to the US (0900 hours). And yet he couldn't be more specific than a window of an hour or so when he received the horrible news that the fabulous pictured were ruined?

Morris spent considerable effort over the ensuing years explaining the tension and drama as he and the still photo pool editor anxiously awaited Capa's film: "I felt, as did the pool editor from AP, that the whole world was waiting on these pictures."[16] And yet, the news that this very film was—supposedly—ruined by the incompetence of his own staff, made so little emotional impact that he could only place its occurrence in a loose hour or so timeframe? That's incredibly unlikely. In fact, it is the exact kind of vagueness on vital details that leads one to suspect that the event did not actually happen.

Consider Morris's original timeline as he gave in the Jozefa Stuart interview. From receipt of the film at 2130 hours until the bad news that "the emulsion ran" was received, the elapsed time would have been 2½ to 3½ hours. That's a very long period for processing the two hottest rolls of film (the number of rolls he cited in the original Jozefa Stuart interview) his bureau had ever handled. It's a clear indication Morris wasn't telling us everything that transpired.

Custody

Let's step back for a moment and reconsider. Morris's saga is based on the unstated assumption that Capa's film was handled as if it were unclassified material and somehow bypassed the initial screening at the MoI. But that is clearly false, and the film—presumptively considered secret—would have first been sent to the MoI for initial classification review. As much of his film must have shown extensive coverage of the might of the naval armada and the waves of landing craft approaching the beach, the initial review would have tentatively upgraded the undeveloped film to top secret. So, let's re-examine the handling of Capa's film in light of what we now know of the SHAEF censorship process.

First, let's eliminate Capa's embarkation photos, which were sent off to London *prior* to the *Chase*'s sailing. We know they were sent off in that timeframe as three of those photos show censor stamps clearing them for release on 6 June. This film included shots of the Navy assault craft crewmen being briefed in the *Chase*'s gym, as a photo of this briefing also had a censor's stamp releasing it on 6 June. So, the handling of this film took place while Capa was locked down aboard the *Chase* in Weymouth Harbor, at sea or participating on D-Day, and was cleared for publication a day before his later D-Day photos arrived in London. The elimination of these photos is important, as Morris's later versions of events attempt to claim that these, too, arrived for processing the evening of 7 June. That is clearly false.

So, the packet of film received by the SHAEF Message Center at the MoI on 7 June would have included only the film Capa took after he had been locked down on the *Chase*. This included the photos of troops idling aboard the *Chase* in Weymouth Bay prior to sailing (one roll of 35mm film, roll number "Contax 3" per the caption notes sheet, with no subject—I've dubbed it the Troops Sunning on Deck roll—and no date). It also included film shot in the late afternoon and early evening of the convoy departing the UK (one roll of 35mm film, roll number "1 Contax" dated D-1 and subject "Last Glimpse of England"). The next film included the photos he took of the Army briefings around the terrain model in the *Chase*'s cargo hold (one roll of 35mm film, roll number "Contax I", undated, subject "Briefing to Invasion") and film from a Speed Graphic camera (for which some negatives exist, but no caption note pages). Then there were the photos he took in the period beginning with his debarkation from the *Chase* and ending as he fled the beach (one roll of 35mm, no caption notes). His final photos included those he shot aboard *LCI(L)-94* and aboard the *Chase* after his return (five rolls of 120 film, for which there are no caption notes).

When the film reached the SHAEF Message Center at the MoI, a public relations officer/censor "from the parent service" (in this case an Army officer as Capa was embedded with the ground forces) would be summoned to review the caption notes and make an initial judgement on the classification of the film. His interest would have been immediately drawn to the film showing the departure of the invasion convoy as well as all film of the D-Day landings. These could potentially show far more than the FORTITUDE deception would allow, so that film would have been temporarily upgraded to top secret, placed in a separate bag and a custody officer summoned. Capa's remaining film (of troops aboard the *Chase* at anchor in

Weymouth Bay and the briefing in *Chase's* hold) should be fairly harmless. Some minor editing to remove background details or unit patches might be necessary, but the film would not demand tighter handling procedures. Given this, that film would have been sent separately to the *Life* lab for routine processing. Morris's lab, then, would have received two separate packets of Capa's film on the evening of 7 June, although Morris himself would not have initially been given access to the more sensitive packet's contents.

For the moment, we'll follow the custody officer who would take Capa's more sensitive film to Morris's lab for developing. The custody officer would have ensured that the film was developed with the absolutely minimum of personnel present, possibly just a single technician, and quite probably meaning the lab was temporarily shut down until the job was done (unless the lab was large enough to devote an isolated area for this task). Who would have performed the development under the custody officer's gaze?

Morris's narrative jumps the tracks at this point. Supposedly H. C. Bradshaw was the lab chief, and Hans Wild and a 15-year-old assistant named Dennis Banks (or Sanders, according to Whelan's Capa biography)* were working in the lab that night. Morris claimed Bradshaw gave the film to the 15-year-old to develop. It's difficult to believe that the job to develop these critical rolls of film was placed in the hands of a young teenager, literally the least-experienced and least-qualified member of the lab, not to mention one of the last people who should have been entrusted with access to potentially top-secret material. It's impossible to imagine what other task that night was so important that it could have diverted Wild and Bradshaw from developing Capa's film. But that is what Morris claimed did happen. Whatever did take place in the lab that night, it must have taken place under the watchful eye of the custody officer who would have ensured the minimum number of people had access to the film.

After the film had been developed Hans Wild then supposedly looked at it while still wet from developing solution and relayed his "fabulous" comment to Morris. That provides an important clue. If Wild saw the complete film at that point, then it was probably he who did the developing. There would have been no need for a 15-year-old to be given access to potentially top-secret images, much less be solely trusted with their development.

Once developed, the custody officer would have taken the film, two sets of prints and contact sheets back to the MoI. Less than two miles away and facing only late-night wartime traffic, this trip would not have taken long. And after reaching the MoI, Capa's D-Day film, being film from one of the only three photographers

---

* In the Jozefa Stuart interview Morris mentioned only the young man's first name. Unaccountably Whelan called him Dennis Sanders in his 1985 biography. Both Morris and Kershaw called him Dennis Banks in their respective books (1998 & 2002).

to step ashore that day and eagerly awaited by all, would have had top priority for review by Army censors. Negatives and prints that were deemed too sensitive for release would have been confiscated, as would have been the contact sheets. The surviving film would then have been sent back on the short trip to Morris's office for preparation of the necessary number of prints to meet the demands of the various organizations that would receive the finished products. And it was only then, when the surviving film was returned to Morris's office, that he would have first learned that the bulk of the film had been retained by the censor.

And this sequence of events, involving a trip to the MoI, censoring and a trip back to Morris's office, much more reasonably accounts for the time between receipt of the film (2100 or 2130 hours) and Morris learning of the how little film had "survived" ("midnight or 1 o'clock").

In fact, the custody officer scenario explains another incomprehensible aspect of Morris's narratives. In the Jozefa Stuart interview Morris did not mention examining the "ruined" film himself. He just took the teenager's word for it.[17] However, in *Get The Picture,* Morris stated that when he learned the bad news he went to the lab to see for himself.[18] Reviewing the four rolls of 35mm (the larger tally cited in his later tellings of the story), he said that on three rolls there was nothing to see, but on the fourth there were "eleven frames with distinct images."[19] In later retellings, when he examined the film he just saw gray smudge—the supposedly melted emulsion—except, again, for the 11 images. Years later, when the Darkroom Accident fable was demolished, Morris changed his story, suggesting Capa took no more pictures than the 11, and the rest of the four rolls of film were never exposed.[20] But this ran into another factual problem. Unexposed film that has been developed is clear; it does not show gray smudge. In light of that, Morris dropped his story of personally inspecting the damaged film and came full circle back to the version in the Josefa Stuart interview: he simply believed the 15-year-old's explanation. In this moment of crisis, if we are to believe Morris, he sought neither Bradshaw's nor Wild's far greater expertise. In this final narrative, the youth would no longer be blamed for the loss of the film, but he would be guilty of not realizing that almost all the four rolls of film had never been exposed and be blamed for misleading Morris. To be believable, it requires one to believe neither Bradshaw nor Wild examined the film and told Morris the truth, which strains credulity.

Although these conflicting narratives present nearly incomprehensible confusion, one key point seems to have emerged from the revised story: Morris never saw the original film from the two (or four) rolls. Again, this fits with the premise that the film was handled as top-secret material. If the lab hadn't been locked down by the custody officer, Morris surely would have been there to see the film "come out of the soup" himself given its importance. But he wasn't. The alternate explanation, that he later inspected the 'ruined' film himself, but could not tell the difference between exposed, ruined film and unexposed film is plainly unbelievable. Just as

254 • BACK INTO FOCUS

unbelievable is the revised story in which he simply took the 15-year-old's word for what happened to the film and never sought Bradshaw's or Wild's expert judgement. None of it makes sense. And that's because none of it apparently happened. It would seem Morris's several narratives were fictions which were inexpertly woven for the sake of drama. The custody officer's lockdown of the lab would have prevented any of this from taking place.

Morris's conflicting stories collide on another point. Wild's original excited report that the shots were "fabulous" conflicts with Morris's revised version that most of the film had never been exposed. Surely Wild would have reported with some alarm that there were only 11 exposed frames and the other 141 were blank (assuming four rolls of 38 exposures each;[*] or 65 blank frames based on Morris's two-roll version). But apparently, he did not. The only scenario in which Hans Wild's "fabulous" comment makes sense is the one that has the custody officer overseeing the film development and sometime during that process, Wild saw all Capa's exposed film before it was taken to the censors where the bulk of it was confiscated. Confirming this is the fact that Morris never thought to ask Wild what he saw when he made his "fabulous" comment. Instead, all Morris could say was: "But I don't even know what he saw."[21] As bizarre as it seems, he never actually tried to confirm what, if any, film had been lost in the developing process. With the Darkroom Accident myth debunked, it would seem the complete set of Capa's film—however many rolls that might have been—made it through the developing process and into the hands of the censors.

As Coleman's research has shown, none of the secondary players in this drama ever confirmed Morris's version of events that night. The mysterious Dennis Banks/Sanders seems to have vanished off the face of the earth, and there would be ample grounds to suspect the lad was an invention to provide a fictitious scapegoat for the fictitious drying accident, were it not for Bob Landry's widow. In an interview with Coleman, she stated that the young man's name and phone number had been in her husband's address book. Nevertheless, he has never since been located. Neither Bradshaw nor Wild ever publicly commented on the "ruined" film incident. All we have is Morris's obviously flawed word for it, and there is no public record of Morris's version of events until after those two men had died.

High Stakes

These lab staffing questions aside, the custody officer would have arrived back at the MoI and placed the film products, and their fate, in the censor's hands.

It's important to remember that while Capa was employed by the weekly *Life*, his D-Day assignment was as a still pool photographer whose primary responsibility was to provide immediate photos for all news services to use as soon as humanly possible.

---

[*] Although the rolls nominally held 36 exposures, Capa's surviving negatives from the beach prove that he managed to get two more exposures on that roll.

But SHAEF, which directed and coordinated the still photo pool cameramen, had other, far more serious priorities in addition to feeding pictures to a hungry press corps. SHAEF was also concerned with what German intelligence would see in Allied newspapers on 7 June and in the following days, and that concern could trump media interests.

In the wake of the landings the German command structure was in complete disarray and badly informed. Dummy parachutist dolls had been dropped to create false alarms. The actual paratrooper drops were badly scattered but had the beneficial effects of completely confusing German reports and cutting communications over a wide area near the invasion beaches. Many key German commanders were away from their units on 6 June, attending a wargame rehearsal of their own war plans. Others, such as General Wilhelm Falley of the 91st Air-Landing Infantry Division, tried to reach their headquarters or move forward to control the defenses but were killed by roving bands of paratroopers as they travelled. French resistance cells carried out widespread sabotage missions, creating more chaos over a much wider area. Massive Allied feints of air and naval movement toward the Pas de Calais—many being electronically created phantoms—kept the German high command in Berlin transfixed. While Rommel understood the urgency of the situation, Berlin did not. There the preconceived idea that the real invasion would take place at the Pas de Calais outweighed the uncertainty raised by the badly confused and vague reports coming from Normandy. The confusion among Rommel's command structure can be inferred from the fact that by the end of June, his units had lost 28 generals and 354 senior commanders.[22] Beyond this, both Rommel and von Rundstedt (Rommel's superior, commanding German forces in the west) had previously been sacked by Hitler and were rapidly losing favor again.

And while the Allied leaders had no idea how successful these deception measures would be, neither were they willing to risk undermining any potential benefits by permitting the press to let the cat out of the bag when the first shots from the photo pool hit the wires.

In the age of the internet, anyone so inclined can get online and within just a few minutes gain access to literally thousands of pictures about the Normandy invasion. But this is misleading. There was no internet in 1944—obviously—and the only source for pictures of the fighting was the trickle of photos coming through the SHAEF censors. Daily papers wanted up-to-date photos for their next editions, and the only way they could immediately get these was by means of the Army Signal Corps radiotelephoto service. But the only way a photo could get to that service was if it had been selected by the SHAEF Pictorial Review Board as being worthy of this limited, rapid means of transmission.[23] Otherwise the images had to travel by the slower air courier flights.

So, although a tremendous volume of still and motion photography was being produced, very little made it to the press in a timely fashion. A review of the daily editions in the immediate wake of D-Day shows that all the papers were drawing from the same small batch of new photos each day. The weeklies could devote more space to photos, and often included photos not printed by the dailies, but again it was a very small trickle compared to the total photo production, and it was closely monitored by censors. And a very large majority of photos that were published were of the 'B roll' variety, such as grainy pictures of ships at sea. Those images showed so little that most of them could have been taken at any time previously, during one of the landing rehearsals for example.

Nor were the photographs and newsreels the only ones affected by the media brownout. SHAEF's twice daily communiqués went into some detail about sea actions along the entire northern French coast and air strikes throughout France but said virtually nothing about the land actions. At the end of the second day of the invasion, 7 June, SHAEF's communiqués had mentioned just a single location ashore where fighting was taking place: Caen. On 8 June a second location was mentioned: Bayeaux. It was not until June 9 that a location was mentioned in relation to American forces ashore, and that was behind Utah Beach. Typically, only 10–15 percent of the communiqués' content dealt with land fighting and even then, in remarkably generic terms. Which was a very odd fact, given that this was, after all, supposed to be the Allies massive opening of the Second Front. It was the kind of muted official statements that just might encourage the German high command to conclude this was not the main invasion, and that the Allies were husbanding their forces for the large attack at the Pas de Calais.

And in fact, in a midnight meeting on 9/10 June, indications of an imminent landing in the Pas de Calais were so urgent that Hitler was persuaded to reverse an earlier decision to move armored and infantry units from that sector to join the Normandy battle. Instead, he actually diverted *more* troops to the Pas de Calais. It was a decision that would prove decisive for the Allies. As a result, on D+4 (10 June) German commanders would have just 10½ divisions in the line to fight the battle of Normandy instead of the 20½ divisions Allied intelligence had predicted by that date. The vast network of FORTITUDE deceptions, coupled with resistance attacks and the Allied bombing campaign against the French transportation network, was working.[24] And the press was not going to be given a chance to—accidentally and with all the best intentions—sabotage it.

Nowhere was this media brownout better illustrated than in *Life* itself. In its 19 June issue (on the newsstands on 12 June), it included the rather awkward admission that, "According to the Germans, from whom most news of the actual fighting is still coming …" The situation was even further emphasized by another comment later in the same paragraph: "Meanwhile, according to the Germans, who threatened to stop giving out news unless the Allies gave out more news." Yes, the media of a free Allied nation was depending on the information office of a totalitarian enemy state for the most current news of the fighting by Allied forces.

Simply put, the Allied press was free to print millions of words of vague pronouncements, purple prose, hyperbole and brave sentiments, and call it all news. But SHAEF was not going to permit concrete evidence of the scope and power of the invasion to reach the media, not before it had to. The more trumpeting by the press, supported by little actual evidence, the more likely the Germans were to dismiss the Normandy landings as an elaborate distraction from the coming thrust at the Pas de Calais. And as more Allied units were gradually identified in Normandy, and the scope of the fighting was gradually acknowledged, the German high command was caught in the trap of making plans for next week, based on incorrect information from one or two weeks previous.

On the Side of Caution

In this context it is easy to imagine how the censors approached Capa's most sensitive film.

The first photos to come under strict scrutiny would have been those described in Capa's caption notes sheet titled "Last Glimpse of England" (dated D-1 and labelled "1 Contax"). Only one photo seems to have survived from the 36 exposures Capa claimed to have made. That picture shows troops lining the rails of the *Chase*. In the background is a unit of seven LCIs and behind them a stretch of anonymous coastline. The other 35 shots have been lost to us. Neither negatives, prints nor contact sheet have apparently survived. And that is a telling fact, because this roll was never associated with the Darkroom Accident fable. The loss of all that film has been quietly ignored. The likely explanation is that his shots showed far too much of the invasion fleet which was carrying the 1st Division from Weymouth to Normandy, so the censors retained virtually all the negatives and prints as well as the contact sheet, which seems to explain why they are not among the various archives of Capa's work.

The next set of photos that would have been in the top-secret packet were those taken during his landing. Recall that Capa's debarkation series began with frame 29 from one of his Contax cameras and the preceding 28 are missing. I think it is safe to say the preceding 28 frames were exposed between the time he embarked and his LCVP's ramp lowered. These photos should have shown a good deal of the weight of power employed for the invasion. The serried ranks of attack transports, LSTs and command ships in the Transport Area would prove an accurate template of the forces being landed. Then there would have been the naval preparatory bombardment; the types and numbers of ships involved; the scores of LCTs and LCIs which made possible the projection of those forces ashore; secret specialized equipment, such as rocket-firing LCTs for shore bombardment; other LCTs used for firing platforms for

Army self-propelled artillery; LCTs modified so tanks could fire over the bow ramp during the run in to shore. And the list goes on. None of those details would the censors let pass, for obvious reasons. So, all of it was blocked. It's important to realize that very little film from other correspondents or military photographers showing those same items made it into the press in the immediate wake of D-Day, either, and that which did showed equally little detail. And again, we have no negatives, prints or original contact sheets for any of these missing Capa photos, indicating the censors simply retained them, as their policies dictated.

Capa's landing film (taken from the moment the ramp lowered until he fled to *LCI(L)-94)* was a different story. The reality is that Capa's surviving landing photos present a rather dismal picture. The invasion seems to be stalled at the shingle. Troops are pinned down. Only a few small landing craft can be seen struggling in the surf, at least one of which is wrecked. Hardly the stirring images of victorious Allied troops winning the beachhead. In fact, the photos are disturbingly reminiscent of those from the failed Dieppe Raid. We know from Ruley's motion picture film—which was not immediately released after D-Day—that Capa's images present a false impression of the conditions at that point and time. So, it is fair to conclude that the evidence we have seen of Capa's film, as well as that of others, being censored was part of a larger effort to present German analysts an impression of a weak and faltering landing.

And this was certainly consistent with the picture painted by SHAEF's official communiqués—the only authorized public disclosures of the scope and location of fighting—which consistently drew attention away from the Omaha sector. These communiqués had highlighted action behind the Canadian and British beaches and noted successful advances across the Cherbourg Peninsula (from Utah Beach). This image of weakness in the Allied center either spawned or reinforced the same view in Berlin, and German reinforcements and attention had been hurried to the flanks. But the communiqués had been nearly silent about activity beyond Omaha Beach, where German units were virtually destroyed in the immediate days after the landings. It was only on 11 June that an action that could be attributed to the Omaha beachhead was finally announced, and that announcement came two days after the event. All that silence and distraction obscured the reality. By 12 June, American advances from Omaha had been so successful, they were nearly twice as deep as anywhere else in the Allied invasion area.

Capa's culled photos alone were not by any means responsible for misdirection of German efforts. They were just a small part of a much larger deception effort, one which luckily exploited initial German reports that the landings at Omaha had been repulsed.[25] While that report was soon corrected, the initial accurate impression of weakness in the Allied center endured for several days.

It is important to note that while we have negatives and prints for most of Capa's *surviving* landing photos, the original contact sheet(s) which Morris's lab produced on 7 June is missing. And this is what we would expect. If the censors put a hold on the initial 28 frames of his landing roll, they also would have confiscated contact sheet(s) in addition to the offending negatives and prints. Only the acceptable individual negatives and prints would have been returned to Morris. So, the absence of contacts sheets for this phase of Capa's saga perfectly fits with the censorship explanation.

Capa's film taken during his return from the beach and while back aboard the *Chase* is an entirely different matter. We have evidence of 60 shots taken during this period, but the nature of the shots is notably different. Four are indistinct shots of the beach as he pulled away, again showing an invasion apparently stalled at the shore. Four are pointed to the west and east in the boat lanes and show virtually nothing of the 1,500 ships, craft and boats off Omaha Beach that day. In fact, they are remarkable for how little they do show. By comparison, Figure 75 was snapped by CPT Herman Wall, commander of the 165th Signal Photo Company, while his LCT was held up at the Line of Departure off Easy Red shortly after Capa snapped Figures 62 and 63. Wall's photo shows the actual extent of the volume of traffic involved in the landings, but that reality was not the image censors wanted to make public.

The totality of Capa's photos during this phase paint a bleak picture. Of the surviving 31 negatives on the contact sheets, two-thirds (18 images) focused on the dead, dying and wounded. Four more negatives featured a sinking LCI, and the dead and wounded aboard it. From what we can infer from the entire 60 images, only 15 did not focus on casualties or wreckage. Of these 15, 12 seemed to show an invasion stopped at the shore or showed very little in the way assault shipping carrying reinforcements. Only Figure 32 (and it's presumed two mates) did not focus on death and destruction. This is not the visual record of a successful invasion. But it fit quite nicely with what the censors wanted to portray to the enemy: visual evidence that showed anything but the full force of the landings. And *Life's* photo story for this phase reflected that precisely. Five photos: one showing the landings apparently stalled at the shore; two photos showing almost nothing of the assault shipping; and two more photos showing the dead and dying.

Figure 75. CPT Wall's photo of landing craft congestion off Easy Red beach sector. (NARA, US Army Signal Corps)

Now, did Capa restrict the subjects of his camera because he was aware of the censor's concerns? Or was he just following the print media mantra of "if it bleeds, it leads"? Most likely the latter, as he could not have been aware of the invisible hand of FORTITUDE SOUTH hovering above the operation.

Since Capa's focus during this phase, whether accidental or deliberate, was concentrated on negative subjects, the heavy hand of the censor was not required to any noticeable extent. In fact, there is little evidence of censoring beyond the one exposure in which the *Augusta's* antenna array was marked out. Nor do the missing 35 negatives seem to be a result of censoring. Most of these missing negatives fall within sequences of scenes for which there are multiple surviving negatives which the censors passed. It's possible there may have been one or two scenes with a small number of exposures that were completely stopped by the censors, but it seems unlikely given the sequencing of the negative numbers.

There was a great deal of additional photo and motion picture coverage of Omaha Beach that day. Some showed better conditions and more evidence of success; some worse. But the vast majority of that film, which is so familiar to us today, would not see the light of day for weeks, and in some cases years. A few of Capa's photos, however, would quickly make it into the dailies, followed soon thereafter by the weekly magazines. So, I suggest that close attention was paid to the visual story those few pictures would tell. In a photo story which admitted that the details of the fighting came from enemy sources, a key indication of the invasion's true nature (at least to a German intelligence analyst in Berlin) was the evidence of the photos themselves. And it seems SHAEF's censors were very careful what story those photos told.

The Second Packet

But what about Capa's other film, the film that initially didn't appear to have sensitive images? This would have included the film of soldiers sunning on deck and playing cards and the troops receiving briefings in the hold of the *Chase*. They would show scenes of limited scope and no operational detail, requiring minor editing of details and background images. The public relations officer reviewing the caption notes sheets would have let the presumptive secret classification stand and sent that film packet to the *Life* bureau for routine developing. To be clear, it would have arrived at *Life's* office in a packet separate from the one carried by the custody officer.

That packet may have included more than just Capa's film. Since Scherman dropped off his film in Weymouth about the same time as Capa did, it's probable both their takes arrived in London by the same courier and received an initial review of their caption notes at the same time. So, the less sensitive film from both men quite probably arrived at Morris's office in the same packet.

Once at Bradshaw's lab, that film would have been quickly developed, assuming Morris was accurate when he claimed the entire lab staff was standing idly by, waiting for the first film to return. When that film was developed and the corresponding prints and contact sheets prepared, they would have been taken back to the censors for clearance, a job Morris said was part of his duties.

If a photo had nothing objectionable, it received a rectangular "Passed for Publication" stamp. If there were something minor that could be easily obscured or removed, the photo would receive an oval "Passed for Publication as Censored" stamp, with red ink on the photo indicating the offending detail. As noted before, the photo of Sam Fuller sunning himself on the deck of the Chase (Figure 4) showed marks placed by a censor indicating what should be edited before being published. And the reverse of another photo of that same roll shows the "as censored" stamp. Interestingly, that same photo also shows an oval stamp which said "No Navy Objection as Cut" indicating more than one censor might have to vet film depending on the content.

Even more interesting is the fact that this photo was cleared by the censors on 7 June. That's correct. By midnight on 7 June, Morris had received the second film packet from Capa which contained the less sensitive film, then had not only developed it and produced contact sheets and prints but had also hand-carried it all back to the censors at the MoI, and had it passed for publication by 2400 hours, 7 June. That provides a clear indication how quickly film could be processed and censored. And that drives the final stake into Morris's narratives. If we take the timeline in Morris's Darkroom Accident story seriously, then it took his lab longer to simply ruin the two (or four) critical rolls of Capa's D-Day film, than it did to completely process and get censor's approval of several rolls of low-priority film from two photographers. That makes no sense. More to the point, why would Morris or Bradshaw divert the lab's efforts to these secondary, low-priority, pre-D-Day rolls of film before developing the critical rolls from D-Day? They wouldn't, of course, if the D-Day film was in their hands. From which we can infer it was in someone else's hands. The delays in handling Capa's more sensitive film can only be explained by the more deliberate custody officer scenario. The steps in that scenario would fill the timeframe Morris established, whereas the drying cabinet accident scenario could not.

This second packet casts even further doubt on Morris's reliability. It is simply not present in his long-standing narratives. Any of them. But obviously he did receive and process it. Indeed, he must have carried it himself to the MoI for clearance, as he claimed that was his duty. And he had to have arrived there some time before midnight, as evidenced by the censor's date stamp. But it was not until Morris's 2015 response to Coleman's investigation that he suddenly remembered receiving a second packet of film. In this revised version he claimed he received "an advanced packet" from Scherman on 7 June, along with film from Capa. Morris stated, "Capa had somehow managed to get his pictures of life on the U.S.S. *Samuel Chase* over to Scherman when Capa changed ships."[26] Capa, of course, did not change ships to the *Henrico*, and it isn't clear why Morris felt he needed to invent a transfer of film *before* the convoy sailed for the invasion. Morris, 99 years old at the time of that response, can be excused if his grasp of facts had become less than accurate. In reality, Capa's "advanced packet" had been received before the fleet set sail and had been cleared by censors on 6 June. Any packet Morris received from Scherman and Capa on 7 June would have consisted of the film from the invasion that had been sent by the Press Message Center in Weymouth upon their return. After being reviewed by the public relations officer at the MoI, Scherman's film and Capa's less sensitive film were simply forwarded to Morris at the same time by a single courier.

Worse for Morris, however, is that he also stated that he had no need "to edit or use" Capa's film in that packet. That statement is disingenuous. Whether or not Morris edited or used them, he was obliged to provide *all* of them to the still picture pool. Which meant his lab processed them, produced the prints and contact sheets and he himself had to get them passed though the censors, which, as we've seen, he did on 7 June.

The topic of the second packet is important. As we noted earlier in this chapter, Morris's harrowing account of the difficulty in getting Capa's film delivered for its flight to the US blithely glossed over the censorship process. In fact, the way he told it, the sole time he encountered the censors was early 8 June as he was trying to make the courier for the Prestwick flight. But the evidence of the censor's stamps proves that was simply not true.

In some accounts, Morris seemed to try to proactively defuse the censorship issue, claiming his photographers were all veterans and knew what items to avoid so as not to incur the censor's red pen. But this is quite obviously not the case. We know that at least five of Capa's embarkation photos had details obliterated at the censor's direction. Figure 4 shows that at least one picture from his film at anchor in Weymouth was also tagged for editing by the censors, and probably much of the rest of that roll as well given that his caption notes indicated there were many shots of the same scene. That last roll was among the packet of film Capa brought back 7 June and which Morris developed the same night. If Capa ran afoul of the censors while anchored in Weymouth Bay, one can only wonder what he must have captured off Omaha Beach.

Given Capa's near disastrous blunder with the Norden bomb sight just two years earlier, this self-proclaimed 'enemy alien' photographer quite likely was marked for scrutiny by the SHAEF censorship organization. But in his narrative, Morris takes the *Life* film packet to the censors seemingly almost as a formality. Indeed, the censor's role in Morris's story is little more than a comical incident involving adhesive tape. There is absolutely no discussion of the actual censoring process. In his version, it was not just a minor formality, but also the very last step before sending off the photos. That was far removed from the reality wherein he could not even start final printing of finished photos until the censors had reviewed the film, contact sheets and proofs. Yet the fact that Morris purposefully omitted such a complex part of his duties, forgetting to even mention he'd already been to the censors at least once before midnight, would seem to indicate he was trying hide something. And that something, apparently, was the truth behind the Darkroom Accident fable.

One Last Nail

The culmination of Morris's story is his thrilling dash through London to drop the film off with the courier who would start it on its way to the US. Due to the delay incurred by the censor's blundering attempts to use the adhesive tape, Morris nearly missed this connection, and he arrived breathlessly just before the courier locked the bag. From there the bag would be flown to Prestwick, Scotland, where it would transfer to a C-54 Skymaster for the transatlantic flight to Washington, D.C. In his practiced narrative, Morris said he had rehearsed every step necessary to receive, process and deliver that film. He had even scouted out a special route that would avoid traffic. All this, it would seem, presupposed that the Preswick flights were an established routine, giving Morris time before the invasion to plan and rehearse his dash from the MoI to the courier at the American Embassy.

But as with the rest of his narrative, this thrilling race doesn't seem to quite stand up to scrutiny. For one thing, there were actually two flights a day, not one. And as it turns out, arrangements for the Prestwick were only completed on 7 June—the day Capa landed back at Weymouth. It was a belated SHAEF initiative to reduce shipping of press material by 24 hours. In fact, it wasn't until 0522 hours, 7 June (London time) that SHAEF sent a cable to the US War Department stating that the Air Transport Command would support the plan for these flights, and asking if the War Department could accommodate the special press deliveries by providing couriers to receive the material when it arrived in Washington.[27] It was very much a last-minute affair. Clearly Morris could not have been aware this plan had been approved and implemented earlier than sometime late the day of 7 June—and that's assuming the bureaucratic wheels had turned rapidly and smoothly at the War Department's end in Washington. So, the twice-daily flights to Prestwick were not an established fact before D-Day and could not have been part of Morris's advanced planning, which means he certainly had no time to rehearse "every step" as he later claimed.

Keep in mind, that the film we are discussing here is solely the film *Life* would have exclusive access to. Capa's best photos had been selected by the review board and sent out by radiotelephoto. So, Morris's "mad dash" was keyed to *Life*'s deadline for its weekly issue. But was the deadline as tight and dramatic as Morris portrayed? Again, no. As noted above, there were two flights a day. If Morris had missed the 0900 hours courier, it would only have delayed his film by just 12 hours. And while that delay may have missed *Life*'s normal Saturday evening deadline for the next issue, that was merely an inconvenience, not a showstopper. That deadline could be very flexible, as demonstrated by the lengths *Life*'s New York offices had gone to on D-Day. That very day, Tuesday, 6 June, their 12 June edition had just begun its printing run, with 750,000 copies already printed, when the first news of the invasion broke very early that morning on the east coast. At 3:35 AM, the presses were stopped and *Life*'s staff swung into operation, reformatted the edition to incorporate the initial reports, and still had the new version printed and on the newsstands later that day.[28] So if Morris had missed the 0900 hours courier on Thursday and had to wait for the second courier that day, and if his images had not reached *Life*'s offices until Sunday, they still would have had two days more to change the edition than they had the previous week.

It would appear Morris's dramatic tale of the race to meet the deadline was very much a dramatic exaggeration. And it masked a notable failure. The first invasion photos to make it into American papers were several of CPT Wall's images and Bert Brandt's single D-Day image, and these were featured in almost all the major American daily papers. Capa's D-Day photos made it into those same papers—if they were carried at all—at least a day later than Wall's and Brandt's. And none of his photos was featured as universally as theirs. Whether the fault lay in the delay in getting Capa's film off the *Chase* and to London, or confusion in Morris's lab, the *Life* team came in a poor second to both the Army and Acme. This failure was all the more bitter given the lack of usable D-Day photos from all the rest of *Life*'s photographers that day. Morris's dramatic recollections of 7 and 8 June could go only so far in masking the reality.

CHAPTER TWENTY FIVE

Origins

"Doctored photographs are the least of our worries. If you want to trick someone with a photograph, there are lots of easy ways to do it. You don't need Photoshop. You don't need sophisticated digital photo-manipulation. You don't need a computer. All you need to do is change the caption."

ERROL MORRIS

At this point we've discovered that virtually every aspect of the saga of Capa's film in London was either an exaggeration or quite simply not true. Which leads to the obvious question: Just who came up with the Darkroom Accident fable in the first place?

In *Slightly out of Focus*, Capa closed his D-Day chapter stating that seven days later he learned all but eight of his photos had been ruined by a drying accident.[1] The actual sequence of events seems to have gone like this.

The first public hint that some of Capa's film may have been lost was a casual comment in *Life*'s 19 June edition, which carried ten of Capa's photos in a seven-page spread. The accompanying text noted that Capa's cameras were thoroughly soaked as he waded out to board a Navy ship. Fortunately, "By some miracle, one of them was not too badly damaged and he was able to keep making pictures."[2] With that statement a matter of printed record, the suggestion of film loss due to seawater was planted in the public's mind, though not explicitly stated.

Wilson Hicks (one of *Life*'s two executive editors and chief photo editor) cabled Capa his congratulations for the D-Day photos. In that cable he informed Capa that his was "the best coverage of the invasion," but that the bulk of his film "had been ruined by seawater that had seeped into his camera." Whelan cited that cable but neglected to mention the date.[3] It seems certain, however, it must have been in the same 10 June 1944 cable Hicks sent to London offering Capa a job on the *Life* staff—he'd always worked on a short-term contract basis up to that point. The problem is, Capa did not see this cable for more than a month.

Why it fell to Hicks, rather than Capa's London picture editor (Morris) to break the bad news about ruined film is a good question. More importantly, this begs the question, where did Hicks get the idea that the film was damaged by seawater?

It's a bit of a mystery. *Life's* hierarchy, from Morris on up to Hicks, must have been well aware that most of Capa's D-Day film was missing, and we can assume answers were demanded. If Hicks meant that seawater comment as a serious explanation, then he was clearly fed that information from someone much lower down in the pecking order. Such as Morris.

The only communication Morris had from Capa was the note stating, "the action was all in the 35 millimeter."[4] None of Morris's many version of the legend indicate Capa relayed the details of his D-Day escapades on 7 June. Never was there a mention of wading out to *LCI(L)-94* with water up to his chin. And never was there a hint that his wet hands had ruined the film he was trying to change on the beach. By the time Morris dropped the film into the courier's bag early 8 June, he had had just that one short, scrawled note from Capa, and it provided no indication of seawater immersion. The only item that possibly could have hinted at the idea was tucked away in the caption notes for the Last Glimpse of England roll of 35mm film.[5] As discussed earlier, inserted between the description of the pictures on that roll and the instructions to the lab for developing the film, Capa had scrawled, "Film like everything got wett by landing." It is at least theoretically possible that Morris did notice that comment and passed on some version of it to New York when he sent off the film; however, he did not mention it in any of his retellings of the saga. And in fact, it would have been incomprehensible if he had, because according to the version he peddled for decades, he "knew" the bulk of the film had been ruined by his darkroom crew hours before he delivered it to the courier. So, "knowing" that, why would he have lied to his New York superiors rather than admit to the blame himself? Or perhaps, that is exactly why he might have lied to his superiors?

But we know better. We now know what Morris must have known then: that the film was lost to the censor, and not to seawater or teenage bumbling. So, should we even take Hicks's use of the seawater excuse as a serious explanation? I would say not. The media was forbidden from mentioning the nature or extent of censorship in their communications both within and outside the theater. Hicks simply could not have sent a non-secure cable into theater blaming the loss of that much film to censorship. So, I'd suggest Hicks's cable, which was intended to deliver and soften the bad news, had to use a euphemism—seawater—that could be transmitted into theater without drawing the censor's wrath. Nor would Capa have accepted that seawater explanation literally. He would have known if seawater had soaked into his cameras because he changed the film in them. So, I suggest Capa would have understood the seawater explanation was not to be taken literally.

On 11 July, Capa left Normandy for London for a break from the front, and probably arrived in London two or three days later. He was still unaware of the loss of the film. It seems impossible to believe that in the intervening five weeks, Morris had been unable to get a message to Capa informing him of the "true" reason for the loss of the film, but that does seem to be the case. The London *Time/Life* office had sent several correspondents to the same press camp in Normandy during that time; Morris had plenty of opportunity to pass along a note or verbal message on the matter to Capa. Yet Morris appears to have been strangely unwilling to address this topic with his star photographer.

In fact, it appears Morris ducked out of London just ahead of Capa's return. Morris landed on Utah Beach on 16 July for his own junket to Normandy.[6] Considering the necessary time at the Press Training Center for processing, orientation and issue of field gear, as was the norm for correspondents deploying to France, as well as waiting for transport to the Continent, he would have left London several days earlier. Neither of their memoirs mentions them crossing paths at this juncture. In fact, Capa completely omitted his trip to London in his *Slightly out of Focus*. Similarly, Morris remained silent on the return of *Life*'s hero photographer and his own "adopted Hungarian brother." It was very curious timing.*

Having failed to pass on both the bad and good news in Hicks's cable, Morris seems to have left it for Capa to discover at the London office. In a letter Capa sent to his brother Cornell in late July, he stated, "I just got back from London where I had a good time and a bad surprise. I found out that 90 percent of my invasion material was ruined by drying ...."[7] He also learned of Hicks's job offer at this time, contained in the month-old 10 June cable, which means he would have seen Hicks's original explanation that the film was ruined by seawater, not drying. So how did Hicks's seawater scapegoat get cleared of the blame, and an accident in the darkroom become the new villain?

When he arrived back in London and learned of the loss of the film, Capa certainly would have had a talk with anyone who had anything to do with developing his film that night: Bradshaw, Wild and Banks/Sanders. What they may have told him will remain a mystery forever, for the first two never spoke of it, and the last seems to have vanished, if he ever existed in the first place. Regardless of what they might have told Capa had happened, his letter to Cornell shows he adopted the Darkroom Accident fable within two months of D-Day. In fact, he was the first person to mention it, as far as the evidence shows. But did he believe it?

Capa's letter to Cornell was coming from France—a combat zone—to the states, which meant it necessarily would pass through a censor. Therefore, Capa could not explicitly discuss the scope or nature of the censorship of his products in that letter. Just as Hicks had likely done, Capa probably used the "ruined by drying" expression as a veiled reference to censorship. Capa's euphemism had the benefit of shifting the fictional blame to an anonymous darkroom technician, whereas Hicks's seawater version might reflect rather poorly on Capa's fieldcraft. The use of the drying accident

---

* Morris justified his four-week junket to France by inventing for himself the title of "Acting Coordinator, Press Photographers, Western Front." The actual still photo pool had been disestablished a month earlier on 11 June, much sooner than planned. Morris and Capa did not encounter one another until late July when Capa returned to France. By then Hicks had placated Capa.

as a code for censorship seems more likely as that letter was addressed to Cornell, who, working first in the PIX agency photo lab and then in *Life's* New York photo lab, would have realized how unlikely such an accident would be in a professional lab. Capa would hardly have tried to seriously pass off that story to Cornell, so it seems probable he used that term as a euphemism for another cause of loss.

The Darkroom Accident next emerged in a muted form in Wertenbaker's 1944 book *Invasion*, which was illustrated by Capa's photos.[8] That book was hastily published in the wake of the Normandy invasion to take advantage of the public's interest of the great event. Wertenbaker merely noted that "A careless darkroom assistant ruined all but seven of them." Although that comment followed a two-page verbatim account given by Capa on D+3 back in the Omaha beachhead, the comment itself was stated in Wertenbaker's voice, and must have been added to the account later, as neither man had heard from the London office by D+3. Since the "careless assistant" explanation so closely follows Capa description of "ruined by drying," Wertenbaker seems to have adopted a vague version of Capa's characterization of events while editing his manuscript in the later months of that year. The two men accompanied each other on several adventures in the last half of 1944, while Wertenbaker was preparing his book, so he likely took his lead from Capa on this point.

Interestingly, while both men were *Time/Life* employees, neither felt constrained to hew to Hicks's "ruined by seawater" explanation. What should we conclude from this? Why would they dare to refute Hicks's version of events? The simplest explanation is that Hicks never meant the seawater explanation to be taken seriously by Capa or anyone else, as we have already discussed. Beyond that, Hicks' seawater comment had neither been released nor circulated. It was contained in an internal communication, so his name and, by extension, his reputation, were not publicly linked to that excuse. Indeed, the public's only inkling of the seawater excuse was hinted at in the 19 June issue, when it stated his cameras were thoroughly soaked when he was wading out to a ship. So, while *Invasion's* "careless assistant" version first explicitly introduced that reason for the film loss to the public, it did not publicly repudiate Hicks. It merely added a new dimension to what very little readers already knew.

The Darkroom Accident version made its first major public splash when *Slightly out of Focus* was printed in 1947. Whether originally a euphemism or not, it offered several advantages as an enduring element of the Capa saga. The idea that film which had survived the horrors of D-Day had, in the end, been destroyed by a developing error in London provided a pricelessly ironic culmination to his D-Day saga. It endowed the surviving images with an intangible measure of value simply because they did survive. They were the miracle photos. And the Darkroom Accident fable teased the public with the tantalizing speculation of just what wonders might have been captured on the lost film. It also provided an excellent excuse for the total absence of evidence that Capa went far enough ashore to reach the shingle. He couldn't try to blame that on the censors, as close shots of men under fire—shots not revealing the full force of the armada or landing force—were freely passed by censors that day. It was far better to claim he took shots at the shingle and blame the Darkroom Accident for their loss.

A brief survey of pictorial coverage of D-Day in major American newspapers bears this out. Capa's "Magnificent 11' photos were handily beaten out, both in terms of date and frequency used, by those of CPT Wall and SGT Taylor (of the 165th Signal Photo Company) and Bert Brandt. Some papers used none of Capa's photos; others only used photos he took after leaving the beach. Of course, virtually none of these photos was credited to an individual cameraman. Having arrived via the pool transmission channel, they were normally attributed to the US Army Signal Corps (who operated the radiotelephoto network), Acme Newspictures (the manager of the still photo pool) or the American wire services feeding the individual newspapers. So, the pictures published were selected by their merit alone, not based on a cameraman's reputation or the power of his publishing house. And in that environment, Capa's D-Day work fared rather poorly. Even *Life*'s 19 June 1944 issue provided merely a brief exposure to the public. The fame of Capa's D-Day photos only came later, due in large part to the mythos of the Darkroom Accident.

And the Darkroom Accident had one other excellent point going for it. If one believed that explanation, then the film was irretrievably lost. End of story. On the other hand, if he admitted the film had been stopped and held by the censors, some enterprising reporter might prod SHAEF to delve back into its vaults and perhaps find the film, which might well have been possible in 1947 when *Slightly out of Focus* was published. And that would have discredited much of Capa's D-Day saga.

As fanciful as it is in most parts, Capa's narrative in *Slightly out of Focus* remains tightly anchored to the surviving images. It is hardly coincidental that his invented passages, characters and events involved sequences not documented by the surviving photos. His own pictures provided concrete constraints to his flights of fancy, but also defined the boundaries beyond which exaggeration and invention could be set free. The last thing he would have wanted was for the complete set of his D-Day pictures to surface. His fear wouldn't be what they showed, rather what they didn't show. None of the many shots he claimed to have taken at the shingle would have turned up, because he never reached that point and invented that incident.

But this eventuality would not come to pass. The Darkroom Accident explanation shut down all further inquiries into the fate of the film, and ensured no photographic evidence would surface that might destroy Capa's evolving D-Day fable. Following the breakout from Normandy, the liberation of Paris, the Battle of the Bulge and the end of the war in Europe, no one was interested in what the censors may or may not have retained on D-Day. To *Life* it was very old news at a period when breaking-news stories were coming in rapid fire succession.

To put this in perspective, in the period 6–24 June 1944—just 19 days—SHAEF's censorship structure handled more than six million words of press material, over 102,000 photographs and more than 284,900 feet of motion picture film.[9] SHAEF could retain merely a token percentage of this volume of material, and even less would eventually make it into the National Archives. And "stopped" film that belonged to press agencies—which had neglected to reclaim that film when the stop had been lifted—would simply sit forgotten in dusty filing boxes while harried SHAEF functionaries focused on more immediate concerns. Nor would any researcher even bother with trying to locate Capa's stopped D-Day film in the SHAEF archives in the years following victory in Europe, because everyone was under the impression it had been destroyed before it even reached the censors.

Here we see clear parallels with his Falling Soldier photos from the Spanish Civil War. For years the negatives were thought to be lost, and the few surviving pictures matched Capa's accompanying narrative. It was only the totally unexpected discovery of the so-called Mexican suitcase that brought the original film to light and revealed the full scope of the deception. The entire set of scenes were mock combat staged for his cameras, which he passed off as actual combat photography.

So, all things considered, converting the casual euphemism used in private correspondence into an explanation for public consumption must have seemed a pretty good idea to Capa. Upon its inclusion in Capa's *Slightly out of Focus* in 1947, the fable became enshrined in popular culture. More than that, the *Slightly out of Focus* version added a new layer to the fable. For the first time the exact mechanism of the film's destruction was specified: the heat in the drying cabinet had resulted in emulsion melt.

And no one questioned it.

The Morris Era

For three decades, Capa's D-Day saga largely remained as he left it in *Slightly out of Focus*. After Capa's death in Indochina in 1954, his brother Cornell picked up the standard and loyally supported and advocated Robert's legacy. Eventually it began to acquire the popular image it has now but did not enjoy in the 1940s and 50s. The legacy-building effort took a major step forward when, as we've seen, Robert Whelan was brought on board to write an authorized biography of Capa. That book, and his later book that also celebrated Capa (*This Is War!*), brought his legacy back into public focus, though it did little more than repeat most of Capa's self-inventions.

But Whelan's 1985 book (*Robert Capa: A Biography*) had an unexpected effect. The Darkroom Accident story was simply too intriguing to be left as a dangling end to the saga. The story needed a more fitting ending; it demanded an explanation of just what had happened in the lab that night. And the only one who could answer that was John Morris. Everyone else present that night was either dead or had apparently fallen off the earth. And Morris appeared to be a credible source. He and Capa had working relationships that extended back to the war, when he was at least nominally in charge of the *Life* photo section in London. After the war, Morris, then the picture editor for *The Ladies' Home Journal*, was initially the first major client for Magnum Photos, the photographers' cooperative agency Capa and others founded. Indeed, Kershaw reported that fully two-thirds of the money Magnum earned in its first five months came from Morris's patronage.[10] And of course it was Morris who partially salvaged the disastrous *A Russian Journal* collaboration between Steinbeck and Capa; Morris convinced *The Ladies' Home Journal* to print a spread of Capa's photos from that junket, and paid Capa an extraordinarily high fee. All this patronage was eventually rewarded when Magnum hired Morris as its executive editor.

In Morris, Whelan found not only a Capa insider and loyalist, but apparently the only living person who could speak to the circumstances of the Darkroom Accident. Whelan was aided by the work of Jozefa Stuart, who, in the early 1960s conducted a series of interviews for a never-completed biography of Capa. Among her notes were a couple pages from her interview with Morris explaining what took place from the time Capa's film arrived at *Life*'s London offices until it was handed to the courier for Prestwick. (Her interview effort did not seem to include H. C. Bradshaw or Hans Wild, who worked in the darkroom that fateful night.) This appears to have been the first time Morris went on record with a version of those events. Whelan incorporated information from the Stuart interview as well as that from his own interview with Morris (conducted some 20 years after Stuart's) in the 1985 biography.

And with the publication of Morris's version in that book, the Capa D-Day saga effectively became Morris's. If anyone wanted soundbites, insights, anecdotes or personal reminiscences of Capa and D-Day, there was one and only one source: John Morris, Capa's boss during the invasion. And in the telling and retelling, the emphasis shifted from Capa to Morris and his labors.

That also meant Morris not only had to embrace the emulsion-melt theory that lay at the heart of the Darkroom Accident myth but incorporate it into his own narrative. And that was no small task given that the emulsion-melt explanation was a fiction, and a fiction that could reflect very poorly on the professionalism of Morris's operation. So additional supporting fictional details had to be invented. A (possibly fictional) teen lab assistant was chosen to take the blame for the fictional emulsion-melt story, thereby keeping Capa's fanciful story intact while avoiding any slight to the reputation of the very able Bradshaw and Wild. Following this, Morris took his trivial role in passing the film through the censors and delivering it to a courier and exaggerated it completely out of proportion such that it became the central dramatic element of the story—at least as told by Morris. The resulting fable stood up well to an adoring and gullible fan base in the media, and actually seemed to improve with constant repetition. Morris's artful retellings were so successful that he was eventually able to avoid any blame for the supposed loss of the film through the supposed ineptitude of his staff, and instead take credit for "saving" the surviving pictures. Though one cannot image how, by any stretch of the imagination, he saved anything.

This façade proved brittle and unable to withstand even the first serious inquiry.[11] Ross Baughman's initial questions (June 2014) were soon followed by Rob McElroy's brilliantly obvious observation that if the emulsion had melted and run on the film, then something was seriously wrong with physics. The apparent direction of the melted elusions' slipping on the film was toward the bottom of the frames, which would only be "down" (in the direction of the pull of gravity) if the film strips were dried horizontally. But the film was hung vertically in the drying cabinet, in which case gravity pulling the emulsion down would have seen it slip to one side of the frames or the other, not toward the bottom. Rob went on to prove the supposed emulsion slippage was actually a small misalignment of the film in the camera due to the slightly non-standard film spools Capa used. There was no running emulsion; the cameras merely exposed the film off center.

And with that, Morris's well-practiced story of the loss of Capa's film rapidly began to unravel. As more details emerged, the scope of the inaccuracies grew until it reached a point that little, if anything, of the story could be believed. And with that, Morris began recanting his story and "remembering" new details, which, as often as not, were equally inaccurate.

In 2021, Tristan da Cunha drove a final stake into the heart of the Darkroom Accident fable. His practical experiments definitively disproved the emulsion melt theory, and proved the seawater excuse to be false. But by then John Morris was dead, having died in 2017.

Numbers

In the introduction, I noted the confusion regarding the number of photos Capa supposedly took (106, 79 or 72) as well as the confusion regarding the number of images (7, 8, 9, 10 or 11) that "survived" the night of 7/8 June. It is a rather amusing, if absurd, situation, considering how iconic they've become. It's also a commentary on a popular culture that has dubbed the surviving photos "the Magnificent 11," despite there never having been a shred of visual evidence of an eleventh photo. And of course, the confusion also extends to the number of rolls of film and their format.

When I set out to research the Capa D-Day saga, I soon realized a key element would be the not-so-small matter of determining what film Capa shot. I didn't expect to identify every single frame he exposed, but I was confident that with enough diligent research, I could nail down what rolls of film, from which cameras, were exposed at each stage of his adventure. After all, there were several surviving pages of caption notes and several surviving photos. I started by reviewing the work Coleman had done and attempted to see what further refinements could be made.

After considerable effort I was able to clarify a couple more points, but most of the details remained as elusive as ever, partly because of the sheer number of missing photos and partly due to conflicting versions Morris has told over the years. The following paragraphs represent my conclusions, and will, I hope, give some small idea of the confusion that still exists. This discussion does not include the Speed Graphic film Capa exposed on the *Chase*, as information on that film is virtually nonexistent. (Note: the titles used below mostly come from those pages of caption notes that included titles; where no title was listed, I have used appropriate titles of my own making.)

- Embarkation. This phase appears to be the simplest to decipher. We have a page of caption notes titled "Embarcation" which states he used two rolls of film from his Rolleiflex camera and one roll from his Contax (as much as 24 frames of 120 film and 38 frames of 35mm film). There are at least 16 existing photos from this lot, documenting the arrival of the troops at the quay in Weymouth to their boarding the USS *Chase*. Seven of these include the reverse side showing typed captions and the censor's stamps. The typed captions closely correspond to the general description of action written on Capa's "Embarcation" page of caption notes. The censor's stamps on these photos prove they were cleared for release on 6 June, which confirms this packet of film was sent to London before the *Chase* sailed on 5 June for D-Day.

- Briefing the Coxswains. This is a mystery roll of Rolleiflex film. There is no surviving sheet of caption notes for this roll and there appear to be only four surviving photos from the 12 that would normally be on a roll of 120 film, assuming only one was used for these scenes. One of these photos is not in either the ICP or Magnum archives but was printed in the 7 June edition of the *New York Daily News*. One of the three photos in the archives includes a reverse side with a caption that reads: "Briefing of the coxswains who will bring in the first assault troops in the gymnasium of the ship. On the floor are painted lines where the different boats are going in." This caption clearly came from one of Capa's pages of caption notes; only someone on scene could have provided the details. That caption does not remotely fit any other surviving page of caption notes; so, we must assume the images came from a separate roll with a separate page of caption notes, one that apparently did not survive. The censor's stamp shows the picture was also cleared on 6 June, proving this film was sent to London before the *Chase* sailed on 5 June, and suggests this roll of film was in the same package as the embarkation film. This conclusion tends to be supported by the fact that the censor's stamp proves that briefing photo was cleared by one of the same censors who cleared Capa's embarkation photos. When Coleman examined the negatives held by ICP, he reported that there were additional negatives in 120 film format that did not match any of the pages of caption notes. My working assumption is that they were part of this roll. Interestingly, a clip of stock motion picture film shows the exact same scene with the same sailors in nearly identical positions as seen in Capa's close shot of the briefing.[12] Once again, Coast Guard cameramen and Capa duplicated each other's work.

- Troops Sunning … The next set consists of a single roll of 35mm film from one of his Contax cameras. We have a page of caption notes for this roll, but it is untitled. It describes troops on the upper deck of the ship playing cards, reading and sunning themselves as they wait. There are three surviving photos from this roll of film, including the reverse side for one of those three, which states the film came from Capa's Contax. The typed caption on the reverse closely follows Capa's page of caption notes. The censor's stamp on the reverse proves this roll was cleared on 7 June, which confirms Capa took it with him when the Chase sailed and passed it to the Press Message Center in Weymouth when he returned on 7 June.

- Last Glimpse of England. This page of caption notes accompanied a single roll of 35mm film from Capa's Contax camera. Unfortunately, only a single photo from this role has survived. The caption notes sheet shows he exposed all 36 images of this film, and the captions themselves show they all focused on the tension prior to embarking on landing craft. This was also the page of caption notes on which Capa scrawled his "everything got wett" comment at the bottom. We can be sure this film was not sent to London until 7 June for the simple reason that the surviving photo shows the *Chase* underway for the invasion on 5 June.

- Briefing to Invasion. This set of one roll of 35mm film is described by a page of caption notes indicating 36 frames were exposed. Only four pictures from this roll seem to exist, and there are no images of the reverse of any of them. One of the images shows COL Taylor briefing officers in front of a terrain model. Since COL Taylor conducted this briefing the night before the invasion while the *Chase* was underway, the film was not returned to the UK until 7 June, and could not have been transmitted to American dailies until 8 June, at the earliest.[13] Supporting this conclusion is the fact that none of these photos was printed with the other stock pre-invasion photos which the major dailies relied on up until 8 June. These images only appeared in print on the same day that the first film from the beaches became available.

- From the *Chase* up to and including his time on the Beach. We have no caption note page for this phase, and curiously, neither ICP nor Magnum hold any reverse images showing censor clearance stamps, or the original typed captions for the surviving images. Morris's traditional version holds that all 10 of the surviving images came from the end of one roll of 35mm film. Capa claimed he shot two rolls and ruined a third while trying to load it. There is no evidence he exposed more than one roll.

- From the Beach to the *Chase.* Again, we have no caption note page, but we have identified five rolls of 120 film from the Magnum re-created contact sheets, and all seem to have been completely exposed.

To sum up:

Packet delivered to London before D-Day:	
Embarkation:	1 × 35mm
	2 × 120
Briefing to Coxswains:	1 × 120
Packet delivered 7 June:	
On the Upper Deck:	1 × 35mm
Last Glimpse of England:	1 × 35mm
Briefing to Invasion:	1 × 35mm
From the *Chase* to the Beach:	1 × 35mm
From the Beach to the *Chase*:	5 × 120

Based on this, the pre-invasion packet of film sent to London would have included one roll of 35mm and three rolls of 120. As we've seen, all this film was received and processed before D-Day and released by censors on D-Day itself.

Similarly, the post-invasion packet would have included four rolls of 35mm and five rolls of 120. But this does not jive with Morris, who confused matters by providing different tallies for the film he received on 7 June. He told Jozefa Stuart he received two rolls of 35mm and four of 120.[14] In his own book, Morris provided a higher tally: four rolls of 35mm and six of 120. And Morris made absolutely no reference to receiving the Speed Graphic film Capa exposed aboard the *Chase*.[15]

It might at first appear that Morris's revised total of four rolls of 35mm referred to only the film he received on 7 June, and therefore matches the tally I have for that same day. Not so. Recall from the last chapter Morris claimed that on three of those rolls, and on all but 11 images of the fourth, there was "nothing to see," and in other versions, there was just gray smudge. But we have surviving images from all four rolls of 35mm he received that night, so that does not fit. Later Morris posed a further explanation: Capa's packet included unexposed film that he hurriedly and carelessly included with the exposed film. But three blank rolls, added to the four (at least) rolls with surviving images, totals seven rolls, far more than any tally Morris ever claimed he received. His figures just don't add up. And they never have, no matter which version of events he told.

As his version of events began to crumble under examination, Morris suddenly recalled receiving the second packet from Capa on 7 June. He believed this second packet was the pre-invasion film, and Capa had passed it to Scherman before sailing. Scherman, then, had forwarded it to London with his own take when he returned on 7 June. But this fails on at least two points. First, we know for a fact Capa's pre-invasion film was cleared by the censors on 6 June, so it could not have arrived on 7 June. And second, the film tallies still do not jive.

Still, Morris was probably partly correct. As we've seen, Capa's D-Day film would have been split by the censors into two packets. The first, consisting of the less sensitive film (perhaps as much as three rolls of 35mm), would have arrived in the normal manner. Because Capa and Scherman had reunited at Weymouth on 7 June, their film was probably sent by the same motorcycle courier to the MoI. So Capa's less sensitive film and all Scherman's (which was routine subject matter) would have been delivered to Morris's office in the same packet. Morris's memory seems to have confused this packet with the pre-invasion delivery a few days earlier.

And so it is that Morris leaves us just as confused on this point as he has on so many others.

Nevertheless, we now have a better idea of how much film Capa used on D-Day itself. The five rolls of 120 film totalled 60 images, and the one roll of 35mm totalled 38 images—assuming he exposed 28 on the ride to the beach—for a total of 98 images. Of these, 31 of the 120 film have survived, and it is probable most of the rest survived both the developing process and the censor, as they are merely additional shots of the same scenes the censors passed. The bulk of the missing 120 exposures were probably victims of *Life*'s and Magnum's recordkeeping. And of course only 10 survived of the 35mm film; the remainder are likely casualties of the censor's red pen.

Disposition

Assuming the SHAEF censors retained all or most of the missing photos, what then happened to that film? The censors had a couple of options. If the material contained information that was not likely to be unclassified any time in the foreseeable future, the film could have been simply destroyed.

But most of the information the censors were concerned about consisted of items whose intelligence value was rather short lived. For instance, SHAEF normally delayed confirming the identity of units committed to the fight until they were certain the Germans had discovered it themselves. So, even though the Germans had captured members of the 82nd Airborne Division in the pre-dawn hours of 6 June, SHAEF did not confirm the division's participation in the battle until 11 June.[16] But even then, that delay wasn't very long.

In Capa's case, his film would have been retained due to concern for the FORTITUDE SOUTH deception plan, which, as we've already seen, was expected to last only some 45 days. So, in theory, the sensitive items Capa may have captured on D-Day would have been releasable in mid-July. Even the follow-on FORTITUDE SOUTH II plan, when it was implemented, would only have potentially kept Capa's D-Day photos under wraps for a few more weeks, if that. Knowing this, the censors had two options.[17] If Morris's lab had a secure vault and had been certified for storage of top-secret material, the censors had the option of permitting the news bureau to retain the stopped film until the stop order had been lifted, at which time it could be resubmitted for review and release. There is no indication that Morris's offices possessed such a vault, much less had been certified for storage of top-secret material.

Given that, the censors had the option of simply retaining the stopped film in their own storage facilities until it was no longer deemed sensitive. In theory, then, Capa's film could possibly have been released as early as 20 July, or more likely, late August. In fact, it could have been held until at least the end of the war, so as not to give the enemy a hint of the scope, sophistication and effectiveness of Allied deception activity. But by then would anyone have cared?

The Allied breakout from Normandy had gotten underway at the very end of July and two weeks later the public was engrossed in new spectacles. Armored columns were tearing through the German rear, large German forces were being encircled at Falaise, and the amphibious invasion of southern France had begun. Photos of D-Day were suddenly not of much interest. At least not to a weekly magazine which had already published a fictional account of how the "surviving" photos had been snapped in the First Wave. *Life*'s potential interest in recovering those forgotten pictures can best be illustrated by the fact that during this very time, Morris had taken his battlefield tourist leave from his London office for a jaunt to France where he played amateur photographer himself. And after Paris was liberated on 25 August, Morris moved his office to that city. His focus, like the magazine's itself, was on the next deadline and the heady liberation of France. Not a thought would have been given to unclaimed film lying back in a dusty London vault that documented old news. Especially if that film would have revealed *Life*'s original seawater explanation to have been untrue.

And if *Life* didn't care, the censors certainly weren't going to. They had their hands full with ever-increasing workloads of material generated by the avalanche of additional correspondents pouring onto the Continent. The military and naval photo units had an interest in reclaiming their stopped film, as they had mandates to compile a complete historical record, so much of their censored material was rescued. But *Life*, tied to the weekly news cycle, had no such concerns, and it is hard to imagine its remaining London employees made any effort at all to reclaim film they had already claimed had been ruined.

And so, it is likely that Capa's missing D-Day film simply vanished in the SHAEF vaults, forgotten and eventually purged during a round of bureaucratic housecleaning, victim of the mandatory declassification or destruction regulations.

Last Standing Explanation

In the final analysis, I suggest the censor's red pen is the only reasonable explanation for the loss of so much of Capa's D-Day film. Admittedly, much of the evidence is circumstantial. We know the procedures that should have been followed, and we have a pretty good fix on what Capa's film captured. That tells us how the film should have arrived at Morris's lab and how it should have been processed. We know the timeline Morris laid out in the Jozefa Stuart interview makes no sense unless the film was processed as top-secret material. And the speed with which Capa's less sensitive film was processed and censored proves it. And we have the dates on several censor stamps which match the censor scenario but contradict Morris's. And finally, Morris's complete omission of the actual role of censorship calls his account into question; it just doesn't fit with the reality of the day.

The Darkroom Accident fable was just that, a technically infeasible myth. And once that was discredited, there remains just one other logical explanation: censorship in support of FORTITUDE SOUTH.

CHAPTER TWENTY SIX

High Anxiety

"The text is just the inventor's inventions about himself."
FROM "THE MAN WHO INVENTED HIMSELF,"
JOHN HERSEY'S REVIEW OF *SLIGHTLY OUT OF FOCUS*

"I could never tell a lie that anyone would doubt, nor a truth that anyone would believe."
MARK TWAIN, *FOLLOWING THE EQUATOR*

One of the more constant yet confusing themes in the Capa WWII saga is his association, or disassociation, with the airborne forces. The full story of his flirtation with the airborne is perhaps the best insight into his character and best measure of whatever actual grit lurked below the façade of bravery. Because he invented some incidents and completely omitted others, both to his reputation's benefit, few people have any understanding of the whole story. Let's bring it into focus.

Sicily

In an earlier chapter we touched on his fictionalized account of parachuting into Sicily with the 82nd Airborne Division, an account which bears further examination. Capa was facing a problem. After the Axis forces surrendered in North Africa (13 May 1943), he decided to return to London to see his girlfriend Pinky, arriving there early June. While there, *Collier's*, the magazine sponsoring his accreditation with American forces, had decided they had no need to keep Capa on the payroll, since a photo pool would be in effect for the next operation, and they could simply use the pool photos for free. In short, Capa would be fired on 19 July. Capa sent out feelers to *Life*, then hied back to North Africa to see what could be done. All true, up to this point.[1]

Upon arriving back in North Africa, Capa found he had no position in the upcoming invasion, which he attributed to having been fired. That's a bit disingenuous. Since his termination wouldn't be effective until 19 July, and the invasion was scheduled for 9 July (the first airborne landings), there would have been 10 days in which he could have been productive, and that's not counting anything he might capture during the marshalling and the sea voyage. The more likely explanation for being omitted from the operation was simply due to his absence from the war zone as he diverted himself with another man's wife. He arrived back in North Africa from his dalliance so late that the seaborne elements of the invasion had already embarked (the first convoy embarked the afternoon of 4 July).[2] He wasn't slotted in the invasion for the simple reason that he made himself unavailable until it was too late to participate in the assault. It was not the last time that romantic diversions or well-timed absences would preclude his participation in major events.

But here the fiction crept in.[3] To stay one step ahead of eviction from the theater, according to his account, he, and a friendly public relations officer,* hatched a plan to get him a peripheral role in the invasion. Capa would take the place of a sick reporter who was to ride along for the first night's drop into Sicily. And, Capa claimed, this he did, taking a few pictures of paratroopers in the aircraft. After the drop, he returned aboard the empty aircraft and got his film quickly into the press channels. For dramatic effect, Capa inserted the claim that after delivering his photos to the censors on 10 July, the friendly PRO advised him that the cable from *Collier's* had arrived; Capa was fired. The cable may have arrived, but the effective date wasn't for another nine days, a point Capa omitted.

To avoid being kicked out of theater, he claimed, the friendly PRO suggested Capa actually make a parachute drop with a reinforcing echelon of the 82nd Airborne Division the next night (10 July). Capa portrayed it as a slick maneuver to avoid being ousted from the theater, but with 10 days left on his assignment and accreditation, no one would have interfered anyway. In reality, the reinforcing drop took place a day later (the night of 11 July). Despite having no parachute training, Capa claimed he did jump into the beachhead. He and three other paratroopers were isolated behind enemy lines for three days, "creeping out at night to blow up little bridges." On the fourth day, soldiers of the US 1st Infantry Division finally linked up with the little band.

Except for a few thin facts on which to hang the fiction, that story was mostly utter balderdash. As we know, Capa did not fly on the first night's drop as part of the Sicily D-Day. He did accompany the reinforcing drop two nights later, but only as a non-jumping observer to take photos. He did not jump. He was not stranded behind enemy lines. It was all self-glorifying fiction. The irony is that the second drop encountered much greater antiaircraft fire than did the drop on D-Day. The Allied fleet offshore, followed quickly by Army units ashore, mistook the flights of American drop aircraft as enemy bombers and opened a sustained and deadly fire. Those who are apologists for Capa's lack of candor concerning this invasion point to this friendly fire incident to prove that he faced grave peril despite baldly lying

---

* Capa called this officer Chris Scott in his book. As noted earlier, this fictional character was based on two actual public relations officers, Chuck Romine and William Graffis.

about jumping into combat. True, but being unexpectedly exposed to friendly fire is no proof of bravery; it is merely proof of cruel irony.

Capa snapped several photos which captured the self-contained tension of paratroopers in the aircraft before jumping, and I suspect no one can recognize the hidden power of the photos unless they have jumped themselves. Unfortunately, whatever credit he earned was quickly lost—in my humble opinion—when he used his flash as he captured a paratrooper moving to exit the door. That flash popping at close range to the soldier's eyes would have induced a minute or two of night blindness even as the soldier jumped into the dark void and tried to locate the ground in preparation for a landing. For a man celebrated for his soldierly instincts, it was a stupid and callous act.[4]

If he exaggerated in *Slightly out of Focus*, he was much more honest about his role in the Sicily affair in a letter to Elizabeth Crockett, the secretary in *Life*'s London office. As quoted earlier, in that letter he stated, "I jumped at the chance—and fortunately not out of the plane."[5]

Capa's actual arrival in Sicily was far too banal to be included in *Slightly out of Focus*. He arrived on a supply ship which docked at Licata days later. Although he documented the uninspiring event in photos,[6] it was the fanciful airdrop fable that caught the public's imagination, and those photos of his actual arrival are all but forgotten.

Rome and Salerno

His next near-brush with airborne fame supposedly came early in the invasion of mainland Italy. According to Capa's version of events,[7] as the invasion was drawing near, the correspondents were called together and assigned to various divisions. Despite still not being parachute qualified (a fact he passed over in his telling of the story) he was unaccountably assigned to the paratroopers.

If that was true, he was about to get ensnared in what might have been one of the stranger escapades of the war. Italian dictator Mussolini had been deposed in late July 1943, raising the likelihood of an early Italian surrender. As preparations were afoot for the beginning of the mainland invasion on 3 September, peace feelers were sent out by the Italian government. The ensuing enthusiasm spawned an audacious plan to drop an airborne force on airports near Rome to link up with surrendering Italian forces to save that city from destruction.

Brigadier General Taylor, the division artillery commander for the 82nd, had been chosen to conduct a secret trip to the mainland to coordinate the mission with the Italian forces, and to judge the practicality of it.[8] Capa naturally inserted himself into this event, supposedly lending Taylor a money belt for the mission. He claimed to have deduced the secret mission from the knowledge that General Mark Clark had been on a similar mission before the North Africa landings and had lost his pants and money belt in the surf while trying to reach the submarine that picked him up at the end of the mission.[9] It's doubtful Capa would have even known the details of Clark's mishap at that point, much less been sought out by Taylor for the loan of a money belt, which Capa very conveniently claimed he had, quite coincidentally, just obtained prior to this anecdote. In fact, the differences in the circumstances between Clark's and Taylor's missions were so great, there's no reason to believe Taylor had any need to smuggle bribe money along on his trip. Unlike the uncertain Vichy French of Algeria, the Italians were eager to change sides and just looking for an opportunity to do it. But the anecdote is quintessential Capa: telling a doubtful anecdote that placed himself at the center of every exciting event, there to add his insights and aid, even to the most exalted officers. Whelan didn't even bother to mention the money belt anecdote in his Capa biography.

The first phase of the invasion of the Italian boot took place on 3 September with British forces assaulting across the straits of Messina. The main landings were scheduled for 9 September, and the Italians surrendered the day before, on 8 September, just an hour and a half after General Taylor's return departure from Italy. Taylor had already realized the proposed airdrop was much too far north to be supported by the planned landings at Salerno and initial Italian assurances of support could not be counted on. Based on his messages earlier that day, the drop was cancelled. It was a sound decision. The quick German response to the surrender included disarming most Italian units and occupying the planned airports.[10]

Most of Capa's description of this event should be discounted, though it is possible he could have been assigned to the 82nd despite not being jump-qualified. We know Richard Tregaskis (the highly regarded INS correspondent and author of *Guadalcanal Diary*) was assigned to the division for this mission, along with Seymour Korman (*Chicago Tribune*) and George Dorsey (*Stars and Stripes*).[11] Dorsey was soon replaced by Paul Green, also representing *Stars and Stripes*. Since none was parachute-qualified, plans called for them to come in by glider. So, it is at least theoretically possible that Capa, too, could have been assigned to the 82nd for the invasion of Italy and similarly slotted for the gliders. The problem is, Tragaskis said there were just three correspondents, and Capa was not one of them. Furthermore, Capa was notably absent from key parts of Tregaskis's contemporaneous, detailed and precisely dated diary of the leadup to the invasion. Although Capa claimed he roomed with Quentin Reynolds at the Hotel Aletti in Algiers, Tregaskis would seem to disprove this. Tregaskis actually was rooming with Reynolds, as his diary entries prove, yet Capa's name is absent from the list of roommates.[12] Nor was Capa present when the three correspondents were briefed on the operation and given aircraft assignments by COL Lynch.[13] Continuing this trend, while Tregaskis described how he and Korman were assigned to the 504th Parachute Infantry Regiment after landing by glider, he never mentioned Capa, though Capa's account implies he was as well (placing himself in situations where only that unit was), and

Whelan's version plainly stated he was so assigned.[14] But while Tregaskis's account mentions several interactions with the 504th's commander, COL Reuben Tucker, Capa's account places himself with the generals instead, with not a mention of the men he was to be covering. When the airborne correspondents were given a training ride in a glider in preparation for the landing, Capa was not present.[15] Similarly, as the men of the 504th were aboard their aircraft, waiting orders for Rome that would never come, Tregaskis made no mention of Capa among the correspondents eagerly awaiting orders, or later gathered around a radio hoping to hear news of the Italian surrender. Capa, meanwhile, had placed himself not among the 504th's men, but quite illogically in the plane carrying Major General Ridgeway, the division commander, and that plane was most definitely not a glider.[16]

It seems far more likely that Capa's role, if indeed he was involved at all, was not as a correspondent assigned to the paratroopers. It's far more likely Capa was on the fringes of this mission due to being embedded with this Troop Carrier Command unit. It was, after all, the unit he was embedded with during the Sicily drop, and the unit with which he later landed in Sicily by LST. Indeed, Whelan stated that Capa had been adopted by that unit. Capa didn't even arrive at the marshalling base in the same way the airborne correspondents did. They flew from the 82nd's camp in North Africa to the staging airbase in Sicily; Capa came across on an LCI.[17] Whatever his assignment, it's pretty clear it was not as an embedded correspondent with the 82nd Airborne Division.

In Capa's account, he claimed he was terribly disappointed about not being able to go on the Rome mission, but then completely glossed over the sequel. Although the main amphibious landings did take place on 9 September, while the airborne correspondents were sidelined on the runway due to the Rome operation being cancelled, there quickly followed opportunities to jump with the division. German counterattacks at Salerno placed the beachhead in serious peril. As an urgent reinforcement, most of COL Tucker's 504th Parachute Infantry Regiment jumped into the beachhead within friendly lines the night of 13/14 September. The night of 14/15 September, the 505th Parachute Infantry Regiment also dropped into the beachhead. Despite the fire-eating image portrayed in his book, Capa accompanied neither of these drops.

In fact, we're not sure how or when he arrived in the Salerno beachhead. He claimed, "Three days after the Fifth Army had landed at Salerno, a boat carrying the three airborne correspondents dropped anchor at that fateful harbor."[18] But the three airborne correspondents Tregaskis had identified were himself, Korman and Green. No mention of Capa. And a close reading of Capa's third-person phrasing discloses that he didn't exactly claim *he* was in that boat as part of those three; he left it to the reader to infer he was among them. Capa's first-person narrative voice resurfaced in the next paragraph, furthering the written sleight of mouth. Whelan accepted Capa's sleight of mouth, stating the "three airborne" correspondents were

Capa, Tregaskis and Korman, thus removing Green from the tale and inserting Capa. Even then, Capa was at odds with Tregaskis's account. Tregaskis and crew waded ashore from and LCI, whereas Capa said he reached the beach on a DUKW. And while Tregaskis's diary placed their landing the night of 15/16 September, coming in by ship with the glider regiment of the 82nd Airborne Division, Capa, as he was always wont to do, placed his landing earlier, on 12 September—before even the 504th Parachute Infantry Regiment jumped in!

In fact, Capa had remained totally absent from Tragaskis's account up to this point, leaving one to wonder where he had been spending his time. It certainly doesn't seem to have been with the 82nd. It was not until the 16 September morning press conference at the public affairs center that Tregaskis first encountered Capa.[*] At the suggestion of the briefing officer, Tregaskis stated he, Korman, Reynolds Packard (UP) and Capa headed up to see where the 504th Parachute Infantry was going into the attack. But Capa immediately disappeared from this tale and was equally absent from Tragaskis's gripping narrative of the paratroopers' fight for Altavilla, leaving one to wonder where Capa had gotten to this time. He apparently did not take a single photo during this critical battle or even this general timeframe (16–18 September).

Perhaps not so coincidentally, Capa's book completely skipped over the events of those three days, falsely stating he went directly from the press headquarters to the little hamlet of Maiori to cover the Rangers. That was not true. Capa did not go to Maiori until 19 September, riding in a jeep with Tregaskis and another *Stars and Stripes* correspondent, Lieutenant Kearney.

It's anyone's guess what exactly Capa was doing during the Salerno invasion, especially during the period 1–19 September. All we know is that the few facts that bear on it completely fail to corroborate his claims, and directly contradict them on numerous points. Tregaskis's diary was published in 1944 (*Invasion Diary*). It is quite tempting to believe that Capa adopted the general theme of being embedded with the airborne forces from Tragaskis's book as he drew up his own embroidered version three years later.

Normandy

His next near-airborne experience took place during the leadup to the Normandy invasion. As noted earlier, in the 24 April 1944 list of correspondent assignments, Capa was originally slated for the still photo pool supporting the US Army Air Forces, which certainly fits with his frequent association with troop carrier units in the Mediterranean Theater of Operations. It wasn't long until SHAEF was looking

---

[*] Kershaw stated Capa arrived in the beachhead two weeks after the initial American landings, which would put it about 23 September 1944 (location 1334). However, Tregaskis's account here disproves that.

for correspondents to cover the airborne forces during the upcoming assault. *Life* volunteered Capa and Landry. Although Morris was undoubtedly aware of this, he omitted any mention of it in his later accounts of the management of "his team."

Capa now had the opportunity to perform the airborne feat in Normandy that he would later lie about doing in Sicily and pass on at Salerno. Reality, being so much more difficult than writing about it (to paraphrase his introduction to *Slightly out of Focus*), he again opted to pass on the opportunity to prove his mettle. Lieutenant Barney Oldfield, the SHAEF public relations officer charged with recruiting correspondents for the airborne units, knew a bit about the parachuting business. He'd become a paratrooper in 1942, attending just the 23rd parachute class conducted by the Army, and at one point was the public affairs officer for an up-and-coming colonel named James Gavin who was then commanding the newly formed 505th Parachute Infantry Regiment.[19] Despite Oldfield's paratrooper persistence, he was never successful in getting Capa, Landry or CBS's Larry LeSueur to show up for the parachute training course. All three had to be reassigned to other units for the Normandy invasion.

We find confirmation of this in Jozefa Stuart's research. It includes a note that in her interview with Bill Downs, he stated, "Capa refused to take a training course," which training could only have been the parachute school. Bill Downs had been a United Press reporter before the war, and while covering the war in London was recruited by Edward R. Murrow for CBS. Murrow assigned him to relieve Larry LeSueur covering the Soviet front, and then brought him back to London in early 1944. Working there in the same London office as LeSueur, Downs probably heard of Capa's refusal to attend training firsthand from Capa's cohort in evasion.

John Morris, the nominal head of *Life*'s photographers in London,* omitted this rebellion by two of his subordinates and the need to switch their assignments late in the planning.

Holland

Capa's fourth near-brush with the airborne forces is a bit more difficult to pin down. Although he did eventually attend parachute training, he never mentioned doing so or when that took place. Whelan placed it in late March, claiming he took the training at the 82nd Airborne Division base near Leicester.[20] In his notes for the Capa biography, Whelan indicated he chose this period based on a photo showing Capa sitting in an aircraft wearing a parachute while reading a paper with the headline "Red Army in front of Nikolayev."[21] The Soviet army reached Nikolayev in mid-March 1944 and that city fell on 28 March. I was not able to locate that

---

* There is some disagreement as to his actual responsibilities and title.

photo in Whelan's files or any other files held by the ICP, so I cannot confirm it. Regardless, as covered earlier in Chapter 1, we know this is incorrect for two reasons. First, weeks later, on 24 April, SHAEF assigned him to cover the US Army Air Forces for the invasion. If Capa had been jump-qualified in late March, the SHAEF assignment memo would have slotted him with the airborne units. And second, in May—two months later—Oldfield was still trying unsuccessfully to get Capa to training. Furthermore, Whelan had inadvertently undermined his own claim. It was the 101st Airborne Division that had been tasked to train the correspondents for Normandy, not the 82nd.[22] If Capa attended the 82nd's jump school, it must have been in preparation for another jump. Having incorrectly placed Capa's jump qualification prior to the Normandy invasion, Whelan had to come up with an excuse for Capa not making the drop on D-Day. As noted earlier, he speculated that Capa feared the drop would be cancelled at the last minute and he'd miss out once again. It rings hollow, to say the least.

James Gavin, who we last saw commanding the 505th Parachute Infantry Regiment, was one of the finest American combat leaders to come out of WWII. A captain in command of a company in 1941, three years later he had been promoted five times to major general and placed in command of the elite 82nd Airborne Division. He was intelligent, extremely competent and politically savvy. As a result, he knew how to flatter influence makers and knew better than to pick a public fight with a member of the media. So, when he was asked to write a sketch of Capa for *'47: The Magazine of the Year*, on the publication of *Slightly out of Focus*, he did not outright call the cameraman a liar for the Sicily fable. But he didn't quite let him off scot-free, either.

> Capa first came to the 82d Airborne Division in Africa. He flew with the parachute assault echelon that fateful first night. That one should have convinced him that the best place to be in a parachute operation is back home with Hemingway's Men at War. But not for Capa. From then on he kept mumbling in Capa-language about wanting to jump. We finally got around to it in England when he took the requisite five training jumps. Then he kept after us to make a combat jump.
> Since we could not predict the exact date of our next combat jump it meant he would have to wait around with us and sweat it out. This was not to his liking. Torn between idling about Leicestershire and the flesh pots of Soho, he displayed an understandable leaning toward the latter. September 17 found the division, minus Capa, winging over the North Sea en route to the invasion of Holland. He never quite forgave us.[23]

Without directly exposing Capa's lies, Gavin subtly let the facts be known. In Whelan's 1983 telephone interview with Gavin,[24] the general said that he didn't think Capa jumped into Sicily. Whelan's notes read, "If he had jumped in, he (JG) would have known." So, he threw Capa a crumb in the article by saying he rode along with the assault parachute echelon (he did not), which tended to support part of Capa's version in *Slightly out of Focus*. But Gavin wasn't prepared to validate Capa's lie about jumping in, and let that question hang in the air. When he pointed out that Capa was only jump-qualified later in preparation for another operation, he let those familiar with airborne operations know that Capa's Sicily jump story was false. Gavin was his usual diplomatic self but was not about to let himself be cornered into endorsing a lie. Further, Gavin's parting remark that Capa opted for "flesh pots" rather than doing his job as correspondent was nothing more than a slap to the face camouflaged as an endearing anecdote.

Gavin's anecdote places Capa's parachute training as taking place sometime during the leadup to Operation MARKET GARDEN, the jump into Holland, which did begin 17 September 1944. Since Capa had not been jump-qualified in time for the Normandy invasion, he must have had his training sometime between 6 June and 17 September. I believe the only time this could have occurred was when he returned to London in mid-July for two weeks (in company with Wertenbaker). This interlude from the front was totally omitted by Capa in his book. The reader of *Slightly out of Focus* is left to assume that after D-Day Capa was constantly following the leading troops until the liberation of Paris on 27 August. For some reason he decided there was no room in this part of his war stories for mention of a trip to London or, for that matter, a press junket tourist trip to Mont-Saint-Michel that he managed to squeeze in, and which lasted several days. Whelan did make note of Capa's return to London but covered it in a single paragraph focused primarily on his social activity, with a side note mentioning that Capa had his "good time and bad surprise" at this juncture.[25]

The 82nd Airborne Division had completed its return to the UK from the invasion of France by the third week of July and began the hectic process of training replacements, reorganizing and reequipping the division. Capa would have joined the ongoing parachute qualification courses with the new men who were not already jump-qualified. While the course normally took several days, it could be completed much more quickly. For example, Joseph Dearing, a photographer for *Collier's*, completed all five of his mandatory jumps in a single day in preparation for the Normandy drop.[26]

There is, however, a handwritten note in Whelan's files that would place Capa's jump training a bit later. The note states, "August or early Sept: Capa with 82nd Airborne at their HQ in Leicestershire. Made his 5 jumps to qualify for combat jump." As we've seen earlier, Whelan ultimately chose not to go with this option in his book, and instead decided to place Capa's jump training in the previous March. But if true, the late August, early September timeframe does not enhance Capa's stature. With Capa present in Paris when it was liberated on 25 August, he had a very short period to shoehorn in another trip to the UK for jump training before the 82nd was locked down for Operation MARKET GARDEN on 10 September. It means that having been freshly jump-qualified, and with a combat drop very imminent, Capa did not "idle about Leicestershire." He immediately made himself scarce. I do not believe Capa actually did get jump-qualified in this period. There is no other evidence Capa returned to the UK during this window, and Whelan's handwritten note cited no source.

The best evidence seems to indicate the only opportunity for Capa's jump qualification was during his return to the UK in July.

Whelan claimed Capa returned to France just after Operation COBRA (the breakout from the Normandy beachhead) began on 25 July. To some extent he was probably lured back by the prospect of covering that offensive, doubly so as that offered the chance of seeing his beloved Paris liberated. But it also seems clear he was just as strongly motivated to get out of the clutches of the crazy paratroopers as they readied for their next suicidal mission. After two months of discussions, SHAEF formally created the First Allied Airborne Army on 2 August. Anticipating this and spurred by the breakout from the Normandy beachheads, the airborne forces were hastily preparing for their next mission. At least seven separate airborne drops had been planned and then cancelled by 10 September. Having just completed parachute training in July—which must have been arranged with the obvious intent that he accompany the next airdrop—and with frantic preparations underway for the next mission which could launch in a matter of days, Capa's sudden departure back to Normandy takes on a new light.

While accompanying the ground forces, Capa could pick and choose what stories, which locations and exactly how close to, or far from, danger he wanted to be. Parachute drops behind enemy lines were an altogether different matter. Not only was there the prospect of getting killed in the aircraft or during descent under the parachute, but once on the ground there were no friendly lines behind which one could safely operate. Every paratrooper was himself the front line. This was a combat environment completely alien to Capa, who, despite the mythological basis of his reputation, was never quite as far forward on the battlefield as he claimed. His brief stay on Easy Red, two hours behind the assault troops, was as close as he ever wanted to get.

Gavin's comments soft peddled another aspect. Correspondents did not just decide to go along on a major air assault based on their whims. The number of correspondents was set by SHAEF and the men who either volunteered or could be coerced to fill those slots were identified by name and assigned to that duty. Correspondents didn't just simply opt out because it was more fun in London or Paris. Capa either had to directly refuse the assignment or find a scheme that prevented him from going. Gavin may have said that Capa was merely out of reach in London when the division left for MARKET GARDEN, but the fact is Capa had been in Normandy for more than a month by then, most definitely out of the reach of any airborne units that might expect this newly jump-qualified photographer to come along on their next high-casualty adventure.

In fact, Capa had taken an additional step to ensure he missed the next airdrop. When Allied forces liberated Paris on 25 August, Capa settled in to enjoy the pleasures of the city he loved. But he was still assigned to *Life*'s London office, and therefore still theoretically on the string for the next airborne operation, which would be based out of the UK. He enlisted the assistance of Wertenbaker, now the head of the Paris *Time/Life* bureau, to wrangle a change of assignment, which was approved in early September. Wertenbaker cabled New York in reply, "I am delighted Capa is to remain in Paris, and so is Capa."[27] And undoubtedly Capa was delighted; back in England, the 82nd Airborne Division had just been locked down at dispersal airfields in preparation for yet another abortive operation. Two weeks later the next operation, MARKET GARDEN, would not be cancelled, and the paratroopers would suffer heavy losses. But Capa escaped all that. His flight from the UK, combined with his later providential reassignment to the Paris office had plucked him from a very dangerous airborne operation and ensured his continued stay in the city he loved. As we will soon see, for the next six and a half months, Capa was virtually out of the war.

Across the Rhine

In *Slightly out of Focus*, Capa once again played a bit loose with the timeline following the Battle of the Bulge.[28] Although the First Allied Airborne Army had been created the previous August and had already launched Operation MARKET GARDEN in September, Capa vaguely said this new, sixth Allied Army was just being "prepared" after the Battle of the Bulge (which historians define as ending 25 January 1945). He further claimed he was offered the job as the sole photographer of the three correspondents that would accompany the Allied Airborne Army on its next mission, which was rumored to be a drop into Berlin at the end of the war. Elmer Lower, the new head of the Paris bureau, told Capa that if he took the job, he could remain in Paris until the operation commenced, which, for no apparent reason, he said would give him 60 days in Paris with Pinky. In the immediate wake of the Battle of the Bulge no reasonable person expected the Allies would be in Berlin that quickly. Capa merely crafted this part of his narrative to fit what he knew had already happened.

And indeed, the next parachute assault did take place about two months thereafter in late March 1945, though obviously not on Berlin. But there's no way Capa could have guessed that in late January. As illustrated by the 82nd Airborne Division's series of aborted jumps late the previous summer, predicting the objective or date of a next drop was simply guesswork. Therefore, the idea that his assignment to the Allied Airborne Army would guarantee him the next 60 days off was ludicrous. No one could know when the next operation would be launched. And yet he claimed the assignment would guarantee a two-month break.

Regardless of the liberties he took with the timeline, in early 1945 he was indeed again tagged for duty with the First Allied Airborne Army for an unidentified operation. Given his record for Sicily, Salerno, Normandy and Holland, it is

290 • BACK INTO FOCUS

fair to question whether Capa suddenly chose to jump on the next operation—as he claimed—or had been ordered to do so by his employers. Volunteering seems too far at odds with his character and past record. Despite having become parachute qualified, and despite now being a staff photographer at a very good salary, he'd done very little for his employer in return in more than five months. He was, he admitted, tired of the war and it no longer held an attraction for him. That was about to change, and it is unlikely that change was because of his own initiative.

It seems Capa had finally been cornered. None of his previous excuses would help him at this point. He'd finally become parachute qualified, and his Paris bureau now controlled assignments on the Continent, so he couldn't duck out of the job by means of a last-minute transfer to another office, as he had for Holland.

In response, he lit out of town, though that's not how he told the story. In *Slightly out of Focus* he spun a tale of expecting Pinky to arrive in Paris on 15 February and the elaborate plans to welcome her. Alas, she did not show up, and it wasn't until 20 February that he received a cryptic cable saying she wasn't coming. In the wake of that bad news, he headed to the French Alps to console himself with skiing.

The reality, however, was much different. Capa didn't withdraw into solitary heartbreak, rather he actually took off on another road trip with Wertenbaker. The two had previously left France and travelled to London together in July, and then beginning 11 October, had taken a month-long trip ranging from Vercors and Lyon to the east, and to Toulouse near the border with Spain. This was, of course, the same Charles Wertenbaker who had aided and abetted Capa's avoidance of the drop into Holland. As if that weren't enough to raise suspicions, in a 1 February letter to Eleanor Welch,[29] Wertenbaker wrote that he and Capa were leaving for their vacation the next day. So, the failed Pinky interlude was just a fictionalized subplot to add a note of romantic drama to the tale, and perhaps to divert attention from the fact that his vacation began three weeks earlier than he wanted to admit. Whelan attempted to put a better face on the episode, omitting Wertenbaker's part in the trip, and stating it lasted four weeks.[30] Given the actual dates of the trip, the vacation lasted about six weeks, not four, before the recall reached him.

Despite the extended vacation being in the Alps rather than Paris, Lower supposedly agreed, and planned to notify Capa to return in time to join the operation. It hardly seems likely. The idea that *Life* would let Capa that far off the leash, under circumstances of uncertain communications and when the next job was to be a very short notice affair is simply not credible. At this point, one can be excused for suspecting that Capa was trying a variation of the same tactic he had used successfully to miss the Holland drop, except instead of placing himself out of reach of the London office by transferring to the Paris office, he tried to rely on distance and wartime conditions to place himself out of reach of the Paris office.

As operations unfolded, the next opportunity for using airborne troops was Operation VARSITY, part of the assault across the lower Rhine. The original start date for the operation was 15 March 1945, meaning Capa should have been recalled and been locked down with the 17th Airborne Division's troops by 8 March, at the latest. On that date, however, Capa was still on vacation, and Whelan stated Capa didn't receive the recall cable from Lower until "about the middle of March." We don't know when Lower sent that cable, how long it might have been delayed getting to Capa in his alpine retreat, or when Capa managed to obtain transportation and arrive back in Paris. But if Capa didn't get the recall cable until about the middle of March, for an operation due to start 15 March, that timeline suggests Capa's extended 60-day vacation would have succeeded in getting him out of yet another airborne drop. But SHAEF had its own scheduling priorities, and it had to delay the attack until 24 March. Upon his eventual return from the Alps, Capa found it was not too late to make the jump.

It is easy to see signs of *Life's* growing frustration with their newly hired staff photographer during this period. From the time of the liberation of Paris until this jump across the Rhine, Capa had been distracted and uninterested in covering the war. In the 6½ months from 1 September 1944 to 15 March 1945, Capa had been to the front just three times, totaling fewer than 20 days, and only one of these resulted in decent photos. These were the totally underwhelming shots taken during the momentous Battle of the Bulge (including at least one obviously staged one).* By comparison he spent 10 days near Cannes on vacation, nearly a month touring the south of France with Wertenbaker, and 45 days skiing with Wertenbaker, and almost all the rest in Paris. All that time in Paris resulted in just one story, and it was not focused on the war, rather on Pablo Picasso. This indifference to his responsibilities seems to explain another mystery. Hicks had hired Capa as a staff photographer effective 15 June 1944 as a reward for his D-Day photos. Yet *Life* did not list Capa as such in its masthead for the next 10 months. It would appear *Life's* New York office wasn't willing to grant full recognition to a cameraman more interested in living the high life than covering the war.

This changed with the 23 April 1945 issue (on the newsstands 16 April), when Capa was finally listed on the masthead.[31] What had changed? Why was Capa suddenly granted recognition? The answer can be found in *Life's* 9 April issue (on the newsstands 2 April) which contained a multipage spread of Capa's Rhine jump pictures. He was back in the war with a great set of photos, no matter how hard he might have been dragged kicking and screaming to make his long-delayed parachute jump.

It was not, however, a change that would last. He spent only a single day at the front after parachuting across the Rhine. The very next day he returned to Paris.

---

* Capa's photos of the drive to relieve Bastogne made a splash not for the quality of the images, but because they were virtually the only images of the dramatic counterattack.

His excuse? He needed to get his film back to Paris quickly. Despite the near proximity of Ninth US Army's press camp, which would have expedited his film to the rear, Capa felt he had to personally carry his film back to his bureau. Which should finally kill any idea that Capa planned to stay ashore with the 16th RCT on 6 June. If he wouldn't trust the film-couriering system in a fully developed army rear area in March of 1945, he certainly wouldn't have trusted the ad hoc system to get his film off of Omaha Beach and across the Channel under the chaotic conditions of D-Day.

Capa's one day at the front was followed by more than three weeks back in Paris. Following this he spent just three more days at the front, during which he shot his famous "Last Man to Die" series in Leipzig, as well as a posed photo of a friend mimicking Hitler at the Nuremberg Stadium.* Then, with the war in Europe rapidly reaching its culmination, he flew to London to confront his girlfriend who had just gotten engaged to his PRO friend, Chuck Romine. He returned to the Continent just in time to photograph the jubilant crowds celebrating the German surrender. But his absence had caused him to miss being selected to cover the German signing of the surrender document the day before, 7 May. Lower selected Ralph Morse for the job instead. According to Whelan, Capa was furious. "That was the assignment he had been waiting for."[32] That may be, yet it took a poor second place to having it out with the mistress who had dumped him.

Capa always had a ready excuse for his lack of interest in his job during this period. He'd grown weary of war. Returning to the front was "a dull prospect." He was afraid his work would just be a repetition of his previous photos. He was assigned to Paris so couldn't jump into Holland. He found non-combat themes more to his liking during his brief visit to the brutal three-week battle for the city of Aachen, so avoided all fighting. The smoke screen was too thick during his five days at the Saarbrucken bridgehead to take a single picture. When the Nazi concentration camps were liberated, he begged off on the grounds that everyone else was photographing the horrific scenes. The war had changed from a "shooting war to a looting war" which didn't interest him. And the list went on and on. The reality, it seemed, was that for him the liberation of Paris was more important than the final defeat of Nazi Germany.

Was this the caliber of work that would justify the title of World's Greatest War Photographer? Probably not. And yet many still call him such.

The Curious Case of William Graffis

Just below MG Gavin's article in the October 1947 issue of *'47: The Magazine of the Year*, there was another complementary sketch of Capa, this time provided by a

---

* The friend was a soldier, Hubert Strickland, who was assigned to the press camp as a driver for the correspondents. Months earlier, Strickland had been the soldier assigned to drive Capa and Wertenbaker the day they entered Paris.

Bill Graffin, who claimed to have been an officer in the 82nd Airborne Division. He related an anecdote in which he invited Capa to come along on a small troop carrier mission to drop arms to the French resistance. Capa refused, claiming the likely results, a picture or two, were not worth the risk. Graffin (and many Capa loyalists since) have pointed to this anecdote as proof that the photographer's well-known bravery was wisely tempered by a sober analysis of risk.

This anecdote does not appear in *Slightly out of Focus*. Whelan quoted the magazine article but attributed it to Bill Graffis (instead of Graffin), "a public relations officer with the 82nd Airborne and a close friend of Capa's."[33] Whelan's text places this incident sometime in September. He also noted that although Capa declined to go on that resupply mission, he and Graffis did then go off on a short "pleasure jaunt" to the south of France aboard the personal plane belonging to Chuck Romine's boss, the commander of the troop carrier unit.* Kershaw related the same story, and placed it "later that month" ("later" in relation to Capa's being reassigned to the Paris office in early September).[34] That could put the event almost anywhere that month.

Although *'47: The Magazine of the Year* spelled the name Graffin, the individual involved was William H. Graffis II. Jozefa Stuart conducted a telephonic interview with Graffis in March 1961.[35] Although Graffis does not appear in *Slightly out of Focus*, Stuart's interview indicates that the character of Chris Scott in the book is a composite of the real-life PROs Chuck Romine and Bill Graffis.

Graffis had worked in public relations in Chicago before the war, so it was no surprise that he became a Public Relations Officer in the Army. Graffis claimed he first met Capa "during mop-up operations in Tunisia" (that would be about May 1943) and accompanied him throughout the Sicily campaign (July–August 1943). We have independent verification of Graffis's existence from Tregaskis's *Invasion Diary*, which noted that while waiting on the airstrip for orders to launch the abortive Rome mission (September 1943), "Bill Graffis, one of the P.R.O. officers, came dashing out" to say Eisenhower had just announced the Italian surrender.[36]

Due to their association during the war, Graffis and Capa did become good friends. After the war, Graffis and his bride even lived for a time with Capa and his mother Julia in Hollywood. In fact, Graffis and Capa bought a car together.

Handwritten across the top of Stuart's typed interview record was the comment, "Note: This interview came to light only after my biography of Capa was published. Richard Whelan." This is important because Graffis's interview gave no indication when the airdrop to the Resistance anecdote might have happened. He merely included that comment as an indication of how Capa looked at war. But because both Whelan and Kershaw shoehorned this anecdote into September 1944, it rather confused Capa's timeline.

---

* As noted earlier, Chuck Romine was a PRO for the IX Troop Carrier Command.

The pleasure jaunt to the south of France which Whelan mentioned, followed hard on the heels of Capa being reassigned to the Paris office, and Graffis figured largely in it. Stuart's notes of her interview with Graffis included the following:

> Then later, two weeks after Paris liberation, Capa suggested to Graffis that they should go to the south of France, where he knew some pretty nice spots. General Paul Williams supposed to take off for US so Graffis and Capa persuaded General's crew to fly them down. So spent 10 days at Maxine Elliot's Villa Horizon, which had been used by Germans, stocked with first-rate food and wines. Swimming pool. Luxury. On return, Graffis court martialed, Capa not. Court martial was two-thirds base pay.

Paris was liberated on 25 August. Two weeks later would be 8 September. Assuming they put the idea into action soon thereafter, a 10-day jaunt would place them in a lavish villa overlooking the Mediterranean near Cannes through 18 September.

Which pretty much disproves the idea that Graffis was a PRO for the 82nd Airborne Division as he claimed—at least during that period. Graffis placed the jaunt to the south of France in September, but beginning in late August, the 82nd Airborne Division had been subjected to a series of alerts for a series of abortive airborne operations, which finally culminated in Operation MARKET GARDEN, the drop into Holland on 17 September. The division would fight on in Holland until mid-December. In other words, if Graffis was assigned to the 82nd during this period of desperate combat, it is inconceivable he would have been able to skip out for a holiday on the Riviera.

At this point—fall of 1944—it seems Graffis must have been assigned to the IX Troop Carrier Command. How else to explain his ability to sweet talk their commanding general's flight crew into an unauthorized vacation while their boss was back in the US unless they recognized him as a member of their general's special staff.

But can we believe this interlude on the Riviera happened? Graffis's interview reads more like someone recalling highly exaggerated fratboy escapades than real events. He also told of an unlikely prank he and Capa pulled which involved dropping *Stars and Stripes* newspapers on the troops advancing from the Operation DRAGOON landings in the south of France, a stunt that supposedly had the two of them "banned from the area." If true, that escapade would have had to happen in the first two weeks of September, too. And having freshly been reprimanded for that incident, it seems rather unlikely he closely followed it with a 10-day unauthorized absence that would result in a court martial. Doubt about the truth of this jaunt to the south of France is reinforced by a 9 September cable from Wertenbaker in Paris to *Life's* head office, which stated in part, "Capa and I are leaving for Luxembourg Tuesday at the latest." That following Tuesday was 12 September, which would have prevented Capa from flying south with Graffis. Nevertheless, in his interview, Chuck Romine did confirm the incident of Graffis and Capa diverting the aircraft for a vacation, though Romine mentioned neither the date nor duration of the trip. Wertenbaker and Capa were coconspirators in several escapades, and it is just possible that his

9 September cable to *Life*'s head office, Wertenbaker was establishing an alibi for Capa's upcoming bout of hooky.

Character Counts

Capa should not be faulted for his evident fear of parachuting. It is a risky activity and was much more so back then when equipment was far less reliable than today. Everyone has his own set of fears, and one of the most common is the fear of heights. By no means can we expect everyone to overcome such fears by means of will or discipline; it's simply too much to ask of human beings. When one adds in the prospect of jumping into combat behind enemy lines, it took a special breed to volunteer for that duty. In that light, Capa's reluctance to expose himself to this brand of danger does not reflect badly on him. After all, paratroopers made up a very small percentage of the armed forces, and many who would never even consider jumping nevertheless were superb soldiers.

No, Capa's moral and ethical shortcomings were not that he was afraid to jump. What Capa *should* be faulted for is claiming to have done what he could not bring himself to actually do. His errors were both of omission and commission. As a society we tend not to take errors of omission too seriously. So, when Capa neglected to mention that he refused to attend parachute training before D-Day, people shrug it off, as few readers expect an author to frankly admit to their failures and mistakes. But errors of commission are judged more harshly, and deservedly so. In this light, Capa's claim that he jumped into Sicily is inexcusable. He was taking credit for incredibly brave conduct which he could not and would not perform.* It was an insult not just to thousands of paratroopers who stepped forward and did jump into Sicily, but also to fellow correspondent Jack Thompson, who did what Capa lied about doing. If Capa wasn't guilty of stolen valor, he was damned close to it.

For some inexplicable reason, a good number of people give Capa a pass on this based upon his disclaimer that he let himself "go sometimes slightly beyond and slightly this side of" the truth as he wrote the book. Others dismiss the ethical concerns by explaining he'd hoped the book would be the basis of a screenplay, the implication being that movies always lie and so that is excusable. It is, however, a far different ethical issue for a screenwriter to "pump up" a script involving a third person, than it is for an individual to fictionalize his own life to make money. And this goes doubly when those fictions trade on the valor of others.

The fact that Capa did finally make a combat drop does not change the egregious nature of his claims to have jumped into Sicily. As this chapter has shown,

---

* It was rare, but not unheard of, for men to jump into combat without having first gone through jump training. Silver jump wings were normally only awarded upon graduation from jump school, but the regulations provided that a combat drop would earn the award of the silver jump wings even if the man hadn't first gone through jump school.

Capa worked rather diligently at avoiding parachute operations throughout the war. His eventual jump in March 1945 does not redeem his conduct over the years leading up to that drop. Furthermore, our evaluation of his one drop cannot ignore the twin facts that: 1) he'd exhausted all efforts to avoid the jump, and 2) the jump took place a mere six weeks before the end of the war, as German resistance was rapidly collapsing. His character cannot be whitewashed by this one act.

CHAPTER TWENTY SEVEN

Legacy

Any analysis of D-Day must be caveated. It was a confusing, noisy, deadly environment, and piecing together the often-conflicting perspectives is frequently a frustrating effort. Units and individuals occupying the same ground often had entirely different views of what happened. Reports from LT Spalding's platoon claimed credit for providing covering fire that helped Co. G get over the top of the bluffs. Co. G claimed *their* fire made it possible for Spalding's boat section to make it over. Eyewitnesses are not always the most accurate or unbiased sources.

Life is messy. War is hell. And combat is utter chaos.

Having said that, however, I feel confident that this analysis has provided a far more accurate and authentic perspective of Capa's D-Day adventures. Among the facts that we have established are that:

- The entire "First Wave with Co. E" myth is just that. A myth. He neither landed with Co. E, nor in the first wave (which consisted of tanks, after all). Nor did he land in Wave 3, which was the first wave of infantry and the wave that included Co. E.
- The "First Wave with Co. E" myth did not originate with Capa, rather somewhere in the *Life* hierarchy—either in London or stateside.
- Capa landed on the Easy Red beach sector in the vicinity of the Roman Ruins, very close to where Spalding's boat section and Co. G landed.
- Capa landed between approximately 0815 and 0820 hours in Wave 13, arriving in the same LCVP that carried in COL Taylor, commander of the 16th RCT.
- The combination of time and location of his landing placed him at a point of *relative* safety compared to most other parts of Omaha Beach,
- Based on the corrected timeline for the *LCI(L)-94*, Capa's stay on the beach was fewer than 30 minutes, and most likely fewer than 15 minutes.

- Capa's mission as a ground forces pool photographer meant that going ashore would preclude him from meeting the deadline for rapid return of his photos.
- Capa never intended to debark from his landing craft, as any substantial time on the beach with the troops of the 16th RCT would have inevitably caused him to miss his deadline and achieve a scoop.
- His departure from the landing craft was unintentional and involuntary, and most likely due to the resumption of enemy fire while he was taking his Debarkation set of photos.
- His flight from the beach after just a few minutes there, and on the first craft available, was merely an effort to adhere to his original plan of returning to the *Chase* as quickly as possible. His retreat was likely hastened by a degree of panic resulting from unexpected debarkation.
- Capa's photos taken aboard the withdrawing *LCI(L)-94*, LCVP 26-26 and finally back aboard the *Chase* were taken with his Rolleiflex camera. While we cannot rule out pictures from one of his Contax cameras during this phase, there is no evidence of it.
- That, therefore, Capa shot just one roll of 35mm film from the time he left the *Chase* until the time he returned later that day.

In addition to these points, which I believe have been proven beyond a reasonable doubt, I have also forwarded several hypotheses, which, I believe, fit with known details of Capa's saga, but which cannot be definitively proven. These include:

- The missing first 28 exposures on one roll of his landing film were pictures taken during the run in to the beach.
- Capa boarded *LCIL(L)-94* at the end of its first beaching, and not immediately before it was first hit.
- The limited number of surviving negatives was not the result of the Darkroom Accident fable, but much more likely due to censorship in support of the FORTITUDE deception.

In addition to these many points, there has been an underlying theme that touches upon the reliability of the photographic medium and the ethical issues surrounding how these products are packaged, captioned and presented to the unwary public. A picture may well be worth a thousand words, but when that picture is presented in a false context, the thousand words may misspeak, mislead and deceive.

In this respect, it is important that wise readers should do more than simply accept what they see. They must be aware that the entity providing the photo's context has its own agenda, and frequently that agenda requires the photo be presented in a context that meets the organization's needs, not the reader's.

Having arrived at these conclusions and hypotheses, how should we then view Capa, or rather, Capa's legacy?

Certainly, aspects of the Capa legend remain unaffected by this analysis. He was more than personable, he was charming. He was a raconteur of the first order. His fondness for alcohol and women was unquestioned. His vision for creating Magnum Photos resulted in a new business model for photographers. And he was certainly a self-made man. Or perhaps it would be best to use his own words: he was the man who invented himself.

But is there any reason to elevate him above the host of other war photographers of his era? Was he better than Edward Steichen, who captured some of the greatest images of the naval war in the Pacific? Should we glorify Capa more than Joe Rosenthal, who captured the iconic raising of the American flag above Iwo Jima's Mount Suribachi? Should we even place Capa in the same league as Phil Stern? Better known now for his iconic Hollywood celebrity photos after WWII, few are aware Phil was assigned to Darby's Rangers as a uniformed combat cameraman. Yes, *assigned* to the Rangers. He lived with them, fought with them and documented actual combat with them; he did not show up for a short period, snap a few shots in the rear of the action, then return to the press camp for the evening. He was a frontline soldier who happened to carry a camera.

So why exactly have we lionized Robert Capa? I suggest there are several reasons.

The most obvious explanation is that he snapped several iconic photos. In particular, his Falling Soldier and D-Day photos. But these are thin reeds indeed. The Falling Soldier's status as a fake is beyond question, and the photo stands now as a classic fabricated propaganda image, manufactured to serve a political agenda. It is in fact a lie, made acceptable merely because it is a lie that supports a certain political bias. But this does not make Capa a great photographer; it only marks him as an able producer of disinformation.

And of course, his D-Day photos stand similarly unmasked. We now realize that the context in which they have been presented for eight decades is false. He did not land when he claimed to have, and he was met by conditions far different than he claimed. Far from setting foot ashore with the men of the first wave, we now know he came ashore after virtually the entire assault regiment had already landed and did so at a spot relatively undefended by Omaha Beach standards. Would those photos have become iconic had they been placed accurately in context? Undoubtedly not. Furthermore, after eliminating his D-Day photos that duplicated the work of other photographers that day, there are only five Capa photos which are truly unique. Yet none of these portray fighting ashore during this, the pivotal operation of the war in the West. No. His five "unique" photos are *all* pointed offshore. It's nearly impossible to understand why these images have achieved iconic status. The few that were published didn't even draw undue attention when first printed by dailies hungry for any news of the invasion. So, why have subsequent generations allowed themselves to be seduced by these photos?

Having stripped away the images that were falsely granted iconic status, what can we say about the rest of his wartime photography? That's a highly subjective question and impossible to adequately answer here. Perhaps it is best to say he did some very good work, but largely on a par with many other fine photographers covering the war. After all, the same scenes, themes and topics tended to be common focus for all photographers. For instance, Phil Stern's photo of Rangers occupying a hilltop position overlooking an Italian village[1] is nearly identical to Capa's photo that led his "It's a Tough War" spread in *Life*.[2] If anything, Stern's photo is technically superior, and being closer to the soldiers, does a far better job of capturing the human essence of men in combat. It does not help Capa's case that Stern's photo was taken earlier in the campaign than Capa's.

And this leads us to a second point, the technical merit of Capa's photos. Or rather, perhaps, the lack of it. Very few people rate Capa's photos highly for their technical merit. Indeed, neither did Capa himself. As noted in the Introduction, Leon Danielle (PIX) quoted Capa as saying, "The main thing is to get the right mood and feeling. Technique is not important."[3] The question one must ask then is just what is the "right" mood and feeling? If we compare Sargent's debarkation set of photos with Capa's, we find Sargent's are far superior, better focused and show more detail. To be completely honest, Capa's look almost amateurish by comparison, so much so that critics must excuse their quality by embracing a false context: the poor focus and exposure were due to the stress of landing under fire with the first wave! But the hard reality is that Sargent's LCVP landed much earlier than Capa's, when enemy fire was much greater, and the unit landing in Sargent's photos took far higher casualties. Another example is his series of six shots of the same group of American dead on Omaha Beach taken on D+2 when he returned after his trip back to Weymouth. Although the casualties were real, his negatives show he manufactured the context by posing four different groups of men to look as if they were contemplating the bodies, and then shooting the scene from different angles.[4] So, it turns out that the "right" mood and feeling have nothing to do with accurately capturing an event, rather more to do with proper staging to evoke a feeling the photographer wants to convey, even at the cost of misleading the viewers. So, it seems to be less a matter of capturing reality than it is creating an image that will sell. And that's what his art was all about: producing images that would sell.

How inferior this form of photojournalism when compared to the standards set by Stefan Lorant in the 1930s (editor-in-chief of the *Munchner Illustrierte Presse*):

> That photographs should not be posed; that the camera should be like the notebook of the trained reporter, which records contemporary events as they happen without trying to stop them to make a picture …

If anything, this lack of technical merit was something he made to serve his ends. As he told a fellow correspondent during the Spanish Civil War, "If you want to get good action shots, they mustn't be in true focus. If your hand trembles a little, then you get a fine action shot." To illustrate this, we merely need to look at a pair of his photos taken during that conflict. Both purportedly show women running for shelter after an air-raid alarm has sounded. The first is in perfect focus and shows a woman holding a child's hand; the pair is hurrying across a street, but the background figures show no apparent haste, panic or fear.[5] Were it not for the caption, one would think they were just dodging traffic. In the second photo, a woman and a small dog are similarly hurrying across a street. But in this case, the image is badly blurred, conveying the impression of haste and fear in subjects and cameraman alike.[6] Again, the background figures convey no such impression, but the blurring makes it much more difficult to notice this, so the overall impression is more dramatic and apparently fits with the caption. How effective was this trick? Extremely. The blurred image was widely published and is well known. The sharply focused companion photo seldom sees the light of day outside the archives. Photo editors, who were more interested in pictures that had "punch," "impact" and drama, weren't overly concerned if a bit of artifice went into getting the picture "right."

We saw this tactic employed again with his Face in the Surf picture. Superficially it appears to show a wounded soldier under heavy fire creeping in with the surf, a perfect symbol of men struggling against a storm of fire as the first wave fights its way ashore. The blurring of the image again conveys the impression that the ordeal was affecting the cameraman every bit as much as the subject of the shot. Yet Ruley's movie clip of the same scene at the same time strips away this false context and reveals the blurring to be deceptive. And even Capa's own pictures immediately before and after the Face in the Surf show no such artifice.

At its core, Capa's poor technical skills and deceptive blurring are the still photo equivalent of the shaky first-person point of view camerawork seen in films such as *The Blair Witch Project*. Every once in a while, it is interesting solely because it is novel, but one rapidly tires of it, especially as one realizes the often-deceptive purpose of the style.

So, as we search for explanations for Capa's enduring fame, we can safely rule out technical merit.

A more obvious explanation lies with his employers. Although Capa was not employed as a staff photographer until the last year of the war, he nevertheless steadily worked for major periodicals on a contract basis. As a result, when his photos were picked up, they were widely distributed, arriving in most of the living rooms in America. And since he was working for periodicals rather than dailies, his employers could dig up old photos and insert them for fillers months later when the war news was slow. For example, his Sicily invasion photos were again published in January 1944 and once more in May 1944, even though the campaign had ended mid-August of 1943.[7] Capa, then, was not just widely published, but also published far more often than the immediate battlefield developments might otherwise indicate.

And working for a major periodical had another major benefit. Those organizations benefited from star power in much that same way a football team benefits from a popular player. The more well-known their reporters and photographers, the more likely their magazines would be purchased by the man and woman on the street. Naturally, then, *Life* made great efforts to promote their cameramen, following their locations across the globe and profiling them in the text accompanying the photo spreads. In its 26 June 1944 issue, *Life* devoted more than a page to singing the praise of its photographers in the European Theater. This kind of free publicity was a great help in building Capa's image. Chances are that before reading this book, the reader had never heard of any of the military cameramen discussed here, even though many took far better photos than did Capa. And why is that? Because those cameramen operated in an organization that did not allow photos to be credited to individuals, so even though their pictures often made the front page of the nation's dailies, the photographers themselves remained anonymous. *Life*, on the other hand, ensured Capa's name (as well as the names of its staff reporters) received continuing recognition throughout the country.

And *Life* was only one of several media outlets that pumped up Capa's reputation as they published his photos. Recall that it was *Picture Post* that called Capa the "Greatest War Photographer in the World" in its December 1938 issue. Not so coincidentally, that was the same issue in which *Picture Post* published a 10-page spread of Capa's Segre River Battle photos. This means that the "Greatest War Photographer in the World" title was not so much a sober, independent evaluation as it was mere marketing hype to pump up sales. What *Picture Post* also failed to mention was that the Segre River was a secondary front that had been stalemated for months. Worse, a close examination of those photos indicates either they too were at least partially staged, or his accompanying text was largely fictitious.[8] "At dawn I crept back to the Segre," he wrote. "There the last planks of a pontoon bridge were being put into place. Already the first transport mules were carrying across it munitions …"* Except his photo of that bridge showed it must have taken days to build; it could not have been built in the few hours of darkness between the river crossing and dawn.[9] Clearly there was no assault crossing that night; the Republican forces had to have been occupying the far shore for days. His story of the supposed attack on the Rio Segre front seems to have been a manufactured propaganda piece—perhaps partly based on real events at some unknown other time—to deflect attention from the crushing defeat on the Ebro River front, which ended the very day before the supposed Rio Segre assault. And despite the suspicious signs of fakery, Capa was lionized for being a great war photographer. There were obvious advantages to working for a media that didn't question one's photos too closely and had a vested interest in pumping up one's reputation!

As important as *Life*'s patronage (and that of the other periodicals for which he provided pictures) was in establishing Capa's renown during the war, that kind of

---

* His original captions were in French and German, and neither described it as a pontoon bridge. Only the magazine's English translation described it as a pontoon bridge.

fame can quickly fade just as the memories of those violent events themselves fade. It would take additional forces to cement Capa's fame. One step was to die relatively young, with one's greatest work relatively fresh in the minds of the public. This Capa quite unwillingly accomplished in Indochina in 1954 at the age of 40. The reporter who never seemed to be quite as far forward as his photos would have you believe, was, perhaps symbolically, killed not by enemy fire on the front line, but by a landmine in the middle of a very large and long convoy.[10]

A life prematurely cut short arouses natural feelings of sympathy. And if that life seems to be talented or is that of a celebrity, then inevitably there will be those who bewail the loss of someone who had so much to offer. And such was the reaction when Capa died. In some respects, it was the perfect end, solidifying the legend. He did not outlive his fame. He did not live long enough to risk a descent into dissolute alcoholism, which certainly seemed a very real possibility given his lifestyle. Increasingly hampered by a spinal injury and beset by fears it would end his intimate relations with women, it was clear his glory days were leaving him behind. He accidentally escaped the ongoing process of becoming an increasingly unfulfilled businessman at the head of Magnum, and instead saw his life end doing the kind of work that had established his reputation. He was mourned at 40 as the "Greatest War Photographer in the World," rather than pitied at 85 as the fossilized corporate executive who decades before had once been a photographer in a war that ended before most of the public had been born.

But the final element in perpetuating the Capa mythology is perhaps the most critical, for he created an organization which would carry his star forward. Capa was frustrated working on retainer and as a staff photographer. In those positions he could not choose his own assignments; they were dictated by editors, and often by editors who did not share his political views. Worse, whatever media outlet he worked for retained the rights to the negatives. So, in 1947, he and six others founded Magnum Photos, a photographers' cooperative, owned by and operated for photographers. Magnum could negotiate with publishers on behalf of its members, arranging assignments and charging higher fees than individual photographers could themselves. And over the decades, Magnum has served as a powerful force in keeping the Capa legacy alive as part of its brand.

Its efforts were eventually aided by his brother, Cornell Capa who founded the International Fund for Concerned Photographers in 1966, with the object of keeping the "humanitarian documentary" work of Capa and some of his associates in the public eye.[11] This fund established a home for itself in 1974 with the International Center of Photography (ICP), which continues to be a forceful advocate for the Capa legacy.

Between the efforts of Magnum and the ICP, Capa's works and his tales are, naturally, frequently resurrected and recycled, ensuring the Capa legend is seldom out of the public's eye. The two organizations have been dedicated and faithful custodians of the Capa legend and have kept his memory alive where so many others have faded to obscurity. Their efforts have been aided by secondary coverage in periodicals and online sites which repeat the myths, add new layers of invention, and idolize the fabricated persona rather than the actual man. In an era of click-bait metrics, a good, sensational tall tale is much more important than a dull reality.

And that brings us back to the question: what exactly is the Capa legacy?

The answer to that is a bit sobering and more than a bit anticlimactic. If you strip away the falsely iconic pictures, and peel back the institutionalized marketing of his image, and if you acknowledge the lack of technical merit to his work, what is left? Well, there's a very good body of work, but not so different from many other photographers of his day.

And that's a problem. Because Capa's work is objectively difficult to differentiate from that of others of his era, the illusion of his greatness can only be maintained by embracing the legendary, fanciful and fabricated details of the Capa mythos. It is the myth that sets him apart, and therefore it is the myth that is embraced. Unfortunately, that has prevented sober analysis and a realistic appreciation for his work.

And perhaps that's a fitting legacy for the man who invented himself; his legacy is every bit as much a fabricated façade as was his professional persona.

So, it is right that we close with yet another anecdote. In his tribute to Capa, *The Man Who Invented Himself*, John Hersey claimed that Capa was involved

> in a poker game at SHAEF headquarters while waiting for the Armistice assignment. A P.R.O [Public Relations Officer] came in and said cryptically, "I've got a little job for you, Capa." "Little job?" said Capa. "Don't bother Capa. Capa is playing cards." The P.R.O gave the "little job" to another photographer, and Capa missed the Armistice.[12]

Although told in a fond context, the anecdote captured much that was flawed in his character. The excessive ego. The obsession with gambling. The placing his profession second to his vices. And missing many crucial events during the war for various poor reasons.* Beneath the image of the swashbuckling cameraman with the infinite store of Munchausen tales, we once again see the Capa who merely played the photographer.

In his book, Whelan included this Armistice anecdote, but noted that although it was both believable and totally in keeping with Capa's character, Elmer Lower (Capa's Paris bureau chief) said Hersey's tale was apocryphal.[13] Capa was actually back in London on romantic business at the time.

Still, what could be a more fitting than an apocryphal anecdote to sum up a man whose life was itself largely apocryphal.

---

* Recall General Gavin's anecdote that Capa missed his assignment to the Operation MARKET GARDEN parachute drop because he could not resist the pleasures of London (it was Paris) and was socializing there when the 82nd Airborne Division was alerted and sent into combat.

APPENDIX A

Selected Naval Amphibious Craft

Data and diagrams for LCVP, LCM-3, LCT-6 and LCI(L) are drawn from ONI 226, *Allied Landing Craft and Ships*, US Navy Department.

LCVP—Landing Craft Vehicular Personnel

- Length: 36'; beam: 10' 6" wide.
- Crew: 3/4.
- Capacity: 1 × 6,000lb vehicle, or 8,100lb cargo, or 36 troops (limited to 30–32 combat-equipped troops).
- Draft: 2' 2" forward and 3' aft.

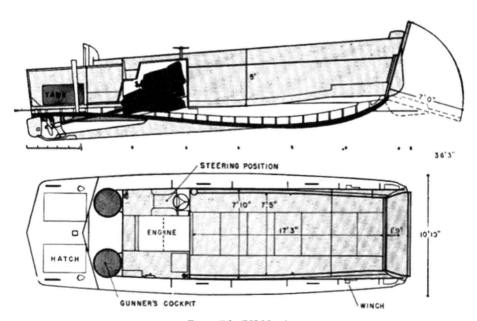

Figure 76. (US Navy)

LCM—Landing Craft, Mechanized

Several versions produced. For the LCM(3):
- Length: 50'; beam: 14' 1".
- Crew: 4.
- Capacity: 1 medium tank, or 68,000lb or 60+ troops.
- Draft: 3' forward and 4' aft.

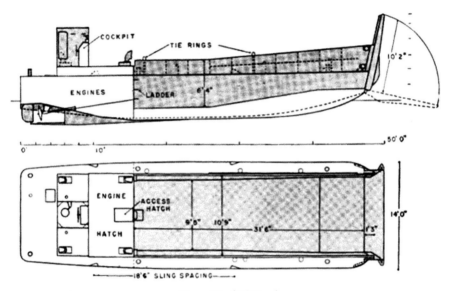

Figure 77. (US Navy)

LCT—Landing Craft, Tank

Two main versions. For LCT(6) class:
- Length: 120' 4"; beam: 32'.
- Crew: 12.
- Capacity: 150 short tons; up to 4 medium tanks.
- Draft: 3' 4" forward; 4 aft

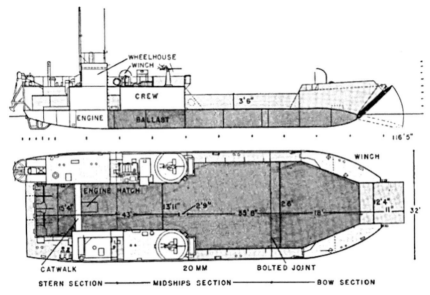

Figure 78. (US Navy)

Landing Craft, Infantry (Large)

- Length: 158' 6"; beam: 23' 3".
- Crew 24.
- Capacity: 188 troops.
- Draft: 2' 8" forward and 4' 10" for landing.
- *LCI(L)-94* had a raised conn, which is not shown in this diagram. The bridge was moved one deck higher than shown in this diagram. An open conning station was constructed above it.

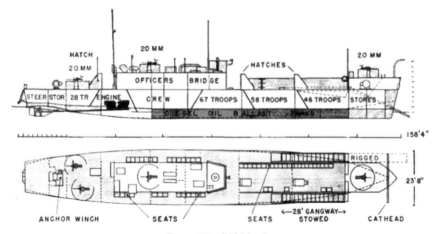

Figure 79. (US Navy)

Attack Transport

Several different classes. For APA-26, USS *Samuel Chase* (originally designated AP-56):

- 489' long; 69' 6" wide
- Crew: 33 officers; 448 enlisted
- Capacity: 98 officers; 1,348 enlisted; 2,700 dead weight tons
- Boats: up to 28 LCVPs and/or 4 LCMs

Figure 80. (NARA)

APPENDIX B

Glossary, Acronyms and Abbreviations

AAA	Antiaircraft Artillery.
AGC	US Navy hull designation code for amphibious force flagships.
AKA	US Navy hull designation code for attack cargo ships.
ANCXF	Allied Naval Commander-in-Chief, Expeditionary Forces. The Allied naval command responsible for landings on D-Day.
AP	Associated Press.
APA	US Navy hull designation code for attack transport ships (primarily personnel).
Bangalore Torpedo	A breaching device consisting of several sections of tubing filled with explosives. The sections were assembled and pushed through barbed-wire obstacles or minefields, then detonated, to clear a path.
Blue Network	A radio network owned by the National Broadcasting Company, it was spun off in a divestiture action in 1942 and rebranded the American Broadcast Network in 1945.
BLT	Battalion Landing Team. An infantry battalion task organized for an amphibious assault.
CA	US Navy hull designation code for heavy cruiser classes of ships.
CAPT	Captain (Navy or Coast Guard). Refers to either the rank of captain (equivalent to an Army colonel), or the position of the commander of a ship.
Co. or Company	An Army unit. An infantry company was about 190 men.
COL	Colonel (Army).
CPhoM	Chief Photographer's Mate (Navy, Coast Guard).
CPT	Captain (Army).

CTF	Commander Task Force. Normally this acronym is followed by the task force numerical designation, e.g., CTF 122.
D-Day	The date an operation is scheduled to begin. When followed by a +/- and a number (i.e., D+3), it denotes days after of before D-Day.
DD or Duplex Drive Tank	A Sherman tank modified to be able to swim ashore. In addition to its normal means of propulsion (its tracks), the tank was equipped with propellers. It also featured a collapsible flotation screen to achieve necessary buoyancy.
Deep Wading Kit	A modification to a standard Sherman tank that enabled it to move though the surf without drowning out the engine. Its most prominent features were two large, curved ventilation stacks mounted to the engine compartment.
Dozer Tank	A tank fitted with a bulldozer blade to conduct engineering tasks under fire.
GEN	General. Commonly used as a shorthand means of address to an officer of any of the four general officer ranks.
H-Hour	The time an operation is scheduled to begin, expressed in hours and minutes. When followed by a +/- and a time using military 24-hour format, it denotes time before or after H-Hour (i.e., H+0045 means H-Hour plus 45 minutes).
ICP	International Center for Photography. An institution dedicated to photography and visual culture, created by Cornel Capa as a home for Cornel's International Fund for Concerned Photography.
LCI(L)	US Navy hull designation code for Landing Craft, Infantry (Large).
LCM	US Navy hull designation code for Landing Craft, Mechanized.
LCT	US Navy hull designation code for Landing Craft, Tank.
LCT(A)	A modified LCT with additional armor.
LCVP	US Navy hull designation code for Landing Craft, Vehicular, Personnel.
Line of Departure	In amphibious operations, a control measure to regulate and coordinate movement of boat waves. It is the last

	control measure before reaching the beach. At Omaha Beach, the Line of Departure was about 3,000 yards offshore.
LST	Landing Ship, Tank.
LT	Lieutenant (either Navy or Army).
LT(jg)	Lieutenant, Junior Grade (Navy, Coast Guard).
LTC	Lieutenant colonel. (Army)
Magnum Photos	An international photographic cooperative agency. It was founded in 1947 by Robert Capa, David Seymour, Maria Eisner, Henri Cartier-Bresson, George Rodger, William Vandivert, and Rita Vandivert.
MAJ	Major (Army).
MoI	British Ministry of Information. Among other responsibilities, was in overall charge of censorship in the UK, to include Allied forces operating there.
MoMM	Motor Machinist Mate (Navy, Coast Guard). Included three grades: 1st Class (1/c), 2nd Class (2/c) and 3rd Class (3/c).
PhM 3/c	Pharmacist Mate 3rd Class (Navy, Coast Guard).
PRD	Public Relations Division. A special staff section within the SHAEF headquarters
PRO	Press Relations Officer.
QM 3/c	Quartermaster 3rd Class (Navy, Coast Guard).
RCT	Regimental Combat Team. And infantry regiment task organized for an amphibious assault.
SGT	Sergeant (Army).
SHAEF	Supreme Headquarters Allied Expeditionary Forces. The combined headquarters that commanded operational forces assigned to European Theater of Operation.
Transport Area	An area off an invasion beach where assault shipping anchored during landing operations. At Omaha Beach, this was approximately 23,000 yards from the beach.
WNTF	Western Naval Task Force. The naval command responsible for landing operations on Utah and Omaha Beaches on D-Day.

Endnotes

CC: Cornell Capa papers, held by ICP
JS: Josefa Stuart notes contained in Whelan's files, held by ICP
NARA: National Archives
SOOF: *Slightly out of Focus*
W/RC: Whelan's *Robert Capa: A Biography*
W/TIW: Whelan's *This Is War!: Robert Capa at Work*
W/n: Whelan author's notes, held by the ICP

Introduction

1   W/TIW, p. 72.
2   W/RC, p. 119.
3   W/RC, p. 100.
4   Susperregui, *The location of Robert Capa's Falling Soldier.*
5   SOOF, pp. 68–70.
6   W/RC, p. 193, footnote.
7   W/RC, pp. 194–96.
8   W/n, "see Crocky's letter."
9   W/n, contained in a draft of Whelan's Capa biography: "Capa was, however, far too busy taking pictures to act as an interpreter, and, in any case, his photographs clearly show an Italian soldier doing the interpreting."
10 SOOF, p. xiv, Whelan's introduction to the book.
11 W/n, Walter Graebner letter dd 12 Jun 1944.
12 JS, extract from Wise's sketch outline for *Battle! The Lives and Wars of Robert Capa.*
13 See also John Morris's account in the *Time* video *D-Day: Behind Robert Capa's Photos of Normandy Beach.*
14 See the *Alternate History: Robert Capa on D-Day* project at Photocritic International.
15 Wertenbaker's *Invasion!*, pp. 42–44.
16 SOOF, pp. 136–49.
17 Annex 3 to Field Order #5, 1st Infantry Division, pp. 21–22.
18 SOOF, pp. 136–37.
19 "The Man Who Invented Himself," Author's Review of *Slightly out of Focus,* in *'47: The Magazine of the Year*, Vol. I, No. 8.
20 JS, Whelan interview with Leon Danielle.

Chapter 1

1   SOOF, p. 119.
2   W/RC, p. 205.

3   JS, Time/Life cable folder on Capa, "exCapa Sans origine to Hicks Feb 3 1944." "Thanks for your cable. I just received travel orders and am preparing to leave for England as fast as possible."
4   JS, Time/Life cable folder on Capa, exLondon, exMorris, 7 February 1944.
5   W/n, notes on Anzio operation.
6   W/n, notes on Anzio operation.
7   SOOF pp. 127–28.
8   Morris, *Get the Picture*, p. 73.
9   Kershaw, *Blood and Champagne*, location 1441.
10 W/n. It isn't clear if the story of the party comes from Pinky's letter, or is a separate letter written by Crockett.
11 W/RC, p. 209.
12 SHAEF Public Relations Division memo to Chief of Staff, subj: War Correspondents, dd 24 April 44, p. 14 of Tab A.
13 Oldfield, *Never a Shot in Anger*, p. 50.
14 Tobin, *Ernie Pyle's War*, pp. 164–65.
15 MacVane, On the Air in World War II, p. 201.
16 SHAEF Public Relations Division memo to Chief of Staff, subj: War Correspondents, dd 24 April 44, p. 17 of Tab A.
17 Oldfield, pp. 55–56.
18 W/RC, p. 209.
19 JS, COL Bert Kalisch interview.
20 Oldfield, pp. 73–74.
21 W/RC, p. 209.
22 Memo from SHAEF Public Relations Division, subj Total List of All Correspondents Accredited to SHAEF, dd 7 June 1944.
23 Appendix A, SHAEF Public Relations Plan "OVERLORD."
24 Jack Lieb's motion picture film, *D-Day to Germany*, features Carroll aboard *LCI(L)-5* during the landings. *LCI(L)-5*'s Report of Operations states that it completed unloading all troops and war correspondents at Utah Beach by 1238 hours, 6 Jun 1944.

Chapter 2

1   JS, Edward K. Thompson interview.
2   SHAEF, Operation Memorandum 33, Photographic Policy, dd May 22, 1944.
3   SHAEF, Public Relations Plan, 1 May 1944.
4   Film and Photo Section, PRD, SHAEF, memo subj: Pictorial Coverage, dd May 1944.
5   *Editor and Publisher* magazine, 18 November 1944, p. 16.
6   ANCXF Operation Neptune—Naval Orders, ON 13—Instructions for the Buildup, Appendix II.
7   MacVane, pp. 203–4.
8   For different perspectives on this incident, see Pogue (pp. 527–28), Voss (pp. 194–97) and Oldfield (pp. 242–55).
9   Fine, *Richmond Times-Dispatch*, 2 June 2014.
10 Tobin, p. 171.
11 Gay, p. 16.
12 *D-Day on Radio*.
13 SHAEF Regulations for War Correspondents, p. 3.
14 Harrison, p. 231.
15 G-3, SHAEF Plan FORTITUDE, dd 23 February 1944.

16 See for example the London Controlling Section's memo subj Plan "BODYGUARD", dd 24 May 44.

17 Brown, pp. 581–82.

18 Annex A (Intelligence Plan) para I.(13), to WNTF Operation Plan No. 2-44.

19 Annex 4 (Administrative Order) para 4.d); and Annex 5 (G-1 Plan) para 18, to 1st Division Field Order No. 35, 16.

20 Annex 6 (Medical Plan) to First US Army Operations Plan NEPTUNE.

21 Censors were listed with the V Corps troops arriving in Force O on D-Day; see Troop List, First US Army Operations Plan NEPTUNE. Censors were not separately listed in the landing tables, but V Corps headquarters troops were scheduled to begin landing at H+120, and 192 soldiers of the unit were scheduled to have landed by H+180.

22 Annex A (Intelligence Plan) para I.(13), to WNTF Operation Plan No. 2-44.

23 Task Organization, and para 3(b), WNTF Operation Plan No. 2-44.

24 Tobin, p. 164.

25 Thompson, p. 108 & Oldfield, pp. 39–41.

26 Oldfield, pp. 74–75.

27 SOOF, p. 132

28 MacVane, pp. 207–15.

29 Tobin, p.164.

30 MacVane, pp. 229.

31 See ICP photo Accession No. 2013.77.131 for example.

32 These assignments were derived from MacVane's narrative and the 1st Infantry Division's Field Order No. 35.

Chapter 3

1 Appendix 1 (Final Ship Assignments), to Annex 3 (Neptune Force O Landing Tables), to 1st Infantry Division Field Order No. 35.

2 USS *Chase* Narrative Report of Operations, 6–7 Jun 1944.

3 Fuller, Ch. 13. The book was finished after Fuller's death, so many of the exaggerations and factually incorrect details it contained may not be of his own doing.

4 Details are from his DD 214. His service number began with 39, indicating he was drafted.

5 Baumgartner et al, Fuller was the last named of the authors of the unit history.

6 G.O. 132, HQ, 1st Infantry Division, award of Silver Star to Technician Grade 5 Samuel M. Fuller, shows his unit of assignment on D-Day was Service Company, 16th Infantry.

7 Again, it is important to note that his autobiography was completed and published several years after his death, so it may be that some of the inaccuracies may be laid at the feet of others.

8 See G.O. 132 above.

9 Annex 3 (Neptune Force O Landing Tables), to 1st Infantry Division Field Order No. 35.

10 Report on Operation "Neptune," Commander, Headquarter Company, 16th RCT, dd 16 Jun 1944.

11 Tegtmeyer, Chapter XX.

12 Kershaw, Ch. 13.

13 SOOF, p. 137.

14 USS *Chase*, War Diaries, 4 Jun 1944.

15 SOOF, pp. 136–37.

16 Appendix 2 (Timetable of Assault), to Annex G (Approach Plan), to WNTF, Operation Plan 2-44.

Chapter 4

1 Zaloga, *D-Day Fortifications in Normandy*, location 365.
2 *Omaha Beachhead*, (6 June–13 June 1944), p. 12 footnote.
3 See Parker's *The Tide Predictions for D-Day*, Physics Today, Vol. 64, Issue 9, 1 September 2011, for an excellent discussion on the various considerations for selecting H-Hour and D-Day.
4 Field Manual 31-5, Landing Operations on Hostile Shores, 1941, "A wave consists of one or more boat divisions which land approximately simultaneously. Waves are designated successively from front to rear, as first wave, second wave." And, "A boat division consists of two or more small boats used to transport a tactical subdivision of the landing group such as a platoon or a company."
5 Appendix 2 (Timetable of Assault), to Annex G (Approach Plan), to WNTF, Operation Plan 2-44.
6 For this and following discussions of the 16th RCT's waves, see Annex 3 (Neptune Force O Landing Tables), to 1st Division Field Order 35.
7 Contrary to some sources, the tank dozers did not tow in trailers with engineer supplies. This error can be traced back to the Army's *Omaha Beachhead* (p. 32). The standard M4 Sherman tanks of Co. A that landed with them, however, towed in M8 armored ammunition trailers with spare tank ammunition. This is confirmed by several photos, the 741st Tank Battalion's after-action report and the LCT manifests contained in the 16th RCT's landing tables.
8 Annex 10 (Tank Employment Plan), to 1st Infantry Division Field Order No. 35.
9 Annex 16 (Special Engineer Task Force Plan), to 1st Infantry Division Field Order No. 35.

Chapter 5

1 SOOF, p. 137.
2 SOOF, p. 119.
3 W/RC, p. 205.
4 Annex 3 (Neptune Force O Landing Tables) to 1st Infantry Division Field Order No. 35
5 W/TIW, p. 222.
6 Wertenbaker, p. 42.
7 The time—0415 hours—is noted in the 16th RCT's S3 Combat Report, as well as the narrative for the Distinguished Unit Citation—forerunner of the Presidential Unit Citation.
8 Appendix 2 to Annex G, OPLAN 2-44.
9 Appendix 2 to Annex G, Western Naval Task Force, Operation Plan 2-44.
10 6 knots was the speed specified in Appendix 2 (Timetable of Assault), to Annex G (Approach Plan), to Western Naval Task Force, Operation Plan 2-44. However, the 1st Division Landing Diagram shows 7 or 8 knots, depending on location in the boat lanes. Regardless, none of these speeds would have been enough for him the cover the necessary distance in the short time required.
11 The 16th RCT's S3 Combat Report is the basic source for details of the events of the actual landings.
12 CTF 122 Mapsheet, OMAHA Beach-East (Colleville-sur-Mer), with obstacle overprint, scale 1:7920, dated 21 April 1944.
13 Ambrose, p. 394.

Chapter 6

1 *Life*, 19 June 1944, pp. 25–31.
2 SOOF, p. 137.
3 A review of seven versions of Morris's tales has the note including anywhere from just seven words up to several sentences.

4   The details of the handling of Capa's film varied over time, and will be addressed in a later chapter.
5   Déjà vu, *The Normandy Project*.
6   Ibid.
7   Morris, pp. 5–6.
8   *Life*, 19 June 1944, pp. 36–37.
9   W/TIW, p. 248.

Chapter 7

1   Except as otherwise noted, the primary sources for this chapter are the "History of the 16th CT Invasion of France," the "16th CT S-3 Combat Report" and the "Covering Citation of the 16th Infantry for the Period of 6 June 1944."
2   Discussion of the tanks is primarily based on the Headquarters, 741st Tank Battalion, Unit Journal covering 6 June to 1 July 1944.
3   Annex 10 (Tank Employment Plan) para 3.b, to 1st Infantry Division Field Order No. 35.
4   Administrative Annex to 741st Tank Bn Field Order 1.
5   SGT Beetson's after action report, contained in 741st Tank Bn Unit Journal.
6   Although 16th RCT reports claim Company L landed on Fox Green, *Omaha Beachhead* shows them landing just across the boundary on Fox Red, and this seems to be confirmed as the cliff, under which the survivors took shelter after crossing the beach was in the Fox Red sector.
7   Plans for these teams were specified in Annex 16 (Special Engineer Task Force Plan) to 1st Infantry Division Field Order No. 35.
8   For the activities of the combined Army–Navy gap-clearing teams, see *The Corps of Engineers: The War Against Germany*, Chapter XV, and Report on Naval Combat Demolitions Units [NCDUs] in Operation "Neptune" as part of TASK FORCE 122, 19 July 1944.
9   SGT Nicol's after action report, contained in 741st Tank Bn Unit Journal.
10 SSG Fair's and SGT Larsen's after action report, contained in 741st Tank Bn Unit Journal.
11 McManus gives the time as 0710 hours and credits the shot to SGT George Geddes's DD tank (p. 108). In *The Devil's Garden*, Zaloga quotes a 0720 hours message sent by the 726th Grenadier Regiment to its division headquarters which included the fact that this 88mm gun had been knocked out (p. 363). Given the normal delays in reporting from a fortification up to regimental level, it's likely that this 88mm had been knocked out even before 0710 hours.
12 In Pogue's 1945 oral combat interview, Spalding placed his landing at 0645 hours, confirming they were roughly a quarter hour late. He did not mention the presence of engineers ahead of him.
13 Beck, p. 323. The activities of this gap assault team will be examined in a later chapter.
14 Ibid, p. 325. Due to the loss of gap marking equipment, so many craft could not tell if some lanes had been cleared. Nevertheless, photos clearly show LCVPs using Team 9's cleared lane 70 minutes after H-Hour.
15 The issue of casualties on this part of Easy Red will be examined in some detail in a later chapter.
16 397th Antiaircraft Artillery Provisional Machinegun Battalion, D-Day After Action Report.
17 The German 726th Grenadier Regiment reported at 0905 hours that WN61 was in enemy hands. See Zaloga, *The Devil's Garden*, p. 375.

Chapter 8

1   Jarreau's oral history, Lewis's diary and West's letter to the editor in *American Heritage* magazine. Allan Coleman discovered a second-hand account by another *LCI(L)-94* crewman—Seaman 2nd Class Victor Haboush—describing Capa's arrival on the craft. Haboush is also identified as one of

the figures in a Capa photo showing a casualty being treated on that craft (See Figure 66). While this account adds to the confirmation of Capa's departure on this craft, the account is tainted to some degree by the inclusion of an incorrect detail—that Capa was wearing a Correspondent's patch. As was the norm for him, he did not wear one for D-Day. Being a second-hand account, this may not be Haboush's fault.

2   W/TIW, p. 235.

3   *LCI(L)-85* Action Report for Operation NEPTUNE.

4   SOOF, p. 149.

5   Jarreau's beaching and general quarters stations (at auxiliary steering and in the engine room, respectively) would not have permitted him to take these pictures. From his interview with Ambrose, it appears the craft's captain (LT Gislason) took the photos, and the camera's position at bridge level certainly seems to bear this out. Jarreau said he and the captain shared an interest in photography and the captain even had a makeshift (and unauthorized) darkroom aboard. He also said the captain took photos during D-Day and gave copies to him. However, as it was Jarreau's family who donated these photos to the National WWII museum, they are often referred to as his photos.

6   Landing Table Index Number 1181, p. 27 of 116th RCT Landing Tables, Annex 3 (Neptune Force O Landing Tables) to 1st Division 16 Field Order 35.

7   USCG Historian's Office, *104th Medical Battalion, 29th Division Aboard LCI(L)-94 on D-Day*, Mark Johnson, COL, USA (Ret.).

8   Ambrose's interview is disappointing. About a third of the pages are missing, and Ambrose's interruptions caused continual digressions, which resulted in a chaotic narrative, a confused timeline and key threads left unexplored.

9   *Movie Makers* magazine 20:6, June 1945, pp. 213, 228–30.

10 USCG Historian's office, "D-Day through the eyes of a Coast Guardsman."

11 Landing Table Index Number 1186, p. 29 of 116th RCT Landing Tables, Annex 3 (Neptune Force O Landing Tables) to 1st Division 16 Field Order 35.

12 *LCI(L)-91, Operation Neptune, Participation in by USCG LCI(L) 91*, 10 June 1944 and *LCI(L)-91, Loss of Ship, Report of*, 19 June 1944.

13 *LCI(L)-92* Action Report.

14 Shepard's *The Story of LCI(L)-92 in the Invasion of Normandy*, and *Soldiers' Stories: Fritz Weinshank*.

15 Appendix 2 (Timetable of Assault), to Annex G (Approach Plan), to WNTF, Operation Plan 2-44.

16 1st Division Landing Diagram.

17 104th Medical Battalion After Action Report for the Month of June 1944.

18 For a crosswalk between ship hull numbers and planning serial designations, see Appx 1 (Final Ship Assignments, Force "O") to Annex 3, (Neptune Force O Landing Tables) to 1st Division 16 Field Order 35.

19 After Action Report, 29th Infantry Division—June 1944—Battle of Normandy.

20 *LCI(L)-94* Muster Roll for June 1944.

21 *Coast Guard Heroes at Normandy*.

Chapter 9

1   See Pogue's comments on his oral interview with LT Spalding.

2   Morgan identifies these tanks as belonging to SSG Shepard (left), SSG Fair (rear) and SGT Larsen (right), and these identifications match the after-action reports of each tank commander found in the Combat Team 16 S-3 Combat Report.

3   W/RC, p. 213.

4   W/TIW, p. 235.

5   *LCI(L)-85*, Action Report for Operation Neptune, 24 June 1944.
6   SOOF, p. 140.

Chapter 10

1   In the commendation for Lt (jg) James Forrestal—the commander of the first wave of *Chase* LCVPs and scheduled to land at 0740 hours—he was praised for bringing his boats in on time. Also see the CT 16 S-3 Combat Report.
2   The Muster Roll for June 44 recorded three crewmen killed at 0850 hours. It also notes two wounded crewmen were later transferred to other ships for medical care.
3   *LCT-305* Action Report, dd 13 June 1944; see also Commander, LCT Flotilla 18 Report of Damage to Landing Craft Due to Enemy Action, dd 11 July 1944.
4   CTF 124 (Commander, 11th Amphibious Force) Action Report, Assault on Vierville-Colleville Sector, Coast of Normandy, Part IV, Resume of Battle Damage (Losses), p. 73. This list shows "one quad unit inoperable," LCIs had two "quad units" of diesel engine, and each quad unit powered one of the two propeller shafts.
5   For wave schedules and composition are from the RCT 16 Landing Tables.
6   Actual landing times are from the CT 16 S-3 Combat Report.
7   Thompson's report on his D-Day experiences accompanying COL Taylor were printed in the *Chicago Daily Tribune* on 9 June, although for security purposes neither the 16th RCT nor COL Taylor could be identified.
8   There is some thought that this position may have been filled by Bert Brandt, however his narrative of D-Day seems to imply he rode in with the 116th Regiment, and his pre-invasion photos show he was embarked on an attack transport carrying elements of that regiment. MacVane, though, recalled that Brandt went with either the 26th RCT (Force B) or First Army Headquarters. As with virtually all correspondents covering the invasion, Brandt was extremely vague regarding details of his landing assignment.
9   Although the landing table extract shows both correspondents slotted to come in on one of the LCMs, MacVane said he came in on the LCVP in this wave. It approached to beach on time but withdrew and moved offshore to consult the commander of a follow-on regiment. He estimated he landed between 1000–1030 hours. Therefore, it is possible that MacVane's craft was thus diverted while BG Wyman and Thompson's craft landed after only a short delay.
10 His LCVP was "rail-loaded"—that is, troops loaded the craft at the rails while it was still in its davits, then the craft was lowered into the water. The other loading method required troops to clamber down cargo nets to reach landing craft already in the water—called "net loading."
11 Information on the Chase's operations comes from its Narrative Report of Operations, 6–7 June 1944 and War Diaries, 4–7 June 1944.
12 The Henrico's Narrative report stated these LCVPs left the ship at 0411 hours; the CT 16 S-3 Combat Report said this wave was lowered into the wave at 0415.
13 History, Medical Detachment, 16th Infantry.
14 See Chapter XX of his Personal Wartime Memoirs.
15 Two reports (CPT Ralph's report for Headquarters Company and the Regimental Medical Detachment's report) cite a slightly earlier beaching time for this wave: 0815 hours. I've used 0820 hours as this was the time listed in CT 16 S-3 Combat Report and was confirmed in the action report of the 741st Tank Battalion. The latter report stated the Battalion Commander landed at 0820 hours; he was slotted to land in the same craft as COL Taylor.
16 Capa never acknowledged this encounter with Thompson. This may be due to the fact that at least one of his fictionalized stories in *Slightly out of Focus*—the combat jump into Sicily—was lifted and embellished from Thompson's real-life adventures.

17 Sargent's position in the first wave of *Chase* landing craft is confirmed in *The Coast Guard at War, Volume XI: The Landings in France.*

18 Data concerning tides and beach gradients here and throughout this work are taken from the reverse side of the CTF 122 mapsheet "Omaha Beach—East (Colleville-sur-Mer)," 21 April 1944. The map had an overprint showing beach obstacles based on 12 May 1944 information. The reverse side of the map listed tabular data, to include sunlight and moonlight data, beach gradient data for various points, current data, and tide data.

19 4 feet per hour (1 foot in 15 minutes) is the figure given in *Cross Channel Attack* (p. 317). The Navy's official history, *The Invasion of France and Germany* (p. 138), cites an even more dramatic rise of 1 foot in 8 minutes. Both of these are merely estimates, as the tide's rate of rise varied, being much slower near the high and low tide states. The rate of 1 foot per 11 minutes is taken from the tide chart for this 60-minute period on 6 June 1944

20 in SOOF, p. 218, Capa said he was on the regimental commander's plane and the time he cited would have placed him in the second regiment to jump. His claim to have jumped as the number two man in the stick, behind the regimental commander, is an exaggeration, as the colonel would have been followed by several key staff members who needed to land immediately in the commander's vicinity.

Chapter 11

1 The 397th AAA Provisional Machine Gun Battalion's after-action report claimed these two batteries had five guns at some point later in the day. The CT 16 S-3 Combat Report, however, states only two guns were successfully landed. The difference is probably due to efforts to salvage guns lost in the surf later in the day.

2 The CT 16 S-3 Combat Report is confused when discussing these two companies. While it describes the activities of both units, it mistakenly identifies both as Company C, and omits reference to Company A. In addition, it mixed up which was delayed in its landing. The information presented in this passage is taken from *The Unit History of the 81st Chemical Mortar Battalion,* written by its commander.

3 The 2015 scandal involving Brian Williams' experience aboard a helicopter in Iraq in 2003, which he claimed was hit by enemy fire and forced down, is a perfect example of the all-too-common practice of correspondents moving with follow-on echelons, but presenting the public with the false impression that they are at the front, in the thick of the fighting.

4 Prior to 6 June 1944, just 20 percent of the Army's divisions had been committed to combat (18 of an eventual total of 90). The last year of the war saw a huge increase in the number of US troops engaged, with a commensurate rise in casualties.

5 "Dagwood" Daily Casualty Report, 060630 June to 081200 June 1944.

6 Strength and Casualty Statistics, 16th Infantry.

7 See Pogue's 1945 oral combat history interview with Spalding.

8 In an interview 47 years after the fact, CPT Dawson claimed that he and two men had exited his landing craft when it was hit and the rest of the boat section was wiped out; his LCVP had 36 men embarked, which would mean there were 33 casualties. If that were true, then all of the losses Co. G suffered on the beach came as a result of that one hit. This is clearly impossible, and his recollections must have exaggerated the event. In a similar vein, he was quoted in another interview claiming that he lost 62 men to the American naval shelling of Colleville. In fact, that figure was two more than the total losses he reported from 0630 hours 6 June through 1200 hours 8 June—a period of 53½ hours that included this friendly fire incident.

9 16th CT S-3 Combat Report, p. 18.

10   Zaloga, *The Devil's Garden*, p. 364.
11   There is some disagreement in types and calibers of weapons among sources; here I have followed Zaloga.

Chapter 12

1   SHAEF PRD memo, subj: Pictorial Coverage, May 1944, p. 5.
2   SOOF, p. 138.
3   SOOF, p. 149.
4   W/TIW, p. 236.
5   SOOF, p. 139.
6   JS, COL Bert Kalisch interview.

Chapter 13

1   Wertenbaker, pp. 42–44.
2   W/n.
3   SOOF, pp. 139–48.
4   *Black and White (online)*, Rearview Mirror, *John G. Morris: Normandy*, 1944.

Chapter 14

1   *Omaha Beachhead (6 June–13 June 1944)*, p. 65.
2   *History of the 16th CT Invasion of France, S-3 Combat Report*, p. 18.
3   Headquarters Company, CT-16, *Report on Operation "Neptune"*, p. 4.

Chapter 15

1   This chapter is a somewhat expanded version of a series of posts that appeared in June 2015 as part of the "Alternate History: Robert Capa on D-Day" project, on A. D. Coleman's Photocritic International website.
2   W/TIW, p. 248.
3   *Omaha Beachhead*, p. 51.
4   CriticalPast, A demonstration about clearing Japanese-type obstacles with explosives at a beach in Florida, United States, clip # 65675058859, time 00:44.
5   Ibid, time 0013 hours.
6   Blazich, Frank A., *Opening Omaha Beach: Ensign Karnowski and NCDU-45*.

Chapter 16

1   Whelan first said the man was Edward K. Regan, W/RC, p. 212, but then identified him as Huston S. Riley, W/TIW, p. 233.
2   CriticalPast, *United States Army 1st Infantry Division soldiers landing at Omaha beach in Normandy, France on D-Day*, clip # 65675038165. This motion picture film shot by SGT Richard Taylor includes a brief sequence showing a still photo cameraman—another member of Detachment L, 165th Signal Photo Company. This clip was taken on Fox Red beach sector.

3   Viemo, *At the Beaches of Normandy June, 1944*, video # 157908080, time 12:57.
4   Ibid, time 14:56.

Chapter 17

1   Scheduled arrival times are drawn from the RCT 16 landing tables.
2   W/TIW, p. 227.
3   For a discussion of the evolution of the several contact sheets for D-Day, see W/TIW, p. 239.

Chapter 18

1   Yerkey, Gary, *Dying for the News*, location 59 and World War II on Deadline website, "Remembering Journalists Killed Covering WWII."
2   Change 3, p. 3, to WNTF Operation Plan 2-44, dated April 21, 1944.
3   Ibid. Change 1, p. 5.
4   *The United States Army in World War II: The Technical Services; The Signal Corps: The Outcome*, Washington D.C. (1991), p. 109. The Provisional Engineer Special Brigade Group's report was more forthcoming. It stated that the boats, RAF seaplane tenders, arrived in such poor condition that they all required overhaul and only one was ready by the evening of D-Day; *Provisional Engineer Special Brigade Group, Operation Report Neptune, Omaha Beach*, 30 September 1944, pp. 313–15.
5   SHAEF, Coordinating Route Slip, subj: Letter of Authority for Major W. A, Ulman, 2 June 1944.
6   SHAEF message, signed SCAEF, Ref No. S-53927, 2109 hours, 15 June 1944.
7   W/RC, p. 210, footnote.
8   *Alternate History: Robert Capa on D-Day* project, Guest Post 30, *The Legend of the Lost Film*.
9   SOOF, p. 122.
10   SOOF, p. 59.
11   Oldfield, p. 86.
12   *The Signal Corps: The Outcome*, pp. 112–13.
13   Office of the Chief Signal Officer, HQs, Eighth US Army, 'Current Information Letter', July 1944. pp. 41–42
14   *Popular Mechanics*, "I Cover the Battlefront" May 1945, p. 84.
15   *Time*, 19 June 44, p. 68 and Oldfield, p. 77.
16   W/n.
17   The opening chapter to Morris's *Get the Picture* is devoted to this episode.
18   JS/n.
19   SOOF, p. 80.
20   ONI-226, *Allied Landing Craft and Ships*, p. 48.
21   History, Medical Detachment, 16th Infantry, November 1940 to May 1945, p. 16, and History of the 16th CT Invasion of France, S-3 Combat Report, pp. 18–19.
22   Memoirs of Staff Sergeant Reuben A. Weiner, Combat Photographer with the 508th PIR.
23   See Lieb's narrative to *D-Day to Germany*, NARA, Archives Identifier: 95634.
24   MacVane, p. 229.

Chapter 19

1   Kershaw, Alex. *Blood and Champagne: The Life and Times of Robert Capa*, location 1561.
2   *American Heritage*, September 1994, Vol. 45, No 5, p. 8.

3   According to Steven Zaloga's *The Devil's Garden: Rommel's Desperate Defense of Omaha Beach on D-Day* (1828) this would be the one remaining operational 75mm gun in WN62. Although the German 726th Grenadier Regiment reported at 0905 hours that WN62 was down to a single machine gun, it's clear that 75mm gun in the lower concrete casemate was in action at least intermittently until about 1000 hours. Hein Severloh, one of two defenders of WN62 who published their accounts of D-Day, identified these guns as "7,65-cm-Feldkanone Modell 1917" (*WN 62—Erinnerungen an Omaha Beach: Normandie, 6. Juni 1944*, (location 85)). However, pictures of the guns bear out Zaloga's identification.

4   *Movie Makers* magazine, "Filming Normandy D-Day," Ruley, David, 1 June 1945.

5   CriticalPast, "A breakwater made up of sunken ships at Normandy" clip # 65675058892.

6   The original source for this photo is unknown. It was found on Yves Cordell's excellent website, Omaha Beach-Vierville, p. 6221. Although it is clearly one of Capa's photos, neither ICP nor Magnum Photos seems to hold it in their archives.

7   LCT-305 Action Report, dd 13 June 1944; see also Commander, LCT Flotilla 18 Report of Damage to Landing Craft Due to Enemy Action, dd 11 July 1944.

8   CriticalPast, "United States soldiers tend to wounded personnel aboard ships during the invasion of Normandy," clip # 65675020542, time 1:03.

9   See Lewis's diary entry for 6 June 1944.

10   Ambrose's interview with Jarreau, p. 33.

11   CriticalPast, "United States soldiers tend to wounded personnel aboard ships during the invasion of Normandy," clip # 65675020542, time 1:36.

12   ICP image accession no. 2010.90.2107.

13   CTF 120 Operation Order No. BB-44, para 3.d, p. 9.

14   SHAEF G4 msg to ETOUSA, Ref # S-52990, dd 1 June 44.

15   W/TIW, p. 235.

Chapter 20

1   This chapter is a condensed analysis of the topic which appeared in a series of five posts in June 2022 as part of the "Alternate History: Robert Capa on D-Day" project, on A. D. Coleman's Photocritic International website. Much of the material in the original posts has been covered elsewhere in this book, and has been omitted from this chapter as it was redundant.

2   Hendley, Pete. LCI-85: *The Military Career of Lt(jg) Coit Hendley, Jr. During the Invasions of North Africa, Italy and Normandy on D-Day, His Papers and Photos*, p. 210.

3   *Movie Makers* magazine, "Filming Normandy D-Day," Ruley, David, 1 June 1945.

4   Hendley, p. 210.

5   The Landing Tables contained in the 1st Infantry Division's Field Order #35 indicate that *LCI(L)-94* had 179 men manifested, but Jarreau's interview mentions 208 embarked troops.

6   See Lewis's diary entry for 6 June 1944.

7   As derived from the tide height chart on the reverse of the CTF 122 invasion map.

Chapter 21

1   *Magnum Stories*, "D-Day and the Omaha Beach Landings."

2   See ICP image accession No. 3001.1992's caption for this photo.

3   Fuller, location 2071.

4   *Life*, 19 June 1944, p. 31; along with a second, nearly identical shot (ICP image accession no. 2010.90.2109).

5 US Coast Guard Report Number 4, Normandy Invasion.

6 Wertenbaker, p. 43.

7 SOOF, p. 149.

8 16th RCT Landing Tables, Index numbers 2213-2218 consisted of six LCVPs carrying various overstrength elements, these were the last elements scheduled to leave the *Chase*.

9 USS *LCI(L) 85*, Action Report for Operation Neptune, dd 24 June 1944, p. 2.

10 USS *Samuel Chase*, "Narrative Report of Operations, 6–7 June 1944," dd 26 June 1944, p. 2, and USS *Chase* War Dairy entry for 6 June 1944.

11 ICP image, accession no. 2010.90.2106, see Also Magnum image PAR77859.

12 W/TIW, photo caption for Figure 308, p. 249.

13 Annex 4, Administrative Order, to 1st Division Field Order #45, dd 16 April 1944, and as amended by Change 1, dd 9 May 1944.

14 See PhotosNormandie video files f00200 and f00244 for images of casualties and survivors arriving in Weymouth on 7 June 1944.

15 W/TIW, p. 224.

16 Annex N (Medical Plan) to WNTF OPLAN N0. 2-44.

17 WW2 US Medical Research Center website, "WW2 Hospital Ships."

Chapter 22

1 W/TIW, p. 211.

2 The Press: Little and Late, p. 48, *Time*, Vol. XLIII, No. 25, June 19, 1944.

3 Getty Images, Editorial # 517438204.

4 W/RC, p. 214.

5 W/TIW, p. 236.

6 W/TIW, p. 249.

7 SOOF p. 211.

8 Fuller, location 2067.

9 W/TIW, p. 234.

Chapter 23

1 SOOF, pp. 149–50.

2 W/RC, p. 213.

3 W/TIW, p. 236.

4 USS *Samuel Chase*, "Narrative Report of Operations, 6–7 June 1944," dd 26 June 1944, p. 2, and and USS *Chase* War Dairy entry for 7 June 1944.

5 Caledonian Maritime Research Trust website, Scottish Built Ships.

6 SHAEF PRD Memo, Subj: War Correspondents, dd 24 April 1944.

7 W/RC. p. 213, n <note number missing>

8 W/n, interview with David Scherman.

9 *LST-317* deck log entry for 7 June 1944.

10 See PhotosNormandie video files f00200 and f00244.

11 USS *Carroll*, Deck Log entries for 6 and 7 June 1944.

12 *SOOF*, p. 152.

13 Magnum Photos, image PAR77858.

14 W/RC, p. 215.

Chapter 24

1 JS interview with Morris for the 6 PM time; Morris's *Get the Picture*, p. 6, for the 1830 hours time.

2 JS interview with Morris for the 2130 hours time and Morris's *Get the Picture*, p. 6, for the 2100 hours time.

3 JS, Morris interview.

4 W/TIW, p. 238.

5 JS, Morris interview.

6 Morris, p. 6.

7 Ibid.

8 JS, Morris interview.

9 SHAEF memo subj: Processing of Still Photographs from War Correspondents, dd June 1944

10 For a description of how the Allies continued the Fortitude deception after D-Day, see NARA, War Cabinet, London Controlling Section memo, subj, 'Present Position Regarding Europan Deception Plans', dd 11 June 44.

11 Heskith, p. 250.

12 Heskith, pp. 235–36 and pp. 282–83.

13 See, for example, SHAEF message to Combined Chiefs of Staff, SCAF 40, dd 30 May 1944.

14 SOOF, pp. 34–37 and W/RC, 183–84.

15 Morris, pp. 70–71.

16 W/RC, p. 214.

17 JS, Morris interview.

18 Morris, p. 6.

19 Morris, p. 7.

20 "Rearview Mirror: John G. Morris, Normandy 1944," *Black and White* magazine, issue 106, December 2014.

21 Ibid.

22 Ryan, p. 303.

23 SHAEF memo, subj: Standard Operating Procedure for Handling and Disposition of Still Photographs (marked Annex F), dd June 1944.

24 Brown, pp. 685–87.

25 *Omaha Beachhead*, p. 113, "At noon [LXXXIV] Corps stated that attempted sea landings from the Vire to the coast northeast of Bayeaux had been completely smashed."

26 Morris, "The A. D. Coleman Attack," January 2015. See Post 19 of the *Alternate History: Robert Capa on D-Day* project on Allan Coleman's Photocritic Internation website.

27 SHAEF PRO message (signed Eisenhower) to Adjutant General at the War Department, message ref # E-31717, 0522 hours, 7 June 1944.

28 W/TIW, p. 237.

Chapter 25

1 SOOF, p. 152.

2 *Life*, 19 June 1944, Vol. 16, No. 25, p. 30.

3 W/RC, p. 214.

4 Morris, p. 6.

5 Caption notes page titled "Last Glimpse of England," dd D-1, Roll 1 Contax.

6 Morris, pp. 80–81.

7   ICP, Cornell Capa archives, letter from Robert Capa to Edith and Cornell Capa, postmarked "Aug 28 1944 New York NY Parcel Post," handwritten note "July 1944."
8   Wertenbaker, p. 44.
9   SHAEF memo, subj: Responsibiliies, Press Censorship Branch, dd 11 July 1944.
10 Kershaw, location 2179.
11 For the detailed dissection of Morris's narratives, see the *Alternate History: Robert Capa on D-Day* project on Allan Coleman's Photocritic Internation website.
12 CriticalPast, "Allied invasion force departs England en route to France for invasion of Normandy, in World War II," clip #65675065480, time 3:37.
13 See Patrick Peccatte's excellent article at the PhotosNormandie Project website on the initial publications of Capa D-Day photos.
14 JS, Morris interview.
15 Morris, p. 6.
16 Appendix to 21st Army Group memo 29767, Publicity and Psychological Warfare, dd 13 July 1944.
17 SHAEF memo subj: Processing of Still Photographs from War Correspondents, dd June 1944.

Chapter 26

1   All the standard sources agree with this outline.
2   Garland, *Sicily and the Surrender of Italy*, p. 108.
3   SOOF, pp. 62–70.
4   *Illustrated*, 15 January 1944, pp. 5–8.
5   W/n, "see Crocky's letter."
6   *Illustrated*, 13 May 1944 carried one of Capa's photos of his arrival in Sicily aboard an LST (ICP's image Accession No. 2013.92.30).
7   SOOF, pp. 87–88.
8   Garland, p. 500.
9   SOOF, p. 89.
10 See Gardner, Chapter XXVI for a complete discussion of this event.
11 Tregaskis, Richard, *Invasion Diary*, 1 September 1944 entry, p. 108.
12 Tregaskis, p. 104.
13 Tregaskis, p. 113.
14 W/RC, p. 199.
15 Tregaskis; 30 August 1944 entry, pp. 106–7.
16 SOOF, p. 90.
17 Tregaskis, p. 110 vs. SOOF, p. 88.
18 SOOF, p. 90.
19 Oldfield, p. 30; and Gavin, *On to Berlin*, p. 5.
20 W/RC, p. 209.
21 W/n.
22 Oldfield, p. 51.
23 *'47: The Magazine of the Year*, October 1947, Vol. I, No. 8. p. 123.
24 W/n.
25 W/RC, p. 217.
26 Oldfield, p. 54.
27 W/RC, p. 226.
28 SOOF, pp. 213–14.
29 JS.

30 W/RC, p. 233.
31 W/RC, p. 218.
32 W/RC, p. 237.
33 W/RC, pp. 226–27.
34 Kershaw, locations 1800–1809.
35 JS, interview with Graffis.
36 Tregaskis, p. 114.

Chapter 27

1 This image was used for the cover of Liesl Bradner and Phil Stern's book *The World War II Exploits of Darby's Ranger and Combat Photographer Phil Stern*, 2018.
2 Magnum image PAR131948, published in *Life*, 31 January 1944, Vol. 16, No, 5, p. 17.
3 W/n, Whelan interview with Leon Danielle.
4 See Magnum Photos images PAR77862, PAR79253 and PAR199388. The same scene of corpses was first photographed alone, then the angle was changed with two more shots each with a different group of posed onlookers.
5 ICP archives, accession no. 888.1992.
6 ICP archives, accession no. 2012.58.98.
7 The 15 January and 13 May 1944 issues of *Illustrated* magazine.
8 Even Whelan had misgivings about Capa's narrative. Capa attended a farewell party in Barcelona for Hemingway the evening of 6 November, the same evening the assault took place. Whelan initially admitted he was not there for the assault. (W/RC, p. 151) Ever the Capa loyalist, Whelan later contrived a scenario in which Capa left after the party and drove the 180 kilometers to the front in wartime conditions, over bad roads and blackout lights, yet still managed to cross the river two to three hours before dawn. (W/TIS, p. 147).
9 See ICP image Accession No. 1368.1992.
10 The task force consisted of 2,000 men and 200 vehicles, W/RC, p. 297.
11 ICP press release, "ICP Celebrates 50th Anniversary of Fund for Concerned Photography," 4 May 2016.
12 John Hersey's "The Man Who Invented Himself," *'47: The Magazine of the Year*, Vol. 1, No. 7.
13 W/RC, p. 237.

Bibliography

Official Records

Principal Sources for official records include:

MRC: Colonel Robert R. McCormick Research Center, First Division Museum at Cantigny.

NARA: The National Archives and Records Administration.

CARL: US Army Combined Arms Research Center.

USCG: US Coast Guard Historians Office.

USN: US History and Heritage Command.

FOLD3: Fold3 Historical Military Records.

1st Infantry Division Field Order No. 35, 16 April 1944, w/changes (MRC).

16th Infantry Daily Journal, 1 to 30 June 1944 (MRC).

16th Infantry Regiment, 1st Infantry Division, *Summary of Regimental Situation on D-Day, 6 June 1944.* (MRC).

18th Infantry Regiment, 1st Infantry Division, *Citation of Unit*, 17 June 1944 (MRC).

18th LCT Flotilla, *Damage Report*, 11 July 1944 (FOLD3).

29th Military Police Platoon, *After Action Report, 29th Infantry Division—June 1944—Battle of Normandy* (MRC).

104th Medical Battalion, *After Action Report for the Month of June, 1944* (MRC).

Combat Team 16, *Annex 3 (Neptune Force O Landing Tables) to Field Order 5*, 15 May 1944 (MRC).

Combat Team 16, *Comments and Criticisms of Operation "Neptune" from the TQM's Point of View*, 30 June 1944 (MRC).

Combat Team 16, *"Dagwood" Daily Casualty Reports for the Period 0630 hours 6 June to 1200 hours, 8 June 1944* (MRC).

Combat Team 16, *Dagwood Daily Casualty Reports, June 1944* (MRC).

Combat Team 16, *Exercise "Neptune"—Intelligence Notes* (MRC).

Combat Team 16, *History of the 16th CT Invasion of France, S-3 Combat Report, Covering Citation of the 16th Infantry for the Period of 6 June 1944* (MRC).

Commander, Assault Force O, Western Naval Task Force, *Action Report, Assault on Vierville-Colleville Sector, Coast of Normandy*, 27 July 1944 (FOLD3).

Commander Task Force One Two Two. Mapsheet, *OMAHA Beach-East (Colleville-sur-Mer), 1:7920*, dd 21 Apr 1944, with beach obstacle overprint dd 12 May 1944.

Commander Task Force One Two Two. *Report on Naval Combat Demolitions Units [NCDUs] in Operation "Neptune" as part of TASK FORCE 122, 19 July 1944.* (Naval History and Heritage Command).

DD Form 214, Enlisted Record and Report of Separation, Honorable Discharge, Fuller, Samuel F. (NARA).

Eleventh Amphibious Force (Task Force 124), Operations Order BB-44, 20 May 1944 (MRC).

Headquarters, 1st Infantry Division, General Orders No. 132, 24 July 1944 (MRC).

Headquarters Company, CT-16, *Report on Operation "Neptune,"* 16 June 1944 (MRC).

LCI(L)-5, Report of Operations in the Invasion of Normandy, France, 29 June 1944 (FOLD3).

LCI(L)-85, Action Report for Operation Neptune, 24 June 1944 (FOLD3).

LCI(L)-91, Loss of Ship, Report of, 19 June 1944 (FOLD3).

LCI(L)-91, Operation Neptune, Participation in by USCG LCI(L) 91, 10 June 1944 (FOLD3).

LCI(L)-92, Action Report of Recent Operations—No. France, 10 June 1944 (FOLD3).

LCT-305, Action Report, 13 June 1944 (NARA).

Headquarters, 397th Antiaircraft Artillery Provisional Machinegun Battalion, *D-Day After Action Report* (CARL).

Headquarters, 741st Tank Battalion, *Action Against Enemy/After Action Report, 19 July 1944* (CARL).

Headquarters, 741st Tank Battalion, *Field Order 1, Operation Neptune, 21 May 1944* (CARL).

Headquarters, 741st Tank Battalion, *Unit Journal covering 6 June to 1 July 1944* (CARL).

Headquarters, First United States Army, *Operations Plan Neptune, 25 February 1944* (CARL).

Johns Hopkins University Operations Research Office, *Strength and Casualty Statistics, 16th Infantry*, 26 May 1953 (MRC).

London Controlling Section's memo subj Plan "BODYGUARD," dd 24 May 44 (NARA).

Medical Detachment, 16th Infantry; *History, Medical Detachment, 16th Infantry, 1st Infantry Division, United States Army, November 1940 to May 1945, 14 July 1945* (MRC).

Office of the Chief Signal Officer, HQs, Eighth US Army, *Current Information Letter*, July 1944. (FOLD3).

Pogue, F. (1945) *John Spalding D-Day narrative*, LT Spalding combat interview (Military History Institute, Carlisle Barracks, Pennsylvania).

Provisional Engineer Special Brigade Group, *Operation Report Neptune, Omaha Beach*, 30 September 1944 (FOLD3).

Service Company, Combat Team 16, *Comment and Criticisms of Operation "Neptune"*, 30 June 1944 (MRC).

SHAEF, Coordinating Route Slip, subj: Letter of Authority for Major W. A. Ulman, 2 June 1944 (NARA).

SHAEF, Operation Memorandum 33, Photographic Policy, 22 May 1944 (NARA).

SHAEF, Pictorial Coverage, May 1944 (NARA).

SHAEF, Public Relations Plan, 1 May 1944 (NARA).

SHAEF, Regulations for War Correspondents Accompanying Allied Expeditionary Force in the Field, 1944 (NARA).

Tegtmeyer, Charles. R. *Personal Wartime Memoir of Major Charles E. Tegtmeyer, Medical Corps, Regimental Surgeon, 16th Infantry Regiment, 1st Infantry Division.*

USS *Carroll, Deck Logs, 4–8 June 1944* (NARA).

USS *Chase, Narrative Report of Operations, 6–7 June 1944* (NARA).

USS *Chase, War Diaries, 4–7 June 1944* (NARA).

USS *Henrico*, Brief Chronological Narrative Report of Operations from Time of Departure for Assault to and Including 17 June 1944, dd 26 June 1944 (NARA).

USS *LCI(L)-94, Muster Rolls, January–December 1944* (NARA).

War Department, General Orders No. 76, Washington, D.C., 22 September 44. Battle Honors, Citation of Units, XII, 397th Antiaircraft Artillery Provisional Machinegun Battalion (CARL).

Western Naval Task Force, *Allied Naval Expeditionary Force, Operation Plan 2-44, 21 April 1944 (with Changes 1–3, 22 May 1944).*

Western Naval Task Force, Assault Force "O" (Task Force 124), *Operation Order BB-44, 20 May 1944* Psychological Operations in the European Theater of Operations; Study 131, A Report to the General Board (CARL).

Books

Ambrose, S. (1995) *D-Day, June 6, 1944: The Climactic Battle of WWII*. Touchstone/Simon & Schuster.

Bamford, J. (2001) *Body of Secrets*. Doubleday.

Bass, R. (2014) *Clear the Way!: A History of the 146th Engineer Battalion from Normandy to Berlin*. Tommies Guides.

Baumgartner, J., A. De Poto, W. Fraccio, and S. Fuller. (1995) *16th Infantry Regiment, 1789–1946*. Cricket Press.

Beck, A., et al. (1985) *The United States Army in World War II: The Technical Services, The Corps of Engineers, The War Against Germany*. Center of Military History, United States Army, Washington, D.C.

Bronfen, E. (2012) *Specters of War: Hollywood's Engagement with Military Conflict*. Rutgers University Press.

Brown, A. (1975) *Bodyguard of Lies*. Harper & Row.

Caddick-Adams, P. (2019) *Sand and Steel: The D-Day Invasion and the Liberation of France*. Oxford University Press. Kindle Edition.

Capa, R. *Slightly out of Focus*. New York: The Modern Library, 2001.

Carell, P. (1995) *Invasion! They're Coming! The German Account of the D-Day Landings and the 80 Days Battle for France*. Atglen, PA: Schiffer Military History. Translated by David Johnson.

Casey, S. (2017) *The War Beat: Europe*. New York, NY, Oxford University Press.

Chazette, A., and E. Ferey. (2015) *Mur de l'Atlantique en Normandie, Les Images Oubliées*. Histoire et fortifications.

Chazette, A., Lemonnier, C. et al. (1996) *Atlantikwall Omaha Beach*. Histoire et fortifications.

Cloud, S., and L. Olson. (1996) *The Murrow Boys: Pioneers in the Front Lines of Broadcast Journalism*. Houghton Mifflin Co.

Coll, B., J. Keith and H. Rosenthal. (1988) *The United States Army in World War II: The Technical Services, The Corps of Engineers, Troops and Equipment*. Center of Military History, US Army.

D'Este, C. (1994) *Decision in Normandy*. Konecky & Konecky.

Eckhertz, H. (2015) *D Day Through German Eyes*. DTZ History Publications. Translated by Sprech Media.

Eckhertz, H. (2015) *D Day Through German Eyes, Book 2*. DTZ History Publications. Translated by Sprech Media.

Ellis, J. (1990) *Brute Force: Allied Strategy and Tactics in the Second World War*. Viking Penguin.

Folkestad, W. (1996) *The View from the Turret; The 743rd Tank Battalion During WWII*. PA, Burd Street Press.

Fuller, S. (2002) *A Third Face, My Tale of Writing, Fighting and Filmmaking*. Alfred A. Knopf; Applause Theatre & Cinema Books.

Gavin, J. (2014) *Airborne Warfare*. Pickle Partners Publishing. Kindle Edition.

Gavin, J. (1979) *On to Berlin*. Bantam Books.

Gay, T. (2012) *Assignment to Hell, The War Against Nazi Germany with Correspondents*. New American Library.

Goldman, K. (2008) *Attack Transport: USS Charles Carroll in World War II*. University Press of Florida.

Gorrell, H. (2009) *Soldier of the Press: Covering the Front in Europe and North Africa, 1936–1943*. Missouri, University of Missouri Press.

Greenfield, K. (1959) *Command Decisions*. Center of Military History, US Army.

Hargreaves, R. (2006) *The Germans in Normandy: Death Reaped a Terrible Harvest*. Barnsley, Pen & Sword Military.

Harrison, G. (1993) *U.S. Army in World War II, ETO: Cross Channel Attack*. Center of Military History, US Army.

Hastings, M. (1994) *Overlord, D-Day and the Battle for Normandy*. Simon & Schuster.

Hendley, P. (2019) *LCI-85: The Military Career of Lt(jg) Coit Hendley, Jr. During the Invasions of North Africa, Italy and Normandy on D-Day, His Papers and Photos*. Yewell Street Press.

Hesketh, R. (2000) *Fortitude: The D-Day Deception Campaign*. The Overlook Press, Peter Mayer Publishers, Inc. Kindle Edition.

Keegan, J. (1984) *Six Armies in Normandy: From D-Day to the Liberations of Paris*. Penguin Books.

Kershaw, A. (2003) *Blood and Champagne: The Life and Times of Robert Capa*. St. Martin's Press.

Knickerbocker, H., J. Thompson, J. Belden, D. Whitehead, A. Liebling, et al. (1947) *Danger Forward: The Story of the First Division in World War Two*. Albert Love Enterprises.

Levine, J. (2012) *Operation FORTITUDE, The Stories of the Spies and Spy Operations That Saved D-Day*. Lyons Press.

McManus, J. (2014) *The Dead and Those About to Die: D-Day: The Big Red One at Omaha Beach*. NAL Dutton Caliber.

MacVane, J. (1979) *On the Air in World War 2*. William Morrow & Company.

Morgan, M. (2014) *The Americans on D-Day: A Photographic History of the Normandy Invasion*. Zenith Press.

Morris, J. (1998) *Get the Picture: A Personal History of Photojournalism*. Random House.

Morrison, S. (1994) *History of United States Naval Operations in World War II, vol XI: The Invasion of France and Germany, 1944–1945*. Little, Brown & Co.

Oldfield, B. (1989) *Never a Shot in Anger*. Capra Press.

Pogue, F. (1954) *The Supreme Command*. Office of the Chief of Military History, Department of the Army.

Pyle, E. (2016) *Brave Men*. Michael O'Mara Books (digital edition).

Ryan, C. (1959) *June 6, 1944: The Longest Day*. Simon & Schuster.

Severloh, H. (2014) *WN 62, Erinnerungen an Omaha Beach Normandie, 6. Juni 1944*. Mythos Verlag (digital edition).

Sylvan, W., and F. Smith. (2008) *Normandy to Victory: The War Diary of General Courtney H. Hodges and the First U.S. Army*. University of Kentucky Press (digital edition).

Thompson, G., and D. Harris. (1991) *The United States Army in World War II, The Technical Services, The Signal Corps: The Outcome (Mid-1943 through 1945)*. Center of Military History, US Army.

Tobin, J. (1997) *Ernie Pyle's War: America's Eyewitness to World War II*. The Free Press.

Tregaskis, R. (2004) *Invasion Diary*. University of Nebraska Press.

Turner Publishing (Ed.). (1995) *USS LCI "Landing Craft Infantry,"* Vol. II. Paducah, Kentucky: Turner Publishing Co.

United States War Department, Historical Division. (1984) *Omaha Beachhead (6 June–13 June 1944)*. The Battery Press.

US Coast Guard, Historical Section. (1946) *The Coast Guard at War: The Landings in France, vol. XI*. US Coast Guard.

Voss, S. (1994) *Reporting the War, The journalistic Coverage of WWII*, Smithsonian Institution Press.

Wertenbaker, C. (1944) *Invasion!* D. Appleton-Century Co.

Whelan, R. (1985) *Capa: A Biography*. Alfred A. Kopf.

Whelan, R. (2007) *This Is War!: Robert Capa at Work*. ICP and Steidl Publishing.

Whitehead, D. (2004) *Beachhead Don: Reporting the War from the European Theater, 1942–1945*. Fordham University Press.

Whiting, C. (2018) *Hemingway Goes to War: Travels with A Gun, 1944–5*. Bookzat Publishing, Ltd.

Williams, G. (2020) *The U.S. Navy at Normandy: Fleet Organization and Operations in the D-Day Invasion*. McFarland & Co., Inc. (digital edition).

Yerkey, G. (2015) *Dying for the News*, GK Press.

Zaloga, S. (2013) *D-Day Fortification in Normandy*. Osprey Publishing (digital edition).
Zaloga, S. (2013) *The Devil's Garden: Rommel's Desperate Defense of Omaha Beach on D-Day*. Stackpole Books (digital edition).

Online Sources

Blazich, F. 2022. Opening Omaha Beach: Ensign Karnowski and NCDU-45, US Navy Seabee Museum, accessed 18 March 2024, https://seabeemuseum.wordpress.com/category/dday/.
Blegen, R. 1998. "LCT(5) Flotilla 18 at Omaha Beach, D-Day, June 6, 1944." WWII Landing Craft Tanks, accessed 18 March 2024, http://ww2lct.org/history/stories/flot_18_at_omaha.htm.
Caledonian Maritime Research Trust. "Queen Empress." Scottish Built Ships, accessed 18 March 2024, www.clydeships.co.uk/view.php?ref=16576.
Coleman, A. D. 2014 "Alternate History: Robert Capa on D-Day Project." Photocritic International, A. D. Coleman on Photography and New Technology, accessed 18 March 2024, www.nearbycafe.com/artandphoto/photocritic/2014/06/10/alternate-history-robert-capa-on-d-day-1/.
Cordelle, Y. 2020. "The Landings at Omaha Beach." Omaha Beach-Vierville, accessed 18 March 2024, https://omaha-vierville.com/indexcolleville.htm.
da Cunha, T. 2022. "Historical Research About the Photos by Robert Capa from June 6, 1944." Tristan da Cunha, accessed 18 March 2024, https://tdacunha.com/robert-capa/.
D-Day on Radio, www.jimramsburg.com/d-day-on-radio-audio.html.
D-Day through the eyes of a Coast Guardsman. www.uscg.mil.
Harris, Mark E. 2014. "Rearview Mirror: John G. Morris." *Black and White* magazine, no. 104, accessed 18 March 2024, www.bandwmag.com/articles/john-g-morris-normandy-1944.
Johnson, M. "104th Medical Battalion, 29th Division Aboard LCI(L)-94 on D-Day." USCG Historian's Office, accessed 18 March 2024, www.history.uscg.mil/Browse-by-Topic/Conflicts/World-War-II/D-Day-June-6-1944-Normandy/Aboard-LCI-L-94-on-D-Day/.
Lancaster, M. 2021. "Remembering Journalists Killed Covering WWII," World War II on Deadline, accessed 18 March 2024, https://ww2ondeadline.com/2021/05/31/ww2-war-correspondents-killed-world-war-ii/.
Leib, J. 1944. "D-Day to Germany." NARA, Archives Identifier: 95634, accessed 18 March 2024, www.youtube.com/watch?v=fJVaa0RAUGg.
Lewis, C. 1944 "Excerpts from WWII Diary of Clifford W. Lewis, MoMM 1/C, UNITED STATES COAST GUARD." USCG Historian's Office, accessed 18 March 2024, https://media.defense.gov/2021/Dec/15/2002909575/-1/-1/0/NORMANDY_DIARY.PDF.
Magnum Stories. "D-Day and the Omaha Beach Landings." Magnum Photos, accessed 18 March 2024, www.magnumphotos.com/newsroom/conflict/robert-capa-d-day-omaha-beach/.
Pecatte, P. 2015. "Robert Capa's D-Day photos—Another Story and New Interpretations." Déjà vu, The Normandy Project, (24 June 2015, updated 16 October 2018), accessed March 2024, http://dejavu.hypotheses.org/2298.
PhotosNormande, accessed 24 March 2024, www.youtube.com/@PhotosNormandie/videos.
Shepard, S. 2021. "The Story of LCI(L)_92 in the Invasion of Normandy on June 6, 1944." Defense Media Activity, accessed 16 March 2024, https://media.defense.gov/2021/Dec/15/2002909573/-1/-1/0/1944-LCI92-SETH_SHEPARD_D-DAY_ARTICLE.PDF.
Susperregui, J. 2016. "The location of Robert Capa's Falling Soldier," *Communication & Society*, Vol. 29(2), accessed 18 March 2024, https://doi:10.15581/003.29.2, 17–43.
US Coast Guard. "Coast Guard Heroes at Normandy." Defense Media Activity, accessed March 18, 2024, www.history.uscg.mil/Browse-by-Topic/Notable-People/Award-Recipients/Coast-Guard-Heroes-at-Normandy/.

Weiner, Reuben. "Memoirs of Staff Sergeant Reuben A. Weiner." 162nd Signal Photographic Co., accessed 18 March 2024, https://162spc.tumblr.com/Weiner.

Weinshank, F. "Soldiers' Stories: Fritz Weinshank." *LCI(L)-92*, accessed 18 March 2024, www.geocities.ws/lcil_92/Pg24.htm.

WW2 US Medical Research Center. "WW2 Hospital Ships." Accessed 18 March 2024, www.med-dept.com/articles/ww2-hospital-ships/.

Magazines and Articles

Brandt, Bert, (1945, May). I Cover the Battlefield, *Popular Mechanics*, 94.

Butler, E. K. (1994, 18 November). Invasion Pictures Took Long Preparation, *Editor and Publisher*, 16.

Gavin, J. (1947, October). Letter to the Editor. *'47: The Magazine of the Year*, 123.

Graffin, W. (1947, October). Letter to the Editor. *'47: The Magazine of the Year*, 123.

Hersey, J. (1947, September). The Man Who Invented Himself. *'47: The Magazine of the Year*.

Life, 19 June 1944, Vol. 16, No. 25.

Parker, Bruce. (2011, September). The Tide Predictions for D-Day. *Physics Today*, 64–9, 35–40. *Extracted from "Sea, Surf & Hell," & USCG History Website Extracted from Sea, Surf & Hell & USCG History Website.*

Ruley, David. (1945, 1 June). Filming Normandy D-Day. *Movie Makers* magazine, 213, 228–30.

Sheehan, V. (1947, October). Letter to the Editor. *'47: The Magazine of the Year*, 122.

Time, Vol. XLIII, No. 25, 19 June 1944.

Interviews and Oral Histories

Jarreau, Charles, interviewed by Stephen Ambrose, on file with the National WWII Museum Oral Histories, Personal Diaries and Journals.

Spaulding, John, interviewed by Forrest C. Pogue, on file with the Military History Institute, Carlisle Barracks.

Newspapers

"Thompson Lands with Yanks on Assault Boat." (1968, 1 June). *Chicago Tribune*, A1–2.

Fine, R. (2014, June 2). "Uncovering D-Day Coverage." *Richmond-Times Dispatch*.